QUEST FOR DIVINITY

Modern Intellectual and Political
History of the Middle East

Mehrzad Boroujerdi, *Series Editor*

Muhammad, riding his horse Buraq and accompanied by the angel Gabriel, ascends to heaven and comes before the angel glorifying God with seventy heads and seventy tongues. *Courtesy of the Bibliothèque Nationale de France.*

QUEST
for
DIVINITY

A Critical Examination of the Thought of Mahmud Muhammad Taha

MOHAMED A. MAHMOUD

Syracuse University Press

Permission to reprint text from Arthur J. Arberry's *The Koran Interpreted* is gratefully acknowledged. Reprinted by permission of HarperCollins Publishers Ltd. © A. J. Arberry 1955.

The paper used in this publication meets the minimum requirements of American National Standard for Information Sciences—Permanence of Paper for Printed Library Materials, ANSI Z39.48–1984.∞™

For a listing of books published and distributed by Syracuse University Press,
visit our Web site at SyracuseUniversityPress.syr.edu.

ISBN-13: 978-0-8156-3100-2
ISBN-10: 0-8156-3100-6

Library of Congress Cataloging-in-Publication Data
Mahmoud, Mohamed.
Quest for divinity : a critical examination of the thought of
Mahmud Muhammad Taha / Mohamed A. Mahmoud.—1st ed.
p. cm.—(Modern intellectual and political history of the Middle East)
Includes bibliographical references and index.
ISBN 0–8156–3100–6 (hardcover : alk. paper)
1. Taha, Mahmud Muhammad. 2. Scholars, Muslim—Sudan—Biography.
3. Islamic renewal—Sudan. 4. Islam and politics—Sudan. I. Title.
BP80.T224M34 2006
297.2092—dc22   2006031486

Manufactured in the United States of America

To my mother,

my father,

my sisters,

and my brothers

Mohamed A. Mahmoud taught at the Faculty of Arts at the University of Khartoum and at the Oriental Institute at the University of Oxford. Currently, he teaches at the Department of Comparative Religion at Tufts University.

 Contents

✒ Abbreviations

IN CITING Mahmud Muhammad Taha's works, the following abbreviations are used:

AJi	*As'ila wa ajwiba*, Part I
AJii	*As'ila wa ajwiba*, Part II
AS	*Adwa' 'ala shari'at 'l-ahwal 'l-shakhsiyya*
DH	*Min daqa'iq haqa'iq 'l-din*
DJ	*Al-Da'wa 'l-Islamiyya 'l-jadida*
DI	*Al-Dustur 'l-Islami: Na'am wa la*
DT	*Al-Din wa 'l-tanmiyya 'l-ijtima'iyya*
IF	*Al-Islam wa 'l-funun*
IQ	*Al-Islam wa insaniyyat 'l-qarn 'l-'ishrin*
IS	*Al-Islam*
LL	*La Ilaha Illa 'Llah*
MM	*Al-Markisiyya fi 'l-mizan*
MS	*Mushkilat 'l-sharq 'l-awsat*
QF	*Al-Qur'an wa Mustafa Mahmud*
RMi	*Rasa'il wa maqalat*, Part I
RMii	*Rasa'il wa maqalat*, Part II
RS	*Risalat 'l-salat*
RT	*Al-Risala 'l-thaniya min 'l-Islam*
RU	*Al-Islam bi-risalatihi 'l-ula la yasluh li-insaniyyat 'l-qarn 'l-'ishrin*
SA	*Al-Sifr 'l-awwal*
SM	*The Second Message of Islam*
TK	*Ta'allamu kaifa tusallun*
TM	*Tariq Muhammad*
TS	*Tatwir shari'at 'l-ahwal 'l-shakhsiyya*
TT	*Al-Thawra 'l-thaqafiyya*
UD	*Usus dustur 'l-Sudan*
ZJ	*Za'im jabhat 'l-mithaq fi 'l-mizan*

Mahmud Muhammad Taha.
Courtesy of Muhammad Sadiq Ja'far.

 Preface

MAHMUD MUHAMMAD TAHA came to brief international prominence in January 1985 when he was publicly hanged by General Ja'far Nimairi's regime in Sudan. Few scholars of modern Islam were aware of Taha's thought and his movement before his tragic death. Although an increasing number of scholars are recognizing the importance of his intellectual contributions on many key issues of Islamic reform, there is still a dearth of studies of Taha's scholarship and a great need to examine the nature of his thought and its relevance in the light of the serious challenges facing contemporary Muslims. This book is an attempt in this direction.

The methodological approach of this study is based on the premise that thinkers are a product of an active interchange between an objective, cumulative, and collective intellectual process spanning several centuries (or what may be called "tradition") and a personal intellectual process rooted in individual experience. A thinker's "epistemological horizon" is defined by the coming together of these two processes, by the creative fusion of the objective and the subjective. Taha is thus approached from two vantage points: the historical context that shaped him and his own personal experience.

The book is divided into a preliminary background discussion, six chapters, and a conclusion. The preliminary background is aimed at the general reader who has no prior knowledge about Islam in the Sudan. Chapter 1 introduces Taha and his world. The main influences that shaped his spiritual and intellectual formation are highlighted: the early conditioning of his family's Sufi tradition and ethos, his formal education within the context of a colonial modernity, and his informal education within the larger context of competing Islamic and European schools of thought and ideological projects. The chapter stresses Taha's role as a public intellectual and political activist and analyzes some aspects of the movement he tried to create.

Chapter 2 deals with Taha's controversial theory of prayer and Islamic worship. By casting his own mystical experience in the light of this theory and by offering his theory as a new framework that redefined the nature of Islamic prayer and worship, Taha established himself as a radical Sufi par excellence. Taha's theory is examined in the context of his Sufi heritage on the one hand and his modernist sensibility with its emphasis on the notion of individuality *(fardiyya)* on the other. This dynamic interplay between mystical and modernist also provides a foundation for the way Taha approached the Qur'anic text, which is the subject of chapter 3. Taha's Qur'anic hermeneutics is examined in the light of his attempt to reconcile the text's historicity with its purported divinity.

Chapter 4 focuses on the central theme that lies at the heart of Taha's metaphysics, namely the issue of determinism versus free will. The long history of the debate and the current relevance of some of its key concerns are underlined. The related issue of divine punishment and the problems it poses are examined. In chapter 5 the focus shifts to Taha's social message, or what he called the "second message" of Islam. In formulating his social message, Taha was responding to a deep sense of crisis in modern Islam and what he perceived as a complete failure on the part of traditionally trained scholars to address it. Nor was he satisfied with the answers of other modernists that he found inadequate. What he proposed as the "real" message of Islam does certainly present us with the most radical social message of a modern Muslim reformer. Chapter 6 covers three themes that figure in varying degrees in Taha's work: science and in particular evolution, the status of Islamic law and in particular the penal code, and fine art. His position on these issues provides us with a fuller view of his thought and the scope of his reform project.

Taha was first and foremost a mystical thinker who viewed individual and collective human action in terms of a "salvific determinism": human life is intrinsically oriented toward God; it is only through God that humans can de-alienate themselves and realize their freedom, ultimate fulfilment, and salvation. But Taha was also a radical Sufi who did not accept the absolute alterity of God and insisted that the human is in fact a "God in the making": the human's journey will never come to an end because the human is involved in an eternal quest for divinity, an eternal quest to be God.

The writing of this book could not have started without the support of Leila Fawaz, who as dean for humanities and arts at Tufts University kindly agreed to release me from my teaching and administrative duties and hence afforded me the opportunity to concentrate on my research and writing. I owe a great debt to her. I also wish to express my thanks to my departmental colleague Joseph Walser for his continual support.

During the writing of this book I divided my time between Oxford and Birmingham. I would like to express my thanks to the staff of the Oriental Reading Room at the Bodleian Library, the staff of the library of the Oriental Institute, and the staff of Birmingham University Library, particularly at the Selly Oak campus. My stay in Oxford was made the richer on the personal level by the warm welcome and hospitality of Robin and Doke Ostle, Ron and Bonnie Nettler, Ibrahim al-Salahi, Edmund Gray, Hashim Muhammad Ahmad and Iman Bashir, Muhammad 'Umar Bushara and Fatma Khalid, and Ali al-Zubair and Nafisa Lutfi. In Birmingham, the Open End group, under John Hick, and the Sudanese Reading Group provided me with a highly stimulating intellectual atmosphere. I would also like to thank Sigvard von Sicard of the Centre for the Study of Islam and Christian-Muslim Relations at Birmingham University for his support.

Over many years, I have discussed Taha's thought and movement with many colleagues whenever we meet. Some of these were or are still disciples of Taha. I am privileged to have had access to the knowledge and insights of these colleagues. An exhaustive list of them is not possible, but I would like to acknowledge the following: Muhammad Bashir Ahmad, Salah Hasan Ahmad, Haidar Ibrahim 'Ali, 'Abd al-Rahim 'Abdin Hillawi, 'Abd Allah Ahmad al-Bashir (aka Bola), Ahmad al-Mustafa Dali, al-Nur Hamad, 'Abd al-Salam Hasan, Stephen Howard, al-Baqir al-'Afif Mukhtar, Abdullahi An-Na'im, Ahmad al-Nimairi, 'Abd al-Salam Nur al-Din, Haidar Badawi Sadiq, and 'Abd al-Salam Sidahmad.

Many people aided me in bringing this book to fruition. I should like to thank Mehrzad Boroujerdi, editor of the Modern Intellectual and Political History of the Middle East book series, to which this book belongs, and the two anonymous readers of my manuscript, from whose valuable comments and advice I greatly benefited. I have been particularly fortunate to have worked with the staff of Syracuse University Press. I wish to single out for thanks Mary Selden Evans, for her constant support and encouragement, and John J. Fruehwirth, to whom I owe a special word of thanks. I am also grateful to Carolyn Russ for the meticulous care and attention she showed in copy editing my manuscript.

Most of all, it was the unfailing and boundless loving and caring support of my wife, Corony Edwards, that made the work on my manuscript a most enjoyable undertaking. As a first reader, a perceptive critic, and an editorial adviser, she contributed substantially to the improvement and readability of my manuscript. I will always be indebted to her.

Transliteration and Other Matters

For the transliteration of Arabic words and names I have used a simple, modified system based on that of the *International Journal of Middle East Studies.* Place names, however, follow their established familiar English form (Khartoum, Omdurman, etc). No diacritical marks are used. The inverted comma (') indicates the letter *'ain,* and *hamza* is indicated by ('). The *hamza* of union *(wasl)* is indicated by ('), but this practice is not applied to names (hence *wahdat 'l-wujud* but 'Abd al-Rahman instead of 'Abd 'l-Rahman). Final *ha'* is represented by *a* at the end of the word, with the exception of the word *salat,* and by *at* when in construct. Diphthongs are indicated by *ai* and *aw.* For plurals of words I have added an *s,* except for a few words like *'alim,* whose familiar *'ulama'* plural is used.

Dates for the premodern period are indicated according to both the Islamic *hijra* calendar and the Common Era, with the two dates separated by a slash.

There are now many English translations of the Qur'an. Throughout this book I have used Arthur J. Arberry's translation, *The Koran Interpreted,* which has established itself since its publication in 1955 as one of the best in

English; I am grateful to HarperCollins Publishers Ltd. for permission to quote from it. Where Arberry's translation gives rise to a specific problem, particularly in the light of Taha's reading of the Qur'an, I have supplied an accompanying note. In citations from the Qur'an the chapter number is followed by the verse numbers, separated by a colon.

QUEST FOR DIVINITY

Background

Beginnings of Sudanese Islam

ALMOST EXACTLY five hundred years ago, the defining event in the history of what we know today as the Sudan took place. In 1504–5 C.E. the last Christian Nubian kingdom, Suba, was overrun by an alliance between the Funj, a nomadic cattle-herding people who extended their influence as they moved northward, and migrating Arab peoples under the leadership of the ʿAbdallab clan, who pushed southward.[1] The origins of the Funj are shrouded in mystery,[2] but what concerns us here is their decisive role in establishing the first Muslim state in eastern *bilad ʾl-sudan* (land of the blacks, as the Arab geographers called the Saharo-Sahelian sector of Africa). Their dominance provided the stable, historical context within which the country's people were gradually Islamized and Arabized.

In the new context of the Funj kingdom, the interrelated though distinctive processes of Islamization and Arabization assumed a hegemonic nature. An example of the impact of the process of Islamization is found in the observations of Scottish traveler James Bruce about the consumption of pork in Sennar, the capital of the Funj Kingdom: "Hog's flesh is not sold in the market; but all the people of Sennar eat it publicly; men in office, who pretend to be Mahometans, eat theirs in secret."[3] Bruce was not impressed by the conformity of seventeenth-century Sudanese Islam to normative Islam, but his observation about the secret consumption of pork is a good example of the gradual success of Islamization in claiming the "public space" of Funj society.[4] On the other hand, Arabization expressed itself chiefly through the spread of Arabic as a lingua franca and the language of religious and literary culture. When this process of Arabization eventually

1

came of age, it led certain groups to identify themselves genealogically with the Arabs and appropriate an Arab memory.[5]

A crucial role in the spread of Islam and Islamization was played by the *shaikh*s (masters) of Sufi orders *(tariqas)*.[6] The political stability and economic order of the Funj regime allowed these orders to develop and flourish and play a pivotal role in shaping Sudanese Islam and defining its character. The earliest order that entered the country was the Qadiriyya, which came to dominate the Sufi scene. The Qadiriyya were soon followed by the Shadhiliyya order.[7] Besides the interorder rivalry, there was also the traditional conflict between Sufi *shaikh*s and the *'ulama'* (scholars of the religious sciences, jurists). Perhaps the most dramatic illustration of this in the hagiographic memory of the Funj period was the confrontation between Muhammad al-Hamim, a venerated *shaikh* who was one of the first initiates of the Qadiriyya and a member of the Rikabiyyun group, and Dushain, a Shafi'ite judge. The author of *Kitab 'l-tabaqat,* our major source on religious life during this period, tells us that the *shaikh,* while in "a state of divine ecstasy," did not abide by shari'a rules; he married more women than was permissible and compounded his breach by marrying two sisters at the same time. The following account of the celebrated clash between the two men is given:

> When Shaikh al-Hamim came to Arbaji for the Friday service, Justice Dushain condemned what he had done. As [al-Hamim] was on his way out [of the mosque], the judge grasped his horse's bridle and said to him, "You have married five, six, and seven wives. All this has not been sufficient; [and now] you combine two sisters [in marriage]." The *shaikh* said to him, "So, what do you want?" [The judge] said, "I want to nullify your marriage because you transgressed against God's Book and the Way of the Messenger of God." [The *shaikh*] said, "The Messenger of God gave me his permission."[8]

In recounting this confrontation, the hagiographic memory demonstrates a clear sympathy for the *shaikh,* who is vindicated in two ways: the divine and revered *shaikh* Idris b. al-Arbab (d. 1059/1650) did not denounce what al-Hamim had done, and the disrespectful judge was later punished with a nasty skin affliction.[9] A deep hostility to the *'ulama'* was expressed by Abu al-Qasim al-Junaid, al-Hamim's grandson and successor as a Qadirite *shaikh,* who declared that "the hearts of the *fuqaha'* (jurists) are concealed from God."[10]

This state of discord and antagonism, however, was not the norm. Although the Sudanese Sufi tradition allowed for an "ecstatic space," it tended on the whole to stress the ideal of soberness and a balanced synthesis of the esoteric and the exoteric. The main institution around which the *shaikhs'* educational activities revolved, namely the *khalwa* (lit. "retreat" but conventionally "Qur'anic school"), offered a traditional syllabus involving Qur'anic studies, *hadith* (prophetic traditions), and *fiqh* (jurisprudence).[11] The education of the *shaikhs* themselves varied; some were illiterate and others highly learned.

What really mattered to the believers was the perception of the *shaikh* as a possessor of *baraka* (blessing) and, at times, as a performer of *karama* (a miraculous act). The *shaikhs'* spiritual status often translated into economic power and political influence. The already mentioned Idris b. al-Arbab is a case in point. Granted land by the state, he established a center in al-'Ailafun, southeast of Khartoum, that attracted people from various parts of the country who brought gifts of "honey, textile, slaves, and camels."[12] He played an important political role as mediator between subject and ruler.[13]

During the final years of the Funj regime the Sammaniyya order came to prominence. This order, founded by Muhammad b. 'Abd al-Karim al-Samman (d. 1189/1775), was introduced into the Sudan by Ahmad al-Tayyib al-Bashir (d. 1239/1824), who hoped to establish a new order that would replace the prevalent Sufi fragmentation by a unity under his spiritual guidance. During his time, al-Bashir represented the intellectual peak of Sudanese Sufism. He not only broke the isolation characterizing the *shaikhs'* world by forging close links with the great centers of Mecca, Medina, and Cairo, but he also authored numerous works that revealed a great philosophical depth.[14] Besides showing the influence of Abu Hamid al-Ghazali (d. 505/1111), he notably showed the influence of the theory of Muhyi al-Din b. 'Arabi (d. 638/1240) of the "unity of being" *(wahdat 'l-wujud)* and other influences coming from the mystical philosophies of al-Husain b. Mansur al-Hallaj (d. 309/922), Shihab al-Din al-Suhrawardi (d. 587/1191), 'Abd al-Karim al-Jili (d. ca. 832/1428), and the esoteric teachings of the Isma'iliyya.[15] After the death of al-Bashir, the Sammaniyya did not escape the fragmentation that had plagued other orders.[16] About six decades after the founder's death, the order was to give the country its greatest religious revolutionary.

Competing Islams under the Turco-Egyptians

The Funj regime ended in 1821 when riverain Sudan was invaded by the army of Muhammad 'Ali (d. 1849), the viceroy of Egypt, marking the beginning of what came to be known as the Turco-Egyptian period. Muhammad 'Ali, nominally ruling on behalf of the Ottoman sultan, had his own ambitions; in invading the Sudan he was motivated by the desire to raise "a docile slave army" and have "access to the region's fabled gold mines . . . which, could they be located and exploited, would provide [him] with the means to assure his position in Egypt and his independence of the sultan."[17] The role that religion could play was not lost on the invaders, and so their expedition was accompanied by three religious scholars who were to persuade the population that "obedience to his majesty the [Ottoman] sultan, the prince of believers, and the successor of the Prophet was a religious duty."[18] The choice of these scholars, who represented the three Sunnite rites of Hanafism, Shafi'ism, and Malikism, was significant as it highlighted from the start the intimate connection between the 'ulama' class and the colonial regime that was on the point of being established.

The religious policy of the Turco-Egyptian regime was not different from that implemented throughout the rest of the Ottoman empire, namely the establishment of a central judicial system run by jurists who were closely allied to the state and dependent on it. It soon became clear that this policy necessitated the creation and training of a sufficiently numerous indigenous 'ulama' class, as the reliance on expatriate jurists from Egypt was impractical. Accordingly, the regime instituted an educational policy that privileged *fiqh* training. Education in traditional Sufi institutions was discouraged because their graduates were not perceived as qualified to join the state service. Al-Azhar University, the bastion of Sunnite Islam, played a major role in the creation of this class of 'ulama', and a lodge for Sudanese students (*riwaq 'l-Sinnariyya*) was established. This educational policy notwithstanding, the Turco-Egyptians, recognizing the widespread influence of Sufi Islam in the Sudan, sought to win *shaikhs* over, granting them privileges and providing their orders with subventions.

Toward the end of the Funj period the Khatmiyya order entered the country and experienced a remarkable rise during the Turco-Egyptian period. This order was founded by Muhammad 'Uthman al-Mirghani (d. 1268/1852), a disciple of Ahmad b. Idris (d. 1253/1837), the great Moroccan Sufi reformer whose teachings gave a fresh impetus to a revival of Sufi organization at the beginning of the nineteenth century.[19] Al-Mirghani was initiated into several orders, hence his sense of total confidence in calling his own order the Khatmiyya, that is, the "seal of orders" that brought all Sufi paths into a final synthesis and a higher unity. Al-Mirghani's Sudanese offspring spread his teachings and consolidated his order, which became influential throughout the country but with greater dominance in the northern and eastern regions.[20] Later, when the deterioration of the political situation led to the outbreak of the Mahdist revolution against the Turco-Egyptians, the Khatmiyya threw in their lot with the regime, delegitimizing the revolution's messianic claims and bolstering the *'ulama'*-led campaign against it.[21] This position had far-reaching consequences as it changed the nature of the Khatmiyya order and defined its future history and role.

Triumph and Demise of Sudanese Mahdism

The leader of the great revolution that was to galvanize large sections of the Sudanese into a unified act of resistance and rebellion and succeed in driving the Turco-Egyptians out of the country was a product of a profound condition of revolutionary ferment on the one hand and a heightened religious sensibility with a deep sense of political and social commitment on the other. Muhammad Ahmad b. 'Abd Allah came from the northern part of the country from a modest background. On joining the Sammaniyya order, his intense commitment to religious learning and his spiritual charisma soon caused him to stand out in the order's circles. The order's fragmentation allowed him to rise to the position of head of one of its branches. This could have been the peak and the end of his religious career, but he saw himself as destined for a special vocation. The time was pregnant with a messianic expectation of the rise of the Mahdi, the guided one, who would "fill the earth with equity and justice as it has been filled with inequity and injustice," as the hadith put it.[22] Muhammad Ahmad believed that his mystical experience and religious calling were meant to realize the Mahdist expectation vibrating around him. When in 1881 he declared his divine mission and routed in the same year a government expedition sent to arrest him, his Mahdist claim and his call for jihad (holy war) against the "infidel Turks" struck a timely chord with a great number of people throughout the country.

Muhammad Ahmad's religious ideology reflected to a large measure the overconfidence of the heroic moment of his Mahdism. He saw his moment as a direct continuation of the heroic prophetic moment when Islam was founded. His Mahdism entitled him to no less than the "supreme succession" *(al-khilafa 'l-kubra)*, and as such he was the "successor of the Apostle of God" *(khalifat rasul 'llah)* in a very special sense: what he performed placed him in parallel with Muhammad as he was specifically charged with the revival of the "prophetic moment" (by extension, the careers of his own successors were to parallel those of the caliphs of the Medina state who inherited the Prophet's mantle). Furthermore, in al-Mahdi's view the prophetic "unity" *(tawhid)* paradigm meant the abrogation of all *madhhabs* (rites, or normative schools of law) and *tariqas* (Sufi orders), for the Mahdi's way had to be the only valid legislative source and the only redemptive spiritual path.[23]

Sudanese Mahdism lost its impetus when al-Mahdi died in 1885 shortly after the fall of Khartoum and the founding of Omdurman as the capital of the new state. Under his successor, al-Khalifa 'Abd Allah (d. 1899), the ideological oppression of Mahdism was coupled with political oppression. Al-Khalifa 'Abd Allah's attempts to realize the Mahdi's dream of expanding his state (particularly northward into Egypt) came to naught. The Mahdist state made its last heroic stand in September 1898 at the battle of Karari when its army was crushed by a British-led army acting in the name of the khedive of Egypt. This marked the country's entry into what came to be known as the condominium period.

The Condominium and the Rise of the Nationalist Movement

The condominium was a creation of Lord Cromer (d. 1917), Britain's consul general in Egypt—an arrangement under which the Sudan would be governed by Britain and Egypt, with the former being in effective control of the country's administration.

In its early days, the Sudan government, as the British colonial administration came to be known, perceived the major threat against it as coming from the Ansar (supporters, as the followers of al-Mahdi were known) and from the Sufi orders. Hence, an important aspect of the government's religious policy was forging an alliance with the 'ulama', the representatives of orthodox Islam, to combat the influence of Sufi orders. A board of 'ulama' was created in 1901, and the government actively promoted orthodoxy by financing the building of mosques and Qur'anic schools.[24] Being acutely wary of a backlash, the government firmly resisted any Christian missionary activity in the country's Muslim regions. Furthermore, when it came to the judicial policy, although the penal code was based on the model of India, the personal status laws were determinedly kept under the jurisdiction of shari'a.[25] While the north was considered a Muslim sphere where policies were shaped by special concern for Muslim sensibilities, the south was treated as a separate and distinctive sphere subject to a different set of policies. Here, indigenous religions were subject to gradual annihilation. While Muslim influence was systematically checked, Christian missionary activity was given free hand.

The government's suspicion of the Ansar, and its willingness to suppress them, served the interests of 'Ali al-Mirghani (d. 1968), the spiritual leader of the Khatmiyya, who was well disposed to position himself as a reliable ally. On its part, the government "welcomed the support [of the Khatmiyya], trusted [the order] on its record during the Turco-Egyptian administration, and was therefore prepared to make an exception to its general rule of suspecting all [Sufi orders]."[26] International developments, however, were soon to lead to an unexpected reversal of policy as regards the Ansar. When the First World War broke out and the Ottoman sultan sided with Germany and Austria and declared a jihad against his enemies, the Sudan government found itself in a potentially exposed position. 'Abd al-Rahman al-Mahdi (d. 1959), the posthumous son of the Mahdi and the dynamic and ambitious leader of the Ansar, was readily willing to pledge his support and loyalty to the government, and it swiftly embraced him. Under 'Abd al-Rahman's leadership, the Ansar were to become a formidable force.[27] Despite the fact that al-Mahdi was opposed to Sufi orders, the Ansar effectively became a new order, though with a distinctive nature that set it apart from other orders. The Ansar were a community in whose memory the "Mahdist moment" was freshly alive, and this defined them as a religio-political community. Furthermore, the rise of the Ansar redefined the Khatmiyya. In allying himself with the condominium government, al-Mirghani was motivated by his desire to block the rise of the Ansar rather than to turn the Khatmiyya into a political force. Consequently, the new development pushed the Khatmiyya into the political arena and the Ansar-Khatmiyya polarization led to the birth of what came to be known as *ta'ifiyya* (sectarianism).

A key objective of the British administration was the replacement of Egyptian employees by Sudanese ones. This was gradually achieved by investing in education and creating a class of what came to be known as the *afandiyya*. For the first time, the Sudanese received an education radically different from what was offered by indigenous institutions: a modern education based on a secular curriculum. By virtue of this education they were able to read not just in Arabic but in English as well, and this undoubtedly provided them with a wider intellectual horizon. Ahmad Khair, a politically active member of this class, describes his generation in the following terms: "[It] is a generation that has acquired a measure of modern knowledge and a great deal of training and skill in government bureaucracy. Hence, this generation started looking at life and Sudanese society through a modern perspective and through modern criteria; it was formed by a mixture of sound religious culture and a sweeping European culture."[28] It was in fact this "sweeping European culture" component that came to represent the basis of their worldview, and what Khair describes as "sound religious culture" tended to be a recasting of Islam in the light of the values of the new world created by their colonial encounter. This generation readily embraced the reformist project of Muhammad 'Abduh (d. 1905) that attracted them because of its bold rejection of traditionalism and its call for religious liberation.[29] In their view, what 'Abduh articulated was to have a profound impact on Islam similar to that of the Reformation on Christianity.[30]

Although the education of this generation had a major impact in shaping their attitudes and sensibilities, there was a certain receptive willingness on their part to accept change that could, ironically, be explained in the light of their hostility to the Mahdist state. This attitude is best summed up by Muhammad Ahmad Mahjub (who went on to become a leader of the Ansar-supported Umma Party):

> The Mahdiyya came to rescue people from the moral chaos and the injustices [of the Turco-Egyptians]—an objective it succeeded in achieving in its earlier phase. However, ignorance thwarted its intentions and led in its latter phase to a reanimated provocation of tribal disunity. The oppression by those in authority led to moral decline . . . and so intrigues and hypocrisy prevailed and commitment to high ideals waned except in the case of those who were granted strength of belief [and] fortitude in the face of misfortune.[31]

This new elite was to play a key role in the articulation and mobilization of a nationalist consciousness and movement that was to lead the country to its independence. The nationalism *(wataniyya)* that the educated Sudanese evoked was a politically motivated ideological construction based on what was perceived as the real interests of the country's people as opposed to the interests of the colonial "other."[32] However, despite the immense cultural diversity within the Sudan, it was the hegemonic voice of the Islamized, Arabized center that had defined this nationalism. Moreover, the idealized construction defended by the nationalists was a notion of "Sudanese-ness" that transcended tribalism *(qabaliyya)* and acted in opposition to it.[33]

Sudanese nationalism developed in the shadow of Egyptian nationalism and in opposition to it. In its early stage, it was a subsidiary expression of Egyptian nationalism through the pro-Egyptian slogan of "the unity of the Nile Valley." The culmination of this stage and at the same time its point of disintegration was the events of 1924 in which Sudanese and Egyptian troops staged an abortive revolt against the British.[34] The latter stage of Sudanese nationalism was characterized by a higher sense of self-confidence as the nationalists started increasingly to stress an independent identity, the shared key components of Islam and Arabism with Egypt notwithstanding. This was clearly articulated in the mid-1930s by Muhammad Ahmad Mahjub, who championed the call for a Sudanese culture and in particular a Sudanese literature and a Sudanese literary sensibility that was consciously autonomous. In making his case he argued:

> It is surprising that people shrink from the notion of separate Sudanese and Egyptian literatures and cultures. Such separation is natural and inevitable and does not mean a severing of relationships between brothers. . . . If Egyptians work on creating and developing their national literature and if the Sudanese do the same, there will come a time when Egyptians would feel a pressing need to study Sudanese literature and examine all that is produced by Sudanese thought, and the Sudanese would do the same. Both would find in the literature of the other what would complement their own deficiencies.[35]

This sense of a distinctive Sudanese culture that had to express itself through a distinctive literature was part of a growing nationalist assertion that, like Egyptian nationalism, was soon to assume a political character. In 1938, the politically active elements of the educated elite formed the Graduates' Congress, ostensibly to press for the particular interests of the *afandiyya,* but it soon developed into an organization voicing the political aspirations of the Sudanese and spearheading the fight against colonialism.[36] The Congress elite perceived themselves as a modern, nationalist force that represented the Sudanese irrespective of their regional backgrounds or religious affiliations, and this led them to the development of an anti-*ta'ifiyya* political discourse. For many of them, 'Ali al-Mirghani and 'Abd al-Rahman al-Mahdi represented the traditional face of the country with its regional and religious divisions.[37]

However, both al-Mirghani and al-Mahdi recognized the importance and dynamism of the educated elite, and it was through the alliances they could form with this force that they entered the modern world of party politics. In 1943 the Ashiqqa' (Full Brothers) Party was born under the leadership of Isma'il al-Azhari (d. 1969) and with the blessing of al-Mirghani. In 1945, the Umma (Nation) Party was created with the endorsement and support of al-Mahdi. The *ta'ifiyya* that was initially rejected by the new political force thus became an indispensable ally. Yet to make these alliances workable, to manipulate the educated elite, and to attract greater public support from beyond their traditional constituencies, the two sects had to modify their discourses along lines that accommodated nationalism. It was this discursive convergence that made it possible for the sectarian and political forces to come to a brief consensus that brought the country its independence in January 1956.

1 ✐

The Context, the Man,
and the Movement

Early Life and Struggle Against Colonialism

MAHMUD MUHAMMAD TAHA was born sometime between 1909 and 1911 in the town of Rufaʻa in the central Gezira region. He lost both parents when he was still a child. His family belonged to the Rikabiyyun clan, and Muhammad al-Hamim was his great-grandfather.

Because the socialization and home education of children in the Sudan involves making them aware from an early age of their clan origin and clan memories, it is likely that certain memories played a significant part in Taha's childhood conditioning. It is reasonable to assume that Taha would have been made aware of the purported sharifi (noble, prophetic) origin of the Rikabiyyun, who trace their ancestry to al-Husain b. ʻAli (d. 61/680), the prophet Muhammad's grandson.[1] It is probable that he would have heard many stories about his great-grandfather al-Hamim. It is likely that he heard the story about why the holy man earned the epithet of "al-Hamim" (the high-minded, the resolute): how his *shaikh*'s wife wanted a *dawka* (clay griddle), how he bought the *dawka,* carried it on his head, and covered great distances on foot trying to find his *shaikh*.[2] He probably heard about al-Hamim's dramatic initiation into the Qadiriyya when he offered himself to be sacrificed[3] and about the celebrated confrontation and exchange between him and the orthodox Dushain; and how al-Hamim saw *lailat 'l-qadr* (the Night of Power) in Rufaʻa and how he was thunderstruck by it, losing not only his consciousness but also its special blessing, which was conferred on another *shaikh*.[4]

Taha was also likely to have heard about the miracle of ʻAli al-Nayyal, al-Hamim's son and successor, the mention of whose name was enough to press elephants to service.[5] He would likely have been told about Abu al-Qasim al-Junaid, who might have cut a heroic figure with his sudden leap from being a cattle herdsman to becoming a Sufi *shaikh,* and his miraculous ability to read people's minds.[6] Furthermore, he was likely to have heard about the radical and unprecedented decision of the *shaikh* Abu Dulaiq, who appointed his daughter 'A'isha as his successor to the leadership of al-Hamim's branch of the Qadiriyya.[7]

Taha grew up in a post-Mahdist world that was being actively shaped by condominium policies, and he received the type of secular education that eventually enabled him to join the privileged *afandiyya* class.[8] He entered the highly competitive Gordon College, where he studied engineering and graduated in 1936. He briefly worked for the Sudan Railways, but because he wanted to take an active part in the political movement and struggle for independence and as the regulations of civil service debarred him from doing so, he resigned and went into private practice.[9]

During the Second World War, political forces in the Sudan were unanimously supportive of the Allied nations in their war against the Axis powers. The postwar international atmosphere with a new balance of power in favor of the United States and the Soviet Union and the establishment of the United Nations, whose charter stressed respect for the principles of equal rights and self-determination for peoples, spurred the momentum of the nationalist movement. However, beyond the dismantling of the condominium, the nationalists were divided. On the one hand there was the unionist movement that called for a unity with Egypt, ranging from full unity to a confederal arrangement, and on the other there was the independence movement pressing for the country's full independence. A further division concerned whether the country should be a republic or a monarchy.

When Taha and a few other educated colleagues founded the Republican Party (al-Hizb 'l-Jumhuri) in October 1945, they were determined to fight against both colonialism and sectarianism. By the early 1940s some influential sections of the Graduates' Congress were willing to enter into alliances with the sectarian leaders who commanded large popular power bases. The intense dissatisfaction of Taha and his colleagues with the programs and performance of the Congress prompted them to establish their own party.[10] The party's call for the establishment of a republic was inseparable from its denunciation of unity with Egypt or the acceptance of a sectarian leader as monarch.

From the start, the Republicans were characterized by the intensity of their hostility to sectarianism. This can be explained in the light of their ideological commitment to an Islam-based outlook *(madhhabiyya)*. Though vaguely defined at this early stage, such a commitment still provided a basis for a self-perception that set them on a collision course with any other political (and, for that matter, religious) force that claimed Islam as an ideological frame of reference. Taha and his colleagues were modernists, although their attachment to Islam made them more of Islamic modernists (as opposed to the active elements of the Graduates' Congress, who tended to be secular modernists). The young Republican activists believed that Islam and modernity were fully compatible and that Muslim societies could be radically transformed through a dynamic combination of a revitalized tradition and modernity.[11]

To expound the nature of their political vision, the Republicans produced a pamphlet with the pedestrian title of *al-Sifr 'l-awwal* (The First Pamphlet). Taha was not only the party's president but its only theoretician as well. The pamphlet echoed a number of ideas that were prevalent among the *afandiyya* class and encapsulated many themes that remained central in Taha's thought until the end of his life. According to the pamphlet, the Sudan was to be immediately evacuated by the forces of colonialism because it was mature enough to exercise its independent will. Like the vast majority of the educated class, Taha was committed to democracy, and because "the republican system is the best that humans have arrived at in their long search for an ideal system," the Sudan was envisaged as a democratic republic (SA 27).

In stressing the case for independence, the pamphlet referred to what it described as the "authentic characteristics" *(khasa'is asila)* of the Sudan. Speaking about what distinguished Sudan and its culture was, understandably enough, a theme close to the nationalists' hearts and minds. In Taha's case this was taken to a point that effectively made the Sudanese a "chosen people." He expressed this most unequivocally in 1951 in connection with his call for a Qur'an-based constitution when he declared:

> I submit that from this present time Islam is what the world is turning to and that the Qur'an will be the law of humankind. Sudan, by virtue of present-ing this law in its practical form that reconciles the need for social security and the need for absolute individual freedom, is the center of the circle of existence [*markaz da'irat 'l-wujud*] on this globe. This statement should not startle people because Sudan is ignorant, obscure, and small. Through His grace, God has preserved among the Sudanese a solidity of moral character that qualifies them to act as the meeting point of heaven and earth. (RMi 8)

This celebration of a divinely preserved moral character and spiritual excellence pertaining to the Sudanese dovetails with a celebration of the East *(al-sharq)* as Taha embraces the simplistic and clichéd equation of the East with spirituality and the West with materialism. The identity of the Sudan is defined with reference to a triple heritage represented by Islam, Arabism, and the legacy of the Orient—a notion espoused by a consider-able number of intellectuals at the time.[12]

The pamphlet outlined the position of Republicans regarding such di-verse issues as the economic system, the southern problem, education, and the women's question. As far as economics were concerned, the pamphlet envisaged the implementation of a developmental program that focused on human resources, particularly in the south. The pamphlet dealt with the southern problem in exclusively economic terms as a problem of uneven development, overlooking the cultural and religious aspects. In the sphere of education, the duality separating secular and religious education was re-jected in favor of an integrated system. The women's question drew special attention because it was believed that the failure to tackle it would have "dark consequences" and would lead to "an endless moral degeneration" (SA 24). Taha's solution to the perceived problem is educational in nature. He proposed a gender-specific educational program expressly designed to prepare women to carry out their responsibilities in their "special sphere." Although Taha was to adopt a progressive and generally equalitarian stance on women, he retained this conservative aspect of his thought.

Taha's notion at this time of Islam as a theoretical foundation for change was vague or even naïve. The pamphlet refers to what it describes as "'Umar's Islam" as the ultimate ideal that the party aspired to revive, a position that Taha later abandoned. The idealization of 'Umar and his reign was widespread among intellectuals in Sudan and Egypt and was considerably enhanced by the publication in 1945 of Muhammad Husain Haikal's celebratory biography of the caliph titled *al-Faruq 'Umar*. An essential prerequisite for national reawakening was the stimulation of what Taha described as *al-fikr 'l-hurr* (liberal thought). By this was meant a quality of thought that did not recognize restrictions and that subjected everything to questioning *(tasa'ul)* and methodical doubt *(tashkik)*. Although this might sound radically Cartesian, it was in reality an expression of a religioideological and political rather than a philosophical position. When Taha said that this "liberated thought" was the real foundation on which "religious awakening" *(al-nahda 'l-diniyya)* rested, it was then clear that the questioning and methodical doubt he recommended served as ideological weapons to discredit a particular kind of religious consciousness, namely that of sectarianism and traditional understandings of Islam.

In propagating their ideas, the Republicans adopted a tactic of direct engagement—distributing leaflets and addressing ordinary people in the streets and at mosques, clubs, and cafés. This confrontational method led to the arrest of Taha and several members of the party in 1946. When Taha refused to sign a pledge to desist from political activity for one year, he was given a one-year sentence. The Republicans launched a vigorous campaign and the authorities were forced to release him unconditionally after fifty days.[13]

Barely two months after his release and flush with his victory over the colonial administration, Taha was involved in what came to be known as the "Rufa'a episode," whose consequence was instrumental in bringing about the most significant transformation in his own life and the future direction of the Republican Party.

In 1946, the Legislative Assembly passed a law making pharaonic circumcision (an extreme type of female circumcision) a criminal offense punishable by fine and imprisonment. The passing of this law was preceded by debates about the harmful effects of pharaonic circumcision on physical and psychological health.[14] The legislators were careful not to outlaw another type of female circumcision called "sunna" (i.e., Prophet-sanctioned) that was perceived as less harmful.[15]

Although Taha and his colleagues shared the abhorrence of pharaonic circumcision felt by the socially progressive sections of the educated class, they still condemned the legislation. They read in the law a calculated attempt on the part of the colonialists to stigmatize and humiliate the Sudanese and project them as barbaric and backward and hence unready for independence at a time when the nationalist movement was gathering irreversible momentum. The Republicans argued that the practice was so deep rooted that it had to be eradicated through a gradual educational process rather than by resorting to the sanction of law. By rejecting the law, they believed that they were defending the "dignity" *(karama)* of Sudanese women and championing the cause of the country's freedom.[16]

In September 1946 and following the arrest of a woman who performed a pharaonic circumcision in Rufa'a, Taha led a local revolt to release the woman. This led to his arrest, along with others.[17] The authorities were anxious to affirm that Taha and his colleagues were arrested on account of committing the offense of riot and not because of what they thought of circumcision, as citizens were entitled to express their views in conformity with the law. When Taha was put on trial, he refused to cooperate with the court unless the law on pharaonic circumcision was reopened for discussion. He was sentenced to two years' imprisonment and was to remain under surveillance for one more year after his release.

Finding the Sufi Path and a New Vision of Islam

When Taha went to prison, he felt that his confinement was a providential act that gave him a chance to be alone with God. He applied himself to a rigorous mystical discipline of praying, fasting, and meditating.[18] After his release, Taha continued his discipline and withdrew into a *khalwa* (spiritual retreat) in Rufa'a for another two years, until November 1951.

In a revealing letter published in *al-Sha'b* newspaper on January 27, 1951, Taha wrote about what went on inside his mind. Since the founding of the Republican Party and his active involvement in politics, he apparently felt more acutely the need to deepen his knowledge of Islam. Despite his commitment to Islam as the ideological basis of his political vision, Taha was in a state of perplexity *(haira)* as to the nature of the Islam that he should advocate. Like all reform-minded idealists, he thought that he could go back to a pure and unadulterated source from which he could imbibe, that he could reproduce a foundational heroic moment. For him this meant going back to the "pure fount from which Muhammad, Abu Bakr, and 'Umar drank."

Like Muhammad when he started his mission after ending his retreat around the age of forty, Taha came out of his seclusion at about the same age with a strong sense of mission and a clear perception of a radical reform program dealing with problems on both the individual and the social levels. The Republican Party was to be reinvented; it was to adopt Taha's vision as its official ideology, and those who did not accept his ideas had to leave. Though politically and ideologically vociferous, the party remained numerically small and, consequently, politically insignificant. The party was identified with Taha, who was the fount of its thought and its life president. In the early 1970s Taha and his followers felt the need to adopt a new name that would reflect the nature of their outlook more accurately. For a brief period they experimented with the name "New Islamic Mission" *(al-Da'wa 'l-Islamiyya 'l-Jadida)*. This name, however, gave their opponents a chance to tarnish the group's image by suggesting that they were propagating deviation from Islam. They eventually continued using their historical name with a slight variation, the "Republican Brothers" (al-Ikhwan 'l-Jumhuriyyun).[19] Besides reflecting the apparent influence of the name of their major opponents, the Muslim Brothers (al-Ikhwan 'l-Muslimun), this name, with its patriarchal overtones, did injustice to their feminism and the movement's increasingly active and visible female members.

The vision that Taha offered as the basis of radical Islamic reform is described herein as "neo-Islamist." In understanding what is meant by neo-Islamism it is appropriate to start by an understanding of Islamism. Islamism is characterized by subscription to the following five basic tenets:

1. Islam is a religion of a comprehensive nature that addresses human needs on all levels.

2. Our present time is in the grip of a deep and global crisis characterized by a pervasive state of depravity.

3. Islam can address this crisis and indeed provides the only solution.

4. The Islamic solution is revivalist in nature, calling for reestablishment of the Prophet's model state and shari'a (the Law).

5. This model state and its law are envisaged in universal, transnational terms.

Although Taha shared these principles with other Islamists (some of whom may be described as fundamentalists), what is significant in his case is the degree of his willingness to open Islam to change, a willingness that led him to develop a distinctive and separate revivalist project and discourse. It is on account of the counterorthodox nature of his project that it is described as neo-Islamist.[20]

Postindependence: Elusive Horizons and Martyrdom

The first fruit of Taha's neo-Islamism was borne in December 1955 when, on the eve of independence, he produced the Republican Party's most important political document, *Usus dustur 'l-Sudan* (Fundamentals of the Constitution of the Sudan). The document envisaged a federal, democratic, and socialist republic guided by the principles of the Qur'an. According to the document, the most serious dilemma facing humankind was the conflict between the individual's need for "absolute individual freedom" and society's need for "total social justice." The document contended that Islam offered the only philosophical-religious worldview and social system that could reconcile the two needs through the creation of a democratic, socialist system. The document purported to offer an "Islamic" model that addressed not only the problems of an independent Sudan but also the problems of the rest of the world. Hence, it articulated a neo-Islamist universalism that was offered as an alternative to other ideological global models. Furthermore, the document emphasized a notion that came to play a vital role in Taha's reformist project, namely, constitutionalism.

The document's adoption of federalism was in agreement with the views voiced by some southern politicians.[21] After the mutiny of August 1955 in the south, setting off the civil war between south and north,[22] it was clear that the country's unity was still fragile and that short of the adoption of a federal system the alternative was secession. The northern political parties were vehemently opposed to federalism because they believed it would undermine the country's unity. Taha showed marked foresight and courage in accommodating the country's diversity by embracing the federal ideal on the political level. As far as Taha's overall position was concerned, by virtue of his reformist project he pitted himself against *ta'ifiyya*, the Islamist ideology of the Muslim Brothers, the thought of liberal capitalism, and Marxism.

The Republican Party, along with the other parties, was dissolved in November 1958 when General Ibrahim 'Abbud staged a coup d'état that met with no popular resistance. Bitter divisiveness and a marked lack of direction characterized the 1956–58 democratic period and its party politics, to the extent that the coup itself was engineered by the democratically elected government of the day.[23] The Sudanese had their first taste of a military dictatorship: a state of emergency was declared, martial law was proclaimed, and security forces were given supreme powers to enter houses, search and detain without warrant, censor mail, and confiscate any written materials deemed subversive. Taha supported the military takeover, arguing that it saved the country from the *ta'ifiyya* of the Umma Party and the unionist tendency of al-Azhari that could have thrown the country back into the sphere of Egyptian dominance.[24] The Republicans (henceforth "Jumhuris") reconstituted themselves as a religious group and resigned themselves to a quietist phase.

In October 1964 a popular uprising, the Sudanese "October Revolution," brought down 'Abbud's regime. The country enjoyed anew multiparty democracy. Although Taha was particularly impressed by the peaceful nature of the revolution, a characteristic to which he attached a special significance that came to be the cornerstone of his criticism of Marxism, he was deeply disappointed because the change meant that the promoters of *ta'ifiyya* could once again exercise their political influence. This sense of disenchantment was the basis of his claim that what happened was an "unfinished revolution." He maintained that the momentous revolutionary event itself was no more than a "noble sentiment," an emotional drive expressing a national will to bring down the military regime. This, however, was an initial phase to be followed by a mature phase in which a program of radical change should be adopted (LL 7).

The second period of party democracy was a time of great change and turbulence including an increase in the importance of the Communist

Party on the left and the Muslim Brothers on the Right. The Communist Party had played a leading role in the popular uprising by mobilizing the new forces of students, professionals, workers, and farmers into a general strike that forced the military regime to hand over power to a civilian government.[25] The Muslim Brothers, on the other hand, came late onto the scene, playing a decisive role barely a year after the revolution in spearheading a campaign that succeeded in pressuring the Constitutional Assembly in December 1965 into amending the Constitution, dissolving the Communist Party on account of its being inspired by an "atheistic" ideology, and expelling its parliamentary representatives.[26]

This plunged the country into a constitutional crisis and, for the first time, injected its political life with an element that was to prove most detrimental to its democracy and stability, namely the mobilization of Islam as the basis of political legitimization. The Supreme Court decided in December 1966 that the amendment passed by the Constitutional Assembly was unconstitutional, and in February 1967 the Court of Khartoum Province decided that the dissolution of the Communist Party and the expulsion of its parliamentary members were unconstitutional acts.[27] The government dismissed the courts' decisions. The views of the right were articulated by Hasan al-Turabi, the leader of the Muslim Brothers, who produced a government-sponsored pamphlet justifying the Assembly's decisions. Taha, who was active in a broad alliance opposed to the dissolution of the Communist Party, wrote a searing attack against al-Turabi's pamphlet, describing it as "incoherent, superficial, infused with prejudice, and characterized by a lack of basic discernment" (ZJ 2). He stressed a fundamental point that the clause pertaining to "freedom of speech and the right to form associations in conformity with law" was the essence of the constitution and the foundation of all laws (ZJ 13). However, Taha's position had a more complex nature. He was motivated not only by his belief in the Communists' right to freedom of speech and association but, paradoxically, by his profound antipathy to communism and Marxism as well. He argued that when the Communist Party was forced underground, communism would acquire an attractive aura and consequently pose a potentially greater threat.[28]

The success of the Muslim Brothers and their allies in dealing a severe blow to the left encouraged them to launch a fierce campaign calling on the

Constitutional Assembly to adopt an "Islamic" constitution. It was in this feverish atmosphere that two of the *'ulama'*, in collaboration with the Muslim Brothers and other orthodox religious forces, decided to take a drastic move against Taha and the Jumhuris. In November 1968, al-Amin Da'ud Muhammad and Husain Muhammad Zaki, who taught at the Islamic University of Omdurman, took a *hisba* legal action against Taha, asking the Supreme Shari'a Court to declare his *ridda* (apostasy).[29] The litigants' petition also requested that the court declare the dissolution of the Republican Party, order Taha's books be confiscated, dissolve his marriage, prohibit him and his followers from speaking in the name of Islam or interpreting the Qur'an, and punish those who believed in his ideas by a range of measures including the dissolution of their marriages. This action on the part of the *'ulama'* was a twentieth-century reenactment of the trial and execution of al-Hallaj in tenth-century Baghdad and a replay of the centuries-old ideological battle between orthodoxy and what was perceived as "nonconformist" Sufism.[30]

Although Taha was absent because he did not recognize the court's jurisdiction, a session was held on November 18. The proceedings took three hours during which the litigants and their witnesses made their case. After a twenty-minute recess the court passed its verdict, ruling that Taha was indeed guilty of apostasy. Although according to classical Muslim jurists apostasy is a capital offense, both the litigants' petition and the court's decision were careful not to press for the death penalty. Granting the litigants' first request, the court convicted Taha of apostasy and ordered him to renounce his ideas and activity. However, pending Taha's declaration of his "repentance," the court decided not to take action on the rest of the petition's requests. In confining itself to these decisions, the court was apparently acting in the full knowledge of the limits of its powers and the likely backlash any more drastic decisions might provoke. To carry out the full measures of the litigants' petition, the Muslim Brothers and Taha's orthodox opponents had to wait another seventeen years.[31]

One of Taha's most important interventions during this period was the publication of his *Mushkilat 'l-Sharq 'l-Awsat* (The Problem of the Middle East) in October 1967, shortly after the Arab defeat at the hands of Israel in June 1967. Taha's response to this devastating and shocking defeat was both pragmatic and religious. He saw in it the hand of God: this was a rude awakening to show the Arabs (and Muslims) the folly of their ways. This much was shared by Taha and some Islamists who believed that God shared their loathing of Arab secularist regimes, particularly Nasser's regime.[32] However, Taha's position set him apart when it came to the problem's solution because, unlike other Islamists, he did not subscribe to a jihadist model. Rather, he wanted to see a just peace based on recognition of the right of Israel to exist alongside a Palestinian state. This, however, he viewed only as a short-term, political solution. By making this compromise, the Arabs would be able to buy time to bring about a long-term solution that would address this and other problems on a more profound, civilizational level. The solution Taha suggested was based on his particular notion of Islamic revival and entailed the return *('awdat)* of Islam on a global level to heal all human divisions (MS 186–91).

In May 1969 another coup d'état brought the country's democracy to an end. The coup of Colonel Ja'far Nimairi and his "free officers" was a leftist response to the hegemony of the right, the dissolution of the Communist Party, and the proposed introduction of an Islamic constitution. The coup came with the avowed commitment "to consummate the unfinished agenda of the October Revolution."[33] Taha was among the first to welcome and support this military takeover, maintaining that the new regime was a bulwark against *ta'ifiyya*. Again, Taha's animosity to *ta'ifiyya* proved to be greater than his commitment to democracy. Although political parties were banned, the Jumhuris were allowed to continue their activity as a religious association. Taha was banned in the early 1970s from giving public talks, but this did not prevent him from effectively and tirelessly directing the steady and vigorous activity of his followers throughout the country. The largest growth of the Jumhuri movement occurred between the early 1970s and the early 1980s.[34] The social background of the movement's membership was predominantly lower and middle class,[35] and its members enjoyed a high degree of literacy.[36] The Jumhuris tended to be young people[37] who lived in urban centers, and their overwhelming majority came from the central Gezira and northern regions. A notable characteristic of the movement was the visibility of women in its public activities.[38]

The first serious challenge against Nimairi's regime came from the

Ansar, who were crushed in a grisly massacre in March 1970 in Aba, the small island in the White Nile from which al-Mahdi had started his revolution.[39] Soon afterward, disagreements developed between the regime and the Communist Party, which insisted on keeping its autonomy and that of its organizations among the youth and women. After the failure of a Communist-inspired coup in July 1971, the regime executed leading military and civilian Communists and started a slow and relentless shift to the right.[40]

The regime's major achievement in the early 1970s was the signing of the Addis Ababa accord in February 1972, which put an end to the seventeen-year-old civil war and granted the south regional self-government. With the recognition of southern autonomy, the national discourse of the 1970s was predominantly of a secular nature stressing "unity in diversity." There was a euphoric sense that by bringing the country's Arab and African elements together, the agreement "promised the continent of Africa its first optimistic framework of Afro-Arab cooperation."[41]

In July 1976, the major northern opposition forces staged an invasion of Khartoum that was aborted. The regime's realization of the threat that a militant opposition could pose, and the opposition's failure to dislodge the regime, led to a reconciliation between the regime and the Umma Party and the Muslim Brothers. It was the Muslim Brothers who gained most from this reconciliation. With the appointment of al-Turabi as attorney general, a drive to Islamize laws was soon set in motion. But more crucially, the Muslim Brothers took advantage of their alliance with the regime to launch Islamic banking, a process that helped turn them in a few years into a formidable economic force.[42]

Throughout all these vicissitudes, the Jumhuris remained persistently supportive of the regime despite their occasional disagreements with some of its policies.[43] However, the reconciliation alignment was the most alarming development as far as they were concerned because it gave *ta'ifiyya* (represented by the Umma Party) and the Muslim Brothers a foothold within the regime and its institutions. In August 1977, they submitted to Nimairi a memorandum and a charter of national conciliation warning against the return of *ta'ifiyya* and advising on the course of action that should be taken to prevent it. They were adamantly opposed to the return of the "traditional, reactionary parties" and stressed that the regime's one-party system was most appropriate for the country's needs. They suggested that the political parties should be replaced by "ideological and intellectual associations" that would operate as free, though closely supervised, platforms. The Jumhuris were certain that in this market of free ideological competition all their ideological foes would crumple one by one. Hence, by leveling the political and ideological plane, the regime would perform the historical mission of preparing the ground for the Jumhuris to take over.[44] The Jumhuris' proposal reflected a clear failure to grasp the nature of political parties as representatives of social forces and conflicting interests.

Taha's orthodox opponents felt that the new circumstances provided them with a fresh opportunity to sway the regime against him. The 'ulama' had already obtained two fatwas (legal opinions) declaring Taha's apostasy from the Islamic Research Council at al-Azhar University in 1972 and the Mecca-based Islamic World League Organization in 1975. Barely two months after the conciliation agreement, the official orthodox body of 'Ulama' 'l-Sudan submitted a memorandum to the People's Assembly accusing Taha of distorting Islam and of colluding with foreign powers, and calling for action to be taken against him.[45] Nothing came of this bid.

In 1983 and following Nimairi's persistent interventions in the parliamentary processes of the southern region, culminating in his unilateral redivision of the south, the Sudan People's Liberation Army/Movement was launched and the civil war broke out again. In August and September of the same year Nimairi decided to introduce shari'a and in particular the *hudud* (sing. *hadd*) punishments.[46] The Muslim Brothers were his right hand in implementing what he described as his "legal revolution," and the country was immediately engulfed by a shari'a frenzy that reached its climax in April 1984 when a state of emergency was declared.[47]

Shortly before the imposition of shari'a, Taha and about fifty of his disciples were detained without charge or trial. Their detention was on account of a pamphlet they had produced criticizing the vice president for having sponsored an Egyptian preacher who ceaselessly inveighed in his preaching sessions against Taha's views and described them as heretical. As Nimairi had announced his intention to impose shari'a shortly after the detention of the Jumhuris, it has been plausibly suggested that at least Taha's detention might have been a deliberate measure to curb his likely opposition.[48]

On December 19, 1984, Taha and his disciples were released. A routine practice of Nimairi's regime was to make detainees sign pledges to the effect that they would not engage in oppositional activity after their release. Had Taha and the Jumhuris been asked to sign such pledges, it is highly unlikely that they would have complied, repeating Taha's actions under the colonialist regime. The fact that they were released unconditionally gives substantial credence to the assumption that they were being manipulated by the regime, which was counting on Taha's expected active opposition to shari'a implementation.[49] Despite Nimairi's Islamist lurch there still were secularist elements within his regime who disagreed with his new religious policies and worked hard to counter the rising power of the Muslim Brothers. It was predictable that under a military and repressive regime like Nimairi's, Taha would be arrested on account of his opposition to shari'a implementation, just as Sadiq al-Mahdi, the leader of the Umma Party, was arrested for taking a similar position. The fact that Taha was singled out for more drastic treatment cannot be adequately explained solely in terms of his opposition. His treatment was related to the particular agenda of the forces on which Nimairi relied in his shari'a drive, namely the Muslim Brothers and the other Islamist allies of the regime (particularly members of some minor Sufi brotherhoods who found themselves in competition with the Jumhuris). These groups saw his opposition as their irresistible opportunity to revive the charges of the shari'a court of 1968 and complete what they perceived as an unfinished job. The internecine conflict within the context of Sudanese Islam resonated with the echoes of centuries-old conflicts between orthodox scholars and Sufis and what they perceived as "deviant" Sufis.

Following his release, Taha wasted no time. In an address to his followers he said that the regime was targeting him and told them that God would not accept their worship unless they sided with the oppressed and fought against the regime's shari'a laws. He maintained that through their act of resistance the Jumhuris were redeeming the entire nation.[50] Taha's uncompromising position was not surprising given the nature of his reform program and his belief as to what the regime was about. In an interview he gave in 1972 he dismissed the regime's plans to promulgate a constitution, stressing that the regime was overstepping its bounds and failing to recognize its "transitional nature" *(marhaliyya)*. As such, the best that the regime could do was to produce a "national charter" *(mithaq watani)* and leave the task of promulgating a "true Islamic constitution" for a subsequent stage.[51] Consequently, the implementation of the shari'a laws of 1983 was an even more serious failure on the regime's part to recognize its transitional nature. By venturing into the shari'a domain, the regime had crossed a boundary that, in Taha's view, it had no right to cross. Taha was thus willing to give the regime, despite its oppressive nature, his full support as long as its credentials were secular; when these credentials became Islamist, the regime placed itself on a collision course with the Jumhuris. As a guardian of (in his phrase) "true Islam," Taha's religious duty was to resist the distortions that the regime and its Islamist allies were propagating and, worse still, implementing.

On December 25, 1984, the group issued a leaflet entitled "This or the Deluge." The leaflet denounced the 1983 shari'a laws, declaring that they "violate shari'a and violate religion itself." It charged that the laws "have . . . humiliated and insulted [the Sudanese] who have seen nothing under [them] except the sword and the whip." The threat the laws posed to the country's national unity owing to discrimination against non-Muslims was stressed. The leaflet called for the repeal of the laws, the ending of the civil war in the south and the implementation of a peaceful solution, and the adoption of a more enlightened understanding of Islam.[52] The leaflet was written in the spirit of "genuine and honest advice" and made its criticisms and demands without calling the regime's legitimacy into question. In this respect, it did not mark a significant departure from Taha's basic line of support for the regime.

When the Jumhuris started distributing their leaflet, the police authorities were not alarmed by it. The Jumhuris were treated leniently, and in some cases police officers intervened to release those Jumhuris who had been arrested by their subordinates.[53] This initial reaction on the part of police authorities indicated that they were in the dark about what other quarters within the regime were hatching.

Then, the state minister for criminal affairs stepped in and instructed prosecutors to "press charges of sedition, undermining the Constitution, inciting unlawful opposition to the government, and disturbing public tranquillity . . . as well as membership in an unlawful organization."[54] Literally overnight, the Jumhuris found themselves facing an array of capital offenses. From that moment on, events unfolded with breathtaking speed.

On January 5, 1985, Taha was arrested. Two days later he and four of his disciples were brought to trial before a special criminal court.[55] Nimairi directed that a section be added to the article of law authorizing the court to impose sentence for any *hadd* offense even if it was not provided for in the statutory penal code. In effect, this allowed the court to charge Taha and his disciples with apostasy.[56] The Jumhuris refused to recognize the court's authority, and Taha's last public words were, "I am not prepared to cooperate with any court that has betrayed the independence of the judiciary and allowed itself to be a tool for humiliating the people, insulting [freedom of thought], and persecuting political opponents."[57]

After a session lasting under two hours on January 7, the court, manned by a single junior judge of limited experience, met the following day. In his judgment, the judge addressed himself to an assessment of Taha's thought, focusing on Taha's claim that the shari'a as implemented by Prophet Muhammad was no longer capable of meeting the needs of modern Muslims. The judge went on to counter this by voicing the familiar orthodox objection that human beings are not endowed with the required capabilities or the right to change the Prophet's shari'a, which was an immutable system. Echoing the charge of "disturbing public tranquillity," the judge deployed a peculiar argument rooted in a particular attitude toward mystical knowledge: although mystical knowledge could be valid and valuable, it was not meant for common people as it could lead them astray and engender a state of *fitna* (dissension). As such, it became clear that the judge was trying Taha and his disciples not just on the basis of the formal charges brought against them but also for the incompatibility of their views with orthodoxy and, furthermore, for what he perceived as a presumptuous act of "throwing pearls before swine."

The judge declared all five guilty of all the charges brought against them, and they were all sentenced to death with the conditional stipulation that the sentence could be mitigated if they renounced their views and repented.

The judgment did not establish any substantial connection between what the accused had done and the provisions of the sections under which they were being charged. The judgment's reasoning and the repentance requirement (which had no basis in the penal code) clearly indicated that the judge had the offense of apostasy in mind although he did not refer to it explicitly.

The explicit mention of apostasy was to be made by the special court of appeal, which accepted on January 15 the trial court's reasoning and sentences. Furthermore, the special court of appeal separated Taha's case from that of his disciples, ruling that his repentance would not be accepted and that he should be immediately executed. The others were to be allowed a one-month grace period to reconsider their beliefs and recant.

On January 17, Nimairi confirmed the sentences, directing that Taha be executed the next day and that the grace period given to the disciples be reduced to three days.

The next morning, a swelling crowd of thousands gathered in the Justice Square of the Khartoum North prison to attend Taha's execution. The Muslim Brothers and other Islamist allies of the regime had mobilized their crowds to demonstrate their support for the sentence. When Taha was led into the prison courtyard with his hands tied behind him, some in the crowd jumped to their feet to revile him. He approached the execution scaffolding with firm and peaceful steps. Describing the moment before the execution, one journalist wrote, "I managed to catch only a glimpse of Taha's face before the executioner placed an oatmeal-colored sack over his head and body, but I shall never forget his expression: His eyes were defiant; his mouth firm. He showed no hint of fear."[58] Others reported catching a serene smile. Two guards pulled a noose tight around his neck and then they "suddenly stood back, the platform snapped open, the rope became taut, and the sack that covered Taha wriggled in the air. A few seconds later, the sack merely swayed a bit at the end of the rope."[59] Taha's body was hurriedly removed into a helicopter that immediately took off to an undisclosed location. Neither Nimairi's regime nor the regimes that came after it revealed where his body was taken.[60] The man whose exact date of entry into the world was not known was to leave it at a date and precise point of time that was to be engraved in his country's memory and in the memory of the rest of the Arab world.[61]

On January 19, Taha's four disciples were forced to go through a public renunciation of their views that was broadcast on radio and television. They were subjected to the humiliation of reading out a prepared statement declaring their rejection of the "false and anti-Islamic" teachings of the "apostate, infidel Mahmud Muhammad Taha." This was compounded by the further humiliation of reappearing before the trial court to make a formal recantation declaring their return to the fold.[62]

As far as the secular forces of the opposition were concerned, Taha's death sealed the regime's fate. The abhorrence and revulsion felt by the majority of the Sudanese was undoubtedly an important catalyst that contributed to the regime's overthrow only eleven weeks after his execution. The Professionals' and Trade Unions' Committee that was formed on the eve of the confirmation of his sentence to protest the decision and mobilize for a stay of execution went on to lead the popular uprising against the regime. Shortly afterward, Taha's elder daughter, Asma, and his leading disciple, 'Abd al-Latif 'Umar Hasab Allah won a constitutional suit when the Supreme Court ruled in November 1986 that the trial, the confirmation proceedings, and the legal basis of Taha's execution were all null and void.[63]

Jumhuri Movement: From Messianic Zeal to Paralysis

Despite Taha's rejection of organized, traditional Sufi *tariqa*s, he created in effect a new mystical brotherhood that revolved around him. He passed on his own sense of spiritual distinction to his disciples, who developed a strong sense of a distinctive spiritual identity and destiny. The Jumhuris saw themselves as having the most intimate relationship with the Prophet by virtue of being the guardians and truest followers of his *sunna*, his way. On account of this relationship and their call for a special message—the Second Message of Islam—they saw themselves as a spiritual vanguard of a new global Islamic era. The belief in this second message was underpinned by a messianic sense; the Jumhuris were a group in a state of waiting.[64]

On closer examination we find that the movement had a virtual, theoretical center represented by the Prophet and a real center represented by Taha. In this it did not differ on a certain level from other mystical brotherhoods as they all claim a chain *(silsila)* connecting the founding *shaikh* and his successors, with the Prophet at the source. Yet on another level there was a crucial difference that made the Jumhuris stand apart, for Taha was not a *shaikh* in the conventional sense. According to Taha, the spiritual starting point of the mystical seeker *(salik)* is a particular relationship with the Prophet that leads to the establishment of a direct relationship with God. The mystical experience can hence be perceived in terms of two spiritual modes: a mediated, prophetic mode and a direct, divine mode. For the Jumhuris, the first mode evidently corresponds to the Prophet and his way, while the second corresponds to Taha's experience. Although Taha had always stressed that it is the Prophet who should be imitated and held as a universal prototype, his particular spiritual claim does effectively turn him into another prototype. Unlike a conventional *shaikh,* Taha did not directly interpose himself between his disciples and their prophetic prototype, but on the other hand his own understanding of the nature of the seeker's relationship with the Prophet and his own particular spiritual claim determined his disciples' understanding of the nature of their religious experience and made it necessary for them to live their spirituality in his shadow.

Despite its establishment as a political party, the Jumhuri movement functioned as a religious brotherhood for most of its history, owing to the abortions of democracy at the hands of the military. Taha was antisecularist, and his anti-*ta'ifiyya* position, just in this respect like that of the Muslim Brothers, did not translate into an adoption of a polity based on the separation of religion and politics. Rather, as an Islamist, he insisted on the conjunction of the two spheres, provided that one advanced what he described as "true Islam."

Hence, the movement that Taha created was politico-religious, with the emphasis placed on its religious aspect. In addition to instilling his followers with the cosmic consciousness of Sufism, he inculcated them with a strong global messianic sense. Paradoxically, this global messianic sense was rooted in the movement's strong locational identification with the Sudan. This is made starkly clear by Taha's claim that when the Sudan implemented the Jumhuri version of a Qur'an-based constitution, it would be "the center of the globe's circle of existence."

The movement produced a distinctive and highly cohesive community where collective prayers were performed intracommunally and members were encouraged to keep company mainly with other members.[65] Acting as a solid anchor and a supportive enveloping milieu, the Jumhuri community was the most effective agency in the resocialization of individual members.

Owing to Taha's anti-intellectualism, the Jumhuris developed an internal culture that was mistrustful of book knowledge. The community's oral tradition provided members with some encapsulations of Sufi knowledge, but the main source of their knowledge and their constant intellectual diet was Taha's own writings. A notable characteristic that the internal life of the Jumhuri community shared with other mystical groups was their strong identification with Sufi masters through the extravagant tales of their miracles. A traditional practice that the Jumhuris belatedly borrowed from other mystical brotherhoods was that of *dhikr* (remembrance) and *inshad* (Sufi singing) in which the human voice is unaccompanied.

The movement had a hierarchical structure at the top of which stood Taha, who enjoyed ultimate spiritual and organizational authority.[66] Taha was a man who exuded charisma, gentle charm, and energy. He led a life that conformed with his Sufi ideal of asceticism: he lived in a simple adobe house, wore simple clothes, made a point of never carrying money on him, and did not eat meat.[67] Following Taha in the group's hierarchy was a small elite of senior *(kibar)* members, and at the base of the pyramid was the rest of the membership or the juniors *(sighar)*. The ranking of the members was determined by Taha. The relationship between Taha and his disciples rested on a tacit understanding whereby they accepted his final authority not just as regarded the group's stance on public issues and internal organizational matters but also, more significantly, concerning their own spiritual states and the judgment of their progress along the mystical path. The internalization of Taha's authority within the community's consciousness was so deep and effective that the movement hardly experienced any division.

Taha's confrontational engagement that characterized Republican activities under colonialism inspired the vigorous activities of the young Jumhuris of the 1970s and 1980s. Jumhuris walking around in groups of two or more, distributing their publications or engaging passers-by in discussions, became a familiar sight in the streets of most cities and towns. At the University of Khartoum, the country's liveliest center of political activity, the Jumhuris were the first to initiate what came to be known as discussion corners, a practice that soon spread to other university campuses. A striking aspect of Jumhuri practice was the active participation of women, whose engagement of the public in streets and in the group's events challenged the prevailing stereotypes and expectations of Sudanese patriarchal traditions. It is important, however, to emphasize that the Jumhuris did not engage in this activity in the spirit of open-minded discussions; theirs was an activity of elitist propagation in which they saw themselves as transmitters of the truth of Islam and educators of the nation while strongly believing that it was only a matter of time before their recipients recognized that truth.

The Jumhuri movement presents a bewildering phenomenon: despite all its ideological stridency and aggressive missionary zeal, the movement immediately and completely withdrew from public space after Taha's execution. It was understandable that the Jumhuris would be traumatized by the judicial murder of their leader and that some of them would altogether opt out of the movement, but how can we account for the movement's wholesale paralysis and total inaction despite its assertive claims of leading a divinely sanctioned, global Islamic revival?[68]

What made the Jumhuris' shock particularly poignant was the fact that it involved a distressing implication that was hard for the Jumhuris to accept in light of their particular mystical outlook. Taha not only preached nonviolence but he also stressed that the time of martyrdom was over because mankind had already entered a higher stage that required serving by living rather than serving by laying down one's life.[69] He viewed himself as a sober mystic who was rooted in the Prophet's way and followed the traditions of sober mystics. Sober mystics like Abu al-Qasim al-Junaid (d. 298/910), whom Taha sometimes quoted, recommended esoteric prudence. Despite al-Junaid's close friendship with al-Hallaj, who was executed on the pretext of his Sufi "theopathic statements" (shatahat), he censured al-Hallaj's position because he did not approve of divulging one's mystical experience to the public. This censorious view called into question the balance and sober judgment of the martyred Sufi and saw in his final fate an element of divine punishment and estrangement. The negative implication that this mystical standpoint would project on Taha's execution was not lost on the Jumhuris' mystical sensibility. One effective way through which they tried to make sense of the situation was to assert that Taha's death was in fact a willing act on his part. Accordingly, he chose to make the ultimate sacrifice of giving his life in order to atone for the nation and save it from the disaster of the regime's shari'a laws.

Undoubtedly, Taha's death left the Jumhuris with a leadership crisis. As he was the movement's spiritual and organizational center, it was not surprising that this would occur. This does not provide a complete explanation, though, for the Jumhuris' drastic response. The movement's underlying crisis was not one of leadership but rather of what may be described as a lack of intellectual independence. Despite Taha's theoretical emphasis of the notion of freedom, and for that matter of "absolute individual freedom," this was precisely what he failed to offer his disciples. The movement he created reflected his notion of guardianship *(wisaya)* according to which a person who attains to spiritual and intellectual maturity (like the Prophet, for instance) has a natural right of guardianship over others by virtue of their "spiritual minority." The outcome of this culture of guardianship and total intellectual dependency was a movement with impoverished inner intellectual and spiritual resources, intrinsically incapable of surviving Taha's death.[70]

On Taha's Intellectual Formation

As a mystic and thinker, Taha belonged to the school of Islamic mysticism that may be described as "radical Sufism." Radicalism is defined here in terms of the mystic's relationship to tradition; a radical mystic deemphasizes tradition (at the center of which stands Muhammad) and shifts his emphasis to his own raw and direct experience of having a union *(wasl)* with the Divine. Perhaps the starkest representative of radical Sufism was the little-known Muhammad b. 'Abd al-Jabbar al-Niffari (d. ca. 354/965), whose writings seldom refer to Muhammad or quote the Qur'an, exclusively focusing on his communion with God.[71] However, this type of mystical expression is usually associated with the names of other great mystics such as Rabi'a al-'Adawiyya (d. 185/801), Abu Yazid al-Bistami (d. 261/874 or 264/877–78), al-Hallaj, and Shihab al-Din al-Suhrawardi. It reached its greatest theosophical expression at the hands of Muhyi al-Din Ibn 'Arabi, who was known as *al-shaikh 'l-akbar* (the greatest master). The major themes of those radical Sufis came to influence and shape Taha's thought.

Rabi'a provides the sharpest expression of the mystical doctrine of "pure divine love" *('ilm 'l-mahabba)*. Rabi'a reportedly said that she did not worship God from fear of hell or in hope of paradise but only for His own sake and for His eternal beauty.[72] Her attitude toward the Prophet was summed up in a statement according to which she said that she was so possessed with the love of God that she had no room for loving except Him.[73] Whether such statements were actually made by her is not important; what is significant is that they expressed a mystical perspective whose attitudes must have struck a responsive chord among some Muslims of the second Muslim century and afterward.

Al-Bistami pushed the notion of mystical union to the ultimate horizon of a merger and identification with God *('ain 'l-jam')*.[74] Constantly setting his sight on God as his goal, everything, even his own self *(nafs)* became an obstacle *(hijab)* that had to be overcome. In articulating his mystical states, he used the hyperbolic language of theopathic utterances, coming up with seemingly shocking statements such as "Glory be to me! I am my Lord, Most High!";[75] "I am the totality of the Preserved Tablet";[76] and "If hell sees me it will die out."[77] A similar mystical impulse consumed al-Hallaj, who spoke in the language of *wahdat 'l-shuhud* (lit. "unity of witness"), expressing the belief that the saint can attain to a state of mystical union that makes him a living witness of God. It was on attaining this state that al-Hallaj made theopathic statements such as "I am the Truth"[78] and "Oh, He who is I and I who am He, there is no distinction between my I-ness [*annayati*] and Your He-ness [*huwiyyatak*] except in that I am created and You are eternal."[79] Like a number of other mystics, al-Hallaj made a distinction between the external aspect of obligatory rites (such as prayer and fasting, which he viewed as *wasa'it,* or means) and their internal aspect (the *haqa'iq,* or ultimate realities of the means), placing the emphasis on the latter aspect, which he saw as the ultimate goal.[80]

The name of al-Suhrawardi is associated with the school of illumination *(ishraq)*. His thought was rooted in several traditions that he strove to bring into a creative theosophical synthesis: Sufism (with the particular influence of al-Hallaj and al-Ghazali), Zoroastrianism, hermetism, and Neoplatonism. According to al-Suhrawardi's illuminationism, existence is perceived in terms of light and darkness, with the first element corresponding to corporeal existence and the second corresponding to incorporeal existence. God is the Essence of the First Absolute Light; He is the Light of Lights *(nur 'l-anwar)* who has brought all things into existence. Illuminationism entails a spiritual geography that invests the notions of East and West with its own symbolism, equating the East with light and the West with darkness, and human existence in this world is perceived in terms of an "occidental exile."[81] Escape from this exile, the goal of the mystical endeavor, could only be realized by attaining to the illumination of the Divine Essence.

Ibn 'Arabi was the most creative and prolific mystic produced by Islam. Like al-Suhrawardi, he came under the influences of hermetism and Neoplatonism and developed a theosophical system that combined mysticism and philosophy. By virtue of his central notion of the unity of being *(wahdat 'l-wujud)*, Ibn 'Arabi's mystical thought has been characterized as pantheistic.[82] For him the natural starting point is not proving God's existence, who is beyond proof, but rather understanding why God created the world. In accounting for this he quotes a tradition according to which God said, "I was a hidden treasure, and I wanted to be known. So, I created the creatures. I made Myself known to them, and it was through Me that they knew Me."[83] God as "hidden treasure" is perceived by Ibn 'Arabi in terms of the infinite multiplicity of His names (or attributes or aspects). In creating the world God wished to regard these names as existent entities *(a'yan,* sing. *'ain)* or, as Ibn 'Arabi puts it, "[God] wanted to regard His own existence in an encompassing cosmos that encapsulated everything. . . . for the regarding of a thing of itself by itself is not like its seeing itself in another thing that acts as its mirror."[84] As such, the phenomenal world is a self-manifestation *(tajalli)* of God. Moreover, the world is anthropomorphized as it is perceived as the "greater human" *(al-insan 'l-kabir)*. This divine self-manifestation reaches its highest realization in the Perfect Human *(al-insan 'l-kamil)*. Ibn 'Arabi grounds this notion of the Perfect Human in the prophetic tradition about God creating the human in His image and fuses it with the Qur'anic notion of human vicegerency *(khilafa)*. Hence, the world constitutes the external image of the human, whereas the human's internal image corresponds to the divine image. The existence of the world is made possible by virtue of God's permeation *(sarayan)* through all its manifestations.[85]

Ibn 'Arabi expresses the philosophical notions of the One and the Many, or Reality and Appearance, in terms of the opposition between *Haqq* (the Real) and *khalq* (the phenomenal world). This, however, is a dualism beyond which he asserts an ultimate unity. What he ultimately sees, in the light of the monistic logic of his Unity of Being theory, is the One Reality that is God. This is a Reality that can only be perceived by undergoing a mystical experience, because its knowledge requires the attainment of "esoteric sciences" *('ulum 'l-asrar)*.[86] Among the radical Sufis, Ibn 'Arabi is the one who exerted the most influence and, consequently, who was subjected to the severest attacks by classical and modern exponents of orthodoxy.[87]

It is not clear at what point in his intellectual development Taha became attracted to Ibn 'Arabi and in particular to his theory of the Unity of Being that became the cornerstone of his metaphysics. With Taha's independence of mind and his acute sense of distinctive spiritual rank, it was no surprise that he would eventually signal his own coming of age vis-à-vis the "greatest master." Although Taha did not deny Ibn 'Arabi's influence on him, he liked to emphasize his own distinction. He stressed that his own project was completely original and hence transcended all past projects, even that of Ibn 'Arabi.[88] Taha was keen to deny his intellectual discipleship (what he called *talmadha*) to any mystic or thinker. What he acknowledged was a discipleship of methodology *(minhaj)* that helped him along his mystical progress and realization, and this was an aspect with which he credited the Prophet and al-Ghazali.[89]

Taha places methodology against reading *(qira'a)*—that is, the attainment of knowledge through scholarly effort. This is embedded in the Sufi oppositions of internal *(batin)* and external *(zahir)*, or esoteric and exoteric, or knowledge based on direct experience and received knowledge (what al-Bistami describes as taking knowledge from the Living One as opposed to taking it from the dead). This is a point about the right and ultimate manner of acquiring knowledge and as such has a special significance not just as regards Taha's epistemology but also in connection with the particular spiritual claim he makes when he expounds his theory of prayer.

It is in the light of this position that Taha, on being asked about his readings, asserted, "I followed the methodology and read little—fragments [*shadharat*] from here and there." These fragmentary readings did not include modern Muslim thinkers but covered writings by "Marx, Lenin, [Bertrand] Russell, [George Bernard] Shaw, and H. G. Wells."[90]

Taha's statement that he did not read modern Muslim thinkers should be read, on the one hand, as an affirmation that he was not a systematic reader and, on the other, as an extreme way of asserting the originality of his thought and his independent authority. This statement notwithstanding, Taha was fully aware of the major trends and debates of modern Islam. The Islam of his generation's *afandiyya* class was very much conditioned by the progressive influence of Muhammad ʿAbduh and his school. This was an influence whose impact was particularly significant in the Sudan, owing to Egypt's cultural domination on the one hand and the willingness of the educated class to open themselves to Egyptian influences on the other. Taha's antitraditionalist and reformist discourse is undoubtedly indebted to ʿAbduh's project despite his tendency to accentuate its shortcomings.[91] This project has been summed up in four points: (1) purging Islam of all corrupting trends and practices that influenced it; (2) reforming higher education; (3) reformulating Islamic doctrine in conformance with modern thought; and (4) defending Islam against secular and Christian attacks.[92] Although all these were objectives with which Taha did identify, his own project chiefly focused on the third element.

Although Taha was ideologically and politically opposed to the Muslim Brothers, particularly in their Sudanese expression,[93] the movement he created shared a fundamental characteristic with Sayyid Qutb's (d. 1966) notion of the ideal revivalist movement. In Qutb's view this movement has to be separationist; it has to dissociate itself from the rest of society, which is deemed as living in a depraved state of *jahiliyya* (spiritual ignorance) not dissimilar from that of Meccan society when Muhammad started his mission.[94] The notion of *jahiliyya*, popularized by Muhammad Qutb's 1964 work *Jahiliyyat 'l-qarn 'l-ʿishrin* (The *Jahiliyya* of the Twentieth Century), was used as a sweeping judgment applying not only to non-Muslim societies but also to Muslim societies. The Jumhuri movement was in effect a separationist community with a highly developed sense of self-distinction. Like the thinkers of the Muslim Brothers, Taha also used the term *jahiliyya* in referring to the modern condition, though with the important positive qualification that present-day *jahiliyya* is a higher and more refined state than that of the Prophet's time.

In comparing the contributions of 'Abduh and Hasan al-Banna (d. 1949), the founder of the Muslim Brothers, Taha lauded the political consciousness and activist reformism of the latter. He used the same criterion as a basis to condemn the Ansar 'l-Sunna group, the Sudanese offshoot of the Wahhabi movement, whose quietism during the period of the struggle against colonialism he did not approve. More importantly, he was dismissive of their reform views, maintaining that "nothing good can possibly come out of them" (AJii 76). When it came to mystical orders, Taha wanted them to dissolve and unite in the all-encompassing "Muhammad's *tariq* [path]" as the ultimate order. In saying this he was both stressing their irrelevance and laying the foundation for his own reformulation of Islamic worship and ethics in the light of his theory of prayer.

As far as European trends of thought were concerned, Taha's mention of "Marx, Lenin, Russell, Shaw, and Wells" indicated his indebtedness to the two major trends of socialism and liberal democracy—trends that played a decisive role in shaping the social and political content of his Second Message of Islam. Although he does not make an explicit reference to Sigmund Freud or any of Freud's works, he clearly had been exposed to his theories as shown by his employment of some psychoanalytic notions.

Another domain of Western provenance that has been used (and abused) by modern Muslim thinkers is that of modern science. The physical notions of matter and energy and the biological notion of evolution are central in Taha's account of the nature of the world and life. He borrows and uses these notions, creatively incorporating them into his metaphysical scheme. Like 'Abduh and other modernists, Taha's willingness to incorporate the principle of change into his understanding of Islam was the solid foundation of his modernism. This becomes clear in the discussion of his theory of a Second Message of Islam.

The principle of change is pivotal in Taha's own perception of his role as an intellectual. In his view, the ideal intellectual is someone who goes through an "intellectual revolution" *(thawra fikriyya)* that frees him from his ignorance, his intellectual prejudices, and his fears. This is an intellectual who combines the pursuit of knowledge with his activism to change the world or, in Taha's words, combines ‘*ilm* (knowledge) with ‘*amal* (action, praxis), as the daunting task of changing the world requires constant self-change and self-regeneration. In saying this Taha was inspired by his reading of a Qur'anic verse he often quoted, namely verse 55:29, which describes God as engaging every day in new deeds. He maintains that this refers to God's ceaseless self-renewal, which should provide humans with their ultimate and constant example.

Taha believed that his own life was an active attempt to realize this ideal, and, moreover, he believed that he could provide others with the necessary guidance to realize it, namely through a combination of a spiritual striving based on prayer and a social and political activism that seeks to change the world.

2

Theory of Prayer

Worship, Individualism, and Authenticity

Divine Intention, Human Response

MAHMUD MUHAMMAD TAHA'S THEORY of prayer lies at the heart of his reformist project. He expounded his theory in 1966 in a major work, *Risalat 'l-salat* (A Treatise on Prayer),[1] and a complementary text, *Tariq Muhammad* (The Path of Muhammad), also published in 1966, as well as *Ta'mallamu kaifa tusallun* (Teach Yourselves How to Pray), published in 1972.

Throughout his writings, Taha stresses that prayer is the most important and most noble of works, work that is God-oriented par excellence and hence at the very root of the human relationship with the Divine. Like many a great religious and mystic thinker, Taha saw this relationship as the ground of being, and he was preoccupied with the means through which such consciousness could be made to permeate human existence. This, in his view, was only realizable through prayer in its Islamic sense *(salat)*.

Taha's theory of prayer is characterized by its radicalness in rejecting the orthodox consensus of Muslims in the past and the present as regards the nature and function of prayer. Although he invariably appeals to the Qur'an and Muhammad's traditions as his ultimate frame of reference in making his case, the rupture with the body of traditional beliefs is clearly marked.

The conceptual foundations of Taha's theory of prayer are the notions of servantship *('ubudiyya)* and individualism *(fardiyya)*.

The Islamic concept of human relationship to God rests on the interrelated notions of service and servantship. The Qur'anic verse usually ad-

41

duced in connection with these notions is verse 51:56, "I have not created jinn and mankind except to serve Me [*li-ya'buduni*]."² Traditional exegetes have generally understood the verb *ya'bud* in the sense of "to worship, to serve."³ Another opinion attributed to Ibn 'Abbas (d. 68/687) introduced the substantive *'ubuda*, which he explains as submission, whether out of willingness or through coercion.⁴ An isolated exegetical opinion attributed to Mujahid (d. between 100/718 and 104/722) holds that the verb means "to know."

The verb has thus been generally understood in the light of the notion of *'ibada* (worship, service): God created the jinn and humankind to worship Him. This interpretation, however, gave rise to a problem: if that is the case, then how can one explain the fact that not all humans recognize God and worship Him? In accounting for this conundrum, an exegetical tradition attributed to 'Ali b. Abi Talib (d. 40/661) maintained that the verse really meant, "I have only created jinn and mankind *so that I may command them to serve me*."⁵ Another prevalent view among the exegetes was articulated by Zaid b. Aslam (d. 136/753), who maintained that the verse meant, "I created the righteous for my worship and the damned for my disobedience."⁶ Further substantiation of this point of view was offered through a variant reading attributed to 'Abd Allah b. Mas'ud (d. ca. 33/653) according to which the verse reads, "I have only created *the believing* jinn and mankind ['*l-jinna wa 'l-insa mina 'l-mu'mina*] that they may serve me."⁷ In addressing the problem, al-Zamakhshari (d. 538/1144) placed his emphasis on human free will, arguing that had God willed all humans to worship Him this would have taken place, but in reality He wanted His worship to be a willing act.⁸

❦

Unlike the traditional exegetes, the Sufis made a key distinction between the notions of service and servantship. They perceived of service as a preparatory level to be transcended by a higher level of spiritual realization, that is, that of servantship. Abu 'Ali al-Daqqaq (d. 405/1014–15 or 412/1021–22) suggested a threefold spiritual path progressing from *'ibada*, which was for the commonalty *(al-'amma)*, to *'ubudiyya*, which was for the spiritually elect *(khawas)*, and culminating in *'ubuda*, which was for the spiritually superelect *(khass 'l-khass)*.⁹ This tripartite scheme did not catch on with later Sufis, who preeminently articulated their thoughts and described their experiences in terms of a creative interplay and opposition between the categories of service and servantship.[10]

Furthermore, the Sufi perspective went beyond the service/servantship duality, placing it within the context of what it perceived as the ultimate duality that invests human life with its vital spark and meaning, namely, the *rububiyya/'ubudiyya* (lordship/servantship) dichotomy to which everything ultimately points. For Ibn 'Arabi, for instance, it is in fact this dichotomy that lies at the heart of verse 51:56: "[God] said this only about these two species [jinn and humans] since it was only they who claimed lordship [*uluhiyya*] or attributed it to others than God or treated the rest of His creation with haughtiness."[11] As far as the Sufis were concerned, this dichotomy constituted the ground of their experience. Ibn 'Arabi once described the dichotomy in the following terms: "I have realized the ultimate of servantship; I am a pure and absolute servant without the merest hint of lordship [*rububiyya*]."[12]

As in the thought of other Sufis, the assumption of this dichotomy is a central premise in Taha's thought. It is a dichotomy that started in fact even before humans appeared on the scene in their Adamic, bodily form, as verse 7:172 intimates:

> And when thy Lord took from the Children of Adam, from their loins, their seed, and made them testify touching themselves, 'Am I not your Lord [*alastu bi-rabbikum*]?' They said, 'Yes, we testify'—lest you should say on the Day of Resurrection, 'As for us, we were heedless of this.'

It has rightly been noted that this idea of a transhistorical primordial covenant between God and humanity "has impressed the religious conscience of the Muslims, and especially the Muslim mystics, more than any other idea."[13] According to Taha, the verse not only reminds humans of the original state of their servantship but also rebukes them for the state of *ghafla* (heedlessness) in which they constantly live. Putting an end to this heedlessness plays a key role in his theory of prayer.

The other foundational notion in Taha's theory of prayer is that of individualism *(fardiyya)*. Although he would insist on stressing its Qur'anic provenance, Taha is undoubtedly indebted to the ideas of Western liberalism for the ways in which he developed and emphasized *fardiyya*. Concerning the Qur'anic source of individualism he quotes verse 6:94, which states that humans shall come to God "bare and alone [*furada*]" and verses 17:13–14, which emphasize individual fate and responsibility on the Day of Judgment (RS 79). Although the context of these verses is eschatological and hence concerns events that transcend history or are part of a special salvation history, Taha subjects them to a *tawhid*-based ontological principle that asserts that everything that was, or will be, is (AJi 25).[14] Accordingly he reads them as revealing a fundamental aspect of the human/divine relationship not just in the hereafter but also in this life.

Hence, Taha's chief focus is the spiritual universe of the individual: "The individual man or woman is the ultimate end [*ghaya*], and everything else is a means [*wasila*] to this individual, including the whole of creation [*al-akwan*] and the Qur'an" (RS 61). But since the individual does not live in a vacuum, it is natural that Taha would raise and problematize the question of the nature of the relationship between individuals and their society, for individuals need to attain their "absolute individual freedom" *(al-hurriyya 'l-fardiyya 'l-mutlaqa)*, and society needs to achieve "total social justice" *(al-'adala 'l-ijtima'iyya 'l-shamila)*.

The Prophetic Ascension Event

It is in the light of the notion of servantship and his affirmation that the individual is the ultimate end that Taha approaches the nature and function of prayer in Islam. In expounding his theory, he starts by drawing on a particular set of Islamic and mystical perceptions of Muhammad's spiritual and religious experience.

With respect to this experience, two climactic events defined Muhammad's prophetic career. The first was that of receiving his initial revelation *(wahy)*, when, according to Muslim belief, he encountered the archangel Gabriel (Jibril), who revealed to him the first verses of the Qur'an.[15] The second was that of his ascension to heaven *(mi'raj)*, when he reportedly met God. It is this second event that concerns us here with regard to Taha's theory of prayer, for it is believed that Islamic ritual prayer as practiced by Muslims was instituted when Muhammad performed his ascension.

Muslim sources tell us that the ascension event was preceded by another, seemingly preparative, subevent, that is, Muhammad's night journey *(isra')* to Jerusalem, where he met all the prophets and led them in prayer.[16] This event is only briefly referred to in verse 17:1. By contrast, the ascension event is addressed more extensively in verses 53:5–18:

> [5.] [He was] taught . . . by one terrible in power,
> [6.] very strong; he stood poised,
> [7.] being on the higher horizon,
> [8.] then drew near and suspended hung,
> [9.] two bows'-length away, or nearer,
> [10.] then revealed to his servant that he revealed.
> [11.] His heart lies not of what he saw;
> [12.] what, will you dispute with him what he sees?
> [13.] Indeed, he saw him another time
> [14.] by the Lote-Tree of the Boundary
> [15.] nigh which is the Garden of Refuge,
> [16.] when there covered the Lote-Tree that which covered;
> [17.] his eye swerved not, nor swept astray.
> [18.] Indeed, he saw one of the greatest signs of his Lord.

Despite its elliptical nature, the Qur'anic account of the ascension event gave rise to elaborate, fantastic, and colorful accounts in the *sira* (prophetic biography), the hadith, and the *tafsir* (Qur'anic exegesis) materials. Some aspects of the hadith and the *tafsir* materials provide a context for Taha's treatment of the ascension event.

According to one tradition, Muhammad gave the following account of his ascension experience: "While I was at Mecca, the roof of my house was opened, and Gabriel descended, opened my chest and washed it with Zamzam water.[17] Then he brought a golden tray full of wisdom and belief and having poured its contents into my chest, he closed it. Then he took my hand and ascended with me to the heaven." The hadith recounts Muhammad's admission into seven heavens and his meetings with Adam, Idris, Abraham, Moses, and Jesus.[18] At the climactic moment when he met God, prayer was prescribed. This, however, was not a simple event of divine command and unquestioning human submission; rather, it was a delicate consultative and negotiatory process as described in the rest of the hadith.

"Allah enjoined fifty prayers on me. When I returned with this order of Allah, I passed by Moses, who asked me, 'What has Allah enjoined on your followers?' I replied, 'He has enjoined fifty prayers on them.' On that Moses said to me, 'Return to your Lord (and appeal for reduction), for your followers will not be able to bear this.' So, I returned to my Lord and asked for some reduction, and he reduced it to half." This, however, did not satisfy Moses, who again pressed Muhammad to go back to his Lord and ask for further alleviation. When prayers were reduced to five and Moses still insisted on reduction, Muhammad replied, "I feel shy of asking my Lord now"—a decision on his part that finally fixed the number of Muslim prayers at five. On the way back, Muhammad was taken by Gabriel to see the dazzling "Lote-Tree of the Boundary" *(sidrat 'l-muntaha)* and was afterward shown paradise.[19]

The hadith material also provides the answer to the crucial question of how Muhammad learned the manner of the prayer gestures that he communicated to his community. According to the traditions, Gabriel is the central agent through whom prayer as a ritual act of specific, prescribed gestures was instituted. According to one tradition, Gabriel descended five times and acted as Muhammad's prayer leader *(imam)* in order to teach him how to perform each obligatory prayer.[20] Another tradition places the ritual act within a communal-prayer context: Muhammad called five times on the believers to perform the prayer in a position behind him while at the same time he himself was performing it behind Gabriel.[21]

In dealing with the ascension event, the *tafsir* material methodically posed several key questions, and in addressing them the exegetes substantially drew on hadith materials. They were unanimous that the passage of chapter 53 describes a spiritual encounter involving the Islamic "revelatory trinity" of God, Gabriel, and Muhammad. An early problem that arose was whether the event was a purely spiritual, visionary experience or whether it was also corporeal, involving Muhammad's physical being. Al-Tabari threw his weight behind the second point of view, which came to characterize the orthodox position. He argued that a physical ascension is more miraculous and would more effectively serve as proof of Muhammad's prophethood.[22]

Furthermore, the specific referents of the respective verses in the passage were widely debated. Exegetes agreed that verses 53:5–7 refer to

Gabriel. Beyond this, however, they took divergent points of view in interpreting the rest of the passage. In reading verses 53:8–10, some exegetes maintained that the object of reference here is still Gabriel, whereas others argued that the verses in fact refer to God. Disagreement also arose in reading verse 53:13, as some authorities interpreted this as seeing God for a second time while others maintained that it was Gabriel that the Prophet saw again.[23] An important issue raised in connection with verse 53:11 was the nature of the Beautific Vision. The literalists insisted that the believers could see God with their own eyes, whereas their opponents advocated a metaphorical reading, maintaining that it is only the heart that can see God.[24] The enigmatic reference to "one of the greatest signs" in verse 53:18 led the exegetes to speculate in two directions: some applied a vivid imagination and maintained that he saw a green expanse *(rafraf akhdar)*[25] that blocked the entire horizon, and others held that he saw Gabriel in his real form.[26] Another inscrutable reference that sparked disagreement was the one to "the Lote-Tree of the Boundary." It was clear from the second noun of the genitive construction describing the tree *(muntaha,* "end, extreme, utmost limit") that it demarcated a boundary. Hence, the question with which the exegetes grappled was what kind of boundary was intended. On this, the *tafsir* material offered three views. The first was that the tree represents the point where human knowledge reaches its limit and beyond which prevails the realm of the unseen *(al-ghaib),* known only to God. The second view was that it represents the point where all that ascends from below ceases its ascension and all that descends from above ceases its descent. The third view was Islamocentric in nature, maintaining that it is the point where the spiritual progress of all those who do not belong to Muhammad's community or follow his way comes to a standstill.[27]

Mystical Ascensions

For the religious imagination of the orthodox Muslims, the ascension event was a unique, Prophet-specific experience. Sufis, though, and in particular radical Sufis, saw in it a spiritual model and a pressing call to meet God by actively engaging in one's own ascension.[28] Two noteworthy mystical-ascension accounts were furnished by al-Bistami and Ibn 'Arabi. The claims of these Sufis of having performed ascensions were found credible by other

Sufis. They were, however, subjected to an important qualification summed up by the fifth/eleventh-century mystic al-Hujwiri, who said, "The ascension of prophets takes place outwardly and in the body, whereas that of saints takes place inwardly and in the spirit."[29]

In describing his ascension, al-Bistami used a language that belongs to a special category of Sufi statements characterized as *shatahat* or *shathiyyat* (ecstatic utterances). The Sufi author al-Sarraj (d. 378/988) defines such an utterance as "an unusual statement that describes an overpowering, burning, and overwhelming state of passion [*wajd*]."[30] He not only views these utterances as an expression of a profound mystical state but also tenaciously defends the right of Sufis to declare them.[31] This contrasts with a later, post-Hallajian stance that dominated Sufi circles and showed a marked hostility toward making public statements about ecstatic states.[32] This position is summed up by al-Jurjani (d. 838/1434), who defines *shath* as "a statement indicating foolishness and presumption. It is pronounced by the people of gnosis [*ma'rifa*] while they are in an impulsive and unstable state and it is a lapse on the part of those who have achieved a high rank of realization [*muhaqqiqun*]. It is a truthful claim that the gnostic reveals without divine permission."[33]

Al-Bistami is attributed with the following account in describing his ascension:

> I saw that my spirit *(sirr)* was borne to the heavens. It looked at nothing and gave no heed, though Paradise and Hell were displayed to it, for it was freed from phenomena and veils. Then I became a bird, whose body was of Oneness and whose wings were of Everlastingness, and I continued to fly in the air of the Absolute *(huwiyyat)*, until I passed into the sphere of Purification *(tanzih)*, and gazed upon the field of Eternity *(azaliyyat)* and beheld there the tree of Oneness. When I looked I myself was all those. I cried: "O Lord, with my egoism . . . I cannot attain to Thee, and I cannot escape from my selfhood. What am I to do?" God spake: "O Abu Yazid, thou must win release from thy 'thou-ness' by following my beloved (i.e., Muhammad). Smear thine eyes with the dust of his feet and follow him continually."[34]

In another account, al-Bistami describes his experience in terms of a personal, dialogical encounter with God. He writes:

Once, I was raised up [*rufi'tu*] until I stood before Him.[35] He said to me, "O Abu Yazid, my creatures want to see you." Abu Yazid said, "O my Beloved ['*azizi*], I do not want to see them but if Thou want me to do so I cannot object to what Thou want me to do. Then adorn me with Thy Oneness so that when Thy creatures see me they will say: We have seen Thee! Thou will then be That [*(dhaka)*] and I would not be there." He did that—He stood me up, adorned me, raised me up, and said, "Go forth to my creatures!" I took a step away from Him toward the creatures. When I took the next step, I fainted. He called out, "Bring back My beloved, he cannot be away from Me."[36]

In another account God disappears only to reveal Himself in an unexpected manner: "I reached the Throne ['*arsh*] and found it empty. I threw myself on it and said, 'My Lord, where do I seek Thee?' He unveiled [Himself] and I realized that I was I [*anni ana*] and that I am I [*fa-ana ana*]. [I realized that] I am in charge of what I seek and it is only I and nothing else in what I perform."[37]

Like al-Hujwiri, Ibn 'Arabi asserts the corporeal nature of Muhammad's ascension as opposed to the purely spiritual ascension of the saint *(wali)*. In writing about this experience, he mostly uses the term *isra'* (night journey) and describes it as an experience in which the saints "witness reified meanings [*ma'ani mutajassida*] in concrete forms [*suwar mahsusa*] accessible to the imagination [*khayal*], and they will be given knowledge of the meanings contained in these forms."[38] God makes these spiritual journeys possible for His saints in order to expand their knowledge and make them more perceptive, and the experience of each saint corresponds to his level of spiritual progress. Ibn 'Arabi places all this within a larger metaphysical framework in which God, the world, the human, and God's Names *(asma')* interconnect. The world is created in God's image and the human is created in the world's image, but it is only when humans realize that they are created in God's image that their spiritual journey toward God starts. God would take the seeker through the realm of His Names (whether those described as His Beautiful Names or His other countless Names), and it is by virtue of experiencing these Names as his own names that the seeker can attain spiritual self-realization.[39]

Ibn 'Arabi's notion of ascension involves going through an initial state of dissolution *(hall tarkib)* to be followed by a state in which the seeker would reintegrate his self in a new unified whole *('ada yurakkib dhatahu).*[40] Whereas al-Bistami describes his encounters with God through a highly subjective imagery, Ibn 'Arabi takes Muhammad's ascension as his model and articulates his experience through its imagery.[41] His experience was to bear witness to his theory of divine Names, that is to say that the mystic's identification with God is made possible through God's self-disclosure through His Names. It is by virtue of these Names that God becomes concretized and familiarized and the mystic can reach God and talk to Him.

Following in Muhammad's footsteps, Ibn 'Arabi ascends through seven heavens before he meets God. In each heaven he meets a prophet from an earlier era with whom he discusses issues that preoccupied the Muslim scholars of that time.[42] After meeting Abraham in the seventh heaven, he proceeds to witness the "inhabited house" *(al-bait 'l-ma'mur),*[43] symbolizing his heart. The divine hadith according to which God says, "I am contained by neither heaven nor earth but it is the heart of my believing servant that contains Me," is recaptured by Ibn 'Arabi in terms of divine epiphany through "seventy thousand veils of light and darkness," for "if He manifests Himself without [these veils], the lights of His face would burn the world of creation."[44]

While some traditions rendered Muhammad's experience of seeing the Lote-Tree of the Boundary with marked mundaneness, Ibn 'Arabi describes his experience in purely spiritual terms.[45] When he saw what he described as "the seating of gnostics" (the Prophet's "green seating"), he was overwhelmed with light until he himself became all light. He describes his experience at this moment in the following terms: "I called out, 'O My Lord, the signs [*ayat*] are in a state of fragmentation [*shatat*].' " God's response was to "reveal" to him *(anzala 'alaiyya)* verse 3:84.[46] In describing the experience of this revelation, Ibn 'Arabi says, "In this verse, He gave me all the signs, made things more accessible, and gave me the key to all knowledge. I knew I was the sum total of all those He had mentioned to me."[47]

A supreme insight produced by this state of intimate communion was that the meanings of all the Names refer to a single Named One *(musamma wahid)* and a single Object *('ain wahida)*—that is, the divine Essence. The climax of his experience was witnessing this Named One and subjectifying the single Object of which his own being *(wujud)* became a part.[48] He sums up his realization by saying, "My journey was but in myself and my act of indication was but to myself."[49] He was rewarded by numerous gifts of knowledge that filled him with a sense of uniqueness. It was this sense that made him declare, "As far as I know I am not aware of any person who has attained to the station of servitude [*maqam 'l-'ubudiyya*] at a higher level than myself. If there is such a person, this person is then like me."[50]

Taha's New Perspective on Ascension

Although Taha does not refer to the ascension accounts of al-Bistami and Ibn 'Arabi, it is reasonable to assume that he was aware of them and that their daring perspectives influenced his own experience and perspective. To make sense of what Taha says about prayer, his writings have to be placed not only within the broader concerns and aspirations of the Sufi tradition but also within the context of his experience. Although Taha does not provide a vivid and detailed account of a mystical ascension as al-Bistami and Ibn 'Arabi did, the nature of his experience can be inferred from his theory of prayer.[51]

In tackling the ascension event, Taha is not concerned with a systematic scrutiny of the materials of the classical sources; rather, his point of departure is a direct engagement of the Qur'anic passage of chapter 53. It would, however, be wrong to presume that he engaged the text in a neutral and detached manner informed only by what the verses disclose. Rather, he read this highly opaque and mystifying passage in the light of a particular theological perspective and a particular exegetical approach.

Taha offers a reconstructed notion of God that draws on Sufi theology. Accordingly, the notion of God (Allah) is treated as an equivalent to the mystical notions of the Muhammadan Self *(al-dhat 'l-muhammadiyya)* or Reality *(al-haqiqa 'l-muhammadiyya)* or Light *(al-nur 'l-muhammadi)* or the Perfect Human *(al-insan 'l-kamil)*. The notion of Muhammad's Light was accorded authority notably through two traditions: a tradition according to which the Prophet told his companion Jabir b. Abd Allah al-Ansari that the first thing God created was Muhammad's own light and a tradition in which Muhammad said that he was already a prophet while Adam was still "between water and clay." It is, however, important to bear in mind that when Sufis used the phrase "Muhammadan Reality" they were not referring to the historical Muhammad. Ibn 'Arabi, for instance, uses it as an equivalent to the active intellect of Hellenistic philosophy or the Logos of Christian philosophy. Taha employs the idea in the same sense. When he addresses this theme there is an unmistakable Neoplatonist resonance in what he says. The Muhammadan Reality or the Perfect Human is the first form through which the Absolute *(al-mutlaq)* manifested Itself; it is the first particularization *(qaid)* of the Absolute.[52] In light of all this, he affirms that when Muhammad performed his ascent he met this Muhammadan Reality that can also be called God. In going through his ascent, the Prophet in fact met his own Reality; his ascent was a journey from his lower self to his higher self. Taha's use of the word "Allah" is characterized by ambiguity as he sometimes applies it to the "person" of the Muhammadan Reality or the Perfect Human but at other times uses it to signify the ineffable divine Essence *(dhat)*.

Like the exegetes, Taha places the ascension event within the larger context of the human/divine relationship. He stresses the dynamic and reciprocative nature of this relationship as both God and humans reach out to each other. Quoting verse 55:29, which refers to God as engaging every day in new deeds *(kull-a yawm-in huwa fi sha'n-in)*,[53] Taha points out that God's *sha'n* (deed, affair, work) is His engagement in continually disclosing Himself to His servants (RS 70). It is by virtue of this act of divine descent *(tanazzul)* from the absolute obscurity *(bahamut)* of the divine Essence to the world of creation that the corresponding human act of ascension is possible. This notion is expressed most dramatically in two holy traditions *(hadith qudsi)*.[54] In the first, God reportedly said, "My servant draws closer and closer to Me by works of supererogation [*nawafil*] until I love him. When I love him I am the hearing by which he hears, the sight by which he sees, the hand by which he strikes, and the leg by which he walks."[55] In the second hadith, He declares, "If the servant approaches Me a span I approach a cubit and if he comes walking I come hurrying."[56]

In addressing Muhammad's experience, Taha argues that he saw God on two levels: an initial level of seeing Him through His creation (as embodied by Gabriel) and an ultimate level of encountering the divine Essence (RS 73). Muhammad's experience on the ultimate level, hinted at in verse 53:17, takes place in a fleetingly ephemeral moment because human nature cannot sustain it for long. Describing the nature of this unique experience, Taha writes,

> Since the Lote-Tree [*sidrat 'l-muntaha*] is the end of dual perception [*shuhud shaf'i*] and the beginning of unitive perception [*shuhud witri*], the Qur'an did tell us about this, saying "when there covered the Lote-Tree that which covered," describing the impact of divine Self-manifestation on it. The Prophet reached the station *(maqam)* indicated by the Qur'anic statement "his eye swerved not, nor swept astray." Here, "eye" or "sight" *(basar)* and "insight" *(basira)* mean the same thing, as this is a station of unity *(tawhid).*[57] The verse refers to the Prophet's thought *(fikr),* which never swerved in that it was not preoccupied with the past, "nor did it go wrong" in that it was not preoccupied with the future. Witnessing the divine essence, the Prophet was totally overwhelmed. As such, his own self, space, and time were all unified. Thanks to this total unification he could release himself from time and space and be free of them. This made it possible for him to see Him who is not circumscribed by space or time; he could see God directly, an experience that cannot be expressed through language. (RS 73–74)

Taha's proposition that Muhammad saw God on two levels holds crucial significance to his theory of prayer. Contrary to orthodox Muslim belief, he maintains that the Prophet came back not with one but in fact two modes of prayer. When he experienced God as an essence he received what Taha describes as the "prayer of communion" *(salat 'l-sila)* or prayer in its "ultimate sense" *(ma'na ba'id).* According to Taha, this mode of prayer was a "direct communion with God in the station indicated by 'his eye swerved not, nor swept astray.'" He further characterizes this state in the following general terms: "The servant's created self [*dhat muhdatha*] is annihilated, and his eternal self [*dhat qadima*] remains in direct communion with the Eternal [*al-qadim*]. Here, means and ends vanish and only the One [*al-wahid*] remains" (RS 75).

In contrast, another prayer was stipulated when Muhammad saw God through His creation. This corresponds to prayer in its familiar ritual sense, which Taha describes as prayer in the "immediate sense" *(ma'na qarib),* or the "prayer of gestures" *(salat 'l-harakat),* or the "prayer of ascension" *(salat* 'l-mi'raj) (RS 75). A notable difference between the two prayers is that although Gabriel left Muhammad at the Lote-Tree and was not present when the prayer of communion was stipulated, he was in fact the intermediary of the prayer of ascension.[58] It was the archangel who showed Muhammad the manner, times, and ablutionary preparation for ritual prayer, as the hadith material indicates. Taha takes his defining terms of *sila* and *mi'raj* from two traditions in which Muhammad reportedly said, "Prayer is a communion [*sila*] between the servant and his Lord," and "Prayer is the ascension [*mi'raj*] of the servant to his Lord" (LL 45).

Moreover, Taha characterizes the ascension mode of prayer as "subsidiary" *(salat far'iyya)* and the communion mode as "essential" *(salat asliyya)*. The determining factor here is that of "time." Ascension prayer is time-specific in that it is performed at stated times and its ritual soundness is inseparable from the fulfillment of this condition. Communion prayer, on the other hand, is not subject to this time specification; its time is a mystical time that simply becomes "every moment," or, as Taha puts it, "The time of this prayer is every single moment a human breathes in or breathes out" (IF 20).

Although the communion prayer evidently enjoys a higher spiritual status, it is the ascension prayer that is the focus of Taha's attention because it is by virtue of the systematic methodology of ritual prayer that one can eventually realize one's communion with God or what verse 17:79 describes as one's "station of praise" *(maqam mahmud)*. Even after his ascension, Muhammad strove hard to realize this station of praise through his prayer. Muhammad once reportedly said, "Three of your world were made dear to my heart: women, perfume, and my supreme joy [*qurrat 'aini*] is in prayer." Taha argues that prayer was the Prophet's "supreme joy" because it opened his way to this "station of praise" through the realization of a state of total self-unity *(jam'iyyat nafs)* (TM 24).

By virtue of this constant striving, Muhammad set the perfect example for Muslims. There was, however, a very significant difference that set him apart from his community: in performing the prayer of ascension he was not engaged in an act of imitation *(taqlid)* because he was "authentic" *(asil)* (RS 75). What invested him with authenticity *(asala)* was the fact that he was directly granted his own individual prayer on his ascension.

By constantly performing the prayer of gestures Muhammad was engaged in what Taha calls a "minor ascension" *(mi'raj asghar)* that prepared him for his moment of communion with God or "major ascension" *(mi'raj akbar)* (RS 78). Not only did the Prophet differ from his community in being authentic, but he also stood apart in terms of the scope and intensity of the spiritual discipline to which he subjected himself. Besides the five obligatory prayers of his community, he continually performed night prayer as an extra obligation. This went hand in hand with a more rigorous discipline of fasting and other acts of ascetic piety that were not incumbent upon his community. Yet Muhammad also stressed that "religion is being good to others" *(al-din 'l-mu'amala)*, and hence his worship was inextricably linked with his service to others.

In connection with this perceived distance between Muhammad and his community, Taha makes a clear distinction between the shari'a and the sunna. The shari'a stands for the (holy) law in its entirety, it is the comprehensive body of dictates to which a Muslim ought to conform in relating to God *('ibadat)* and to his fellow human beings *(mu'amalat)*. The shari'a draws on primary and secondary sources: the former being the Qur'an and the prophetic traditions and the latter being the body of knowledge constructed by juristic schools. The sunna, on the other hand, is Prophet-specific in that its origin and legitimation are traced to Muhammad. Traditionally, the sunna has been defined as what the Prophet said or did or confirmed. This definition is, however, contested by Taha, who sees the sunna as Prophet-specific in a narrower and more stringent sense: the sunna is what the Prophet performed on the personal level. Accordingly, what the Prophet confirmed was shari'a pure and simple and what he said should generally be subsumed under the shari'a, with the exception of those statements that "indicated the gnostic state of his heart " (RT 13).

This category of the "gnostic state" of the Prophet's heart is further refined to indicate the distinctive category of "reality" *(haqiqa)*. This tripartite state of affairs is summed up by a tradition according to which Muhammad reportedly said, "What I say is shari'a, what I perform is *tariqa* [path], and the state of my heart [*hali*] is reality [*haqiqa*]." What Muhammad said was relative to what his historical community could have received as indicated in one of his statements: "We prophets have been commanded to address [our] peoples in accordance with their understanding" (TM 17–19). His own actions, nonetheless, flowed from another higher level, that is, that of his *tariqa* (path), or *sunna*. It is the totality of this sunna that constitutes, in the final analysis, "Muhammad's path" *(tariq Muhammad)*.

For Taha, there is a close connection between the prophetic tradition quoted above and another tradition, according to which Muhammad said that God put His hand on Muhammad's shoulder and bequeathed to him three levels of knowledge: knowledge that he was not allowed to disclose for it was only he who could bear it, knowledge whose communication was left to his discretion, and knowledge that he was commanded to communicate to everyone. In fact, Taha maintains, these levels of communicatory disclosure correlate with Muhammad's three roles: that of *wilaya* (being a friend of God), *nubuwwa* (being a prophet), and *risala* (being a messenger of God) (TM 19). To the first level belonged Muhammad's esoteric knowledge, to the second a higher knowledge that was esoteric in nature and a lower knowledge that could be revealed to everyone, and to the third the knowledge of shari'a.

This perspective comprises the basis of Taha's contention that Muhammad, in performing his task of preaching God's message to his community, did in fact continually engage in an act of *tanazzul* (descent). Taha then proceeds to make the bold assertion that Muhammad's community knew him only partially because "[he] was not from the society of seventh-century [Arabia]. He came to [his community] from the future.[59] . . . Although he lived with them, he [in fact] only mingled with them without [really] being one of them" (TM 21).

The Modern Seeker's Way

Taha applies his theory to the Muslim worshipper or seeker *(salik)*, drawing a sharp distinction between present-day seekers and seekers of the past, including the highly venerated companions of the Prophet *(sahaba)* and the great Sufi masters.[60] According to him, present-day seekers are in a far more privileged position than those of the past, owing to the nature of their relationship to the Prophet. In making this argument he draws on two traditions in which Muhammad reportedly told his companions about the future of Islam and Muslims.

In the first tradition, the Prophet expressed his yearning for his "brothers" *(ikhwan)* who were yet to come. When those accompanying him asked whether they were not his brothers, he told them, "You are my companions." In clarifying the difference he said that his brothers were people who would come "at the end of time" and whose recompense would be seventyfold that of the companions, owing to the adversity of the conditions within which they would act (TM 21–22). In the second tradition, the Prophet declared that inasmuch as Islam had started as unfamiliar *(gharib)* it would return as unfamiliar, thanks to the efforts of some who would revive his sunna after it had died out (TM 22).[61]

On the basis of these traditions Taha advances two fundamental interrelated claims, first, that the present time is the time for the emergence of the "brothers" heralded by the Prophet, and second, that it is by living on the level of the sunna rather than clinging to the shari'a that a present-day Muslim can meet the challenge of his age and realize his spiritual potential. Like many modern Muslim reformers, he is scathingly caustic about the state of modern Muslims, whom he views as all but superficial believers, but he is still wholly positive and optimistic about their potential and future. This positive attitude stems from his evolutionary and progressivistic notion of history.

Taha holds that by virtue of the fourteen centuries separating them from Muhammad's contemporaries, present-day Muslims enjoy a greater spiritual experience and potential owing to the upward movement and progress achieved in the span of these centuries. Although Taha admits that contemporary Muslims live in a state of *jahiliyya,* he insists that they nonetheless stand at a relatively higher level than that of the Arabs of seventh-century Arabia, as present-day Muslims enjoy a superior degree of knowledge and sophistication.

Having fallen heir to this progress, present-day Muslims are not only on a higher plane but also the horizon of their religious experience is extended. Whereas Muslims in the past were only required to follow the shari'a, that is no longer the case as far as present-day Muslims are concerned. Muslims are now required to engage in an active revival and application of the sunna in its sense of special prophetic practice. The main thrust of Taha's notion of sunna revival is the performance of night prayer *(qiyam 'l-lail),* which should assume the nature of an obligatory rather than a supererogatory act.

The seeker should thus consciously and meticulously follow "Muhammad's path." In the course of this spiritual journey, the seeker should be fully aware of the fact that he is constantly engaged in imitating Muhammad as his spiritual paradigm and that it is only through him that he can reach God (TM 29). Furthermore, in holding Muhammad up as his model, the seeker should distinguish between the Prophet's cultic actions *('ibadat)* and his personal habits *('adat)*. Consequently, he should follow the Prophet's example in worship with scrupulous rigor while following the example of his personal habits to the best of his ability.

When the seeker prays, he acts in accordance with the prophetic injunction to "pray as you have seen me praying!" In Taha's view, this tradition is not only about the external form of the act of imitation but about its spirit as well. In complying with the Prophet's injunction, the seeker engages in a dual act of imitation: an external imitation of the Prophet's ritual gestures and an internal imitation of his "attitude of mind" or what Taha describes as "the sincere state of his heart" (RS 76). To achieve this, the seeker calls on his sight *(basar)* and insight *(basira)*, seeing the postures of the Prophet's body through his sight and the attitude of his mind through his insight. The seeker enters his prayer session through the act of ablution that Taha, like his Sufi predecessors, invests with a high degree of symbolism.[62] Since the real impurity *(najasa)* that the seeker tries to remove during his ablutionary act is not of the limbs he washes but rather of his heart or state of mind, the emphasis should shift to a close self-examination and the evocation of a penitent and contrite frame of mind (TK 51–56).

The seeker's presence *(hudur)* during his ablution session is carried over into his prayer session. This presence is in fact the "communion" element of the "ascension" aspect of the seeker's prayer; it is the spirit without which prayer would be reduced to mere empty bodily gestures. When the seeker recites the Qur'an (a cardinal element in prayer), he induces a state of "remembrance" *(dhikr)*, which Taha points out is essential to "illuminate one's heart and purify one's thought" (TK 37). He maintains that a close interrelationship between one's communion prayer, ascension prayer, states of mind, and mundane daily actions is underlined by verse 29:45, which reads, "prayer [*salat*] forbids indecency and dishonour. God's remembrance [*dhikr*] is greater." Although the word *salat* here has a general denotation, Taha insists that it specifically refers to ascension prayer because of the direct relationship the verse establishes with good conduct. The word *dhikr*, on the other hand, alludes to communion prayer.

The seeker has to be fully conscious of his prayer for his cultic act to be of value. This intimate connection between prayer and consciousness is a key feature of Taha's theory of prayer. He perceives of thought in terms of a movement that constantly fluctuates between the opposite poles of memory (or the past) and imagination (or the future). This thought fluctuation is dialectical in nature as it seeks to reach a point of synthesis where its vacillating pendulum reaches a point of equilibrium *(istiwa')*. The best that the Qur'an offers by way of educating and training thought is its unity-proclaiming formula of "There is no god but God" *(la ilaha illa 'Llah)*. The formula's negation and affirmation confirm that the truth is "in between" *(baina bain)* (LL 38); accordingly, the truth is at its starkest when it is neither on the end of negation nor on the end of affirmation. This in-between point is the point encapsulated in "his eye swerved not, nor swept astray," the point of living in the present (for the present is the only real time), the point of *istiqama* (rectitude, uprightness).

This in effect makes a prayer session a "psychotherapeutic session" *(jalsa nafsiyya)* during which the seeker examines and grapples with the complexes *('uqad nafsiyya)* of his personal unconscious and his collective unconscious. Taha places this psychological dimension at the heart of a larger scheme into which he weaves some of his major themes:

> [Prayer] is a method that makes it possible for us to detach ourselves from the maelstrom of modern life and find a retreat within which we can examine our inner world. We know of the world that surrounds far more than we know of our own selves. . . . We are surrounded by divine manifestations, and to live in peace [with ourselves and with others] we must know God and the mystery of His creation. . . . This knowledge will help us address our collective and individual complexes that were generated by ignorance [*jahl*]. By closely scrutinizing them we bring them out of their dark recesses to the full light of life and freedom. This will infuse our lives with freedom and perfection. (TK 43)

This state of profound inner peace is intimately bound up with the state of contentment *(rida)* that verse 20:130 mentions. This prayer, which is capable of reaching the seeker's innermost layers of consciousness, is what Taha also calls "intelligent prayer" *(salat dhakiyya)*.

Besides employing some of the notions of modern psychology, Taha brings into play the psychological scheme of Islam as well, particularly in its Sufi formulation. Accordingly, the seeker's spiritual journey is perceived as ascending progress along a seven-stage path, each stage of which corresponds to a particular soul or self *(nafs)*. These souls are the lower self *(ammara)*, the conscientious self *(lawwama)*, the inspired self *(mulhama)*, the soul at peace *(mutma'inna)*, the well-pleased self *(radiya)*, the well-pleasing self *(mardiyya)*, and the perfect self *(kamila)*. At the heart of this septenary scheme is a simpler tripartite scheme comprising a lower self *(nafs sufla)*, a higher self *(nafs 'ulya)*, and reason *('aql)*. Reason mediates between the two selves; it functions as a censor that represses the lower drives of the self and helps it in its upward progress. Since "intelligent prayer" is perceived as playing a comparable role in enlightening the self to realize its perfection, does this mean that prayer in essence is a "rational act," that it is a tool of reason in its meditative activity between the lower and higher selves? This is an implication that Taha's theory of prayer does not accept, as prayer in his view performs a higher function that places it above reason. The first step in conceiving this higher function is to look into the significance of the ritual gestures of prayer.

In elucidating the significance of the ritual gestures, Taha uses a highly mystical language. He resorts to the esoteric significance attached to the number seven and deploys the moon/sun opposition and the shari'a/*haqiqa* (reality) duality. His symbolic parallelisms are inspired by verse 41:53, which affirms, "We shall show them Our signs [*ayatina*] in the horizons [*afaq*] and in themselves [*anfusihim*], till it is clear to them that it is the truth."[63] The verse's reference to God's signs on the levels of external "horizons" and human "selves" *(nufus)* indicates a broad opposition between "outer signs" and "inner signs," between outer landscape and inner landscape, between the world and human beings. Regarding this verse, which Taha quotes frequently, he draws on traditional Sufi symbolism that treats the sun, the moon, and the earth as a triad representative of outer landscape and corresponding respectively to the heart, the mind, and the body *(jasad)*, which represent a triad of inner landscape. Furthermore, the correspondence between the external and the internal is firmly established through a recurrent septenary pattern that governs existence: God created the world in seven days,[64] human embryonic development, as verse 23:14 indicates, goes through seven stages, and the human path to perfection is a journey through seven selves.

Taha applies the same symbolic logic when he approaches prayer gestures. Since each genuflection or prayer cycle *(rak'a)* is made up of seven gestures (involving the sequential acts of bowing and prostrating), two *rak'a*s would in fact symbolically correspond to the number of mansions *(manazil)* that the moon covers from its new moon phase to its full moon phase. Addressing the seeker, Taha writes,

> If you were to perform two *rak'a*s in a state of presence, you should then know that each of your fourteen postures differs from the one preceding it despite their [outward] resemblance. This is the case because each posture is a new mansion of the "moon" of your shari'a relative to the "sun" of your *haqiqa*. When you finish the two *rak'a*s, your moon would have become a full moon. Your mind [*'aql*] would be illuminated by the light of the knowledge flowing out of your spirit [*ruh*], and your mind and your heart [*qalb*] would correspond to each other. (TK 39)

This symbolism of the number seven is accentuated most dramatically through the belief that each *rak'a* gesture is respectively performed by the angels of each of the seven heavens (TK 65–66). The neatness of Taha's lunar symbolism requires a prayer session whose length is ideally two genuflections, which applies only to the dawn prayer *(fajr* or *subh)*. He does not clarify why one need perform two lunar cycles in the midday *(zuhr)*, late afternoon *('asr)*, and evening *('isha')* prayers or, more strikingly, a cycle and a half in the sunset *(maghrib)* prayer.

As a formal service, prayer is almost always linked in the Qur'an with alms giving *(zakat)*.[65] In two verses (2:45 and 2:153), however, the word *salat* is mentioned in conjunction with the word *sabr* (patience). Although exegetical opinion has on the whole simply interpreted this word in the light of its given denotation stressing the virtue of perseverance and fortitude in the face of adversity (as exemplified for instance by Job), there was also a view maintaining that the word specifically meant "fasting." [66] Taha adopts this latter view and sees in the Qur'anic reference a basis for the stringent mystical discipline of "eating less, sleeping less, and talking less" (RS 92–93).

Hence, in projecting Muhammad as a paradigm of imitation, Taha not only emphasizes the importance of prayer but also highlights the close link between prayer and fasting in the Prophet's ritual practice (TM 35). Quoting a prophetic tradition that proclaims, "Satan circulates inside you like your blood; constrict his flowing by fasting [*sawm*]," he argues that fasting acts on the spirit, sharpening intelligence *(dhaka')* by purifying the blood and restraining craving *(shahwa).*[67] Juxtaposing another tradition that declares, "Fasting is radiance [*diya'*] and prayer is light [*nur*]," with verse 20:5, which affirms, "It is He who made the sun a radiance and the moon a light," he infers the symbolic opposition of fasting/sun and prayer/moon. This is evidently a perspective that places fasting in a particularly privileged position vis-à-vis prayer, hence undermining Taha's repeated assertions that prayer is the greatest of works a human being can perform.

While Taha holds that a proper imitation of the Prophet involves both his gestures and the attitude of his mind, he places a special emphasis on the latter element, which he perceives as constituting the "spirit" of prayer. He establishes a close correlation between this mental state and the notion of the "presence of prohibition" *(hadrat 'l-ihram)* that sacralizes the entire prayer session.[68] In Taha's view, the final ritual act signaling the end of the prayer session is not the end of the prayer act. Rather, it is an entry into another mode of worship that Taha identifies with the Qur'anic reference to the "middle prayer" *(al-salat-u 'l-wusta)* to which 2:238 alludes.[69] This middle prayer is the totality of the seeker's physical and mental actions during the periods separating his performance of ritual prayers. Like ritual prayer, these intervening periods are also characterized by their own *hadra* (presence), that is, *hadrat 'l-salam* or the "presence of peace."[70]

According to Taha, the action aspect of this presence of peace is summed up in the prophetic tradition that "religion is about good conduct" *(al-din 'l-mu'amala).*[71] On one level, the message of Islam, as one tradition puts it, may be seen in primarily ethical terms: "I have been sent to bring the best of morals [*makarim 'l-akhlaq*] to completion." In reading this tradition, Taha maintains that what it in fact confirms is that the full realization of God's ethical message constitutes the only reason why Muhammad was sent (TK 67). The seeker should thus assiduously subject his life practice to the code encapsulated in the tradition that "a Muslim is he who does not verbally abuse or physically harm other Muslims" *(al-muslim man salima 'l-muslimun min lisanihi wa yaddihi)*. In reading this tradition, Taha holds that the object "Muslims" here refers in fact to *all* of God's creation (RS 91). To translate this into an attitude of mind and action, the seeker should live in total peace with others, desist from doing harm, tolerate harm done to him, and do good to others. He who leads such a life would have brought his external conduct and internal life into complete correspondence and harmony and would realize the ultimate goal of approaching God with the "sound heart" *(qalb salim)* to which 26:89 refers. Yet, on another level, this clearly defined ethical-action-oriented theory is impaired by Taha's adoption of the orthodox position that adheres to a salvific doctrine negating the relevance of human action and placing exclusive emphasis on divine grace (RS 90).[72]

The other integral part of this imitative practice concerns the conscious adoption of the Prophet's habits. Taha highlights particular aspects of the Prophet's actions, such as that of "giving the righthand side precedence over the lefthand side."[73] Taha argues that this was a deliberate and conscious plan on the Prophet's part to combat any tendency to do things out of habit by infusing all his actions with constant awareness *(fikr)*. Quoting verse 16:44, which affirms that God sent down the "Remembrance" *(al-dhikr)* so that people would reflect *(yatafakkarun)*, he places the emphasis on what he perceives as a close interconnection between worship and the raising and sharpening of one's consciousness (RS 93). Through his conscientious performance of these simple acts the seeker would, Taha maintains, effect a profound change in his state of mind and life because he would know how to "give everything its due," which is the essence of wisdom *(hikma)*.

Realizing Authenticity

The quest for wisdom is inextricably linked to the seeker's ultimate horizon, that is, the imitation of God. Taha holds that this horizon is intimated by the tradition in which Muhammad urged, "Take God's virtues as your model [*takhallaqu bi-akhlaq Allah*], my God is on a straight path." The seeker's overall imitative process is thus described by Taha in the following metaphorical terms:

God, the Almighty, walks before all of us, but His footprints are invisible and can only be seen by a powerful light. It was only Gabriel who possessed this light, so he followed in the track of God, stepping accurately and precisely in His footprints. Gabriel's footprints, in their turn, were invisible and could only be seen by a powerful light. Muhammad possessed this light and he followed, walking accurately and precisely in the footprints of Gabriel and trying his utmost to make them clear by pressing his own footprints on them. They become clear to each one of us in varying degrees. At their minimal visibility, the Prophet's footprints are clear enough for those with the least light among his community. Some people, however, are content to walk behind the Prophet without paying attention to the impressions of his footprints. Such are the common imitators. Other people walk behind the Prophet while stepping in his footprints accurately and precisely; their footprints would be neither larger nor smaller than those of the Prophet's. Such are the imitators who perfect their imitation.

Thanks to this imitation, the lights of Muhammad would be reflected on the imitator, in accordance with his striving. The lights of such an imitator would be strong enough to enable him to see the impressions of Gabriel's footprints, which he could not see at first. He would perfect his imitation till he sees the impressions of God's footprints. . . . When the imitator who has perfected his imitation of the Prophet sees the impressions of the Divine footprints, he becomes independent in his perspective [*ru'ya*] and observance [*ittiba'*]. In the end and thanks to his perfection of imitating the Prophet, he imitates God without the mediation of the Prophet (RS 80).

This passage sums up what stands at the heart of Taha's theory of prayer: prayer is a means *(wasila)*, and as such the imitation of Muhammad is a means that comes to an end when one "meets God." Meeting God is not a spatio-temporal experience but rather a realization of the prophetic statement, "Take God's virtues as your model," through an active striving to bring one's qualities ever closer to God's attributes or what Taha describes as *"taqrib 'l-sifat min 'l-sifat"* (TK 11).

It is clear from the way Taha describes the seeker's quest that worship, and in particular prayer, is, in the first place, an individual act. On the face of it, such a position is at variance with the special merit that Islam attaches to communal prayer. Only once does Taha justify the orthodox position by claiming that what makes communal prayer hold greater worth is the higher intensity of the "spiritual" bodily vibrations *(dhabdhaba)* associated with it (AJii 30). What he says in this respect is based on his contention that the seeker's continual work on his ascension does not result only in spiritual progress but also in a process of "physical sensitization" whereby he becomes more sentient and alive (QF 199). It would hence seem logical that Taha should emphasize communal prayer as an effective means to accelerate the seeker's progress. The fact that he does precisely the opposite is a function of the central role that the notion of individuality plays in his thought.

This individuality is the starting point and, at the same time, the ultimate flowering of the seeker's experience. Following the shari'a, the seeker realizes his *haqiqa.* Imitation leads him to realize what the Prophet had realized—that is, his "authenticity." The Prophet acts as the seeker's Gabriel, taking him all the way up to his Lote-Tree. Like Gabriel, the Prophet would leave the seeker to meet God—this is the moment when the "great veil" *(al-hijab 'l-a'zam)* or the "prophetic veil" *(al-hijab 'l-nabawi)* falls away and the seeker realizes the state indicated by "his eye swerved not, nor swept astray." This is the seeker's moment of mystical union during which God, as He did in Muhammad's case, gives him his testimony *(shahada)*, prayer, fasting *(siyam)*, alms giving, and pilgrimage *(hajj)* (RS 78). From this moment onward, the seeker's relationship to the Prophet is no longer one of imitation but of emulation *(ta'assi).*[74] Whereas imitation is a vertical relationship in which Muhammad is above and ahead of the seeker, emulation is a horizontal relationship whereby Muhammad and the seeker are on a level plane of direct access to God.

Taha is at pains to assure his Muslim audience that although imitation comes to an end, prayer does not (RS 84). The "prayer of gestures," where the model is the Prophet, gives way to a "personal, authentic" prayer where the model is God. This act of following the example of God is the essence of the supreme realization of servantship. The transition is one from prophetic constriction to divine freedom, from belief to knowledge. Quoting verse 4:103, "surely the prayer is a timed prescription for the believers" *(kitab-an mawqut-an),* he affirms that the seeker's realization is in fact a movement from the immediate, surface meaning of the Qur'anic phrase alluding to the fixed times of ritual prayer to what he describes as its ultimate, deeper meaning that confirms the temporary nature of imitation (suggested by the word *mawqut).*

It is important to stress the comprehensive nature of Taha's concept of authenticity. Inasmuch as authenticity is the highest expression of individuality on the level of one's relationship with God (what is technically known as *'ibadat),* it also has an important bearing on the relationship with one's fellow human beings (the *mu'amalat).* Since Taha does not recognize any formal separation between the realm of the legal and the realm of the ethical, he views shari'a as leading from public ethico-legal conduct to individual moral conduct. Consequently, the seeker who is a gnostic *('arif)* does in fact live on the higher level of his "individual shari'a," which is more stringent than that of the general shari'a of the *umma* (the community of believers). Taha adduces the part of verse 5:48 that declares, "To every one of you We have appointed a right way [*shir'a*] and an open road [*minhaj*]," as a Qur'anic underpinning of this notion of individual law. Although the verse's context is about the competing claims of the faith communities of Judaism, Christianity, and the new religion of Islam, Taha insists that the verse is equally applicable to individuals. He reads the terms *shir'a* and *minhaj* as respectively connoting the notions of shari'a as general law and sunna as individual law. In this regard he affirms that "the gnostic's shari'a is an integral part of his *haqiqa,* and in his case both aspects are individual" (RS 79); this individual shari'a of the gnostic is immeasurably higher than general shari'a.

In dealing with individuality in the context of the individual/society relationship, Taha stresses the notion of freedom. This freedom is, however, a means to an even higher freedom, that is, the state of servantship that one realizes in the context of the human being/God relationship. The state of total transformation brought about by the realization of servantship is both spiritual and physical. In demonstrating this, he quotes verse 39:23, which reads, "God has sent down the fairest discourse as a Book, consimilar in its oft-repeated, whereat shiver the skins of those who fear their Lord; then their skins and their hearts soften to the remembrance of God." Taha puts a literalist construction on the references to "shiver" *(taqsha'irr)* and "soften" *(talin)* in connection with the skin. Worship, particularly prayer, equips seekers with their most potent instrument to free themselves from fear. When fear is vanquished, "the heart expands, becomes energized, rhythmic, sending forth vigorous and pure blood into all the cells of the body and the skin. . . . The entire body springs to perfect life and no trace of thickness or lack of sensibility remains" (QF 198). This "perfect life," a life of total mental serenity to which prayer leads, is intimated by the reference to the softening of the skins. This state is also expressed in terms of *rida* (content-ment, satisfaction) and "soundness of heart." Taha perceives of content-ment as a "struggle [*mujahada*] on the level of servantship" (RS 62). On this supreme level, contentment also expresses itself in renouncing *tamanni* (wishing), as this in reality is a remonstration against God's will.

Taha extends the impact of prayer from this physico-spiritual level to the level of *rizq* (sustenance, provision). Quoting verse 20:132, which ad-dresses the Prophet, saying, "And bid thy family to pray. . . . We ask of thee no provision, but it is We who provide thee," he argues that when prayer reaches its spiritual apex it in fact becomes the means through which one sustains oneself instead of through one's hard work and exertion. This is a level of prayer where the seeker is always with God as God is always with him; it is a level where prayer is a constant, dynamic movement from a state of heedlessness to a state of presence, from a state of distance *(bu'd)* to a state of nearness *(qurb)*, from a state of ignorance to a state of knowledge *(ma'rifa)* (RS 5–6). The heedlessness/presence opposition is furthermore articulated in terms of a sleep/wakefulness opposition. Quoting a prophetic tradition that declares, "People are asleep and when they die they wake up," and another tradition that exhorts, "Die before you die," Taha confirms that prayer can lead to a "metaphorical death" or a "resurrection" that makes the seeker fully awake and alive.

It may be argued that Taha's theory of imitation and authenticity could not have been advanced by the Sufis of former times; it is a theory that requires the incubatory context of a century with a different sensibility. Taha's theory is intimately bound up with the notion of individual freedom—a notion that attracted a number of Muslim modernists in the twentieth century. In Taha's thought, the radical Sufi's insistence on experiencing God directly blended with the notion of individual freedom, giving rise to a unique theory of Islamic prayer.

In addressing individual freedom, Taha tends to use the phrase "absolute individual freedom." He defines absolute individual freedom as a state of affairs where individuals have resolved their inner conflict, that is, the conflict between the conscious *(al-'aql 'l-wa'i)* and the unconscious *(al-'aql 'l-batin)*. As such, individuals realize their full integrity, with the "exterior" *(zahir, sira)* fully corresponding to the "interior" *(batin, sarira)*. Such individuals will "think as they wish, speak as they think, and act as they speak. They will realize a life fully infused with [deep] reflection [*fikr*] and [intense] awareness [*(shu'ur)*]" (UD 33). Although Taha employs the modern psychological notions of the conscious and the unconscious (along with other notions such as repression [*kabt*] and instinct [*ghariza*] that he often uses throughout his work), he offers in fact an unmistakably Sufi theory and ideal of personality—that is, a personality that carries the seed of divinity, a personality capable of achieving a divine-like state of "oneness" *(tawhid)* by bringing about a complete identity between its "outside" *(zahir)* and its "inside" *(batin)*.[75]

In Taha's view the absolute nature of individual freedom stems from the inextricability of the human and the divine. He maintains that when God said to the angels, "When I have shaped him [Adam], and breathed My spirit in him [*wa nafakhtu fihi min ruhi*], fall you down, bowing before him," this did not convey an act of "breathing" *(nafkh)* that came to an end with the creation of Adam. *Nafkh* is a continuous act on the part of the Divine (RS 27). Because the Divine is characterized by absolute freedom, this freedom then becomes, by necessity, part of what God imparts to human beings, and since *nafkh* is a ceaseless act, then human freedom is continually expanding and deepening as humans are ever propelled by the aspiration (ultimately never realizable) to attain to a freedom as absolute as God's freedom.

It is on this level of absolute freedom that the imitation of Muhammad, a human being, gives way to the imitation of God, the Absolute. It is on this level that one is Muslim not in the sense of a "submission" to a body of laws and rituals dictated by an organized religion but in the deeper sense of an existential submission to God where He permeates one's existence and radiates from one's every thought and act. Just as Gabriel had no place in Muhammad's "higher presence" with God, Muhammad has no place in the seeker's higher presence with God. This is a presence of unity where the seeker identifies himself with God—a state that has best been articulated by al-Hallaj's lines,

> I have become the One I love, and the one I love
> has become me!
> We are two spirits infused in a (single) body.
> And to see me is to see Him,
> And to see Him is to see us.[76]

Taha's theory of prayer thus offers a radical solution to the mystic's problem as regards prophetic mediation. Although Sufis never refer to Muhammad as a "problem," surely the fact that Muhammad acts as a mediator between humans and God constitutes a major problem as far as the inner logic of Sufi experience is concerned. Since this inner logic presupposes the possibility and indeed the necessity of experiencing God directly, then ultimately there is no place for the mediation of any human agency. Taha's crucial break lies in his claim that this moment of mystical union also marks a final break with the seeker's state of imitation. Having "met" God, the seeker has realized an elevated degree of spiritual maturity that frees him from the imitative mould of prophetic mediation. His ascension to God results in a state of direct and constant communion with Him.

Taha: Between Being Authentic or "The Authentic"

It is reasonable to assume that Taha's theory of prayer is not a mere theoretical scheme outlining the mystic's journey toward God but is meant in addition to reflect his actual experience of realizing his authenticity. He couches his experience in a language closer to that of Ibn 'Arabi's than that of al-Bistami's, though without the detailed density that is present in Ibn 'Arabi.

By the time Taha wrote his letter to *al-Sha'b* newspaper in 1951 (see chapter 1), outlining his politico-religious philosophy, he was clear about the mystical nature of his quest and had a positive feeling about the possible outcome of his experience. Regarding this, he asserted, "I have not gone into retreat in search of (exoteric) knowledge [*ma'rifa*] but rather in search of a greater goal that lies beyond knowledge, that is, knowing my own self, which I have lost in the midst of a welter of illusions and deception. I must find it in the light of the Qur'an, spread it out, and be in peace with it before I call others to Islam." At that point he felt confident enough to say the following about his spiritual progress: "I am on the point of achieving [my] goal and putting my affairs straight in the best manner" (RMii 3).

It is noteworthy that in following the Sufi path Taha did not place himself under the guidance of a *shaikh*. In the practical mysticism of Sufi orders, the role of the *shaikh* is so central that it is always asserted that "he who has no *shaikh*, his *shaikh* is Satan."[77] There has been, though, an alternative tradition of recognized Sufis who embarked on the mystical path without the help of a *shaikh*. Such Sufis are called Uwaisiyya, an epithet derived from the name of Uwais al-Qarani (d. 37/657), a contemporary of Muhammad who never met the Prophet but was believed to have been in a kind of telepathic connection with him.[78] An Uwaisi mystic hence claims to have attained his illumination through a direct guidance by Muhammad's prophetic light or through the agency of another saintly figure. Taha belonged to this class of Sufis. Despite his religious background and his heightened religious sensibility, he did not join a mystical order. It may be argued that his secular education, his own antisectarianism, and the prevalent negative attitude among the educated class toward the popular Islam of Sufi orders all contributed to draw him away from adhering to organized Sufism.

When Taha emerged out of his seclusion he stopped practicing the "prayer of gestures." By that time, he was certain of two things: that he had realized his authenticity and that his concept of a Second Message of Islam (see chapter 5) was not only the true understanding of Islam but also the only global answer to the problems of human beings in the modern age.

Taha's disciples believed in his authenticity, vehemently defending it and viewing it as the solid anchor of their own prayer practice.

Besides the category of "authentic" *(asil)* that is open to everyone, Taha's esotericism proposed another category, that of "the Authentic One" *(al-Asil)*, which is open to only one person. According to him, the Authentic One corresponds to the classical Sufi entities of the Muhammadan Self *(al-dhat 'l-muhammadiyya)* or Reality *(al-haqiqa 'l-muhammadiyya)* or the Perfect Human *(al-insan 'l-kamil)*. Although Taha's disciples recognized that he was authentic, a question that arose among them was whether he was also the Authentic. The issue was addressed by Taha in an internal meeting of the group in April 1982. Reflecting his disciples' state of mind, he said, "You may be asking yourselves—in fact you should be asking yourselves, people would undoubtedly ask you: am I the Authentic One? I spoke about the doctrine of authenticity, wrote about it, and I am following the path of its practical application. Am I the Authentic One? I hope to be he, but I am in doubt." [79] Quoting verse 19:78, which says reprimandingly, "What, has he observed the Unseen, or taken a covenant with the All-merciful?" he affirms, "I have neither had access to the Unseen nor have I taken a covenant with the All-merciful." The crucial point in his view is that one cannot "feel secure against God's devising [*makr*]" as this entails the presumption that one knows as much as God knows. A gnostic is always inhabited by the uncertainty that he may not be the "real one" but only a "temporary one," or, as Taha puts it, "Am I going to finish the journey or does God have someone else, better than me, to finish the journey? Someone whom He would pick from where I stop?" [80] The best that the gnostic can do, and this is what Taha claimed to be engaged in doing all the time, is to be "in a state of constant preparedness" at the receiving end of God's ceaseless act of descent. This state of mystical doubt and its accompanying gnostic existential anguish bestow upon Taha's theory of prayer a marked dynamism and openness within the mystical tradition of Islam.

Exclusivism and the Problem of Authenticating Authenticity

Taha attaches a special importance to the distinction between Muhammad's companions and his brothers. Another important corresponding distinction he advances is that between belief *('aqida)* and knowledge *('ilm),* belief being the defining mark of the companions and knowledge that of the brothers. Since the understanding of Islam he offers is on the higher level of the brothers, it is knowledge based (IQ 3). As such, the theory of imitation and authenticity is not offered just to Muslims but to all men and women—whether believers in other creeds or nonbelievers.

But why should Muhammad be the ultimate model of imitation with the view of realizing one's communion with God? Why should he be the only gate to God? In accounting for this issue, Taha expresses a typical Islamocentric position. He draws on a particular reconstruction of Muhammad's prophecy on the one hand and on an exclusivism informed by the Qur'an on the other.

Taha stresses that the foundation of Muhammad's spiritual career was his *nubuwwa* (prophethood). His *nubuwwa* occupied a middle position between the lower rank of *risala* and the higher rank of *wilaya*. When Muhammad was ready to receive God's message, verses 74:1–7 were revealed. This readiness is viewed by Taha in the light of Muhammad's personal history from the moment of his birth to the moment he proclaimed his mission, usually put at the age of forty. The tradition in which Muhammad says, "My God nurtured me" *(addabani rabbi),* reflects, according to Taha, a process of spiritual maturation that spanned these forty years (TM 18).

What is at work here is a doctrine of what may be described as a double election: a "prophetic election" (translated more specifically into a "Muhammadan election"), and a "communal election." In spelling out this Muhammadan election, Taha embraces the curious belief that Muhammad was special even during his prenatal period (TM 18).[81] This emphasis of Muhammadan election functions within the comprehensive context of another election, that is, the election of Islam as a religion and those who believe in it as a chosen people, which constitutes the foundation of what may be described as Islamic exclusivism. This exclusivism is informed by the Qur'an, which explicitly states, "Whoso desires another religion than Islam, it shall not be accepted of him; in the next world he shall be among the losers" (3:85). Taha, however, shifts the locus of this exclusivism from the time of revelation to the present time, arguing that the "Islam" to which the verse refers is of the higher, knowledge-oriented level of the brothers and not the belief-centered Islam of the companions (RT 116–17).

When dealing specifically with prayer in Islam, there is yet another possible type of election, that is, the privileging of Arabic over other languages. Although Taha does not discuss the possibility of reciting the Qur'an in translation by Muslims who do not speak Arabic, it is reasonable to assume that his mere silence indicates that he agrees with the orthodox consensus that the recitation of the Qur'an in prayer can only be in Arabic.[82]

It is thus by virtue of the election of the Prophet of Islam and exclusion of other prophets and the election of Islam and exclusion of other religions that Muhammad and his path become the only gateway leading to God's presence, the state of mystical union, and the realization of authenticity. Muhammad is thus reconstructed as a dehistoricized figure who comes from the future and speaks the language of all ages.

The major weaknesses of Taha's theory lie in this act of dehistoricizing Muhammad on the one hand and in its psychology on the other. On account of being the most recent major founder of a global religion, Muhammad's career, in comparison with other major religious figures, provides us with the richest tapestry of events. Both the Qur'anic text and a great deal of the hadith material provide an accurate picture of his message. The wealth and detail of the *sira* and hadith materials have made it possible for Muslims throughout the centuries to subject Muhammad to their own reconstruction. This has particularly been the case among Muslim reformers in the twentieth century. In Taha's case we find that his theory of a Second Message in Islam rests on a reconstructed modernist Muhammad whose "real" message is expressed through modern ideas such as democracy, constitutionalism, and socialism. Additionally, Taha emphasizes a mystical and ethical Muhammad who is always in a state of presence with God and with others as manifestations of God. Taha hence projects Muhammad as a progressive mystic who is constantly engaged in a spiritual struggle to realize his absolute individual freedom and a social struggle to realize the objective of total social justice. Hence, to accept Taha's theory of prayer one has to reject all other possible counterreconstructions of Muhammad and entrench oneself in the specifics of Taha's method and selective citations.

The psychology of Taha's theory presupposes an indivisible link between the categories of imitation and authenticity: there is no way that we can be authentic without first engaging in a willing and conscious process of imitation. Taha distinguishes in the act of prayer between the two levels of the Prophet's external gestures and his internal state of mind and stresses that the seeker should imitate the Prophet on both levels. Although it is possible to speak about imitation in connection with bodily gestures, the notion is problematic with regard to mental state. Since the Prophet's mental state is unique to him, there is no way for the seeker to claim that he can somehow reproduce the Prophet's mental state in the process of his imitative act. What the seeker does is to perform a ritual to the best of his ability and live his unique psychoreligious experience in the process. This raises a fundamental problem: if authenticity is a state of being oneself or of realizing one's individuality or one's individual freedom, then why should it be predicated on its negation, that is, imitation, in the first place? Furthermore, even if one accepts for the sake of argument what Taha says, then how can authenticity be authenticated? If a Muslim comes forward and makes the claim that he or she is authentic (as in Taha's case), then how can other Muslims, who are imitators, recognize that person's authenticity?[83]

In addressing this problem, Taha quotes what Jesus says in Matthew 7:15–16 about false prophets who can readily be recognized by their bad fruit (RT 11). This democratizes the issue; the implicit assumption here is that the common believer is in a position to judge for himself and distinguish between the authentic and the false. Naturally enough, Taha says this with the complete confidence that his own "tree" had borne "good fruit." But what happens when the common believer is uncertain of his verdict or shrinks away from a fruit he is offered on account of its unfamiliarity? In responding to this Taha counters with a doctrine that makes a virtue out of this very consideration: the unfamiliarity and novelty *(gharaba)* of what he says is in fact a hallmark of its veracity.[84]

Taha's ideal believer is someone who accepts a rule stipulating that to reach certainty one has to start with "mere belief" *(tasdiq)*. The mirror he holds for this believer is his own experience that he sums up by saying, "I should like to acknowledge that I started with mere belief because I was born to Muslim parents. Faith did not, however, lead me to fanaticism or blind me. That could have twisted the outcome of my experience. With God's help, I could proceed with my eyes open to realize an outcome that confirmed my simple belief and transformed it into certainty" (IS 14–15). But if there are competing "mere beliefs" and belief systems, how can the potential believer decide on the correct belief that leads to the correct certainty? Neither Taha's experience nor the theories he offers provide us with a satisfactory answer to this problem.

3

The Qur'an and the Hermeneutics of Semantic Fluidity

The Status of the Qur'an

AS THE CENTRAL SCRIPTURE around which the Islamic tradition historically evolved, the Qur'an has always played a key role in Islamic thought. This special status is pointedly articulated in a tradition related by 'Ali b. Abi Talib. According to the tradition the Prophet forewarned, "There will be dissension [fitna]." When 'Ali asked him how this could be averted, he responded:

> Through the Book of God. It informs you of past events and future happenings. It provides the conclusive resolution of your disagreements. Its ruling is final, and it is not to be taken lightly. He who abandons the Qur'an and goes the way of oppression, God will destroy him. He who seeks guidance in anything else, God will lead him astray. It is God's firm rope. It is the wise remembrance, the straight path. Thanks to it no vain desires would lead one astray and no uncertainty would prevail. [Studying it] the learned would never be satiated. It will always provide fresh answers and will never be exhausted. Its wonders will never come to end. . . . He who speaks in agreement with it speaks the truth; he who acts according to it will be rewarded; he who judges according to it will be just; he who calls to it will guide [others] to the straight path.[1]

As "the Book of God," the Qur'an thus has the unique characteristic of being the source of all knowledge and wisdom, a self-ascriptive claim based on verse 6:38, which affirms that "nothing has been neglected from it." Ibn 'Arabi says that by virtue of this Qur'anic "complete knowledge" *(al-'ilm 'l-*

kamil), the Muhammadans *(al-muhammadiyun)* live up to the Qur'anic description of them as "the best nation ever brought forth to men" (3:110).[2] This sense of the uniqueness of the Qur'an and, by extension, the uniqueness of Muslims and their sense of spiritual distinction, election, and vocation rests on the belief that the Qur'an is God's speech *(kalam Allah)* in that both its content and form communicate the literal "word of God."[3]

The Qur'an as a revelatory event involves the revelatory trinity of God, Gabriel, and Muhammad. This can further be reduced to a primary revelatory relationship involving God and Muhammad. Muhammad's Qur'anic utterances were later to be transcribed and codified as a Qur'anic text that came to represent, according to Muslim belief, God's last and eternal message for mankind. It is in the light of Muhammad's apostolic mission and the way Muslims perceive their holy scripture and relate to it that one can extend the revelatory trinity to a "revelatory quaternity." By virtue of this, the recipients of the Qur'an (during Muhammad's time and after him) were and are part of the revelatory event and witnesses to it.

Taha's treatment of the Qur'anic text is dealt with in this chapter under four topics: the nature of the Qur'an, its function, its language, and the hermeneutic procedures that should be applied to understand it. Although his starting point is the central Islamic belief that the Qur'an is God's speech, Taha situates this belief within a larger mystical imagination that invests the notion of divine speech with a much broader significance.[4]

The Qur'an as the Locus of the Divine

The key element in Taha's Qur'anic theory is the act of divine *tanazzul* (descent): the Qur'an is God's essence *(dhat)*, and this essence, through sheer grace, engaged in an act of descent so that humans can know God. In making this point, Taha, like his Sufi predecessors, adduces a divine tradition according to which God says, "I was a hidden treasure and I wanted to be known. So, I created the creatures. I made Myself known to them and it was through Me that they knew Me."[5] He maintains that the expression "hidden treasure" indicates the "absolute essence," an entity that is in fact beyond expression *('ibara)* and signification *(ishara)*. However, for Taha what the divine statement conveys is expressed through a tripartite divine descent. According to him, when God wished to make it possible for His creatures to know Him, He descended from the absoluteness of His essence to that of name *(ism)*, calling Himself God *(Allah)*. He then descended to the rank of attribute *(sifa)* and called Himself the All-Merciful *(al-Rahman)*. This was followed by a further descent to the rank of action *(fi'l)* in which He called Himself the All-Compassionate *(al-Rahim)* (AJi 76).

Verse 24:35, along with the "hidden treasure" tradition, has always exercised Sufi imagination and creativity.[6] The verse reads, "God is the Light of the heavens and the earth; the likeness of His Light is as a niche wherein is a lamp (the lamp in a glass, the glass as it were a glittering star) kindled from a Blessed Tree, an olive that is neither of the East nor of the West whose oil wellnigh would shine, even if no fire touched it." The Sufis set out to uncover what they perceived as the allegorical meanings of the verse's references to the mundane elements of niche *(mishkat)*, glass *(zujaja)*, lamp *(misbah)*, tree *(shajara)*, and oil *(zait)*. In applying his imagination to this problem, al-Ghazali came up with a scheme according to which these elements corresponded to five ascending degrees of the mind. Hence, the verse's "niche" corresponds to "the sensible mind" *(al-ruh 'l-hassas)*, that is, a mind informed by the five senses; the glass corresponds to the "imaginative mind" *(al-ruh 'l-khayali)*, that is, the site of memory that mediates between the sensible and the rational minds; the lamp corresponds to the "rational mind" *(al-ruh 'l-'aqli)*, which is analytic in nature, subjecting the perception of the sensible and imaginative minds to its scrutiny; the tree corresponds to the "conceptual mind" *(al-ruh 'l-fikri)*, which is synthetic in nature, operating on the level of abstractions; and the oil corresponds to the "prophetic mind" *(al-ruh 'l-nabawi)*, which is open to the realm of the "unseen" *(al-ghaib)*.[7]

Taha establishes an intimate connection between the reference of the "hidden treasure" tradition to the divine self-disclosure and the description in verse 24:35 of God as "the Light of heavens and earth." Taha reads the verse in the light of the divine descent idea, which he reformulates in anthropomorphic and phenomenal terms. Hence, the descent of the divine Essence to the ranks of name, attribute, and action are respectively manifested through the Perfect Man *(al-insan 'l-kamil)*, the Perfect Woman *(al-insana 'l-kamila)*, and the phenomenal world. When it comes to the verse's mundane elements he presents us with an imaginative scheme different from that of al-Ghazali's: the "niche" is the body *(jism)* of the Perfect Man, the "glass" his mind *('aql)*, and the "lamp" his heart *(qalb)* (RMii 39–40).

In describing divine descent, Taha also uses the language of theology. Accordingly, God engages in a descent through a seven-rung ladder made up of the "attributes of essence" *(sifat nafsiyya)*, which are life *(al-hayat)*, knowledge *(al-'ilm)*, will *(al-irada)*, power *(al-qudra)*, hearing *(al-sama')*, sight *(al-basar)*, and speech *(al-kalam)*.[8] These attributes are compressed into three that run parallel to the aforementioned tripartite manifestation of descent. Hence, the following triad of correspondents emerges: the name/God's knowledge, the attribute/His will, and the action/His power (QF 19). Like the Mu'tazilites, Taha seeks to safeguard the absolute unity of God by adopting the (originally Aristotelian) doctrine of the unity of essence and attribute in God.

Taha applies the same tripartite structure to the Qur'an. In doing so, he does not view the Qur'an as a space- and time-specific text expressed in a particular language and stabilized as a fixed codex through the editorial decisions of those who oversaw its collection.[9] Rather, he treats the text as an atemporal, esoteric entity. As such, the word *qur'an* is used as an inclusive term to designate God's descent through three stages: *dhikr* (remembrance), *qur'an* (recitation), and *furqan* (capacity to discriminate between truth and untruth) (RT 166). In particularizing these stages of divine descent, Taha quotes 17:106, which reads, "(It is) a Koran We have divided [*faraqnahu*], for thee to recite it to mankind at intervals [*'ala mukth*], and We have sent it down successively [*nazzalnahu tanzilan*]." The root q-r-' from which the word *qur'an* is derived can mean "to recite" or "to collect together, gather." Taha, like Ibn 'Arabi before him, uses the word *qur'an* here in the second sense.[10] *Dhikr* acts as a primary fount from which both *qur'an* and *furqan* flow, *qur'an* being *dhikr* on its level of "collection" or "conjunction" and *furqan* being *dhikr* on its level of "fragmentation" or "disjunction" (RS 70).[11] The stage of *furqan* is one of multiplicity, duality, attributes, and action. This is a stage that, paradoxically, combines both unity *(tawhid)* and multiplicity *(ta'addud)*. Taha further elaborates on this scheme through the preceding verse, which reads, "With the truth We have sent it down [*anzalnahu*], and with the truth it has come down [*nazala*]." He reads the first phrase, *anzalnahu*, as indicating *dhikr* as "ultimate togetherness" *(jam' 'l-*

jam'), or that facet of the name in its descent that reflects an aspect of essence. The second phrase, *(nazala),* indicates the descent to the rank of the "togetherness" *(jam')* of *qur'an,* or that facet of the name in its descent that reflects an aspect of the attribute (RS 71).

The Qur'an as the Locus of the Human

Taha holds that the seed of the Qur'an is the word "Allah." This word, however, has a dual sense: on one level it denotes God, and on another level it denotes the Perfect Human through whose agency the divine descent from a state of absolute unicity to a state of multiplicity is mediated. As such, the Perfect Human functions as God's partner *(zawj)* and enjoys an identity of essence and attribute. As an objectification *(tajsid)* of the divine essence (which is beyond expression and signification), the Perfect Human serves as bearer of God's Beautiful Names and attributes.[12] Would such a perception of the divine name mean that the anthropomorphism that we come across in the Qur'an may be exclusively applicable to the Perfect Human? Taha opts for such a view only partially, insisting that the divine name refers equally to both God and the Perfect Human. When it comes to a classic problem such as God's "sitting on the throne," he adopts the position of the early traditionists and the Ash'arites, who argued for belief in the act's truth without knowing its modality (AJi 19).[13]

Although the Qur'an categorically states, "Like Him there is naught" (42:11), confirming thus the absolute transcendence and otherness of divinity, it nevertheless posits a counterperception, professing divine proximity on the one hand and intimating similarity between the human and God on the other. Proximity is strikingly expressed in verse 50:16, which declares, "We indeed created man; and We know what his soul whispers within him, and We are nearer to him than the jugular vein." With respect to similarity, it is underlined in a prophetic tradition that proclaims, "God created Adam in His own image" *(inna Allaha khalaqa Adama 'ala suratihi).*[14] For Taha, this prophetic tradition implies a general statement and a particular one. On the general level, the human/divine similarity can be perceived in the light of the "attributes of the essence": God enjoys life, knowledge, will, power, hearing, sight, and speech, and so do humans. The crucial difference, however, is that God enjoys these attributes in a state of absolute perfection *(kamal)* while humans enjoy them in a state of inadequacy *(naqs)* (QF 21). On the other hand, the prophetic tradition refers more specifically to God's objectification or the Perfect Human (AJi 19). This is the case despite God's transcendence and incomparability *(tanzih)*. It is in the light of this special status enjoyed by the Perfect Human that the Qur'an, besides being God's essence, represents the attributes of the Perfect Human or God on the level of His first "specification" or "entification" *(ta'ayyun)* (RMi 54). This intimate link that Taha establishes between the Qur'an and the Perfect Human is further emphasized through his assertion that the phrase *umm 'l-kitab* (lit. "Mother of the Book") in verse 43:4 signifies the "perfect human soul," which is with God (QF 207).[15]

The close connection between the human soul and the Qur'an is further extended to include the human body. The Qur'an as "God's Book" *(kitab 'Llah)* is "in reality the totality of creation. It is, in the first place, the human being. This is so because all the signs [*ayat*] of the external [*zahir*] and the internal [*batin*] are united in the human being. . . . The human body is God's Book. The Qur'an that is preserved between 'two covers of a book' and read in Arabic is but a verbal, phonetic, and noetic representation of this great Book" (TK 3). What Taha says in this respect is inspired by Ibn 'Arabi, who, in treating the tradition of Adam's creation in the image of God, says,

> Adam is the totality of the world in its realities. He is an autonomous world and everything else is part of the world. . . . The whole world is the specification [*tafsil*] of Adam, and Adam is the inclusive book [*al-kitab 'l-jami'*]. . . . The human being is the spirit of the world, and the world itself stands for the body. The totality of the world is the "greater human [*al-insan 'l-kabir*]" that contains all humans. . . . The human is breathed [*manfukh*] into the body of the world, and it is the human who is the ultimate goal of this world.[16]

The Qur'an as Divine Speech

Although speech is one of God's attributes, it is important to bear in mind, Taha reminds us, that God does not speak in a human manner. It would hence be wrong to assume on the basis of the language of the Qur'anic text that God speaks Arabic. God's speech is conceived by Taha on phenomenal and essentialist *(dhati)* levels. On the first level, His speech is simply His creation: "The sun rises, it sends light and heat; heat evaporates water, blows the winds, stirs air; winds carry condensed vapour in black clouds . . . and it rains; rain waters the earth and revives it; plants grow and life, in all its forms, blossoms. This is . . . God's speech" (IS 15).

On the other, essentialist level, Taha subscribes to the view that God's speech is an eternal attribute inseparable from His essence; His speech is ultimately nothing but His essence (LL 24). As such, God's speech also means His virtues, or *akhlaq*. We have already come across the tradition according to which Muhammad said, "Take God's virtues as your model [*takhallaqu bi-akhlaq 'Llah*], my God is on a straight path." The word *akhlaq* is the plural of *khulq* or *khuluq*, and as a plural it covers the neutral sense of character, nature, quality, course of conduct, manners, or morals. In addition, the word covers the positive sense of good morals, rectitude, high ideal, or virtue. Taha maintains that as God's speech, the Qur'an is God's virtues or *akhlaq* in His absoluteness. But as humans are incapable of relating to divine absoluteness, the Qur'an as divine virtues was substantialized and hypostatized through the ideal of Muhammad. In making this point, he quotes a tradition according to which 'A'isha, one of the Prophet's wives, was asked about his character, and she answered, "His character [*akhlaq*] was the Qur'an" (QF 209).

An issue related to belief in the Qur'an as God's speech is the controversial question of whether the Qur'an is created or eternal. The question was brought to the fore of theological debates by the doctors of the Mu'tazilite and Jahmite schools in the eighth century.[17] The Mu'tazilites argued that God's attributes and essence are identical. Believing otherwise, they maintained, would lead to a dichotomized perception of God that would entail a belief in a plurality of "eternities" involving His essence on the one hand and His positive attributes on the other. By insisting on this, they were reaffirming their uncompromising belief in God's transcendence and otherness. It has been rightly suggested that the Mu'tazilite rationalization of the unity of God was "influenced by the Aristotelian concept of God as the pure actuality of thought, in whom essence and attribute, thought and the object of thought, are identified, as well as the Plotinian view that God, who transcends thought and being altogether, can only be known negatively."[18]

On account of their rejection of the eternity of God's attributes, the Mu'tazilites could not accept the notion of the eternity of God's speech or word, which they viewed as created.[19] They tempered their position, however, with their subscription to the orthodox belief in a nonhistorical heavenly Qur'an inscribed in a preserved tablet *(lawh mahfuz).*[20]

The Mu'tazilite position was fiercely opposed by the traditionist and orthodox camp led by the learned, pious, and defiant Ahmad b. Hanbal (d. 241/855), who declared that the Qur'an was uncreated.[21] Ibn Hanbal and his school rejected any allegorical interpretation of the Qur'an and placed severe restrictions on the scope of using reason in matters of religion. The conceptual framework within which he perceived the Qur'an as God's eternal speech was due partly to a degree of anthropomorphic emphasis[22] and partly to his equation of God's speech with His knowledge.[23] In his view, the issue was of such decisive significance that it became the litmus test on the basis of which one could draw the line between belief and unbelief.[24]

Another school opposed to the Mu'tazilite position was that of Abu al-Hasan al-Ash'ari (d. 324/935–36), himself a former Mu'tazilite. In proving that the Qur'an is uncreated, al-Ash'ari turned to the Qur'an itself with the view of demonstrating that the logical implication of some verses proves his point.[25] The Ash'arite theologian Abu Bakr al-Baqillani (d. 403/1013) made a distinction between mental speech *(kalam nafsi)* and articulated speech.[26] This distinction was taken up by 'Abd al-Malik al-Juwaini (d. 478/1085), for whom mental speech was eternal whereas articulated speech was created. As such, although God's speech is written down and learned by heart, it does not exist in a written document or someone's heart; the medium of writing is created but what is communicated by the writing is eternal.[27] This distinction between a physical form and a mental content might have been at the heart of a particularly unorthodox view that al-Juwaini expressed regarding the revelation of the Qur'an. Accordingly, the *inzal* (sending down, revelation) of the Qur'an consisted of Gabriel understanding the speech of God in God's station above the seven heavens and then descending *(nazala)* to make Muhammad comprehend *(afhama)* what he had comprehended at the Lote-Tree of Utmost Boundary without conveying *(naql)* the self-same speech.[28] As such the created element is limited not only to the physical aspects through which the Qur'an is preserved or expressed but is further radically extended to include the language of the Qur'an itself.

The highly controversial and intractable nature of the issue of the createdness of the Qur'an has deterred many modern Muslim thinkers from plunging into its vortex. The issue was thrust upon Taha by a questioner who asked him to comment on a piece of research on the createdness of the Qur'an by a certain Taha al-Kurdi. Taha's treatment of the issue draws heavily on Ibn 'Arabi's theory of the Unity of Being on the one hand and on the nature of the relationship between language and meaning in the Qur'an on the other.

On the basis of the Unity of Being doctrine, Taha affirms that in fact there is no place for alterity or otherness *(ghairiyya)* in the relationship between God the Creator and His creation: the entirety of being is nothing but a manifestation of God or, as Taha puts it, "There is nothing in the universe but God and His names, attributes, and actions. The creature is God's manifestation on the level of action" (AJi 72). Such a pantheistic theory raises within Islam the problem of the nature of the opposition between good and evil, or truth *(haqq)* and untruth *(batil)*. Taha fully embraces the logical implication of the Unity of Being theory and declares that as everything is a manifestation of God as the Truth *(al-haqiqa)*, there is no place for "absolute untruth" *(batil mutlaq)* in being. He expresses the relationship between truth and untruth in the following relativistic terms: "Truth [*haqq*] is a manifestation of the Truth [*haqiqa*] in which untruth [*batil*] is subordinated, whereas untruth [*batil*] is a manifestation of the Truth [*haqiqa*] in which truth [*haqq*] is subordinated" (AJi 75).

This is the conceptual framework within which Taha tackles the problem of the createdness of the Qur'an. Accordingly, he contests, the Qur'an is both created and not created: it is created in the sense of creating truth *(haqq)* but not in the sense of creating untruth *(batil)*. Quoting verse 14:1, which refers to the Qur'an (while addressing Muhammad) as "A Book we have sent down to thee that thou mayest bring forth mankind from the shadows to the light," Taha comments that "the Qur'an is all but truth [*haqq*] with which God destroys untruth and all but light through which God guides humankind out of darkness. The Qur'an is created on this level. It is the manifestation of God. It is God in His descent from the level of pure essence to the level of the Truth [*haqiqa*] and the level of truth [*haqq*]" (AJi 77–78).

In light of the claims that Taha makes about the nature of the Qur'an, the text acquires what may be described as a "textual ontology" of its own, setting it apart from any other text: the text only partially exists in its external linguistic form *(zahir)*; on the level of its internal dimension *(batin)* the text encompasses the "mysteries of the human soul" *(asrar 'l-nafs 'l-bashariyya)*; the text exists to help humans realize their "unity" *(tawhid)*; and the entirety of the text exists in every single letter of it, indeed its entirety exists in the very dot from which each letter of the alphabet commences (AJi 79–80).

Taha firmly believed that he had given the definitive answer to this contentious problem. In case modern Muslims fail to see the validity of what he proposes, he counsels them to stick to the orthodox position—a course of action that will ensure them the best guarantee to fulfill the pious act of safeguarding the sanctity of the Qur'an (AJi 80). This may be read as an expedient on Taha's part to mollify orthodox sensibilities.

In examining the issue of the createdness of the Qur'an and formulating his answer, Taha does not refer to the specific traditional problems raised by the respective theological camps. When he says that the Qur'an is not created in the sense in which untruth *(batil)* is created, it is clear that he uses the expression "not created" *(laisa makhluqan)* in a different sense that does not convey the historical technical sense of "eternal." If we overlook Taha's esoteric extravagance, such as his claim that the whole of the Qur'an is encapsulated in a dot, or his attempt to pay court to the orthodox position, it is evident that the camp to which he really belongs regarding this issue is that of the Mu'tazilites. His Unity of Being approach, however, divests the issue of its specificity and focus, as the notion of "speech of God" no longer expressly refers to the text of the Qur'an but can cover the totality of divine creation. This, however, did not prevent Taha from dealing with the Qur'an as a differentiated text rooted in human history (see discussion of Taha's theory of a Second Message of Islam in chapter 5).

Taha explicates his notion that the Qur'an—"God's Book"—is in reality the totality of creation by using key terms according to the Sufi imagination: *(ayat)*, external *(zahir)*, and internal *(batin)*. The Qur'an is perceived as a book that has an exoteric aspect and an esoteric one. This pivotal *zahir/batin* duality is further articulated by Taha in terms of another duality, namely, that of the "signs of horizons" *(ayat 'l-afaq)*, corresponding to *zahir*, and the "signs of souls" *(ayat 'l-nufus)*, corresponding to *batin*. The "signs of horizons" are an aspect determined by the external realities of the specific historical context within which the Qur'an was revealed. Had the Qur'an been revealed in a different place or a different historical context, its signs of horizons would have been different (QT 132). It is on the basis of this logic that Taha ultimately shifts the emphasis to the internal dimension as the aspect more expressive of the essence of the Qur'an.

On the Functions of the Qur'an

A key aspect of Taha's ideas on the Qur'an is the multiple functions it performs. Qur'anic functions are perceived as operating historically and transhistorically.

An example of a Qur'anic function that assumed a primarily historical nature was its engagement of its Arabian audience (which was not atheistic but theistic, with a different notion of divinity) to accept the existence of God in the Qur'anic sense of a monotheistic, personal, omnipotent, omniscient, and omnipresent god. Taha argues that because the people addressed were unlettered *(ummiyyun)*, this determined the line of Qur'anic argumentation.[29] Hence, in demonstrating the existence of the Qur'anic God for its audience, the Qur'an did not use a priori, conceptual arguments but rather world-based arguments. It employed a version of the cosmological argument, appealing to its audience to reflect on the contingent realities surrounding them and their own selves in order to wake to the existence of an all-powerful God.[30] The Qur'anic verses that offer such proof raise, however, a special problem: if the Qur'an is God's speech, why does God point to something else as a proof of His existence when the very act of His speech is sufficient to prove this existence? Unfortunately, Taha does not deal with this problem.

Taha projects the Qur'an as fundamentally a book of guidance *(huda)* in the practical sense of leading humans step by step toward God. He characterizes the human condition as a state of alienation from God, and the Qur'an is further and more specifically projected as a "science of the human soul" *('ilm 'l-nafs 'l-bashariyya)*. In working its way back to its source, that is, God, the human soul must rely on the Qur'an and "hold fast . . . by the rope which God (stretches out for [it])" (3:103) (RT 4).

The notion of the primordial covenant of verse 7:172 is a key element in Taha's concept of alienation (see chapter 2). Another underlying element in this respect is Plato's theory of knowledge according to which knowledge is a recollection of universal Forms.[31] Taha holds that "eternal truth" *(al-haqiqa 'l-azaliyya,* a functional equivalent of the Platonic "universal Forms") dwells inside the human soul. Humans have, however, forgotten this knowledge, as verse 20:115 indicates: "And We made covenant with Adam before, but he forgot." This recollection is a slow process that can be realized through worship—an activity in which the Qur'an plays a central role (RMii 68).

The Qur'an plays this role on account of fulfilling a unique spiritual and psychological task. In expounding this role Taha blends the Islamic notion of soul or self *(nafs)* with the modern psychological notion of the unconscious *(al-'aql 'l-batin),* weaving them into a larger whole, the active elements of which are the notions of archetypal spiritual history, forgetting, recollection, and immortality. With respect to this Taha writes:

> This soul is immortal in essence despite the changes that befall it through different forms and at different times and places. At no time does the soul cease its quest for immortality—to be immortal in form as it is in essence. This story is . . . the story of every human being. However, we all have forgotten it. By "forgetting" it is meant that it settled at the bottom of the unconscious and was then covered by a thick layer of illusions and fears that we inherited from the times of ignorance and superstition. There is no way that we can achieve our happiness unless we break through this thick layer . . . which prevents the forms [*suwar*] of the unconscious to be reflected in the mirror of the conscious and hence reveal the greater truth, the truth of truths [*haqiqat 'l-haqa'iq*] that is shrouded by the veils of light. This long story that flows from the unconscious is made of the same stuff as that of dreams. The Qur'an is made out of the same stuff.[32] It was brought into existence only to remind us of [our] extraordinary story. . . . He who remembers it will acquire knowledge beyond which there is no ignorance and an immortality beyond which there is no perishing. (RMi 36–37)

The function of education, Taha contends, is to remind us of this story. When we learn, we never learn a new thing but remember in fact eternal (*qadim, azali*) knowledge that we have forgotten (QF 123).[33] He cites verse 51:49, which declares, "And of everything created We two kinds [*zawjain*]; haply you will remember [*tadhakkarun*]," as a Qur'anic basis for knowledge as recollection. The crucial words for him here are *tadhakkarun* and *zawjain*. The verb *tadhakkarun* may be rendered as "remember" or "reflect" (on God's omnipotence). Taha prefers the first rendering. The substantive *zawjain* serves in his view to underline the process through which human consciousness acquires knowledge. He argues that because thought only operates by recognizing binary oppositions, the whole point of God's creation of pairs is to make it possible for us to "remember" our "primordial covenant" with Him (affirmed in verse 7:172) through reflective thinking. This is one of Taha's more extravagant assertions as it is not clear how natural or conceptual dualities can make one engage in a recollection of a covenant with God.

Taha might have sensed the logical absurdity of his claim because he supplements what he says by stressing the role of a crucial external agency: the prophets were sent to remind humans of their covenant (QF 123). If this is the case, then how can one justify the Islamic belief of the ending of prophecy with Muhammad? Why did not God continue to send prophets to perform this task as the empirical evidence shows that people tend to be unaware or sceptical of their covenant with God? In addressing this, Taha, on one level, gives the conventional Islamic answer that prophecy was concluded because the Qur'an is a comprehensive book that contains all that humans need know to realize their salvation (IQ 20). But from the standpoint of his mystical perspective this view is nonetheless insufficient. Hence, on another level, he subjects all the elements of Islamic religious imagination to a scheme in which revelation ceases to be prophet-centered. Writing about this he says,

> The universe has been made subject to humans in order to help them in their long journey from their state of distance from God [*bu'd*] to a state of being near Him [*qurb*]. Everything has been made subject to humans to realize this goal: Satan and his offspring, the pure angels, the prophets, the scriptures, divine laws, and in particular the Qur'an, which provides the clearest guide for the route of return. Although the Qur'an has been revealed only recently to the seal of the prophets in its [existing] form, its revelation, in reality, has neither a beginning nor an

end as it continues to be revealed and will never cease to be revealed. (TS 14–15)

In maintaining such a position, Taha is evidently at variance with the traditional position in the Qur'an, according to which the utmost that the believers in a postprophecy time can do is to interpret the text and hope, with the help of God, to find fresh answers. Taha, however, does not speak about interpretation but rather, pointedly, about revelation *(nuzul)*. This makes the Qur'an in effect only a partial manifestation of divine revelation. Inasmuch as one progresses from the imitation of the Prophet to the realization of one's authenticity, one also progresses from a stage of prophetic revelation (where the Prophet is the subject of the revelatory act) to a stage of personal revelation (where the worshipping subject is the subject of the revelatory act). Hence, not only does the act of transcending prophetic mediation apply on the level of ritual worship but it also extends to the level of revelation.

A chief function of the Qur'an pertains to the nature of the knowledge it provides. Taha holds that "the Qur'an, as eternal truth, is a heavenly music. It teaches you everything without teaching you anything in particular. It stimulates one's cognitive powers and sharpens the tools of sensation in the whole of one's being. It then draws back, leaving one face to face with the external world to perceive it in one's own way and to formulate a pattern that informs one's daily interactions with the world of others and things" (RMi 39). The issue of knowledge is closely connected with that of thought *(fikr)*. Taha, not unlike other classical and modern Muslim thinkers, stresses the high esteem in which thought or reason is held in Islam and points to the tradition affirming that the first of God's creation was reason (QF 12). This, however, is a qualified celebration of reason and rationality, for these thinkers emphasize at the same time that reason should realize the limits of its powers vis-à-vis what revelation can offer.

Through his "music" metaphor, Taha confers upon the Qur'an a unique quality of universal presence. This is a presence by virtue of which "Qur'anic music" permeates all being with the ultimate goal of helping reason reach God.[34] When it comes to the limits of reason, Taha is categorical in asserting that it is not possible to fathom what he describes as the "mysterious depths [*asrar*] of the Qur'an" by exercising one's thinking faculty.

This is a view that is rooted in the Sufi perspective, which perceives thought on a certain level as a veil *(hijab)*. At best, reason can grasp the exterior *(zahir)* of the Qur'an. To understand the Qur'an one should be fully engaged in *suluk,* or a sustained spiritual quest through worship and service. *Suluk* is hence a process in which the seeker adopts a cognitive stance of "trusting acceptance" *(tasdiq)* and engages, accordingly, in action *('amal)*: the simple act of belief leads to authentic knowledge or certainty *(yaqin),* and the knowledge of the manifestational *zahir* leads to the knowledge of the hidden *batin.* The Qur'an is the means of this *suluk* in the process of which the seeker as cognitive agent progresses from the exterior, shari'a level of the Qur'an to its interior, *haqiqa* level. This makes it possible for the seeker as experiencing agent to progress from a state of fragmentation to a state of oneness and wholeness.

The seeker can overcome his state of "dismemberment" by engaging in an act of "remembering." His journey is epitomized, Taha argues, by what verse 39:23 imparts: "God has sent down the fairest discourse as a Book, consimilar in its oft-repeated [*mathani*], whereat shiver the skins of those who fear their Lord; then their skins and their hearts soften to the remembrance of God." The key term in the verse is *mathani,* which indicates "duality".[35] This duality is represented in the verse through the "skins" and "hearts" (symbolizing the "outside" and "inside") opposition. The seeker's *taqwa* or pious devotion ultimately makes his skin as soft as his heart—this identity of outside and inside marks his spiritual progress beyond the state of *mathani,* or fragmentation and disunity to a state where he has realized his *tawhid* or unity (DJ 15). *Tawhid* as an ultimate goal to be realized existentially through the practice of worship is closely connected with another important theme in Taha's work: as God does not lack unity and because it is the servant who is in dire need of it, then, in reality, it is an attribute that concerns humans (QF 39).

The firm connection that Taha establishes between the Qur'an, knowledge, and the spiritual discipline of *suluk* is the foundation of a peculiar theory on the basis of which he seeks to reconcile Qur'anic pronouncements with two kinds of contradictions: on the one hand, contradictions that arise within the Qur'anic text (discussed in chapter 4), and on the other, contradictions between certain Qur'anic assertions and human beliefs. An example of the latter type is found in Taha's discussion of the Qur'anic affirmation that the earth is flat.[36]

Taha argues that what the Qur'an asserts about the earth's shape has been determined by its educative method of progressing from external realities to internal ones. As such, he claims, the Qur'an intentionally avoided disrupting what was confirmed by the sensory perception of its Arabian audience, as part of a purposeful educative procedure within what may be described as a gradualist cognitive strategy. As the Qur'an advocated monotheism, God did not deem it wise, Taha argues, to overburden the cognitive capacity of the recipients of His word with a belief about the earth's shape that ran counter to the evidence of their own sense perception. Their sensory illusion was hence confirmed, with the goal of gradually eliminating their illusion when they knew better through the practice and perfection of their worship (RT 66). Taha here takes literally what is affirmed by verse 2:282, "And fear God; God teaches you" *(wa 'ttaqu 'Llaha wa yu'allimukumu 'Llahu)*: through *taqwa* (fear of God translated into worship and service), one is taught by God, not only esoterically but also exoterically, about the phenomenal world. This is one of Taha's flimsiest arguments. In premodern times, neither the history of Islamic thought in general nor that of Muslim geographical thought in particular attested to a Qur'an-inspired counterperception suggesting that the earth is round.[37] Taha is silent as to what the Qur'anic foundation might be for a worshipper's eventual realization that the earth is round, and what the attitude of present-day Muslims should be when they read Qur'anic verses that affirm the flatness of the earth.

On the Language of the Qur'an

The nature of the Qur'an and its function are inextricably linked to its language. Taha's discussion of the language of the Qur'an rests on his reading of verses 43:1–3, which read, "*Ha Mim.* By the Clear Book, behold, We have made it an Arabic Koran; haply you will understand." On the basis of this passage he argues that in reality the language of the Qur'an is not Arabic. The point he makes here is bound up with the process of divine descent he describes as moving from *dhikr* to *qur'an* and then to *furqan*. Hence, he holds, Arabic is the specific language through which the divine revelation expresses itself only on the level of *furqan* or disjunction. As the passage above indicates, the expression of divine speech through Arabic was necessary for its Arab audience to understand it. From a Qur'anic standpoint this takes care of the question of why God communicates His message through the medium of a human language in the first place.

Yet two key questions may be raised: Why did God specifically choose Arabic as the medium of His revelation? And does not such a choice limit the reception of divine revelation and make it Arabic-centric? Taha, without specifically posing these questions, is fully aware of them and their implications and does not shrink from tackling them. In justifying the privileging of Arabic as the medium of divine revelation, he follows a very Arabic-centric view according to which Arabic is the most perfect of languages. This view is based on the convention that the numerical value attached to the last, twenty-eighth letter of the Arabic alphabet is one thousand.[38] Quoting some verses where the number "thousand" is mentioned, he argues that the Qur'an underscores the special spiritual value of this number.[39] From this millenary association and assumption he leaps to a bold assertion regarding an intrinsic distinction of Arabic that qualified it for the ultimate privilege of being the medium through which God communicated His last message to all humankind (RT 113–14).

Then Taha moves to another familiar terrain as regards Qur'anic particularity. Besides the genius of the Arabic language, Qur'anic language has its own genius, which is evidenced by its *i'jaz* or "inimitability": Qur'anic Arabic has unique stylistic qualities that make it rhetorically unsurpassable. Echoing the traditional position on *i'jaz*, Taha sums up the unqualified linguistic superiority of the Qur'an in its "comprehensiveness, subtlety, succinctness, and preciseness" (TS 88).[40] An important point related to the rhetorical nature of the Qur'an that exercised Muslim exegetes and rhetoricians was whether the Qur'an is poetry or not. Qur'anic pronouncements, such as verse 36:69, categorically repudiate the suggestion that the divine revelation is poetry. Furthermore, in renouncing any association with poetry, the Qur'an adopts a sweeping antipoetry position expressed unequivocally in verses 26:221–26, which declare, "Shall I tell you on whom the Satans come down? They come down on every guilty impostor. They give ear, but most of them are liars. And the poets—the perverse follow them; hast thou not seen how they wander in every valley and how they say that which they do not?" This Qur'anic position resonates through some hadith materials, such as the Prophet's dire warning to his companions, "It would be better for the inside of yours to be filled with pus than with poetry."[41]

This extreme Qur'anic and prophetic denunciation is, however, counterbalanced by other traditions in which the Prophet expresses more favorable views about poetry, such as the tradition in which he says, "Poetry can contain wisdom."[42] As such, some authorities were eager to make a distinction between good, Islamically admissible poetry that stresses values agreeable to Islam and bad, Islamically forbidden poetry whose values are objectionable to Islam.[43] Taha holds that the Qur'anic censure of poetry concerns its negative aspects, such as "the lack of commitment [*iltizam*] and the lack of sincerity [*sidq*]"(IF 40). On the nature of the Qur'an itself he expresses an earlier stance echoing the received position that the Qur'an is not poetry (RMi 81) and a later stance according to which he maintains that the Qur'an is "poetry and more" (IF 40).

Despite Taha's acceptance of the orthodox doctrine of the inimitability of the Qur'an, he places greater emphasis on the argument that the use of Arabic in expressing the Qur'an does not prove that divine revelation has a language (as seen in connection with his reading of verses 43:1–3). This line is more consistent with his mystical perspective. In expounding this perspective he uses verse 41:53, building on its distinction between the signs of horizons (or the external domain) and the signs of souls (or the internal domain) to point out that had the Qur'an been revealed in a different historical setting, its signs of horizons would have been different. This implies that the use of Arabic was an accident of the historical place of revelation. Hence, the real language of the Qur'an should be sought on the level of the "signs of souls," for, according to Taha, "The Qur'an has no language. It made use of Arabic as a mediative tool for its [own] language." What then is the Qur'an's real language? Taha maintains that "it is the tunes [*anaghim*] of the human soul that flow in valleys shrouded in veils of light and darkness" (QF 207). Evidently, his prime concern here is to break beyond the linguistic and cultural particularism of the Qur'an to affirm a universalism based on symbols shared by all human beings. What he says in this respect echoes his view that what constitutes the building blocks of the Qur'an is the stuff of dreams.

Going Beyond Language

Despite what he says about Qur'anic Arabic, Taha shifts his ultimate emphasis in dealing with Qur'anic *i'jaz* (inimitability) from the formal, rhetorical aspect to the content dimension. In this regard, he maintains that although the Qur'an uses Arabic with stylistic authority, its real *i'jaz* lies in its meanings *(ma'ani)*. He elaborates on this by saying, "The Qur'an is, in the first place, a science of the soul. . . . This science is the internal music of the Qur'an. The Qur'an uses external tunefulness to generate an internal tunefulness in the recesses of the human soul that has been afflicted and paralyzed by primordial fear" (QF 206). He establishes a close connection between the notion of *i'jaz* and his notion of authenticity. According to Taha, those who realize their authenticity live fully in the present moment, performing to the best of their ability their "immediate obligations" *(al-wajib 'l-mubashir)* while being fully content with what God decrees. He characterizes this kind of conduct and attitude as a "life of reflection and sensibility" that is free of fear, and he insists that it is a life that can be realized only through the Qur'an. It is this unique capacity of the divine text to bring about such a state that constitutes its "abiding" *mu'jiza* (miracle) (QF 210).

In deemphasizing the language aspect, Taha deploys another semantic strategy. He argues that the Qur'anic (read: *furqanic*) revelation has a pyramidical structure with infinite gradational levels of meaning between the base and the top: the more one ascends toward the top, the subtler the text's meanings are. Taha insists that this constant ascent to finer and higher levels of Qur'anic meanings is invariably a movement from what is "good" *(hasan)* to what is "better" *(ahsan)* (RT 114). But this is also an ascent that eventually goes beyond language, which is after all only a system of signs rooted in human needs and cannot, no matter how evolved and resourceful, contain all the meanings of God's speech (IS 15). There comes a point where language as we know it breaks down because it can no longer communicate what the Qur'an wants to say. This point is symbolically hinted at in the Qur'an through the letter formations known as the "disjoined letters" *(huruf muqatta'a)*[44] that stand at the beginning of twenty-nine chapters. In dealing with these letters Taha presents two theories, an esoteric one and a psychological one.

Reiterating a view expressed by some classical authorities, Taha declares that the "mystery" of these letters is the "mystery of the whole Qur'an" (RT 114).[45] Accordingly, when words break into letters this does not mean that meaning breaks and disappears or that the Qur'an loses its power of communication. Like words, Qur'anic letters are semantic units and carriers of meaning. Furthermore, the meanings of these Qur'anic letters are inexhaustible because they flow from the attributes of the divine Essence: each letter inheres meanings corresponding to God's life, knowledge, will, power, hearing, sight, and speech (QF 22–23). In signaling the ultimate deficiency of language, letters hence shift the communicative act from the level of *'ibara* to the higher and subtler level of *ishara*.

This is interconnected with another key semantic aspect. In verse 39:23 the Qur'an is characterized as a book of *mathani* (having to do with two, i.e., having a dual nature). For Taha, this self-characterization is clear evidence that the semantic structure of the whole of the Qur'an is dichotomous in that it has an "immediate sense" *(ma'na qarib)* and an "ultimate (or deeper) sense" *(ma'na ba'id)*. The immediate sense can be characterized as falling within the domain of *'ibara,* whereas the ultimate sense goes beyond this into the realm of *ishara.* This is a restatement of two other oppositions in the Qur'an, namely, that of *zahir* (exoteric), corresponding to the "signs of horizons," and *batin* (esoteric), corresponding to the "signs of the souls." Furthermore, the exoteric/esoteric opposition is projected as a progressively endless duality in which each esoteric level becomes an exoteric level for another esoteric level and so on until one reaches the divine essence— an objective that can never be attained (TS 88–89). The grand picture Taha presents is hence of a ceaseless, gnostic advance upward in a semantic pyramid from the limited *(mahdud)* to the absolute *(mutlaq).* The base of this pyramid is language at its most univocal and unequivocal expression of meaning, or what is indicated by verse 3:7 when it refers to "clear" *(muhka-*

mat) verses. The pyramid's apex is the word "Allah," a linguistic expression insofar as it is a word, otherwise more of a sign, a symbolic expression *(ishara).*[46]

In his psychological theory, Taha understands letters as essentially phonemic units expressing the movement of thought. He divides them into three categories: audibly vocalized letters, subliminally vocalized letters, and other, unvocalized letters. As such, letters as speech sounds that we can hear (or "external speech") and sounds that we cannot hear (or "inner speech") are the essential constitutive elements at the root of our conscious and unconscious minds or the totality of our sense of being.[47] The above tripartite division corresponds to another tripartite categorization according to which Taha divides letters into three types: written or representational *(raqmiyya),* vocalized *(sawtiyya),* and mental *(fikriyya).* The first type is represented by the letters of the alphabet; they are the finite audible sounds of ordinary speech.[48] On the other hand, vocalized letters are countless; they are those "subliminally audible sounds" and "inaudible sounds" that generate the thought activity of the conscious part of the mind.

Employing the psychoanalytic notion of the unconscious, Taha recasts it in Sufi terms into an unconscious on the periphery of which lies religion and at the heart of which lies "eternal truth" *(al-haqiqa 'l-azaliyya).* He declares that these mental letters are the essence of everything and that in fact they are the "words" of God alluded to in verse 18:109, which declares, "Say: 'If the sea were ink for the Words of my Lord, the sea would be spent before the Words of my Lord are spent, though We brought replenishment the like of it.' " According to him, verse 20:7, "Be thou loud in thy speech [*tajhar*], yet surely He knows the secret ['*l-sirr-a*] and that yet more hidden [*akhfa*]," indicates the three levels of letters: the "audible articulation" signifies the representational level, and the reference to God's knowledge of "the secret" marks the vocalized level, whereas the allusion to His knowledge of what is "hidden" connotes the mental level (RT 114–15). Taha adduces another Qur'anic basis for his letter typology from the same chapter. Verse 20:108 describes the human eschatological encounter with God in the following terms: "On that day . . . voices will be hushed to the All-merciful, so that thou hearest naught but a murmuring." The moment's heaviness and awesomeness is underlined by verse 20:111, which adds, "And faces shall be humbled unto the Living, the Eternal. He will have failed whose burden is evildoing [*zulm*]." Taha reads the references of the first verse to "voices" *(aswat)* and "murmuring" *(hams)* as allusions to the levels of representational, sound-based letters and vocalized letters. On the other hand, he interprets the word *zulm* in the second verse as "subtle polytheism" *(shirk khafi)*, the locus of which is the realm of the mental letters or the unconscious. Here, again, he subjects the modern psychological notion to his scheme as he suggests that this "subtle polytheism" is at the root of psychological repression and consequently the split of the mind into a conscious and an unconscious (RT 115).

The Qur'an as an Open Text

Like his Sufi predecessors, Taha's gnostic stance leads him to the presupposition of what may be described as an open parallel deep text. This parallel text is a theoretical gnostic construction embedded in the claim of infinite levels of meaning inherent in the totality of the elements making up the Qur'anic text (starting from a preletter level of a mere dot). For Taha this parallel text is a Qur'anic textual reality whose existence is indicated by verse 43:4, "and behold, it is in the Essence of the Book [*umm 'l-kitab*], with Us; sublime, indeed wise." Commenting on this verse, he says, "The beginnings of the Qur'an are accessible to us through the Arabic language . . . but the end of it is with God in the absoluteness of His essence" (DJ 37). Although Taha interprets the phrase *umm 'l-kitab* on another level as the perfect human soul, he reads it here and in other places as signifying the divine essence (see for instance TS 88). This notion of an open parallel deep text brings together three key themes that recur throughout Taha's work: (1) the whole world is God's "book" and His "speech," (2) mankind's progress toward God is eternal *(sarmadi)*, and (3) divine revelation is a neverending process as humans are engaged every single moment in learning from God.

If the Qur'an is such a special text and if it is pervaded on every level by a semantic duality leading to an endless unfolding of an outward/inward opposition, then the hermeneutic questions arising would be how one can approach such a semantically fluid and multivalent text and what methods can be deployed in understanding its language and decoding its signs.

In connection with responding to these questions, Taha declares that one cannot reach a real understanding of the Qur'an solely by relying on language and that the task facing modern Muslims is not one of engaging in *tafsir* (outward, surface interpretation). Rather, they should turn their energies to *ta'wil* (inward, deep interpretation).[49] To be sure, one should start with language or the text's external dimension, while being fully cognizant of the limitation of this approach, through which it is not possible to uncover the deeper meanings of the Qur'an. To accomplish this one must follow a different path. Taha profoundly believes that the Qur'an provides modern Muslims with boundless horizons should they seriously engage in an effort to discover its meanings. Hence he declares, "The Qur'an is the hidden treasure.[50] It is still virgin as early Muslims broke only its outer seal" (RMi 75).

For Taha, understanding the Qur'an is a process that involves divine descent on the one hand and human ascent on the other. God's descent is realized through His constant self-disclosure, as indicated by verse 55:29, which proclaims that God engages in "new deeds" *(sha'n)* every day. Humankind's ascent consists of a constant endeavour to realize His *tawhid* (unity) through worship *('ibada)* with the view of realizing servantship *('ubudiyya)*. What lies at the heart of Taha's hermeneutics is hence this dynamic and creative interaction between the Qur'anic text on the one hand and the experiential act of worship on the other. In the light of this interaction, he affirms two key points: it is *tawhid*, rather than language, that is the basis for uncovering the meanings of the Qur'an, and it is important to draw a clear distinction between the sending down *(inzal)* of the Qur'an and its clarification or explication *(tabyin)*.

Taha uses the term *tawhid* in three senses: first, to denote a psychological category: the state of unity and wholeness that human beings realize through the ending of fear and the integration of mind and heart. Second, *tawhid* refers to an ontological category identical with Ibn 'Arabi's notion of *wahdat 'l-wujud* or unity of being. Third, it is used in an epistemological sense to denote a mode of knowledge that can go beyond appearance and grasp reality.

As far as the clarification of the Qur'an is concerned, Taha discusses this in connection with verse 16:44, which affirms, "and We have sent down [*an-zalna*] to thee the Remembrance [*'l-dhikr-a*] that thou mayest make clear [*li-tubayyin-a*] to mankind what [*ma*] was sent down [*nuzzila*] to them; and so haply they will reflect [*yatafakkar-una*]." According to him, there is a fundamental flaw in the common assumption, on the basis of this verse, that the illumination and clarification of the Qur'an were performed once and for all during the Prophet's time. He maintains:

> The Qur'an cannot be fully explicated. . . . One's quest within its universe is eternal. When the Qur'an says, "The true religion with [*'inda*] God is Islam" (3:19), the word *'inda* here is neither an adverb of time nor an adverb of place. It denotes what is beyond time and place. One's quest through the Qur'an . . . is an eternal quest of God. As such, its explication has not been fully concluded, and it will never be fully concluded. Certainly, the sending down of the Qur'an as a Book has been concluded but not its explication. (RT 135)

With respect to verse 16:44, Taha stresses that it is important to distinguish between the derived verbs *anzala* (fourth verbal form, from *n-z-l,* "to descend, come down") and *nuzzila* (passive voice, second verbal form, same root). He disputes the prevalent exegetical view that the verse's two derived verbs are synonymous.[51] He contends that the indefinite pronoun *ma* does not refer to the noun "remembrance" *(dhikr)* but rather to part of it, namely the part of God's message that has already been explicated to the Qur'anic audience of the Prophet's time (RT 135).

Taha not only emphasizes the intimate connection between the process of discerning the meanings of the Qur'an and the act of worship but he goes on to establish an even more intimate link between the depth of one's Qur'anic understanding and the performance of worship (particularly prayer) at certain times of the day or the year. Pointing out, on the basis of verse 7:204, a distinction between two modes of receiving the Qur'an, namely *'istima'* (hearing) and *insat* (listening),[52] he affirms that the final third of the night and the month of Ramadan are the best times to "listen" to the Qur'an and gain a greater understanding of it because the Qur'an tends to "impart its mysteries" more at these times (TK 85–86).

Interpretive Strategies

Although Taha did not produce a systematic Qur'anic commentary, his constant engagement of the Qur'anic text throughout his work makes it possible to identify the basic characteristics of his hermeneutic approach.

Taha shifts what may be perceived as the Qur'an's real meaning to its internal dimension *(batin)* while at the same time insisting on the importance of the external dimension *(zahir)* as a necessary stepping-stone to reach the text's ultimate meanings. So much does he stress the importance of the text's externality that he is willing at points to adopt a literalist position. An example of this is found in his analysis of verse 47:15, which reads, "This is the similitude [*mathal*] of Paradise which the godfearing have been promised: therein are rivers of water unstaling, rivers of milk unchanging in flavour, and rivers of wine—a delight to the drinkers, rivers, too, of honey purified; and therein for them is every fruit, and forgiveness from their Lord—Are they as he who dwells forever in the Fire, such are given to drink boiling water, that tears their bowels asunder?" Commenting on this verse, the Egyptian writer Mustafa Mahmud said, "This is a metaphor and not a literal description. Such a description is impossible as heaven and hell are unseen matters that cannot be captured in a language familiar to us."[53] Taha rejects this view and declares,

> The literal aspect of the description is intended, as much as its internal aspect. However, Qur'anic metaphors are not like the metaphors we use, for they are gnosis ['*ilm*]. This is so because while Qur'anic metaphors aim at making people understand, they are at the same time not divorced from the truth. When God says, "This is the similitude of Paradise," and so on, this does not mean that the concrete denotation of the words is not intended and that they only function to make the sense accessible. Indeed, the words are meant to be taken literally. Paradise concretely contains what God promises in the Qur'an. (QF 129)[54]

What Taha affirms concerning Qur'anic figurative language has a significant implication. By claiming that Qur'anic metaphors are intrinsically different from the metaphors of ordinary speech on account of their knowledge content, he opts for a hermeneutic strategy that does on one level lead to reducing Qur'anic metaphors to literal statements, as his reading of verse 47:15 demonstrates. So, to what extent can such an approach lead to a gross and absurd literalism similar to the literalism of some scholars in the past?[55] Could Taha be promoting a narrow literalism when he insists that the *zahir* (external or literal denotation) of words in the Qur'an is intended in itself (QF 129)?

Taha's accommodation of literalism takes three forms. The first is what we have seen as regards the literal denotation of words like "milk," "wine," and "honey" in verse 47:15, or what may be described as simple literalism. The second is illustrated by his rationalization of the verses that affirm the flatness of the earth. This may be described as concessionary literalism, that is, the divine revelation making a concession to its original receivers so that it is not out of step with their level of perceiving things. The third can be characterized in connection with his reading of, for example, verse 49:12, which warns admonishingly, "would any of you like to eat the flesh of his brother dead? You would abominate it." The verse denounces slander and backbiting, which is accepted by Taha as its immediate, external sense. He contends, however, that its deep, internal sense concerns the denunciation of eating meat because animals are the "brothers" of human beings (AJI 28). What is striking here is that Taha rereads the metaphorical expression of "eating the flesh of [one's] brother dead" in a different literal sense that extends the metaphorical sense to a new horizon. This may be described as "extended literalism."

Narrow literalism is a function of the first form above. Although Taha espouses, on one level, a simple literalist approach, it would be wrong to characterize his overall position in these terms. What he does in reality is to adapt his radical Sufi position to the orthodox, Sunnite context within which he operates and hence stress the importance of shari'a and an exoteric understanding of the Qur'an. This, however, is only a first step toward the ultimate heights of experiencing *haqiqa* and being exposed to the esoteric meanings of the Qur'an.

As such, in approaching the Qur'an, Taha's starting point is not the Qur'anic text itself but rather a preconceived scheme to which he subjects the text. Some examples serve to demonstrate this.

The hermeneutic method that Taha uses in understanding the Qur'an draws on the rich symbolism of the Sufi tradition. This symbolism is generated by the immediate sense/ultimate sense semantic duality. Hence, the "faithful spirit" *(al-ruh 'l-amin)* of verse 26:193 who came down with the Qur'an, a phrase whose referent is understood to be the archangel Gabriel by the generality of exegetes, is held by Taha to allude on the level of ultimate sense to "reason" *('aql)*. Consequently, the reason of every person is identified as the "Gabriel" of that person (AJii 42). The *ma'un* (vessel, container) of verse 107:7, mentioned in the context of castigating those who refrain from giving alms to relieve the needy, is held to indicate the human heart (TK 88). Both "reason" and "heart" are fused in the notion of *fitra* (original nature) mentioned in verse 30:30 in connection with the Qur'anic notion of the "true religion" *(al-din 'l-qayyim)*.

The categories of "exoteric" and "esoteric," which stand at the heart of the Sufi hermeneutic scheme, allow for an open semantic pattern where dualities are generated endlessly, with the esoteric serving as an exoteric for another esoteric. This scheme, however, remains essentially theoretical as one does not find in exegetical Sufi literature convincing interpretive applications of it. Taha claims that in the Qur'an even the letters are subject to the semantic *mathani* duality that supposedly permeates the entire text. But this, in the end, remains as a mere, excessive claim that Taha cannot substantiate with any interpretive example.

What Sufi hermeneutics has done at best is to posit several simultaneous oppositions that are allegorical in nature and that do not necessarily compete with each other. Take the example of verses 20:9–12: Moses sees a fire and tells his family that he will go and bring a brand from it, but when he comes to it, he hears God's voice commanding him to put off his shoes and telling him that he has been chosen to be a carrier of divine revelation. Moses' *na'lain* (pair of shoes) exercised the symbolic ingenuity of Sufis. Taha opts for a metaphorical reading whereby the discarded pair of shoes stands for one's partner *(zawj)* and one's self *(nafs)*. At the same time, he allows for a symbolic shift whereby the shoes represent worldly existence *(al-dunya)* and the hereafter *(al-akhira)* (QF 154–55).[56]

Taha's readings may sometimes not be in the least warranted by the Qur'anic text. Such an interpretive strategy is at its crudest when he disregards a word's explicit denotation in favor of a forced reading. For example, in reading verse 97:3, which affirms that the Night of Power is "better than a thousand months," Taha declares that the word "month" here means "year." This is motivated by his prior intention to read the entire chapter as a proclamation of the Second Coming (QF 181).[57]

On another level, Taha may impute to a verse an intention that is clearly inconsistent with what it explicitly declares. Chapter 26, for instance, begins by mentioning Muhammad's grief and distress owing to his failure to win the Meccans over to his message, and then verse 26:4 consolingly proclaims, "If We will, We shall send down on them [i.e., the unbelievers] out of heaven a sign, so their necks will stay humbled to it." Despite the conditional nature of the Qur'anic statement (had God willed, He would have sent down His sign, but He did not will) and the historical fact that no such miracle ever took place, Taha asserts that God "had in fact willed and had performed His will. It is only that His act is realized over time. There will come a time when the divine will is carried out in actuality, the sign will be sent down, and necks will bend in humility" (QF 94). Taha follows a similar logic in reading verse 10:99, which states, "And if thy Lord had willed, whoever is in the earth would have believed, all of them, all together. Wouldst thou then constrain the people, until they are believers?" Here, he asserts that "God has willed that all who are on earth will believe but in the future and not at present" (QF 86).

Taha can even go to the extent of engaging in what amounts to a semantic emendation of what the Qur'an says. Quoting verse 53:42, "and that the final end [*muntaha*]] is unto thy Lord," he adds, "and there is no final end" *(wa la muntaha)* (QF 117). For Taha, what the word *muntaha* ostensibly suggests has to be bracketed, as humankind's quest for God is a journey that never comes to an end.

Taha's Qur'anic hermeneutics reveals the acute dilemma of a Sufi reformist in the modern age. On the one hand he views the Qur'an as a God-centered, ahistorical, and undifferentiated revelation. On the other, he deals with it as a humankind-centered text grounded in the history of the human-divine encounter and the story of the spiritual quest of human beings. The former view rests on the belief that the Qur'an is God's speech and His speech is identical with His essence (which makes the Qur'an uncreated, not history-bound). By contrast, the latter view rests on the Qur'an's form as a text expressed in human language and its contents as reflecting the specific context within which it unfolded.

As a Sufi, Taha's point of departure is Muhammad's spiritual narrative and its Qur'anic expression. But he goes further as a radical Sufi, for neither the Prophet's experience nor the Qur'an constitute an end in themselves—rather, they are means to the ultimate end of "receiving directly [*kifahan*] from God" (DJ 36). What is actively at work here is Taha's notion of authenticity with its emphasis of unmediated access to God. In understanding the Qur'an what really matters is not scholarly application and the diverse methodologies it deploys. This path, Taha contends, offers a limited horizon and can lead only to superficial understanding. In claiming that the Qur'an is the story of the human soul, he invests the text with a decidedly existential nature. It is this perception of the text that has determined Taha's hermeneutic approach, which also assumes an existential nature: it is only through a systematic application of *taqwa* that one can work one's way through the infinite layers of Qur'anic meanings. Important characteristics of this *taqwa*-based consciousness are that it eliminates the mediation of any exegetical authority and Qur'anic meanings reveal themselves in correspondence with the seeker's spiritual progress.

Following in the footsteps of Ibn 'Arabi, Taha allows the Qur'anic text to "dissolve." The orthodox belief that "everything is in the Qur'an" is reconceptualized as "everything is the Qur'an." When the latter statement is further abstracted to "everything is a word of God," then the notion of divine text or revelation dissolves to be replaced by an ontological text represented by the totality of being. This totality of being, represented in Taha's thought by the signs of horizons and the signs of souls, is the real, ultimate text that the seeker is called upon to unveil, read, and experience.

4

Determinism, Free Will, and Divine Punishment

The Jabrite and Qadarite Legacy

ONE OF THE EARLIEST and most divisive questions raised by Muslim theologians was whether human actions are predetermined by divine will or whether they originate in man's own autonomous and free will. Although early theologians (and, later, mystics and philosophers) tried to ground their respective positions in the Qur'an, they could not satisfactorily resolve their differences on the basis of what the holy text states. This was the case because the Qur'an presents seemingly conflicting statements on the issue—a state of affairs that was evidently produced by the dictates of the "occasions of revelation" *(asbab 'l-nuzul)* pertaining to the verses in question.

As an example, verse 8:17, addressing the believers and Muhammad at the same time, asserts, "You did not slay them, but God slew them; and when thou threwest, it was not thyself that threw, but God threw." This, the exegetical material informs us, was revealed in connection with the early military confrontations between the newly founded Muslim community and the Meccans at the battles of Badr and Uhud. The verse's references to the specific and concrete acts of "slaying" on the part of the believers and of "throwing" on the part of the Prophet lend powerful plausibility to the exegetical contention that its occasion of revelation was this particular context of violent engagement.[1] On one level, this verse could be read as a Qur'anic assurance to the believers at a time of beleaguerment of God's ever-present help and protection. Yet on another level the verse is an unequivocal expression of a deterministic state of affairs where human beings are not the true authors of their actions.

This belief is confirmed by other Qur'anic verses and in particular those that deal with the themes of guidance and straying from the right path. The Qur'anic assertion that God "leads astray those whom He pleases and guides whom He pleases" appears in verses 14:4, 16:93, 35:8, and 74:31. This total divine sovereignty is articulated in verse 6:125 through the concretely physical images of expansion and constriction: "Whomsoever God desires to guide, He expands his breast to Islam; whomsoever He desires to lead astray, He makes his breast narrow, tight, as if he were climbing to heaven. So God lays abomination upon those who believe not."

Furthermore, Qur'anic determinism resonates throughout the hadith material. One of the starkest expressions of this is a tradition in which the Prophet, after emphasizing the all-encompassing and irrevocable nature of divine decree, concludes by saying, "The pens have stopped writing and the ink of the scrolls has dried up."[2] This image of committal to writing, confirming the inexorability and unalterability of what God preordains, is redeployed in another tradition according to which the Prophet summed up to his companions the story of the entire life and destiny of human beings in these terms:

> In the process of one's creation, each of you is gathered together for forty days in his mother's womb. He thereupon becomes a blood clot for a comparable period and then a lump of flesh for a comparable period. An angel is then sent to record four things. He is told, "Write down his works, his sustenance, his appointed time, and whether he will be damned or saved." The spirit is then breathed into him. A man would be doing [good] works until he is [barely] a cubit away from paradise and then his book takes precedence and he performs the works of those who go to hell. A man would be doing [bad] works until he is [barely] a cubit away from hell and then his book takes precedence and he performs the works of those who go to paradise.[3]

On the other hand, the Qur'an stresses the notion of human free will in accepting the word of God. Hence, verse 18:29 declares: "Say: 'The truth is from your Lord; so let whosoever will believe, and let whosoever will disbelieve.'" What the verse affirms presupposes human freedom and the responsibility associated with it. This responsibility is clearly underlined in verse 3:86, which reads, "How shall God guide a people who have disbelieved after they believed, and bore witness that the messenger is true, and the clear signs came to them? God guides not the people of the evildoers." Here, it is human choice and human action that are decisive, and divine action assumes a reactive nature.

This Qur'anic ambivalence led to sharp disagreements and the rise of competing theological perspectives. Those defending a determinist position (known as Jabrites, from *jabr* "compulsion") threw their weight behind the notion of divine omnipotence, and those advocating volitionism (given the confusing name of Qadarites, from *qadar,* "divine decree") put their stress on the notion of free will. Al-Shahrastani made a distinction between "pure" and "moderate" Jabrites. According to him, "Pure Jabrites attribute no action to human beings and no capability of action in the first place," whereas moderate Jabrites "attribute to humans an ineffective capability of action."[4] Among the pure Jabrites he counts the Jahmiyya, the followers of Jahm b. Safwan.[5] Jahm maintained that one could attribute actions to humans only in a metaphorical sense as one would say that "a tree moved or a celestial sphere revolved or the sun set." It is in fact God who does these acts through the tree, the sphere, and the sun. Likewise, God "created in humans a power through which His act materializes, a will to act, and a choice specific to the act."[6]

For early Muslims, the disagreements about divine omnipotence and human free will did not belong purely to the realm of theological and speculative thinking. The traumatic violence of the *fitna* or the civil war that pitted Muhammad's companions against each other barely two and a half decades after his death eventually led to the establishment of the Umayyad state and dynasty, and it was against the backdrop of the new regime's oppression that the issues were hotly debated. The Umayyad caliphs realized that the promotion of a predestinarian outlook could serve as an effective ideological basis to legitimize their seizure and retention of power.[7] It would, however, be simplistic and inaccurate to assume that those who subscribed to the Jabrite position were pro-Umayyad. Both Jahm and his teacher al-Ja'd b. Dirham (d. 124/742 or 125/743) were executed by the Umayyad authorities.

The volitional, Qadarite position reached the height of its doctrinal development and influence between the first half of the second/eighth century and the first half of the third/ninth century at the hands of the Mu'tazilite school of *kalam* (scholastic theology). At the heart of their philosophico-theological commitment to the notions of free will and human responsibility lay the notion of divine justice. The roots of the Mu'tazilite position may be traced to some early theologians, such as Ma'bad al-Juhani (d. 83/703) and Ghailan al-Dimashqi (d. before 125/743). The most decisive influence, though, may have been that of al-Hasan al-Basri (d. 110/728),[8] the teacher of Wasil b. 'Ata' (d. 131/748–49), the school's founder.

Wasil argued that "God is wise and just. It is not possible to attribute evil or injustice to Him. It is not possible that He would will from humankind what is contrary to what He decrees and that He would predetermine their actions and punish them. Human beings are the agents of their good and evil actions, of their belief or unbelief, of their obedience or disobedience. Human beings are accountable for their actions, and God made it possible for them to engage in all of them."[9] Hence, in advancing the free will case, the Mu'tazilites stressed the inextricable link between human moral responsibility and the eschatological belief in *hisab* (the rendering of human beings' accounts on the Day of Judgment). The logical corollary of this in the view of Abu al-Hudhail al-'Allaf (d. between 226/840 and 235/849–50) was that while a human being's actions are free in this world they are predetermined in the afterworld.[10] The basic belief that one could not attribute evil or injustice to God was further extended by Ibrahim al-Nazzam (d. between 220/835 and 230/845), who argued that God was incapable of performing evil or unjust actions. This was in clear contrast with other members of the school who believed that God in reality is capable of performing such actions but chooses not to perform them owing to their iniquity.[11]

Divine omnipotence was examined by Bishr b. al-Mu'tamir (d. 210/825–226/840) in the light of human moral responsibility. He argued that God has infinite grace *(lutf)* that could, had He willed, turn all people into believers. God, however, is not obliged to grant humans this grace. Moreover, because God's goodness has no limit and as, at every given moment, there is always something better than what is good and more advantageous for humans, God is not obliged to do what is best for them. What God can do is to endow humans with the capability to make choices and to remove any impediments standing in their way by sending His prophets and revealing His messages.[12]

But what about divine and human power *(qudra)*: do they operate within the same or different spheres? With the notable exception of Yusuf al-Shahham (d. after 257/871), the Mu'tazilites maintained that it is not possible to attribute to God what humans do—that which is within the sphere of performability *(maqdur)* differs according to its agency. Conversely, al-Shahham held that an act can be simultaneously performed by the dual agency of God and a human being. As such, while the act is "created" *(makhluq)* by God it is "acquired" *(muktasab,* of *kasb* "acquisition") by a human.[13] In refuting al-Shahham's view and arguing in favor of human autonomy, Muhammad b. 'Abd al-Wahhab al-Jubba'i (d. 303/915–16) contended that God is a creator of acts in the sense of producing acts that are "determined in accordance with what He conceives" *(muqaddara 'ala miqdar ma dabbaraha)* and that humans are creators of their acts in a similar sense.[14]

In employing the notion of acquisition *(kasb)* and arguing that the same act could be performed by God (hence becoming a necessary act, *daruratan)* and by a human being (becoming an acquired act, *kasban),* al-Shahham was apparently influenced by Dirar b. 'Amr (c. 190/805).[15] In Dirar's view, God is the agent of human actions in reality, but human beings are, likewise, the agents of these actions in reality *(fi 'l-haqiqa).*

Dirar's view carried the seed of what later developed into a full-fledged, anti-Mu'tazilite theology that defined the philosophico-theological basis of Islamic orthodoxy. The major exponent of this theology was Abu al-Hasan al-Ash'ari (d. 324/936), a former Mu'tazilite and student of al-Jubba'i.[16] His defection from the Mu'tazilite school was projected by some authorities as a miraculous event prompted by prophetic intervention.[17] On account of his former training, al-Ash'ari did not hesitate in availing himself of the sophisticated methods of reasoning employed by the Mu'tazilites.

In opposition to the Mu'tazilite emphasis on human free agency and moral responsibility, the Ash'arite position stressed complete divine omnipotence: what God wills takes place and what He does not will never materializes.[18] However, al-Ash'ari was careful to construct a version of determinism that was different from the pure determinism of the Jahmiyya. It was with this view that he appropriated the notion of *kasb* (acquisition), drawing a distinction between volitional acts *(af'al ikhtiyariyya)* and compulsory acts *(af'al idtirariyya)*. The first class is comprised of acts that humans perform without determination. By contrast, the second class consists of acts that, although capable of being performed by humans, are, nevertheless, preceded by divine determination. Human beings "acquire" these acts through this divine determination. Al-Ash'ari bases this on his conclusion that because the actions of human beings do not always correspond to their intentions and desires, the real agency of these actions clearly lies beyond humans.[19] So when a human being wills an act of this class, God invests him or her at that particular moment with a power to perform the specific act. The act thus becomes "created, generated, and occasioned by God while at the same time acquired by the human being owing to the power that God generated for him [or her] at the time of [performing] the act."[20]

Al-Ash'ari's reaction against what he perceived as inadmissible and inappropriate limitations placed by Mu'tazilite rationalism on divine omnipotence led him to the defense of a seemingly arbitrary and capricious God not bound by any recognizable code. Because God's sovereignty is absolute ("He shall not be questioned as to what He does," as verse 21:23 affirms), He can do as He wishes without being accused of injustice. Thus, He can mete out severe punishment for a minor sin, punish believers and reward unbelievers, and make the children of unbelievers suffer in hell.[21]

Orthodox Sufis adopted the Ash'arite position. Al-Ghazali, for instance, declared that "all the acts of human beings are created by God and determined by His power," and he embraced the theory of acquisition.[22] This deterministic outlook was likewise shared by some radical mystics such as Ibn 'Arabi, whose Unity of Being theory does not allow for a God/world duality but presupposes a unified order governed by a divine-natural system of laws.[23] As such, humankind or the world as contingent existence is viewed as a manifestation of the Necessary Being or God, and it is in the nature of this contingent existence to seek the Necessary Being. Ibn 'Arabi, however, establishes an indivisible link between God's predetermination of human actions and His mercy, a theme central in Taha's work. Quoting verse 11:56, "there is no creature that crawls, but He takes it by the forelock. Surely my Lord is on a straight path," Ibn 'Arabi comments, "Whoever walks is on the Lord's straight path. In this respect those who walk are neither estranged on account of divine wrath nor are they misguided. As misguidance is temporary, so is divine wrath. The ultimate end that takes precedence is God's all-encompassing mercy."[24] As such, this is an ineluctable, preordained journey leading humans to the sublime station of "determinate nearness" *('ain 'l-qurb)*.[25]

For Ibn 'Arabi, however, determinism is applicable not only to humans but also to God. He holds that it is not possible to speak about free choice *(ikhtiyar)* in connection with God. This is the case because God does not act on the basis of choice but rather on the basis of what is dictated by His knowledge; hence, when God performs an act it is only that specific act that is possible.[26] In arguing this Ibn 'Arabi clearly opted to disregard verse 28:68, which states that God "creates whatsoever He will and He chooses [*yakhtar-u*]."

Ibn 'Arabi's follower, 'Abd al-Karim al-Jili (d. 832/1428), was more cautious and went along with orthodox opinion in asserting divine choice as an expression of divine will.[27] He advances the notion of the "manifestation of actions" *(tajalli 'l-af'al)* through which he tries to reconcile human consciousness, and man's willed observance of shari'a, with divine omnipotence. Accordingly, what humans should develop is a state of consciousness that dismisses human agency and recognizes only divine agency.[28] But what about those who commit a sin and say that their actions were predestined by God and that they could not have done otherwise? Al-Jili concedes the genuineness of some Sufi states where the agent "would share food with you and would swear that he had not done so, would drink [alcohol] and would swear that he had not done so, and would then swear that he had not sworn, while being in all this upright and truthful in the sight of God."[29] This is evidently a messy state of affairs, particularly in light of the fact that even an unbeliever could make similar claims. Al-Jili has no persuasive answer, and his only recourse is to fall back on shari'a, whose dictates, he insists, ought to be followed strictly.

Taha and the Theory of Progressive Reconciliation

Like other modern Muslim thinkers, Taha's starting point in tackling the problem of free will and determinism is the polarity of the Jabrite and Qadarite positions. He maintains that this is a problem whose "niceties have exercised human thought in all times" and one that has contemporary relevance and should be at the center of theological and philosophical investigation today. On one level, the problem encapsulates the fundamental difference between the mystical and the philosophical modes of approaching reality, or the "knowledge of the heart" as opposed to the "knowledge of reason" (RMi 49). He furthermore contends that on another, more practical level the understanding of this problem is an essential prerequisite for the realization of absolute individual freedom and communal freedom (RT 63).

In the course of reviewing the respective classical positions in the debate, Taha is strongly in favor of determinism. He equates the position of libertarians with *shirk* (associationism) and holds that their misconception arose out of a superficial observation of human actions and a superficial understanding of what the Qur'an says. By contrast, the Sufis' insistence on determinism upheld the orthodox position expressed by the Prophet and faithfully followed by his companions (RT 64–65). He identifies orthodox determinism almost fully with the Sufis and hardly credits non-Sufi theologians. However, even though he is appreciative of what the Sufis did, he finds their propositions unsatisfactory and no longer capable of meeting the intellectual and spiritual challenges of modern times.

A good starting point is Taha's response to the challenge of the modern exponents of free will. Since the intervention of Muhammad 'Abduh (d. 1905), the Mu'tazilite position has been revived among the modernist educated classes of Egypt and other Muslim countries.[30] In a letter to an inquirer, Taha provided a succinct exposition of his views on Mu'tazilite volitionism as formulated by the influential Egyptian writer 'Abbas Mahmud al-'Aqqad (d. 1964). Al-'Aqqad wrote:

> The Qur'an explicitly urges humans to depend on themselves and rely on their own power while counting on divine power when they implore God and pray to Him. While God does not accept that humans abandon what

they are capable of doing, He does not deprive them of hope in attaining to the succor of divine power when their own power is wanting. This is the utmost that religion can provide: the power of patience and the power of hope. . . . God inspires people: He shall not forsake them if they help themselves, and He shall not deny them the power they need when they turn to Him. Any religion that does not offer its adherents such hope is pointless and worthless and is as good as nonexistent. This does not mean that belief in God rests on the need for Him. Rather, belief in Him rests on His power, perfection, justice, sovereignty over existence, and relationship with this existence.[31]

Here, al-'Aqqad expresses a volitionist stance that places human ability and autonomy at the center and reduces divine agency to the secondary role of acting in response to the supplicatory pleas of human beings. Furthermore, his insistence that belief in God should not be grounded in human need reflects a typically modernist concern as he seeks to repudiate the Freudian contention that religion is an illusion and a collective fantasy.[32]

In Taha's view what al-'Aqqad expresses represents a most serious misconception of the issues involved. He asserts that belief in God is inseparable from the need for Him.[33] Human need for God flows from the heart and feelings and precedes human knowledge of Him. He contends that knowledge of God deepens one's belief in Him in the sense of deepening one's need for Him (RMi 50). As such,

If a human being sees himself [or herself] as having power over some things whereas he [or she] needs the help of divine power when he [or she] finds himself helpless, such a human being has more belief than he [or she] who sees himself [or herself] as fully capable all the time. . . . Yet the one with more belief has still less belief than he [or she] who sees himself as capable of nothing, no matter how little, and in need of divine help even when breathing. The degree of one's belief in God is [commensurate with] the degree of one's knowledge of the need for Him. (RMi 50–51)

The goal in this respect, as the Sufi tradition stresses, is to witness and actually experience the oft-repeated affirmation, "There is no ability and no power save through God" *(la hawla wa la quwwata illa bi-'Llah).*[34]

This undoubtedly is an extreme expression of the determinist position.

But how, in the light of this position, does Taha read the Qur'anic verses that confirm human free will and that have served as the foundation of the Mu'tazilite position? To harmonize these verses with the ones that proclaim predestination and to defend determinism as the ultimate Qur'anic message, Taha falls back on the Sufi hermeneutic distinction between the outward *(zahir)* and inward *(batin)* dimensions of the Qur'an. As with his discussion of the conflict between Qur'anic knowledge and human knowledge, he advances the theory that the Qur'an follows an educative strategy whereby it initially starts by acknowledging deceptive human sensory perceptions, with the goal of gradually unveiling the reality that lies behind the surface of things. The same theory is employed in accounting for the apparent contradiction between the free will and predestination verses.

A favorite verse that Taha quotes to corroborate his claim is verse 8:17. He maintains that when the verse tells the Prophet, "when thou threwest, it was not thyself that threw, but God threw," the verse not only affirms that the act's author is one and the same, namely God, but also indicates the mode through which God operates. God's action takes place through a generation of an external/internal duality: on the external level a human being's limbs engage in performing actions, but on the internal level it is God who performs these actions (QF 91–92). This duality corresponds to the duality of shari'a and *haqiqa* (truth, reality), with shari'a coinciding with appearance knowledge and *haqiqa* coinciding with reality knowledge.

Hence, the claim of free will is superficial in the literal sense of being solely based on what operates on the external level. Taha holds that the misconception of free will arises out of the particular mode through which divine determination interacts with human consciousness. To demonstrate this, he quotes verses 8:42–44, whose revelation was apparently occasioned by the celebrated Battle of Badr. The first verse underlines the alignment of the Muslims and their Meccan enemies on the day of their confrontation. The second verse refers to a dream in which the Prophet saw his aligned enemies as few; the verse discloses to him and the believers that had God revealed the great number of the enemies the believers "would have lost heart, and quarreled about the matter." The third verse refers to the same experience not only from the point of view of the believers but also that of the unbelievers, who also see their aligned enemies as few. The respective deceptive perspectives of the two parties strengthened their resolve to fight, which corresponds to what God had predetermined. So, Taha argues, divine determination manipulates human action in such a subtle and veiled manner that the conscious wills of human agents are not disturbed in the least (QF 93–94). What Taha says in this regard gives rise to a particularly pressing problem that he fails to address: if God goes to such lengths not to disturb humankind's erroneous belief of having an autonomous and free will, why does He divulge to them at the same time the divine mystery that it is in fact He who performs what seem like volitional human acts?

Although both sets of deterministic and volitional verses are found in the Qur'anic text side by side, Taha insists on situating them in separate, temporal, hierarchical, and epistemological domains. Temporally and hierarchically, the "lower," "deceptive" free will belief comes first to be followed at a later stage by the higher realization of divine determination. Human spiritual and epistemological quests can hence be described in the light of this realization as progress from the domain of shari'a to that of *haqiqa* or "truth," from the domain of externality to that of internality. This journey is succinctly summed up in verses 81:28–29. Although these very short verses cohere within the same passage and can be read as statements that are dialectically interconnected, Taha asserts that they belong to two distinct moments of Qur'anic address. According to him, when the first verse says, "It is naught but a Reminder unto all beings, for whosoever of you who would go straight," it confirms the human illusion of having free will. The verse, however, is what Taha calls a "verse of shari'a," and accordingly the positive message it communicates is that of charging one with the obligation of following the law and rigorously subjecting oneself to the disciplining practice of *suluk*. It is when this sustained activity reaches fruition and one recognizes with certainty that God is the real agent behind one's actions that the Qur'an then addresses its recipient in verse 81:29: "but will you shall not, unless God wills, the Lord of all Being" (QF 83).

Despite all these assertions, Taha is not a determinist in the orthodox, or Ash'arite, or traditional Sufi senses. He sets forth a more complex theory of determinism and free will through which he seeks to resolve the Qur'anic ambivalence on the one hand and satisfy the intellectual and spiritual needs of modern Muslims on the other. He tries to do this through a theory of what may be described as "progressive reconciliation": Starting from determinism as one's foundational belief, one gradually progresses to the attainment of a level of freedom that invests one with free will.

Taha stresses a key point that human will is the spirit that God breathed into humans at the moment of creation (see, for instance, verse 15:29). Furthermore, he perceives will as an integral part of a divine creative trinity comprising knowledge, will, and power through which God brought the world into existence. He maintains, "Human beings, likewise, perform their actions through knowledge, will, and power and hence the similarity between creator and created, as the Prophet indicated when he said, 'God created Adam in His image' " (RT 56). Will is the "trust" *(amana)* mentioned in verse 33:72, eschewed by the rest of God's creation but carried by humankind.[35] "Will" in this sense and on this level is what Taha calls the "will to freedom" *(iradat 'l-hurriyya)* as opposed to the "will to life" *(iradat 'l-hayat)* that is shared among all living beings. This distinction emanates from the three modes of divine determination, namely direct, semidirect, and indirect. Direct determination applies on the level of inorganic matter, whereas the semidirect mode pertains to living organisms, and the indirect concerns the actions of humans who are distinguished by their consciousness. In fact, Taha points out, divine determination of human actions is doubly removed in its indirectness as it operates through the veils of the will to life and the will to freedom.

When he examines these wills more closely, Taha tends to rely on modern, rather than Qur'anic, psychological perceptions. Although he emphasizes that the two wills differ only in degree rather than kind, he underlines at the same time the conflict between their claims. Their nature and functions are defined in Freudian terms. The will to life, like the Freudian id, is identified with the "animal" in the human, seeking immediate gratification and functioning entirely according to the pleasure-pain principle. By contrast, the will to freedom, like the Freudian ego, seeks gratification without incurring the negative sanctions of the social group (or the gods).[36] Considering what took place in early, simple society, Taha maintains that the will to freedom gave rise to what may be described in Freudian terms as an "ego ideal" by "foregoing pleasure when its fulfilment meant the transgression of the laws of the community that [at the same time] were always the commands of the gods. This was done in the hope of procuring greater pleasure, namely the reward of the community and the gods, which was better and more lasting. Thus came into life values that made it possible for the individual to sacrifice immediate pleasures for the sake of anticipated pleasures" (RT 59).

As the two wills differ from each other only in degree, they are viewed as belonging to the same continuum, where the will to freedom is the sublime, rarefied part of the will to life (and as such they respectively correspond to the spirit *(ruh)* and the soul *(nafs)* of the psychological terminology used by Sufis). This opposition is further recast in gendered language where the will to freedom corresponds to the male principle (or the Qur'anic "Adam") and the will to life stands for the female principle (or the Qur'anic "Adam's wife"). Out of the mating of the two principles comes the mind *('aql)*, and on this level the will to life is what we know as "memory" *(dhakira)*, and the will to freedom is what we know as "imagination" *(khayal)* (RT 60). Taha identifies imagination with "intelligence" *(dhaka')*, which is the cognitive power and the will through which humans control their socially unacceptable impulses.

An important dynamic in these processes that has simultaneously acted as a force of stimulation and repression is fear *(khawf)*. Ending fear is a central theme in Taha's thought, intimately linked with his theory of freedom. Human consciousness is plagued by fear that takes three forms: primeval fear that goes back to the remotest beginnings of human social life, fear inherited from the repression of social sanctions, and fear acquired during an individual's lifetime. He emphatically affirms that "fear is the source of all moral vices and behavioral defects. A man cannot attain the full perfection of his manhood and a woman cannot attain the full perfection of her womanhood if they experience fear in the slightest or in any form. Perfection is achieved when one is free of fear" (RT 62). It is in connection with his attempt to provide an answer to how humans can be free of fear that Taha paves the way to his suggested resolution of the problem of determinism and free will.

Taha's answer hinges on two primary distinctions. The first is a distinction between divine will *(irada)* and divine acceptance or pleasure *(rida)*. The second is a distinction between God's *be*-command *(amr takwini)*[37] and His *ought*-command *(amr tashri'i).*[38] These distinctions are intended to reconcile divine omnipotence on the one hand with the potential or actual disobedience on the part of some of God's creatures on the other.

Taha elucidates these distinctions in connection with verses 2:30–37. The passage recounts the creation of Adam, God's command to the angels to bow to him, Satan's refusal to obey the divine command, Adam's and Eve's expulsion from the garden when they eat from the tree, and God's bestowal of His forgiveness when they ask for it. In commenting on Satan's disobedience *('isyan),* Taha affirms that this took place only "on the level of shari'a but not on the level of *haqiqa,*" as "the divine will determines the totality of existence and allows no discordance or disobedience. [On this level] even the one who disobeys would in fact be obeying" (LL 17). Hence, despite his failure to gain divine acceptance on account of his violation of the *ought*-command, Satan was in fact obeying the divine will or the *be*-command.[39]

Quoting verse 11:56 (that Ibn 'Arabi uses in connection with his notion of "determinate nearness" [*'ain 'l-qurb*]), Taha comments that God does not determine human beings will commit sin and that it is the lot of everyone to be rightly guided immediately or at some future time (RT 69). This is the case because obedience *(ta'a)* as an ontological state (reflecting the *be*-command) is not contingent but necessary. However, it is also the case that God desires that obedience be a conscious and voluntary act. These preconditions of consciousness and will draw the boundary between guidance *(huda)* and misguidance *(dalal),* belief, and unbelief. With respect to this, Taha declares, "The difference between belief and unbelief is not one of kind but rather of degree. The believer has more knowledge than the unbeliever. In other words, the believer obeys God knowingly while the unbeliever obeys Him unknowingly" (RT 70).

Taha thus establishes a salvific nexus where freedom, *khati'a* (sin) or *khata'* (error), and knowledge are inextricably intertwined. His starting point is the pre-Fall state, which he does not idealize. He holds that although Adam was a perfect, knowing, and free man, his freedom was nonetheless a mere gift *(minha).* This, in Taha's view, was the deficiency of the pre-Fall state, and hence Adam had to be subjected to a test in order to be worthy of his freedom. Taha reads the Fall event in terms of Adam's failure to exercise his freedom properly. Certainly, he did exercise his freedom by making a choice, but because he made the wrong choice he failed to do so properly. In choosing to eat from the tree, he chose what he wanted rather than what God wanted, and hence, "His freedom was taken away. . . . [H]e was sent down to be punished for his contravention and to start working on restoring a freedom for which he has paid and hence the value of which he knows" (RT 76).[40]

With respect to verse 2:37, which concludes the Fall story by stating, "Thereafter Adam received certain words from his Lord, and He turned towards him," Taha maintains that the forgiveness that Adam received meant in essence giving him the right to err *(haqq 'l-khata')*. This meant that the loss of his freedom was not final, but he was allowed to work on restoring it. As such, life (and, for that matter, afterlife) assumes the nature of a school or training ground where one is constantly learning through trial and error and constantly pushing the horizons of one's freedom through its proper exercise. To demonstrate that his celebration of the right to err has an orthodox legitimacy, Taha quotes a tradition according to which the Prophet said, "If you do not err and ask for forgiveness, God will bring into being people who would err and ask for forgiveness, and He will forgive them."[41]

To exercise freedom, a human being needs knowledge. In commenting on verse 2:255, which confirms, "and they comprehend not anything of His knowledge save such as He wills," Taha asserts that ignorance *(jahl)* is not a necessary condition. God does in fact want humans to know, and He actively engages them all the time through His Self-disclosures. But why does not God equip humans with the knowledge they need in the first place and hence spare them the punishment that goes with an improper exercise of their freedom? Taha responds to such an objection by reasserting his point about punishment as a necessary price to pay for freedom. This freedom cannot be divorced from one's responsibility of bearing the consequences of one's actions. The relationship between knowledge and freedom is one of interdependence: one needs knowledge in order to act and one must act (and hence take the risk of erring) in order to expand one's knowledge. By virtue of this, humans are better than angels. The knowledge of angels makes them incapable of committing sins or making mistakes, but they are not free and hence they are not perfect. Human beings, by contrast, are better and more privileged because they are capable of doing right or wrong and hence of advancing from ignorance to knowledge (RT 87).[42]

Qada' and Qadar

The ultimate knowledge challenge in connection with the problem of determinism and free will is what Taha describes as the "mystery of *qadar*." The word *qadar* usually occurs in the binary technical expression of *qada' wa qadar,* where the term *qada'* can be rendered as "predetermination" or "eternal decree," and the term *qadar* can be rendered as "(time-specific) decree." According to Taha, *qada'* and *qadar* form an integrated whole where *qada'* is the "mystery of *qadar*" in the sense of being its subtle and higher expression.[43] He quotes verses 54:49–50, "Surely We have created everything in measure [*bi-qadar*]. Our commandment is but one word, as the twinkling of an eye," pointing out that *qada'* is the level of divine command that transcends time and space (as the "twinkling of an eye" image indicates); it is a transtemporal decree. *Qadar,* on the other hand, is the instantiation of *qada'* within time and space; it is a temporal decree (RT 89).

Furthermore and more significantly, the temporal decree is a realm of duality involving good and evil, knowledge and ignorance, whereas the transtemporal decree is a realm of unity, "where evil disappears and only absolute good remains" (RT 89). This is realized on the existential level through the unfolding of the *sabiqa* (foreordination)[44] of every creature where what is temporally foreordained can be either good or evil, whereas what is trans-temporally predestined is always good. The notion of *sabiqa* is intertwined with that of *lahiqa* (a human being's subsequent acts), and it is on the basis of these notions that Taha allows for a measure of volitionism. The foreordination/subsequent acts logic is expounded by him as follows: it is not possible to know what God foreordains on the level of temporal decree, that is, whether a human being will be saved *(sa'id)* or damned *(shaqi),* but it is possible to know His law and act accordingly or, in other words, to make one's subsequent acts agree with what shari'a dictates. Taha uses *sabiqa* and *lahiqa* as key technical terms in developing a theodicy that forestalls the "argument [*hujja*] against God" to which verse 4:165 refers. This argument is fleshed out in verse 43:20, "They [the polytheists] say, 'Had the All-merciful so willed, we would not have served them [their deities].' They have no knowledge of that; they are only conjecturing." The polytheists here offer a powerful and sophisticated argument that infers God's intention from the particular state of affairs in which they live; they are in fact deploying against Muhammad a religious argument based on a deterministic logic. The Qur'anic dismissal of what they say on account of their lack of knowledge is elaborated by Taha: "They have no knowledge of the will of the All-Merciful as it is hidden from them. However, they know of His law that commands them to worship only Him" (RT 90). The notion of *sabiqa* hence corresponds to this hidden knowledge, whereas the notion of *lahiqa* corresponds to the revealed knowledge of the law, and it is by virtue of their intrinsic lack of knowledge as regards their *sabiqa* that human beings have no case against God.

So, despite his determinism, Taha develops a philosophy of action that is grounded in the free will to follow the law. According to his scheme, this initial freedom will lead to a further deepening of freedom because acting in compliance with the law will bear no proper fruit unless it goes beyond the external to the internal. Hence free will will bring about a radical transformation in human consciousness. Taha believes that this consciousness transformation can be most effectively brought about through prayer. This transformation or liberation is identified with his notion of "absolute individual freedom," so one would "think as he wishes, speak as he thinks, and act as he speaks." At the root of his definition lies the notion of *tawhid* (unity, oneness) whose focus he shifts from being theocentric to being anthropocentric. *Tawhid* is perceived essentially as a correspondence of thought and action and requalified as "an attribute of the unifier [*muwahhid*] rather than the unified [*muwahhad*]." Taha conceives absolute individual freedom as a state starting with the level of responsibility where one "thinks as one wishes, speaks as one thinks, acts as one speaks, while bearing the full responsibility for one's actions" and culminating in a level of "universal goodness" where one "thinks as one wishes, speaks as one thinks, acts as one speaks, with one's actions always resulting in goodness to all animate beings and inanimate things" (TT 32).

The realization of absolute individual freedom is also a realization of a higher state of *yaqin* (certainty). It is by virtue of this certainty that one can see the "unity of the agent" *(wahdat al-faʿil)* that, according to Taha, is the "root and foundation of divine unity [*tawhid*]" and to which "every letter of the Qur'an beckons" (RT 68). The realization of this level of unity means the realization that "the originator of all things, great and small, is God" (LL 39).

When one sees God's hand in everything, one perceives and confirms the "mystery of divine decree [*qadar.*]" In describing this state, Taha uses a language charged with the promise of mystical rapture and ecstasy:

When one discovers the mystery of *qadar* and ascertains that God is absolute goodness whom one trusts and accepts and to whom one submits and yields, one would then be free of fear and would realize peace within oneself and with the world, animate and inanimate. One would purify one's mind of evil thoughts and hold one's tongue back from obscenities and one's hand back from harming others. One would then realize the unity of one's self and would be pure good, spontaneously spreading good qualities as a sweet-smelling flower would diffuse its fragrance. Here, the heart would forever bow down at the threshold of the first station of servantship [*ʿubudiyya*]. At this point, one is no longer subject to determination; one is free. Determination has taken one to the sublime station of free will. One has obeyed God to the point that God reciprocates by obeying him [or her]. [Now] one is as living as God, as knowing as God, as willing as God, and as powerful as God. One is God. (RT 90–91)[45]

Hence, although Taha vigorously defends determinism as intrinsically good, he evidently acknowledges that free will is more of a perfect state. In starting with the assertion of determination that subsequently culminates in the affirmation of free will, he adopts a theory of progressive reconciliation. Evidently, the key question is whether Taha succeeds in effecting a reconciliation between the two doctrines. It may be argued that his position suffers from the conflicting claims of his Sufi perspective on the one hand and his modernism on the other. By virtue of his Sufi viewpoint he insists on the illusory nature of free will. Yet, he develops at the same time a decidedly modernist and humanist discourse that stresses human autonomy and responsibility.

For Taha, the central problem in the human relationship to God is that of disobedience. When one aligns one's life purpose and efforts with what God wishes, then, no problem arises, and Taha proposes to reward such a person with the ultimate prize of free will. Disobedience, however, poses a serious theological problem as it calls divine omnipotence into question. Taha proposes to address this by resorting on the theoretical level to the *irada/rida* (divine will/divine pleasure) opposition and the *be*-command/*ought*-command opposition while evoking on the practical level the *sabiqa/lahiqa* (preordination/subsequent acts) opposition to justify the necessity of following the law. However, despite his dissatisfaction with the answers of the past, Taha does not make a real breakthrough in solving the problem. At the end of the circuitous route on which he takes his readers, he lands him back at the house of "simple faith." When the Prophet once told his companions that "the seat of every one of you in heaven or hell is preordained," he was questioned about the point of striving, and he responded, "Act! Each one of you is eased [*muyassar*]," and then he recited verses 92:5–10.[46] What Taha proposes to his modern Muslim readers echoes what the Prophet counseled his companions to do: hold tightly onto belief and act in accordance with the law. But what does he say to non-Muslims and unbelievers?

Taha maintains that the difference between belief *(iman)* and unbelief *(kufr)* is one of degree rather than kind. The believer's merit over the unbeliever is that he knows more. But what about believers who belong to other (and maybe competing) religions? Taha deals with this in the context of what he describes as an "Islamic trinity" *(al-thaluth 'l-islami)* that comprises the religions of Judaism, Christianity, and Islam. In this respect he defends what he perceives as the relative excellence of Islam and how it endows its believer with a higher degree of knowledge. Taha subscribes to an exclusivism that asserts that Muhammad's example and his imitation provide the sole path leading to divine presence and hence the realization of one's authenticity or ultimate salvation. Thus, for those who believe in other religions or who are agnostics or atheists, Taha offers the only solution that an exclusivist can offer: believe in my way. Among these, he singles out atheists as the most ignorant. He was, in fact, willing to express at one point his belief that atheists ought not to express their views in public (TM 9).[47]

Divine Punishment and the End of Hell and Heaven

In Islamic eschatological imagination the notions of heaven and hell are inextricably linked with the categories of belief and unbelief. These notions, in their turn, are derived from and controlled by other notions such as reward and punishment, the resurrection of the dead, and the final judgment. In describing heaven and hell, the Qur'an tends to place its emphasis on the sensual delights of the former and the physical torment of the latter, and its descriptions tend to be far more vivid and graphic than those of the Hebrew Bible or the New Testament.

Particular problems are associated with the notion of hell. Qur'anic hell is predominantly portrayed in terms of torture by fire. The key characteristics of this fire are that it is unquenchable and everlasting.[48] Divine punishment and its eternity were accepted as morally justifiable by the proponents of orthodoxy and by the Mu'tazilites. Heterodox positions were, however, expressed by some theologians as early as the second/eighth century. Without questioning the morality of divine punishment, Jahm b. Safwan called the infinite duration of heaven and hell into question, arguing that "the motions [*harakat*] of human beings in the hereafter will come to an end. Heaven and hell will perish . . . as it is not possible to conceive of motions that have no end for eternity, in the same way that it is not possible to conceive of motions that have no beginning from eternity."[49] Likewise, the Mu'tazilite al-Jahiz (d. 255/868–69) did not doubt the morality of punishment but reconceptualized its eternity *(khulud)*, maintaining that the dwellers of hellfire "are not consigned to it forever in the sense of being subjected to [everlasting] tortures. They transmute into the very substance of fire."[50]

The emphasis of Shi'ite extremists *(ghulat)* on the doctrine of metempsychosis *(tanasukh)* led them to belief in the eternity of life, and this in turn led them to rejection of the existence of heaven and hell in their conventional sense. In their view, resurrection *(ba'th)* was purely spiritual and took place in this world. As such, reward meant reincarnation as a righteous person and punishment as a creature of lower existence *(maskh)*. In arguing this, Shi'ite extremists interpreted the Qur'an allegorically.[51]

However, it was the radical Sufis who problematized divine punishment in moral terms and whose perspectives emphasized on the one hand the explaining away and on the other the ending of this aspect of the divine/human relationship. Taking the example of Ibn 'Arabi, we find that he sets divine names such as "the Avenger" *(al-muntaqim)*, "the severe in punishment" *(al-shadid 'l-'iqab)*, and "the Oppressor" *(al-qahir)* against names such as "the Compassionate" *(al-rahim)*, "the Forgiving" *(al-ghafir)*, and "the Benevolent" *(al-latif)* and argues that it is the latter set of names that expresses God's ultimate manifestation.[52] Starting with the assumption that God's compassion always takes precedence over His justice, he proceeds to grapple with the problem of hell. Ibn 'Arabi's strategy is to explain hell away by equating it with what amounts to a state of felicity *(na'im)*, so much so that he establishes a forced derivational connection between the very Qur'anic word for torture, *'adhab*, and the substantive *'udhuba*, which means "sweet taste."[53] He claims that God, from His level of the Merciful *(mustawa 'l-rahman)*, would cast an eye of mercy *(rahma)* on those in the lowest reaches of fire and would turn their state into one of delight. Exercising his creative imagination, Ibn 'Arabi proposes that these dwellers would live in an everlasting state of blissfulness that takes the external form of sleep. Elaborating on this he says,

> The sleeper . . . might be lying in his bed in a state of sickness, misery, and destitution but sees himself [or herself] in his [or her] dreams as a person of power, happiness, and wealth. If one looks at the sleeper from the perspective of what he [or she] sees and enjoys in his [or her] dreams, one would rightly say that he [or she] lives in a state of felicity. Nonetheless, if one looks at him [or her] from the perspective of his [or her] hard bed, his [or her] sickness, misery, destitution, and disfigurement, one would say that the sleeper is in a state of torture. Such will be the state of the dwellers of hellfire. They will be neither dead nor alive, or, in other words, they will never wake from their sleep. This is God's way of showing His mercy.[54]

The same notion of divine mercy is stressed by Taha but with the view of repudiating the eternity of hell. He thinks that it is a grave mistake to believe that punishment in hellfire does not come to an end because such a belief would imply that evil is an original principle *(asl)* of existence, which is not the case. He declares, "When punishment becomes eternal it is the revenge of a malicious self that is devoid of wisdom, and God is indeed exalted above that" (RT 88). His use in this sentence of the word "revenge" *(in-tiqam)* raises the question of the nature of divine revenge—a notion integral to the Qur'anic conceptualization of God (see, for instance, verses 5:95 and 14:47). It is important to note that Taha's logic here is conditional for he does not dismiss divine revenge per se but rather divine revenge under a particular circumstance: if divine punishment (or revenge) is eternal, then it would be devoid of wisdom and would hence qualify as an act of unacceptable vengeance.

So, naturally, a Muslim cannot ascribe to God "unacceptable vengeance." But under what condition or circumstance can a Muslim attribute vengeance to God and have the attribute "the Vengeful" *(al-muntaqim)* elevated to the status of a Beautiful Name? Does the word assume a different, special significance when applied to God? In justifying the Qur'anic use of the word in connection with God, Taha stresses human freedom and autonomy. Like al-Ghazali before him, he grounds divine revenge in a God-human contractual relationship where God's act of revenge is a natural consequence of human disobedience.[55] He contends, "When God was referred to as the Avenger, this indicated what is understood by a [Qur'anic] statement like 'and whoso has done an atom's weight of evil shall see it [99:8]' or a [Qur'anic] statement like 'Every soul shall be pledged for what it has earned [74:38].' The meaning of 'the Avenger' here is He who returns the actions of human beings. The torture of humans is because of their own actions" (AJii 8). The upshot of this logic is that divine revenge is determined by human autonomy: God acts by laying down the law, then humans act (either positively by following the law or negatively by not following it), then God responds.

In addressing the notion of divine mercy, Taha draws a distinction between two levels of divine manifestation: that of the divine name *al-rahman* (the Merciful) and that of the name *al-rahim* (the Compassionate), both of which are derived from the root *r-h-m,* "to have mercy" and both of which occur in the invocatory formula that comes at the beginning of Qur'anic chapters (the *basmala*). He maintains that divine mercy on the level of the Merciful inheres duality and is hence realized through reward and punishment, through heaven and hell. By contrast, the level of the Compassionate is a level of oneness where mercy is free of torture (QF 54). What Taha holds here reverses the denotations assigned to these terms by earlier exegetical authorities and by Ibn 'Arabi. On the basis of a tradition attributed to the Prophet, some orthodox authorities maintained that *al-rahman* refers to God's inclusive mercy, which extends to all His creatures, whereas *al-rahim* refers to an exclusive aspect of His mercy that is accessible only to believers.[56] Ibn 'Arabi adopts this scheme, assigning the name al-Rahman to mercy with the inclusive sense of a "gracious bestowal" *(imtinan)* on all existents while reserving the name al-Rahim to the more restricted mercy of "obligation" *(wujub)*, which applies only to some. Within these terms, *al-rahim* is logically implied by *al-rahman*.[57] In assigning a more universal denotation to *al-rahman*, orthodox exegetes were inspired by a grammatical consideration: *Al-rahman* encompasses more than *al-rahim* because it has a more intensive *(mubalagha)* form.[58] Taha, on the other hand, may have been influenced by the order of the words in the *basmala* formula, projecting upon it his typical preference for a logical progression: *Al-rahman* comes first because it is a lower level that progresses toward the higher level of *al-rahim*.[59]

It is in the light of this belief that Taha discounts the eternity of hell. But what about the Qur'anic verses proclaiming that those who go to hell will "dwell therein forever and ever" *(khalidin fiha abadan)*? Taha's response to this question rests on an ontology that is ultimately informed by his subscription to the Unity of Being doctrine. Taha examines this question in connection with his reading of verses 55:26–27, which affirm, "All that dwells upon the earth is perishing [*fan-in*], yet still abides [*yabqa*] the Face of thy Lord, majestic, splendid." The contrast here is between the two ontological states of *fana'* (perdition, nonexistence, nonbeing) and *baqa'* (remaining, existence, being, permanence). Another term used for this latter state of *baqa'* is *khulud* (eternity, everlastingness). So, what does it mean to say that one thing is impermanent *(fan-in)* and another thing is eternal? In addressing this, Taha says,

All things . . . have a pyramidical form . . . where the top represents the spirit *(ruh)* and the base represents the body *(jasad)* and where the difference between the top and the base is of degree. The base is in a constant process of perishing while continually engaged in a progressive motion to attain to the top. The top, on the other hand, is not unchanging—it is in motion and in constant progress in quest of the point at the center of existence, which is God. Hence, what is *khalid* (eternal) . . . is not that which never changes but rather that which changes or perishes more slowly than the *fan-in* (the perishing). On the other hand, the *fan-in* is that which changes rapidly. (AJi 23–24)

Thus by temporalizing and relativizing the notion of eternity, Taha provides the foundation for his rejection of the eternity of hell.

Taha conceptualizes heaven and hell in terms of this world and the otherworld, contending that the suffering through which one goes in this world is in fact part of the torture of hell and the times of delight one enjoys in this life are part of heaven. This he argues in the light of a *tawhid*-based ontological dictum: everything that was, or will be, is (AJi 25). However, the this-worldly aspect of what is essentially an eschatological doctrine is reemphasized through the Christian-Islamic notion of a Second Coming. When the Christ *(al-Masih)* comes, he will fill the earth with equity and justice as it has been filled with wrongdoing and injustice. This is the time of the "restoration of the earth" *(ta'mir 'l-ard)* or what Taha describes as the "heavenly earth" *(jannat 'l-ard)*. He reads verse 39:74 as a direct reference to this "messianic realization": "And they shall say, 'Praise belongs to God, who has been true in His promise to us, and bequeathed upon us the earth, for us to make our dwelling wheresoever we will in Paradise.' How excellent is the wage of those that labour." Taha seizes on the verse's specific references to "earth" and "paradise" to serve as the basis for his notion of a "heavenly earth."[60]

It should be borne in mind that in his account of heaven and hell what Taha chiefly stresses is the otherworldly, eschatological aspects of these places. In this connection he deals with the nature of the two places and their location. It may be self-evident in the light of Qur'anic and extra-Qur'anic accounts of the two places to conceptualize heaven as a place of absolute happiness and hell as a place of absolute misery. Taha, however, does not accept this and instead characterizes heaven as a state of "delight free of pain, with the exception of very little" and hell as a state of "pain without delight, with the exception of very little" (AJi 26). Furthermore and in the light of his hermeneutic stance that insists on adopting a literalist approach on a certain level, Taha maintains that it is unacceptable to read Qur'anic descriptions of heaven and hell as purely metaphorical. Consequently, the Qur'an's vivid accounts of the sensual pleasures of paradise and the horrifying descriptions of the physical torments of hell signify actual, concrete realities that humans will experience when they go to these places.

Taha identifies the location of heaven and hell within the framework of a cosmogony that he bases on the Qur'an. This basis rests on verses 21:30, which interrogate disapprovingly, "Have not the unbelievers then beheld that the heavens and the earth were a mass all sewn up [*ratqan*], and then we unstitched them [*fa-fataqnahuma*] and of water fashioned every living thing? Will they not believe?" and verse 21:104, which affirms, "as We originated the first creation, so We shall bring it back again."[61] The key terms here are *ratq* (making to coalesce) and *fatq* (dispersing), the first marking the beginning of the present cycle *(dawra)* of our universe and the second indicating its future termination. According to Taha the current cycle of existence started when "the planets of the solar system separated from a cloud of water vapor that constituted the current sun and its planets. They will come to an end when the state of dispersal is restored to coalescence. . . . When the celestial bodies go back to this state of coalescence they would have concluded a cycle of existence" (AJi 26). It is at this point that a new cycle starts, a cycle of heaven that is separate from hell. The sun and the planets rotating around it will coalesce to form a new earth with a cool surface that will be the place of heaven, and a hot interior where hell will be located (AJi 26). Taha's eschatological imagination presents us with the following image of an ascending movement from the nether regions to the paradisial realm: "Life will grow anew in this second cycle from the earth's interior toward its surface as a seed would. Humans would come out of hellfire (the interior of the new earth) into heaven (the surface of the new earth)" (AJi 27). To substantiate this he quotes verse 19:71, which affirms, "Not one of you there is, but he shall go down to [hell]; that for thy Lord is a thing decreed, determined."[62]

The coalescence and dispersal images are essential not only for Taha's cosmogony but also for his metaphysics or more specifically his notion of time. According to him, the coalescence as a static state preceding the dynamic state of dispersal inhered eternity *(abad)*, and eternity, in its turn, inhered change *(haraka)*. When dispersal took place, eternity, change, and time *(zaman)* all came simultaneously into existence. In his view, eternity is a continuum of time extending from the "beginning" to the "end," the beginning being the initial moment when dispersal ruptured the original state of coalescence and the end being the moment when the original state of coalescence is restored again. Time, by contrast, is more of a fragmentary and relative nature. He defines it as "parts of eternity as expressed through the life spans of celestial and terrestrial spheres from the moment when dispersal set in . . . to the moment when coalescence is restored at the end of a cycle of existence that we call life in this world [*al-hayat 'l-dunya*]" (RMi 52). As such, eternity is the "universal" and time is the "particular," eternity is the totality of time whereas time is the realizational manifestations or the objectifications of eternity. However, on another level Taha ontologizes the notions of eternity and time, identifying the former with the being of the Perfect Human and the latter with the being of ordinary human beings and other beings striving to attain perfection.

When it comes to the theodicy of infernal punishment, Taha insists that this punishment entails a higher divine wisdom *(hikma)* as it is ultimately remedial in nature. Consignment of souls to hell is God's way of educating, elevating, and liberating those who failed to be His servants. When human beings find themselves in hell they will realize their utter helplessness and hence recognize God's omnipotence. Once this cognitive and spiritual transformation has taken place, torture will come to an end, for "the knowledge of God extinguishes physical and psychological fire" (QF 137). This transformation is crystallized in an act of *inaba* (turning in repentance) that everyone will eventually perform. To be sure, it is an act that even Satan is destined to perform, but as he is the furthest being from God, he will be the last to turn to Him. This Satanic repentance will mark the end of hell.

With the end of hell, only paradise will remain. However, Taha's notion of paradise does not exclude the idea of suffering. Quoting verse 3:163, which describes those in paradise as being in "ranks [*darajat*] with God," he stresses a hierarchical order in paradise that generates what he calls "psy-chological suffering" *('adhab ma'nawi)*. This notion is grounded in a mysti-cal elitist maxim according to which "the good works [*hasanat*] of the righteous [*abrar*] are the sins [*sayyi'at*] of the intimates [*muqarrabun*]." Ac-cordingly, the paradise of some is the hell of others. Just like hell, paradise will also come to an end.

While hell ends in the temporal space of eternity, heaven ends in poste-ternity *(ba'd 'l-abad)*. Posteternity is a temporal notion that exceeds eter-nity in its duration, such being the case because "heaven is closer to the origin [*asl,* i.e., God] than hell" (QF 138). Heaven, however, cannot be the ultimate mode of experiencing God on account of its spatiality and tempo-rality—conditions from which one has to break in order to experience the Absolute. Citing verses 54:54–55, "Surely the godfearing shall dwell amid gardens and a river in a sure abode, in the presence of a King Omnipotent," Taha comments that they indicate the various ranks preceding the end of heaven, namely the "gardens," the "river," and the "sure abode." Each of these ranks comprises countless subranks through which the godfearing as-cend, to the ultimate rank of "in the presence of [*'inda*] a King Omnipo-tent." He tells us that the word *'inda* here is not an adverb of place or time. Inasmuch as language can convey, the verse's last phrase alludes to a state that transcends space and time.

Here, Taha conveys the ultimate mystical image: the human being in a neverending journey *(sair)* to attain God, to fulfil one's ultimate potential and realize one's perfection, to be God.

5

From the First to the
Second Message of Islam

God, Humankind, and History

THE THEORY of a second message of Islam lies at the heart of Taha's reform and revival project. While he shares some of the basic tenets of Islamism, the nature of his revivalist project is radically different from what is proposed by orthodox revivalist movements, in particular the Muslim Brothers, that came to dominate the Islamist scene in the Sudan from the mid-1960s and eventually succeeded in seizing power in 1989.[1]

Taha's revivalist project as expressed through his theory of a second message of Islam reveals a philosophy of history that in some major respects runs counter to the philosophy that shaped orthodox consciousness. History is perceived by Taha in macrocosmic, objective and microcosmic, subjective terms. On the macrocosmic level, history unfolds through the God/universe opposition. Verse 21:30 recounts the dispersal (*fatq*) of the coalesced mass of the heavens and earth and the creation of every living organism from water. Taha invests the moment of dispersal with the special significance of being the moment whence time and hence history originates.

In dealing with the macrocosmic aspect, Taha's thought shows a marked tension. He describes God's relationship with the world in terms of "direct determination" and posits that this is the case because the world is objective and inanimate. As the world lacks consciousness, its description in terms of objectivity and "thingness" should not, it seems, present any difficulty. The difficulty, however, arises in the light of Taha's Qur'anic frame of reference. Taha often quotes verse 41:111 as a Qur'anic basis of the notion of "direct determination." This verse recounts the following cosmic encounter after the creation of the world: "Then He lifted himself to heaven when it was smoke, and said to it and to the earth, 'Come willingly, or unwillingly!' They said, 'We come willingly.' " Here, in contrast to human perception of the world as a "thing," the Qur'an accords it consciousness and subjectivity; the elements can enter into dialogue with God and choose to be subordinate to His will—the world is, hence, not mere "existence" but also "being."

On another level, though, Taha's espousal of the theory of the Unity of Being results in his subjectification of the world, for the world is but a manifestation, albeit on a lowly level, of divine consciousness. Moreover, unity of being is also perceived as a unity of source to which everything is destined to return. Dealing with the creation of the world, Taha describes the nature of this unity of being and its predetermined course in the following terms:

In the Qur'an, existence has a spiral [*lawlabi*] structure. In all, it is an existence that has no beginning and will have no end. What begins and what perishes is nothing but the crude material form. Existence is God in His descent from His absoluteness, emerging in the form of tangible matter. He has emerged in order to be known . . . by that who is like Him, i.e., the human being—"Like Him there is naught (42:11)." Creation in the Qur'an is [the activity of] the divine will, assuming a state of solidity and concreteness. Creation has descended from the Absolute in the sense of the descent of the will. As such, [creation] traces its way back to the Absolute, as the will, in the final analysis, is the Absolute. (QF 112)

On the microcosmic, subjective level, history operates through a tripartite relationship involving God, Satan, and humankind. The beginning of this history is recounted in the Qur'anic creation story whose climactic events are the creation of Adam, the disobedience of Satan, and the fall of humankind and Satan (e.g. verses 2:30–39). From the start, Adam is endowed with subjectivity, and it is in fact this very subjectivity that serves as the basis of God's command to the angels to bow to him. Although the Qur'anic account does not suggest it, Taha perceives the Fall in terms of a loss of this very subjectivity. In reading verses 95:4–5, "We indeed created man in the fairest stature then we restored him to the lowest of the low [*asfala safilin*]," he not only applies the traditional mystical perspective according to which the fall was from a spiritual, intelligible realm (*'alam al-malakut*) to a material, sensible realm (*'alam al-mulk*), he also adopts an evolutionary perspective in reverse according to which the human was reduced to the most basic life form (see discussion of Taha's notion of evolution in chapter 6). On the level of this microcosmic history, humans occupy an intermediary position between the angels above and the devils below—a rank that makes them "the meeting point of light and darkness, of reason and desire" (TK 17). From the point that "Adam the viceroy" emerged on the scene until our own present time and beyond into the realm of eschatology, the history of humankind, in Taha's view, follows the salvific pattern outlined by the Qur'an and the hadith material.

Qur'anic salvation history starts at the moment of atonement marked in verse 2:37 according to which Adam "received certain words from his Lord" and God forgave him. From that moment onward, human history is depicted in terms of a successive alternation between peak points when God intervenes directly by sending prophets (the mission *ba'tha* phase) and low, intervening lulls (the *fatra* phase) during which divine missionary activity recedes. However, the peak points can also sometimes turn into catastrophic encounters as the Qur'anic "punishment" stories attest.[2] In this salvation history, Muhammad's mission occupies a unique position by virtue of his being the "seal of the prophets" (*khatam 'l-nabiyyin*) as verse 33:40 declares. As such, Muhammad not only performs a mission that confirms and integrates former prophecies but he also holds the unique status of being the last prophet through whom God directly addressed humankind.[3]

In discussing this ending of prophecy (*nubuwwa*), Taha offers the conventional Islamic argument that God set down in the Qur'an "all that heaven wanted to reveal to the people of earth." In this context, the Qur'an is perceived as a transhistorical text whose revelation started with Adam and continued through a long chain of prophets until it reached its final fulfilment in Muhammad's prophecy. Yet, as a radical Sufi, Taha invests the ending of prophecy with another particular significance: the ending of prophecy marked the dawn of a new spiritual era in which it is possible to engage in an unmediated, personal communion with God (RT 10–11). This view is, as already seen, at the heart of his theory of prayer.

Another particularly significant point that Taha makes in connection with verse 33:40 is that although the verse confirms the cutting off of prophecy, this cannot be extended to apply to messengerhood *(risala)*.[4] In expressing this view, Taha not only distances himself from the orthodox position but also from what Ibn 'Arabi holds on this. Pointing out the completeness of shari'a as a legal-prescriptive system, Ibn 'Arabi concludes that this constitutes the raison d'être of the cutting off of both prophecy and messengerhood, substantiating his belief with a tradition to the same effect attributed to the Prophet. As messengerhood is a function of prophecy, Ibn 'Arabi's discussion focuses on prophecy, and in this connection he is particularly concerned with the rebuttal of the notion of a "personal shari'a," to which Taha is wedded.[5]

The belief in the uniqueness of Muhammad's mission was decisive in shaping the Islamic historical perspective. The Prophet's age was recast as the climax of human history; it became the spiritual and heroic age par excellence, to which all subsequent ages had to aspire. According to one tradition, the Prophet reportedly said, "The best of people are those of my age, then those who follow them, and then those who follow them."[6] Another high point in preeschatological Islamic historical imagination is the Second Coming of Christ. The function of this event is "rectificatory": the Christ will destroy the false Messiah *(al-masih 'l-dajjal),* and all religions will perish save Islam.[7] Besides the appropriation and Islamization of the Christian notion of the Second Coming, Islamic imagination developed its own messianic figure, namely, al-Mahdi (the guided one), a descendant of the Prophet. In Islamic imagination both notions fused, giving rise to a utopian vision according to which the Mahdi will "fill the earth with equity and justice as it has been filled with inequity and injustice."[8]

Both the macrocosmic God/universe opposition and the microcosmic God/Satan/humankind relationship are ultimately reduced by Taha to a basic God/humankind relationship. The human being is in fact the "greater universe" *(al-kawn 'l-akbar),* whereas the rest of God's creation is the "smaller universe" *(al-kawn 'l-asghar),* as "the human being is the primary end of God's creation and the locus of His regard. All other universes were created as a secondary end. They serve as the human being's instrument in his journey to God and to perfection" (QF 211). It is this relationship that brings history into being and invests it with meaning. Although, ultimately, this history is determined by divine will, the relationship retains its centrality, as without it there is no history.

Taha perceives existence in terms of a motion that has a spiral form. He maintains that neither space nor time is spherical *(kurawi)*; rather, they have a spiral structure that moves from a base to a pinnacle. Consequently, he accepts the belief that history repeats itself, and he reads the part of verse 21:104 that declares "as We originated the first creation, so We shall bring it back again" as a Qur'anic confirmation of a constant divine act of "repeating" history.[9] Such a belief, however, has to be qualified because "history does not repeat itself in the same manner but in a manner that resembles in some respects what passed before while at the same time differs in other respects from it" (RT 19). Yet, on another level, Taha is ambivalent about the notion of repetition when applied to God because he conceives divinity in terms of constant renewal or, as he puts it, "Divinity does not stop, or go back, or repeat itself" (RS 21).

This scheme undergoes a perceptible shift of emphasis when the human element of the relationship comes into play. When Taha perceives humans as the free agents who create their own history, he infuses his theory with the notion of progress and paints a humankind with a dichotomous history, playing its history out on two different temporal planes. In giving account of this, he says,

> History is spherical like our terrestrial globe, ceaselessly revolving around itself and repeating itself in one way or another. Among backward nations [*umam mutakhallifa*], history repeats itself in a manner that is almost identical with the past. This is owing to the deficiency of thinking and lack of creativity, resulting, consequently, in little progress [*taqaddum*]. [By contrast], among advanced nations [*umam mutaqaddima*], history repeats itself in a manner that differs greatly or slightly from the past, depending on the degree of freedom of thought and capacity for creativity. This leads to progress. Hence, nations that are lacking in freedom of thought move in a vicious circle, always finding themselves where they started. On the other hand, advanced nations move upward a spiral course. (AS 64–65)

What Taha expresses here has a social Darwinist resonance. His use of the terms "backward" and "advanced" echoes the use of the terms "weak" and "strong" by social Darwinists who believe that human individuals and societies are subject to the same laws of natural selection that operate on the level of plants and animals and that social life is a struggle governed by the principle of "the survival of the fittest." [10] This resonance, however, does not make Taha an exponent of social Darwinism, whose philosophy and practical implications (such as the defense of class stratification and the support of laissez-faire capitalism) are totally unacceptable to him.

Taha's occasional lack of consistency and systematicity does him a great injustice. Despite what he says about the virtual circularity of the history of those he describes as "backward nations" (without defining what he means by the term or indicating to what nations it applies), his overall emphasis is on a spiral movement of history governed by a progressivistic teleology that is providential in nature. It is in connection with this spiral movement and its ultimate goal that Taha introduces the key notions of "absolute individual freedom" and "total social justice," which together represent the cornerstone of his theory of a second message of Islam.

Taha places a great deal of emphasis on the notion of individuality *(fardiyya),* which he constructs by dissociating the Qur'anic term *"fard"* (individual) from its eschatological framework and investing it with his notion of "absolute individual freedom." (Taha applies this same notion in his discussion of *tawhid.*) In constructing this notion, Taha progresses from plurality to duality and then to oneness. He posits a triplicity of thought, speech, and action, a binary opposition of externality *(zahir)* and internality *(batin)* and an ideal state of oneness where one's thought, speech, and action or one's outward and inward existences become one and the same and any trace of fragmentation *(inqisam)* disappears. He further identifies this final state of unity and wholeness with the state of servantship *('ubudiyya)* to which ideal worship leads. Taha would agree with Sartrean existentialism that "man is condemned to be free," but he would not agree that this freedom is ultimately based on choice and that human beings have no destiny.[11] In his view, the Qur'anic assertion of verse 84:6 that the human being strives for God laboriously and eventually meets Him confirms that it is God who has chosen the human being and "condemned" him or her to the destiny of realizing freedom through the state of servantship to Him.

Absolute individual freedom is such a pivotal concept in Taha's thought that it is inseparable from his other major themes of free will and determination, freedom from ignorance, freedom from fear, and the realization of one's servantship as a step to the realization of one's lordship *(rububiyya)*. Furthermore, it is at the heart of his moral thinking. Taha's theory of "progressive reconciliation" as regards the problem of free will and determination presupposes a transition from a state of determination to a state of freedom. This is a change that Taha also describes in terms of progress from "ignorance" to "knowledge" and in terms of "freedom from fear." On the ethical level, absolute individual freedom and morality are intimately linked. Quoting the prophetic tradition, "Take God's virtues [*akhlaq Allah*] as your model," he contends that the highest expression of God's *akhlaq* (morality, righteous conduct) is absolute individual freedom. The proper exercise of absolute individual freedom is hence identified with the highest form of worship (AJi 13).

An important aspect of Taha's concept of absolute individual freedom concerns the modality of its realization. In light of his determinism, it might be expected that he would maintain that freedom is bestowed upon human beings. Yet he argues to the contrary that freedom can never be a gift and one has to work hard to attain to it. This hard work has to be systematic and structured and in accordance with the method *(minhaj)* he outlines in his theory of prophetic imitation, wherein he reconstructs Muhammad as a model. The inner logic of his theory of prayer requires that Muhammad be someone who has actually attained absolute individual freedom, and this is precisely what Taha claims.[12]

Taha does not lose sight of the broader context within which individual freedom unfolds and operates. Inasmuch as individuals need to realize their absolute individual freedom, society needs attain total social justice. A key point on which he consistently insists is that the perceived conflict between absolute individual freedom and total social justice is a serious mistake.

The Failure of Western Civilization

In advancing his vision of radical social change, Taha adopts a two-pronged strategy. On the one hand, he sets out to criticize and denounce Western civilization, and, on the other, he promotes Islam, or rather his particular vision of Islam, as the ultimate solution for the problems facing humankind.

His critique of the West hinges on an initial distinction he draws between *madaniyya* and *hadara*. These terms are used in modern Arabic synonymously to designate "civilization," but Taha maintains that there is a crucial difference in what they signify. He equates *madaniyya* with *akhlaq* (morality, good conduct). Morality is indivisible from freedom; morality is in fact "the proper exercise of absolute individual freedom." *Madaniyya* is hence the capacity to distinguish between the values of things; it is the capacity to make the right moral judgments and to act accordingly. Someone who lives on the plane of *madaniyya* enjoys a high level of thought and awareness, and his moral sensibility does not allow him to "confuse means and ends [or] sacrifice the end for the sake of means" (RT 21). *Hadara*, by contrast, is about what one achieves by way of life comforts and material ease; it is about material progress and material well-being. Taha maintains that the difference between *madaniyya* (civilization as moral achievement) and *hadara* (civilization as material achievement) is one of degree rather than kind; he envisages a social pyramid where *madaniyya* stands at the top and *hadara* at the base. The ideal state is a social system that combines both.

He emphatically asserts that Western civilization is a *hadara* but not a *madaniyya*. He maintains that

> present-day Western technological civilization is a coin with a good, agreeable side and an ugly side. Its good and agreeable side has to do with its capacity in the fields of scientific discovery, harnessing material forces to enrich human life, and making use of technology to help humans address their problems. Its ugly face, however, is represented by its failure to achieve peace. Owing to this failure, the West directs far more energies to war, and expenditure on the means of destruction, than it does to peace and expenditure on constructive projects. (RS 55)

Reflecting on the mixture of good and evil in Western civilization, Taha's final verdict is unfavorable: "Its evil is more than its good" (SA 20). Echoing some of the essentializing and reductionist judgments of other Islamists, he asserts that Western civilization lacks the necessary criteria to distinguish between values and denigrates abstract thinking because this kind of thinking cannot be translated into material utility or be subjected to statistical measurements. In his most damning judgement of Western civilization, Taha describes it as a "materialist, industrialist, and technological civilization that has demonstrated its bankruptcy and its failure to make men happy because of its loss of faith in God and in humankind" (SA 20).

When Taha speaks about what he describes as the failure of Western civilization, he is categorical: this civilization has reached an impasse and has nothing of substance to offer. This became glaringly obvious after the Second World War, which in his view ended with "no victor and no vanquished" and the peace in which it resulted was no real peace as it was maintained thanks to a "balance of terror." This failure on the part of Western civilization to achieve peace is symptomatic of another more fundamental failure, namely, the failure to reconcile the two basic needs of absolute individual freedom and total social justice. It is in this respect, Taha sweepingly asserts, that Islam proves its excellence and superiority by offering humankind its real and only hope.

Writing in the 1960s against the background of a global polarization between Western capitalism and Soviet communism, a regional polarization between revolutionary and conservative forces (represented respectively by Nasserite Egypt and the regime of Saudi Arabia), and an upsurge in the prestige and influence of the Sudanese Communist Party after the toppling of 'Abbud's regime, Taha came to see Marxism as a global and regional intellectual and transformative force that presented the only real challenge as far as his project was concerned (MM 4). He drew no distinction between Marxism and Communism and tended to use the two terms interchangeably. When it came to capitalism, he was completely dismissive of it. He stressed that capitalism was a bankrupt system that adopted either a reactionary position favoring the status quo or a proactive position trying to meet Communism halfway (RT 26).

Although Taha's social thought was considerably influenced by Marxism, he vigorously criticizes it on two counts: its atheism and its adoption of violence in bringing about social change. In discussing Marxist atheism, Taha criticizes the dialectical materialist assertion of the primacy of matter over consciousness. In this regard, he reasserts the idealist Hegelian position, which he finds "closer to the truth, though not the whole truth" on account of Hegel's reliance on the rational tools of philosophy that Taha, as a mystic, finds wanting (MM 28–29). He does not investigate the philosophical roots of Marxist atheism or subject Marx's or Engels's statements on religion to any serious critical examination. Rather, he is content to declare that Marx, failing to recognize the existence of God, sought to turn his failure into an advantage by claiming that God does not exist (a sour-grapes type of atheism). On another level, however, Taha applies his deterministic logic and comes up with the peculiar view that Marx's atheism was inspired by God, as atheism (or unbelief) cannot enter into existence except through divine will and as part of an overall divine design (MM 6). When it comes to historical materialism, this is reduced by Taha to four principles: (1) the course of history is determined by economic forces; (2) history is essentially a record of class struggle; (3) the state is fundamentally an apparatus of oppression used by the ruling class against other classes; and (4) violence and power are the only means to bring about radical change in society. He has no quarrel with the first three principles, but when it comes to the fourth, he objects to the role assigned to violence *('unf)* in the revolutionary process of change. He argues that in insisting upon violence as an essential element of social change, Marxism projects onto the future a principle that applied to the dynamic of change in the past. He contends that the social and intellectual development of modern societies has reached a point where new laws of social change apply. Indeed, power *(quwwa)* will always be essential for social change, but violence is no longer necessary.

In demonstrating his point Taha gives the example of the October 1964 popular uprising in Sudan. The key significance of this revolution, he maintains, is that it proved the possibility of a disjunction between violence and power. When such a disjunction takes place, "the door will be open for men to experience a new kind of power, that is, power that rests on the unity of thought and the unity of feeling" (TT 7). Furthermore, when released, this power is such that it neutralizes the violence of the forces of counterrevolution, as these forces would immediately realize the futility of trying to suppress such an overwhelming movement.

In assessing Marxism, Taha recognizes its contributions and merits while at the same time asserting that it is no longer relevant and does indeed constitute an obstacle to the cause of radical social change and liberation. He always asserted that the two major communist systems of the Soviet Union and China were doomed to failure and argued that certain developments such as the introduction of measures of economic liberalization in the 1960s in the Soviet Union or the chaotic upheaval of the Cultural Revolution in China were clear signs of the beginning of the end of both systems. Yet in Taha's view, the communist experiment, just like Marxist atheism, is part of God's plan. In fact, these communist systems pave the way and set the stage for a global Islamic system that will bring the aspired change. When he declares the death of communism and Western capitalism, he simultaneously proclaims the birth of the "Second Message of Islam."

The Two Communities of Islam

Historically, Muhammad's prophetic career spanned two phases: an early phase in Mecca from the time he proclaimed his mission in about 613 to 622 (the Meccan phase), when he emigrated to Medina (Yathrib), and a later phase extending from 622 to the point of his death eleven years later, in 632 (the Medinan phase). Muhammad's emigration *(hijra)* to Medina was a watershed because it laid the foundation for the birth of a new religious community with a sense of a distinctive identity. Moreover, the new community was a political entity whose organization and distinctive interests soon gave rise to a state with a missionary sense of purpose and an expansionist drive. This community perceived itself through two designations, *mu'minun* (believers) and *muslimun* (those who submit), with the latter label gradually gaining dominance and giving the new religion of Islam its name.

The ruptive break and transition in Muhammad's career and the pressing and ever-changing needs of the new community were clearly reflected in the Qur'an. It was not only that the concerns of the Qur'anic passages revealed in Medina were different from those revealed in Mecca, but the Medinan revelations also exhibited a clear legislative feature that came to be known technically as *naskh* (abrogation). Distinguishing between Meccan and Medinan revelations and identifying what constituted their characteristic features was hence not only an exegetical exercise but also, and more importantly, a juristic necessity to establish rulings. A logic of what may be described as textual linearity informed the juristic procedure: what was revealed later (perceived as abrogating, *nasikh*) governed what was revealed

earlier (perceived as abrogated, *mansukh*) and hence provided the conclusive basis for the law.[13]

The Prophet's success in establishing the new religion and its state and
the successes of his immediate successors in consolidating his state and expanding it endowed the period of the Medina state with a unique and
ever-glowing aura in Islamic imagination in the past and the present. So
much so that many a reformist (and Islamist) movement and program is
revivalist in essence in the sense of advocating a return to the model of the
Medina state. Taha, by contrast, is revivalist in a very different sense: he
does not want to go back to the phase of the Medina state; rather, he cham-
pions a return to the earlier Meccan phase. The radical proposition Taha
makes is that the prophetic *hijra* was a clear dividing line between two
messages of Islam: a Meccan message and a Medinan one.[14] Not only that,
but the new community that came into existence after the *hijra* event was a
community that misperceived itself and has since been perceived in the
light of a misnomer.

Taha recasts the difference between Meccan and Medinan revelations in
terms of "essence" *(asl,* lit. "root") and "nonessence" *(far',* lit. "branch") respectively. In this context, the term "essence" has the specific meaning of
"fundamental, primary, intrinsic, ultimate," whereas the term "nonessence"
signifies "subsidiary, secondary, temporary, provisional, transitional." On
the basis of this division, Taha draws the radical conclusion that "Islam" is
an inclusive term designating two messages and, consequently, the term
"Muslims" refers to two communities.

The new community instituted by Muhammad perceived itself as a
community of *mu'minun* and *muslimun.* The first appellation is used, for
example, in verse 2:62, which refers to the new community as "they that believe" *('lladhina amanu)* alongside the other communities of Jews, Christians, and Sabaeans. This reference presupposes that the new community
possesses a distinctive body of belief and doctrine that sets it apart from
other recognizable and established communities. The other term used in
describing the new community, *muslimun,* is also used by the Qur'an in
connection with prophetic figures and communities that came before
Muhammad. On one level, Qur'anic usage suggests that the terms are syn-

onymous. On another level, though, there is a clear technical separation between the two terms as indicated by verse 49:14:

· The Bedouins say, 'We believe [*(amanna)*].' Say: 'You do not believe; rather say, "We surrender [*(aslamna)*]"; for belief [*iman*] has not yet entered your hearts.

Hence, according to this formal distinction, *islam* is a function of an outward state and *iman* of an inward state, with the former serving as a prelude to the latter, and the latter enjoying a higher status over the former.

These two categories were supplemented by another category that figures in the hadith material. According to one tradition, an immaculately dressed visitor called one day on the Prophet, sat close to him, and asked him about *islam*. The Prophet defined *islam* in terms of the Five Pillars. Then the visitor invited the Prophet to tell him about *iman*, and the Prophet explained that it was one's belief in God, the angels, the Holy Scriptures, the prophets, predestination *(qadar)*, and the Day of Judgment. Then the visitor enquired about *ihsan*, which the Prophet defined as "worshipping God as if you see Him, for if you do not see Him, He sees you." When the visitor left, the Prophet told his companions that that was Gabriel who came to teach them the fundamental principles of their religion.[15] On the basis of this tradition, a hierarchical trinity of *islam* (outward submission), *iman* (inward belief), and *ihsan* (perfection) was constructed.

Taha argues that this tradition led to a serious misconception with regard to the concept of *islam*. He contends that when the Qur'an proclaims in verse 3:19, "The true religion with God is Islam," or emphatically declares in verse 3:85, "Whoso desires another religion than Islam, it shall not be accepted of him; in the next world he shall be among the losers," it does not at all refer to Islam in the basic sense defined by the tradition. What the tradition clearly refers to is, on the one hand, a rudimentary Islam that develops from simple beginnings, and, on the other, a formal Islam of mere outward conformity that made it possible even for hypocrites *(munafiqun)* to pose as Muslims. This, in short, is the Islam that the Prophet indicated in another tradition when he said, "I have been commanded to fight against people till they testify that there is no god but God (and that Muhammad is God's messenger). If they do so, they would have secured the protection of their property and persons unless they transgress. Beyond that, their affair is committed to God."[16]

These levels of rudimentary and formal Islam that are below *iman* and *ihsan* are contrasted by a higher level of *islam* that is indicated by the verses quoted above—the ultimate Islam other than which shall not be accepted by God. Realizing the higher level of Islam involves, according to Taha, a journey upward along a spiral, seven-stage path. The initial three ranks are the ones outlined in the tradition. Having reached the stage of *ihsan*, the following challenge is the realization of what is described as the state of *iqan* (certainty), a composite state that takes one through three levels of certainty. The first stage is that of *'ilm 'l-yaqin* (the knowledge of certainty), where one's knowledge is conceptual, one knows about objects without experiencing them directly. This is followed by the stage of *'ain 'l-yaqin* (the very object of certainty), where one partially experiences the object of knowledge; knowledge is no longer merely conceptual or hypothetical, and a greater degree of certainty is hence achieved. The third stage is that of *haqq 'l-yaqin* (the truth of certainty), where the space between knower and known disappears and the knower thus fully experiences the object of his knowledge.[17]

Taha divides this "seven-rung progression ladder" *(sullam taraqqi suba'i)* into three units. The three stages of *islam, iman,* and *ihsan* constitute what he calls the "belief ['aqida] phase" of Islam; the three stages of certainty make up the "knowledge ['ilm] phase" of Islam; and then comes ultimate Islam. It should be noted that although the Islam of the beginning is part of a unit, ultimate Islam, as a stage of culminating perfection, comprises an independent unit. Hence, as Taha likes to put it, the end resembles the beginning and does not resemble it. In contrasting the Islam of the beginning with the Islam of the end, he stresses the superiority of the latter in being knowledge- and certainty-based and in being the ultimate fruit of the realization of the total unity *(tawhid)* of the outward and the inward or, in other words, the realization of absolute individual freedom.

Although Taha is at pains to stress the "progress" aspect in the relationship between these different stages and the belief that ultimate Islam is realized as the final outcome of methodical and rigorous self-application, he nevertheless makes the claim that it was this higher level of Islam that was initially offered by Muhammad to his Meccan audience. He identifies Meccan Qur'anic revelations with the specific message of ultimate Islam. When this level of Islam did not prevail, God implemented a different plan or, as Taha puts it, "Initially people were preached [the message of] Islam, but when they failed to accept it and it became abundantly clear that they could not live up to its precepts, there was a descent to a level they were capable of accepting" (RT 116). In justifying this peculiar course of action on the part of God, he maintains that an effective demonstration to people of their incapacity to follow ultimate Islam was necessary as a conclusive argument before they were subjected to the rigors of the other level of Islam, namely, Medinan Islam, or what Taha calls the "First Message of Islam."[18]

What Taha perceives as a failure of the early community of Islam to embrace and follow ultimate Islam leads him to one of his most radical conclusions: the Prophet's community was not in fact a community of Muslims, *muslimun,* as it has historically perceived itself and been perceived. Rather, it was a community of *mu'minun* (believers). He argues that the Gabriel tradition clearly indicates that the level of that early community did not go beyond the initial three stages of *islam, iman,* and *ihsan,* whereas the three levels of *iqan* and their culmination into *islam* were to be the achievement of another, future community—the community of "Muslims" proper. With this view Taha deploys the tradition of the Prophet's yearning for his "brothers" *(ikhwan)* as distinguished from those with him, his "companions" *(ashab).*

Besides this distinction that the tradition makes, Taha makes a further significant distinction between Muhammad himself and his companions: whereas the Prophet was *muslim,* his companions were *mu'minun.* Applying this differential distinction universally throughout the salvation history of humankind, he contends that it was only the prophetic figures who were *muslim* while their communities never went beyond the point of being *mu'minun.* Prophetic figures like Moses, Jesus, and Muhammad achieved the level of Islam as "the religion of humankind" to which some Qur'anic verses, such as verse 3:85, refer. In the light of his reading of the "brothers" tradition, Taha concludes that the Prophet's use of the term "brothers" was meant to underline parity in spiritual rank between him and the future community he announced, as it would be a community of "Muslims." This promised community would unite humankind and give it its one religion of Islam, as referred to in 48:28: "It is He who has sent His Messenger with the guidance and the religion of truth, that He may uplift it above every religion. God suffices as a witness."[19]

When Taha speaks about Islam as a "religion of humankind," his starting point is in fact a recognition of a "unity of religion" that views polytheism as a necessary preliminary to monotheism and hence an inseparable part of the all-embracing divine plan. When it comes to the "higher religions," he exhibits the familiar Islamic partiality that recognizes and privileges only Judaism and Christianity (his "Islamic trinity"). He depicts the relationship among the three monotheistic religions in terms of a dialectical scheme. The scheme's base is Judaism, which encompasses the legal and the moral but overemphasizes the former. Christianity, with its great emphasis on the moral, is viewed as a radical reaction to the excessive legalism of Judaism. Islam was a point where both Judaism and Christianity met, achieving a synthesis and balance by virtue of which the Muslims became the "midmost community" *(ummat-an wasat-an)* to which verse 2:143 refers. This notion of Islam as a higher synthesis that replaces the chosen communities of Jews and Christians with a new chosen community lies at the heart of the perception of Islam as a "natural religion." To the Prophet is attributed a tradition according to which he said, "Every infant is born in a state of *fitra* (original nature); then his parents make him a Jew or a Christian or a Magian."[20] In commenting on this tradition, Taha maintains that every infant is born with what he describes as "a sound heart [*qalb salim*] and a pure mind [*'aql safi*]" or what corresponds to a mind in a tabula rasa state. This original, pristine state is, however, soon subjected to the distortion of social conditioning. Not unlike other modern Muslim thinkers, he reads the tradition in the light of the assertion that "Islam is the religion of *fitra*,"[21] and he justifies this position by arguing that Islam provides the most effective method to decondition oneself and liberate the mind and the heart (MS 187–88).

Taha presents us with a dichotomous perspective that combines the historical and the ahistorical: whereas the first message of Islam was present-oriented and shaped by the historical context of seventh-century Arabia, the second message is future-oriented in that it responds to the needs of a society to come. In demonstrating the historicity of the first message and its limitations, Taha focuses on the specific issues of holy war, slavery, and gender.

Abrogating Jihad

Taha's teachings about jihad ("struggle, holy war") must be understood in contrast to the historical notion of jihad. With the Prophet's settlement in Medina, Islam assumed a different character. The Muslims were no longer a persecuted minority, and they were able to establish their own polity. One of the earliest decisive measures Muhammad took against the Meccans was making raids against their caravans with the view of destabilizing their trade, compensating some members of his community, boosting the economic base of his nascent state, and creating a new political reality. These raids ushered in a new phase, that of jihad, as a method of propagating the new religion. Jihad came to be Muhammad's overriding concern during the Medinan phase, so much so that almost half of the Qur'anic revelations in Medina were jihad related.

Jihad developed from the notion of a defensive "just war" (as expressed, for instance, by verses 22:39–40) to a full-scale war of aggression against non-Muslims. This later development was formally declared with the revelation of what came to be known as the "sword verse," that is, verse 9:5, which instigated the Muslims: "Then, when the sacred months are drawn away, slay the idolaters wherever you find them, and take them, and confine them, and lie in wait for them at every place of ambush. But if they repent, and perform the prayer, and pay the alms, then let them go their way."[22] The revelation of this verse meant that the verses of *ismah* (peaceful persuasion) and those verses that placed restrictive conditions on jihad were all abrogated.[23] Jihad as a just war of engaging in self-defense against polytheist aggression changed into jihad as holy war, initiating armed conflict with the avowed intention of forcibly converting polytheists to Islam. Hence, with the revelation of the sword verse, the new monotheistic community gave itself the authority and the right to redefine polytheism as a religio-legal status that immediately deprived a person of the right to life.[24] The fortunes of history were on the side of the new community, and jihad eventually led to their success in establishing their religion, its state, and social system.[25]

Taha views the issue of jihad through two perspectives, as an apologist and as a modernist reformer in whose thought the value of freedom occupies a central place. He realized that jihad, as expressed in the Qur'an and as historically practiced by the Prophet and his successors, did not conform with the modern value of religious freedom, to which he was committed. Furthermore, the problem was more acute in his case because of his evolutionary perspective that viewed polytheism as a God-sanctioned necessary spiritual step in the progress toward monotheism.

So, how does he try to solve the problem? On one level, he demotes the verses of jihad to a subsidiary level: jihad in the first place is not a fundamental precept of Islam. On another level, he problematizes the notion of freedom when it comes to the historical context of the Prophet's time. He maintains that freedom is a natural right that corresponds to a duty, that is, the duty to exercise it properly and not to abuse it. When freedom is abused it is then possible to withdraw it, although such a measure should be in accordance with a "constitutional law." He defines constitutional law as a law that reconciles the need of the individual for absolute freedom with the need of society for total justice (RT 118–19). In essence, constitutional law is a law of reciprocity *(mu'awada)* that is best summed up in verses 99:7–8, which proclaim, "and whoso has done an atom's weight of good shall see it, and whoso has done an atom's weight of evil shall see it."

But what gave the Muslims the right to take away the freedom of the polytheists? Taha justifies what the Muslims did by blending the notion of constitutional law with the conventional Islamic argument about the superiority of Islam as a belief system and the moral superiority of the Muslim community: "When people insist . . . on worshipping a stone they had carved, on breaking their bonds of kin, on slaying others, and on practicing female infanticide, then they have abused their freedom and exposed it to the danger of being curbed. As there was no law to enforce this, the only option was the use of the sword" (RT 120). This meant that the polytheists were treated as legal minors *(qasirs)* who had to be subjected by force to a guiding guardianship *(wisaya)* (IQ 22–23). In justifying the use of the sword, Taha insists, "Islam did not use the sword as a butcher's knife but rather as a surgeon's scalpel" (RT 121).

It is to Taha's credit that he could see the untenability of the argument of some modern Muslims that the jihad wars were essentially defensive. He maintains that the concern of these scholars to vindicate Islam led them to misrepresent the nature of its wars. In making his own argument about the polytheists' abuse of their freedom and the right of the new community of Islam to take this freedom away, he effectively places all the responsibility for the rise of the institution of jihad and the violence and compulsion that accompanied it on the shoulders of the polytheists.

Yet despite his defense of jihad, Taha is cognizant of its limitation. The coercive nature of jihad may achieve *islam* as a state of outward submission or subservience to the authority of the state, but it cannot guarantee the achievement of genuine belief *('aqida)* (IQ 23). Muslims in the past were aware of this limitation, and this led to a manifest tension in the construction of the doctrine of jihad. On the one hand, there was a celebratory attitude that invested jihad with a supreme and permanent significance and relevance. So, for example, according to one tradition, the Prophet said, "Jihad never ceases from when God sent me until when the last of my community fights against the Antichrist." [26] This sense is enforced most dramatically by another tradition according to which the Prophet said, "I wish I were slain in God's way then brought to life again, then slain then brought to life again, then slain then brought to life again, then slain." [27] The ultimate reward, paradise, is strikingly described as being "under the shadows of swords." [28]

On the other hand, there was a pacifist tendency that relegated jihad to a secondary activity. This developed into a position that reconceptualized jihad in accordance with a revalorized scale: the familiar physical, combative jihad to which the Qur'an usually refers was redesignated as "lesser jihad" *(jihad asghar),* whereas the struggle against one's "lower self" was designated as "greater jihad" *(jihad akbar).*

This valorization of spiritual struggle over combative jihad was widespread among Sufis. Ibn 'Arabi divides those who undertake jihad into four hierarchical classes: those who struggle without being placed under any restrictive measures;[29] those who struggle only in God's way *(fi sabil 'Llah)*; those who struggle *in* Him;[30] and those who "struggle for God as His due" *(haqqa jihadihi).*[31] In his view, jihad comes to an end. On the basis of his theory of the Unity of Being, Ibn 'Arabi argues that as the grounds for jihad are acts undertaken by those against whom one is enjoined to enter into armed conflict and because these acts are ultimately God's acts, then one's jihad is ultimately directed against what God does. Taking verse 29:69 as his textual basis, he maintains, "It is well known that there is nothing in existence save God and it is (ultimately) God who struggles in God. Had He not guided us in His ways, we would not have known this, and this is why the verse is concluded by 'and God is with the good-doers' [*wa inna 'Llaha la-ma'a 'l-muhsinina*]. *Ihsan* (perfection) is to worship God as if you see Him. When you see Him, you would know that jihad is from Him [*minhu*] and in Him [*fihi*]."[32]

Taha embraces the reduction of the status of combative jihad into a lesser jihad and tries to adduce a Qur'anic basis for this understanding. Reading, for instance, verse 9:123, which says, "O believers, fight the unbelievers who are near to you, and let them find in you a harshness; and know that God is with the godfearing," he applies his "ultimate sense" exegetical method and argues, "The unbelievers who are near to us are our limbs and senses. One should struggle against one's eyes by not casting them unlawfully, and against one's ears, tongue, hands, legs, genitals, and stomach. All one's limbs [and senses] ought to be austerely guarded" (TK 6). Furthermore, he embraces Ibn 'Arabi's radical proposition—though not his reasoning—of the end of jihad, because Taha's argument against jihad is inspired by the realities of the modern world rather than the logic of the Unity of Being doctrine. His antijihad position is inextricable from his consistent emphasis of the need for peace in the modern world. One of the main planks of his criticism of Western civilization is its failure to achieve peace, a failure that he sees as intrinsic and systemic. According to his perspective, the end of jihad takes place within the larger context of what may be described as the end of war.

In underlining his position, Taha dramatically proclaims, "Let it be known that as of the present time jihad by means of the sword is abrogated and that as of the present time greater jihad is declared" (TK 6). In abrogating combative jihad irrevocably, Taha attributes to God what may be described as an "intentionality shift" claiming that "thanks to His grace and thanks to the order of the time, God wants people as of the present time to live rather than die in His way, an exceedingly more difficult task" (TK 6). Taha's evocation of the notion of "the order of the time" *(hukm 'l-waqt)* is of particular significance, as it is this notion, rather for instance than the notion of divine grace, that constitutes the real philosophical (and practical) basis of his position. In recognizing change and the necessity to adapt to it, the notion serves as his operative principle in arguing reform. However, Taha uses this notion not only to provide justificatory grounds for change and reform at the present time but also to explain and vindicate principles and practices that prevailed in past times, as demonstrated by his treatment of the issue of slavery.

Slavery and the Perspective of Moral Ambiguity

Slavery was a pre-Islamic institution that Islam accepted in principle while seeking to reform it. Muhammad himself had slaves, some of whom he manumitted and others he apparently did not, and his wives and companions had slaves.[33] Neither Muhammad nor his companions nor the jurists (or, for that matter, the Sufis and the philosophers) of premodern times entertained the idea of a total abolition of slavery. If we judge by the legal implications of some prophetic traditions, it becomes clear that even manumission was not allowed to be a universal act.[34] Muslim imagination even established a close correlation between a slave's duty to his master and his duty to God as expressed in a tradition that condemned runaway slaves and declared, "If a slave escapes, his prayer would not be accepted."[35]

The discussions by modern Muslims of slavery under Islam usually revolve around the assertion that Islam was in essence a radical emancipatory project. They are usually concerned with highlighting the compassionate treatment of slaves under Islam and the supreme meritorious value placed on manumission. An argument that has gained wide currency in modern Islamic slavery apologetics is that Islam adopted a gradualist approach to put an end to the institution. The argument rests on several assumptions: that Islam viewed slavery as a social evil that had to be eradicated; that from the outset Islam was intent on abolishing slavery; that slavery was so deep rooted that it was not conceivable or possible to abolish it immediately; and that Islam set in motion certain measures that were to bring a gradual abolition of slavery.[36]

In tackling slavery, Taha starts by making the assertion that the principle of freedom lies at the heart of Islam and hence slavery can in no way be viewed as a natural part of the Islamic belief system or social order. He stresses what he sees as an intimate connection between slavery and jihad: "It is a principle of jihad in the way of God that Muslims make a proposition to the infidels [*kuffar*] to embrace the new religion. If the infidels do not accept [Islam], then they must pay the *jizya* (poll tax) and live under Muslim rule while preserving their own religion and enjoying full personal safety.[37] If they, however, resist the Islamic plan, then the Muslims would fight against them, and if they defeat them they take them as prisoners of war [*sabaya*]" (RT 124).

In justifying the enslavement of non-Muslims, Taha advances the following argument: "The higher wisdom [*hikma*] of enslavement lies in the law of reciprocity [*mu'awada*]. When a person was invited to be God's slave and he refused, this refusal demonstrated his ignorance and his need for a period of training during which he would prepare himself to be a willing slave of God. During this [preparatory] period, this person would be a slave of another human being to acquire the training appropriate for a slave of God. This is a situation of reciprocity because when this person, while still free, refused to be God's slave, he was made a slave of another slave of God when he was captured in defeat, 'for a suitable recompense [*jaza'an wifaqan*]' " (RT 124).[38] Taha recognizes in this manner of propagating the new religion a particular form of what may be described as an "Islamic slavery" that expanded the base of the historically inherited institution.

To accept Taha's reciprocity argument as justificatory ground for slavery under Islam one has to overlook the exploitative socioeconomic basis of slavery and its actual history, and reconceptualize it as a religionized and sacralized social institution where the slave master is a mirror of God. This, of course, leaves Taha with a thorny problem as regards the slavery institution in general: if an Islamic, jihad-based form of slavery is defensible as necessary schooling to be a proper slave of God, why then should pre-Islamic slavery be allowed? In addressing this question, Taha adopts a socially conservative position, offering the familiar argument used by other modern Muslim thinkers. He affirms, "In keeping with what religion dictates, it was neither possible nor judicious to introduce legislation that abolished the slavery institution with a stroke of the pen. The needs of enslaved people and the social and economic needs of the community made it

necessary to retain the institution while at the same time working on its reform till every enslaved person was freed" (RT 124–25).[39] Taha proceeds
here from the assumption that the Islamic context of slavery opened the
way for what he describes as a "period of reform" *(fatrat tatwir)*—a transitional phase during which those enslaved could achieve their economic independence while society at large could restructure its economic activity
away from their exploitation. In short, Islam provided a prudent, gradualist
plan serving the best interests of both master and slave. What may be noted
here is that Taha, like other proponents of this argument, completely ig-
nores the actual history of slavery under Islam and instead projects what
may be described as a "prescriptive history" of the institution, or an imagined, "what ought to have really happened" history.

Like other modern apologists, Taha places a heavy emphasis on the legal
and moral protections slaves enjoyed under Islam. This included granting
slaves rights in addition to their duties, encouraging emancipation as a
meritorious or contractual act, and insisting on their humanitarian treatment. In assessing his position it may be said that it is characterized
by a moral ambiguity—although, on one level, he finds slavery morally
abhorrent and hence insists that the ultimate goal of Islam was its abolition,
on another level he is willing not only to justify its existence but also to
sanctify it.[40]

Islam and the Accommodation of Capitalism

Taha's critique and rejection of capitalism reflect the revolutionary and
progressive mood prevalent in the 1960s throughout the Middle East and
the Sudan and his own exposure to the intellectual influence of socialist
thought and Marxism. Yet it may be argued that the roots of this rejection
can be traced to particular socialistic trends within Islam and the Sufi attitude toward material wealth. Early Islamic socialistic tendencies were most
radically expressed by the pronouncements attributed to Abu Dharr
al-Ghifari (d. 32/652), a companion of Muhammad who advocated the giving away of one's wealth beyond the minimum one needs for subsistence.[41]
These tendencies produced an ideal of social justice that informed the ideologies of revolutionary movements such as the revolt of the Zanj, the black
slaves of southern Iraq who rose up against their oppression and threatened

the Abbasid caliphate in the fourth/tenth century, and the Qaramita movement that came to power in Bahrain in the fourth/tenth century and established a state in the organization of which "communal and egalitarian
principles seem to have played an important role . . . especially in terms of
the ownership of property, cultivation of agricultural land, collection of
taxes, distribution of public expenditures, and various types of state assistance to the underprivileged." [42]

The other crucial influence on Taha's social outlook was Sufi spirituality, which tends on the whole to adopt an openly antimaterialist stance that
renounces the world and celebrates poverty. [43] Although this spirituality
tends to present a negative view of this world, whose material achievements
and joys are transient, its ultimate view is optimistic and joy oriented as one
is promised not only the materialist delights of paradise but ultimately the
purely spiritual joy of nothing less than the Beautific Vision, the seeing of
God and being in His eternal presence.

Comparing capitalism and socialism, Taha points out that the gradual
evolution of human society and the human value system made it necessary
that socialism be preceded by capitalism because socialism is a product of
the rule of law that protects the rights of the weak, whereas capitalism is a
product of the rule of the jungle where the weak are oppressed by the strong
(RT 143–44). Considering the global situation, he was highly critical of
both the capitalist and communist systems. He maintained that despite
their apparent dissimilarities, both systems were intrinsically materialistic.
Neither system could reconcile the social and the individual because capitalism discounted the social in favor of the individual and communism dis-
regarded the individual for the sake of the social (DI 36). Furthermore,
under both systems democracy was distorted and falsified.

Despite the fact that the socioeconomic formation that thrived under
Islam since its formative period recognized class division and the private
ownership of the means of production, Taha argues that this took place in
opposition to what Islam really intended. [44] What he views as the ultimate
Islamic socioeconomic system is communistic in nature because property
should be communally owned and each individual should share in the
common wealth according to his or her need. However, this scheme of economic organization was inapplicable in the society to which Islam came

and so the necessity arose to legislate in accordance with its level and needs. The people of that society, according to the depiction of verses 47:36–38, were avaricious and deeply attached to their property. Hence, they were allowed to keep their private wealth and required only to pay the *zakat,* which was both a tax and a devotional obligation. The *zakat* as historically known and practiced was, in Taha's view, a capitalistic measure that functioned within, and adequately met, the needs of what was essentially a property-centered socioeconomic formation (RT 154–55). He furthermore contends that despite this nature, the *zakat* was nevertheless the closest measure to socialism that could have been implemented in the circumstances of early Islam (RT 163).

Women and Gender Discrimination

Taha has always stressed the principle of gender equality. To prove that this equality is a fundamental principle in Islam, he invokes Qur'anic eschatological verses that emphasize individual responsibility, some of the same verses he discusses in connection with his theory of prayer. This gender equality, he contends, was in effect an ideal that could not have been realized in the social context of the Prophet's time. Women's inferior status owing to their economic subordination on the one hand and a deep-rooted male misogyny on the other combined to create a sociocultural context that rendered, according to Taha, both the community as a whole and women themselves unripe for the reception of Islamic legislation at its higher level of equality.[45]

Reflecting the lower level of the early community of Muslims, the Qur'an endorsed the *qawama* (guardianship) of men over women, asserting thus in verse 4:34 that "Men are the managers of the affairs of women [*qawwamuna 'ala 'l-nisa'*] for that God has preferred in bounty one of them over another, and for that they have expended of their property." Furthermore, shari'a subjected women to discriminatory laws in areas such as family law and inheritance. Taha deals with gender discrimination by examining the specific issues of polygyny, divorce, the veil, and gender segregation.

Polygyny and Divorce

Polygyny *(ta'addud 'l-zawjat)* is usually discussed by Muslim scholars with reference to verses 4:3 and 4:129. The first verse is part of a passage that addresses the guardians of orphans. In the process of warning them against misappropriating the property of their legatees, it says, "If you fear that you will not act justly towards the orphans, marry such women as seem good to you, two, three, four; but if you fear you will not be equitable, then only one, or what your right hands own; so it is likelier you will not be partial." The context of the second verse concerns marital discord, where the spouses are advised to reach a settlement. Addressing men, the verse affirms, "You will not be able to be equitable between your wives, be you ever so eager; yet do not be altogether partial so that you leave her as it were suspended." Classical exegetes read into the expression "be equitable" two types of equality: equality in terms of maintenance and equality in terms of emotional and physical attraction. They were unanimous that what the verse confirms here is about the latter type of inequality, and they, along with jurists, confirmed that although it was not possible to exercise an "equality of feelings" among one's co-wives it was possible and indeed mandatory to be equitable in the sphere of maintenance. As far as these scholars were concerned, this was a tolerable and acceptable state of affairs where the verse's warning against not being "altogether partial" was read as an implicit recognition of the admissibility, on account of the frailty of human nature, of "a degree of partiality."

Whereas classical scholars placed their emphasis on the phrase "yet do not be altogether partial so that you leave her as it were suspended," modern reformers shifted the emphasis to the opening phrase, "You will not be able to be equitable between your wives, be you ever so eager." Reformers read this phrase in conjunction with the phrase in verse 4:3 that says, "but if you fear you will not be equitable, then only one," and concluded that the spirit of the Qur'an ultimately prescribes monogamy. Commenting on the two verses, Muhammad 'Abduh says, "On examining the two verses, one recognizes that the admissibility of polygyny in Islam is severely restricted and only allowed on the grounds of necessity provided that justice is maintained. If one examines this restriction and the harmful consequences of polygyny in our times, one must then conclude that it would not be possible for a nation among which polygyny is a common practice to develop." 'Abduh goes on to underline the state of friction and animosity that characterizes polygynous families and concludes that "the harm of polygyny will be carried from individuals to families and from families to the nation as a whole."[46]

Taha does not dwell on the social ills of polygyny because he apparently takes it for granted that his readers can readily see that. He asserts that monogamy is the original teaching of Islam according to which "a woman is equal to a man in marriage, the whole of the man is for the whole of the woman" (RT 127). He maintains that because neither the early Muslim community nor women were ready for a legislative leap, in the circumstance the Qur'anic measure of allowing polygyny while reforming the practice by restricting the number of wives to four was a just measure that struck the right balance.[47] Yet this was only meant as a transitional step to be followed at a later stage by a proscription of polygyny. It should, however, be noted that when Taha argues in favor of outlawing polygyny he does not envision a universal prohibition. He allows for exceptional situations where necessity *(darura)* warrants polygyny, provided that these situations are clearly specified in the law and take into account the wishes of the aggrieved spouse.[48]

Taha views marriage as an "eternal relationship" and accordingly advances the contentious view that divorce is not an original teaching in Islam. Quoting a tradition according to which the Prophet said, "The most abominable [act] of what is permissible in the sight of God is divorce," he comments that what the Prophet says "subtly indicates that what God finds abominable will be prohibited by Him when prohibition is possible and feasible" (RT 128). Hence, for Taha the spirit of the tradition is not a discouragement from an act that remains legally permissible but rather a discouragement from an act that is implicitly prohibited—what is legally binding is inferred from the divine attitude rather than the assertion of permissibility. Taha's argument against divorce is mystical in nature. The experience of love and marital union is described by him in the following allegorical terms: "When Adam and Eve fell on account of their sin and were expelled from paradise, they came down to earth separately and on different places. They both started looking for each other. After great hardship, Adam found Eve and did not find her; Eve found Adam and did not find him. Since that time, each Adam is looking for his Eve and each Eve is looking for her Adam" (RT 130).

Accordingly, one's marriage partner is a projection of one's self or, as Taha puts it, "the totality of the external vis-à-vis one's inner self" (RT 130). Yet the dilemma of human beings, he maintains, is that they do not possess enough "light" *(nur)* to help them choose their right partner. What people possess is what Taha calls the "light of belief" *(nur 'l-iman)*, a light so deficient that divorce is a necessary measure to rectify wrong choices. However, with the coming of ultimate Islam, God shall "perfect His light,"[49] and no mischoice will take place. What Taha presents in this respect is rooted in the Sufi opposition between shari'a and *haqiqa* (truth): marriage that is open to divorce is a function of the level of shari'a whereas the marriage of true partners is a function of the higher level of *haqiqa*.

The Veil and Gender Segregation

As an institution, the veil *(hijab)* was first imposed on the Prophet's wives. This apparently was a measure to check the social familiarity with which the companions treated the Prophet and his wives. The new boundaries were set by verse 33:53, which declared, "O believers, enter not the houses of the Prophet, except leave is given you for a meal . . . and when you have had the meal, disperse, neither lingering for idle talk . . . And when you ask his wives for any object, ask them from behind a curtain [*hijab*]; that is cleaner for your hearts and theirs." Although the verse's ruling specifically concerned the Prophet's wives, there was a juristic consensus that it was a general injunction that applied to all Muslim women.[50] This was a symbolic veil formalizing the already instituted gender separation that banished women from the public domain and confined them to the domestic domain.

But what happened when women ventured into public spaces?[51] This called for the translation of the symbolic into a specific practical measure, that is, the type of veil laid down by verse 33:59. In this verse, the Prophet's wives, daughters, and "the believing women" were instructed to "draw their veils close to them." The verse proceeds to give the following ground for this veiling: "so it is likelier they will be known, and not hurt." The verse's broad description of this veiling was specified by some exegetes as covering the entire head and revealing only one eye.[52] Furthermore, the exegetical material provides us with what was believed to be the social basis for the revelation of this verse, informing us that flirting with women when they went out was a widespread practice in Medina and hence public veiling was stipulated to protect free women by marking them off from slave women.[53] The verse's general reference to "the believing women" was qualified to apply only to free women. So much did this public veiling became an emblem of a woman's free status that when slave women adopted it, 'Umar reportedly used to beat them and tell them, "Reveal your heads and do not imitate free women."[54]

By contrast, verse 24:31 is more detailed. Like men, women are enjoined in this verse to "cast down their eyes." Through this mutual act of what may be described as "visual veiling," both men and women render each other invisible when they move in public spaces. The key word in the verse is *zina* (adornment, clothes, finery, "body") and the central theme addressed is the identification of those to whom a woman may reveal her adornment. A noteworthy prohibition in the verse is that women are not allowed to "stamp their feet, so that their hidden ornament may be known." Commenting on this, Ibn 'Abbas reportedly said, "This refers to when a woman passes by men and jingles her anklets. God forbade this because it is the work of the devil."[55] The "visual veiling" of the casting down of the eyes is complemented by what may be described as "auditory veiling" where the onus falls on women to protect men's sense of hearing from any noises that might prove to be potentially seductive. Hence, from the standpoint of the logic of the veil institution, the requirement that women be physically invisible in public spaces (symbolized by the physical veil) had to be made more stringent by insisting on their physical silence as well.

In accordance with his theory of the transitory nature of most shari'a institutions, Taha insists that the original teaching of Islam is unveiling (*sufur*) and that the veil was a necessary interim measure that met and served the needs of the community of the believers. He treats unveiling as part of a notional nexus that combines the notions of freedom, '*iffa* (chastity), and unity (*tawhid*). His discussion of the issue moves beyond the veil in its technical, shari'a sense to the veil in the basic sense of covering one's genitals and the significance of this act of concealment.

Taha's discussion of veiling and unveiling is based on his reading of verses 7:19–27, which narrate the story of humankind's fall from paradise.

In his view, veiling coincides with this moment of fall. The human original state is alluded to in verse 7:26, which says, "We have sent down on you a garment to cover your shameful parts, and feathers; and the garment of godfearing [*libas 'l-taqwa*]—that is better; that is one of God's signs; haply they will remember." What the verse metaphorically refers to as "the garment of godfearing," which Taha redescribes as "the garment of light" *(libas 'l-nur)* or "the garment of chastity," intimates humankind's original state. The "remembering" that the verse urges is, in his view, "a remembering of the state of purity, innocence, and chastity that prevailed before man had committed his sin. By remembering this state, man can start his return journey" (RT 132). Chastity, unity, and unveiling are inseparable. For Taha, the realization of one's unity of self provides the firm foundation of a moral commitment to chastity that comes from inside rather than being imposed from outside. With the flowering of this chastity, the veil ceases to exist, and unveiling becomes the order of the day. With the disappearance of the veil, gender segregation likewise comes to an end, as the original teaching of Islam is that of a mixed society. Taha does not elaborate on the nature of this mixed society—rather, he is content to characterize it through negation by asserting that it will be "a society free of the behavioral defects that plague present-day mixed societies" (RT 133).

As a social reformer committed to the equality and welfare of women, Taha attached great importance to the reform of the family law. In 1971, he produced *Tatwir shari'at 'l-ahwal 'l-shakhsiyya* (Reforming Islamic Personal Status Law) in which he outlined his proposals for radical changes in Islamic family law that were designed to meet the needs and expectations of present-day Muslim societies.

The Islamic juristic tradition specifies four requirements for the validity of a marriage contract, that is, the presence of two witnesses *(shahids)*, freedom from lawful obstacles *(mahall)*, ratification and approval of a guardian *(wali)*, and payment of a dower or bridal gift *(mahr)*. Taha approves of the first two elements but would like to see the other two invalidated. He is categorical that the era of guardianship *(wisaya)* has come to its end and, hence, a woman has the legal capacity to contract herself in marriage. On the other hand, the dower is a relic of a past when women were bought and, as such, has no place in an age that seeks to assert their dignity. Another significant feature of his reform proposals concerns divorce. As marriage is a relationship into which both husband and wife enter freely, it follows that they should have the equal right to terminate it (TS 76).

A significant aspect stressed by the juristic tradition and reconsidered by Taha is the notion of *kafa'a* or compatibility of status between intended spouses. *Kafa'a* as formulated by classical jurists was reflective of the stratification of their society and their ideological identification with some of the chief factors that defined ascribed and achieved statuses. The Hanafite school, for instance, laid down six qualifications for status equality: Islam, character *(din)*, freedom *(hurriyya)*, ancestry *(nasab)*, wealth *(mal)*, and occupation *(hirfa)*. In dealing with these *kafa'a* factors, Taha argues for their revocation with the exception of character and ancestry (TS 73). Ancestry as a *kafa'a* factor was a racist construction privileging Arabs over non-Arabs within the Muslim community.[56] This notion was rejected by the Malikites and some Hanafite doctors such as al-Thawri (d. 161/778), al-Hasan al-Basri, and al-Karkhi (d. 340–952).[57] Taha does not make clear why he decided to retain ancestry as a marriage qualification, a position totally incompatible with his espousal of social equality.

In trying to secure a firm anchor in the Qur'an for the notion of gender equality, Taha makes use of the part of verse 2:228 that affirms, "Women have such honourable rights as obligations [*wa lahunna mithlu 'lladhi 'alaihinna bi-'l-ma'ruf*], but their men have a degree above them." The key word in this verse, Taha argues, is *ma'ruf*, which he defines as "a customary act to which people conform in accordance with the dictates of their times provided this act does not violate an objective of religion" (TS 4). His definition implicitly recognizes that the primary impetus of reform is change that takes place within the sociohistorical context of the Muslim community and to which Islam has to adapt rather than within a "transition from one Qur'anic text to another" (RT 163), as he sometimes insists on putting it.

Taha's notion of equality is of a legal nature: all the aspects of shari'a that treat women as legal minors or discriminate against them on account of their gender should be abolished. However, when it comes to women and work, he advances what may be described as a traditional view that has always been popular among Islamists, that is, that "a woman's place is the home" (TS 55–56). What distinguishes his position from that of a traditional Islamist is that he places his argument within his commitment to a socialist change that will revalue women's historically devalued mother-housewife role. Although he does not categorically rule out women's entry into the public domain of work, he views their domestic role as their right job and chief duty. "The highest form of productivity for women is to procreate and look after children. As such, women should receive more honor than [those] who produce planes and rockets" (TS 55). This sexual division of labor is so central in Taha's thought that he argues that should women join the labor market, they should be allowed only to perform certain jobs and be barred from others (TS 57).

Despite the strong modernist pull on Taha to recognize gender equality, there is an opposite pull of a perspective that places a higher value on patriarchy, the sources of which are Qur'anic and mystical. The verse that he cites as his ultimate textual basis for equality does not really support his case. Verse 2:228 clearly asserts a subordinative outlook when it declares, "men have a degree above [women]." This, however, is a subordination that Taha does not accept in legal terms, and he sets out to reconstruct the verse in "ethical" terms. He insists that the verse's reference to the preferential "degree" *(daraja)* with which men are invested pertains to "the sphere of morality *(akhlaq)*" (TS 48).

When it comes to his Sufi legacy, Taha ultimately grounds the male/female relationship in a mystical bond of "marriage on the level of *haqiqa* (Truth)." On this level, he maintains, one's wife is one's "second self," an external emanation *(inbithaq)* of his inner self. Quoting verse 4:1, "Mankind, fear your Lord, who created you of a single soul [*nafs-in wahidat-in*], and from it created its mate, and from the pair of them scattered abroad many men and women," he holds that this "single soul" is in the first place "God's soul" or the "eternal soul" from which the "created soul" or the Perfect Man or the "Muhammadan Truth" *(al-haqiqa 'l-muhammadiyya)* descended or emanated. Taha describes the Perfect Man as "God's partner [*zawj*]" and likens the relationship between them to the sexual relationship where God's lordship *(rububiyya)* is action *(fi'l)* while the Perfect Man's servantship *('ubudiyya)* is a receptive act *(infi'al)*. Out of the Perfect Man descended his wife *(zawja),* who related to him in a manner parallel to his relationship with God: he is the source of action *(fa'il),* and she is the recipient of his action *(munfa'ila)* (TS 59).

Taha often contrasts Adam, the male principle, and Eve, the female principle, while retaining a strict hierarchical differentiation between them. Eve is identified with the "will to life" and Adam with the "will to freedom," where the latter is perceived as "the higher, more rarefied manifestation" of the former (RT 60). Furthermore, Eve is identified with Adam's "lower self" *(nafs sufla)* (QF 125), symbolized by the fig tree from which he ate, a symbol that ultimately stands for the "soul that incites to evil" *(al-nafs 'l-ammara)* (AJi 18). If Eve is the *nafs,* which is identified with density and darkness, Adam is the *ruh* (spirit), which is identified with rarefaction and light. Adam or man is hence placed on a higher spiritual plane than Eve or woman, a belief that Taha expresses most dramatically through his image of the order of descent of the expellees from paradise after man's disobedience to God: first Satan (owing to the greater degree of his spiritual grossness *(kathafa),* followed by Eve (owing to the greater degree of her spiritual grossness relative to Adam), then Adam (RT 77). In another place Taha re-expresses this spiritual hierarchy in terms of the descent of the divine essence and its self-manifestation through creation: God's descent to the rank of name is identified with the Perfect Man, and His descent to the rank of attribute is identified with the Perfect Woman (RMii 39). Taha, like his Sufi predecessors, usually uses the term *al-insan 'l-kamil* (the Perfect Man) in an ungendered sense, and it is only in this instance that he departs from ungendered usage in referring to the Perfect Woman. Furthermore, he makes the claim that the Perfect Woman is closer to the "simplicity" *(sarafa)* of the divine essence—a claim that flies in the face of the logic of the order of descent he suggests here and is not compatible with his other claims.

Taha presents Muslim women with a radical vision of legal equality that removes the historical shari'a disabilities imposed on them. Yet, ultimately, his vision is not about dismantling patriarchy, for he replaces "legal subordination" with a theory of "spiritual and moral subordination" that endows masculinity with greater spiritual and moral worth. Masculinity is primary and perceived as a source of creation and action-expression, whereas femininity is secondary and perceived as a site of creation and action-reception.[58]

The Second Message

What Taha advocates as the second message of Islam is a project of economic, political, and social change that draws on the liberal tradition on the one hand and the socialist and particularly Marxist tradition on the other. He insists, however, that his real frame of reference is Qur'anic or, more precisely, early Qur'anic—that is, the early Meccan revelations that were later abrogated by Medinan revelations.

The case for a second message is based on five assumptions. First, it is possible, indeed necessary, to revive (or, as it were, to de-abrogate) abrogated parts of the Qur'an. This is a very revolutionary and radical assumption because it runs counter to the historical consensus on the basis of which Muslims founded their legal, social, and political systems. Second, one can and must apply an evaluative or appraisive measure in the light of which earlier Meccan revelations would be deemed as "higher" than later Medinan revelations. Third, Meccan revelations were revealed in the full divine foreknowledge that they were inappropriate for their time and place; God took this exceptional measure "so that mankind can have no argument [*hujja*] against God."[59] Fourth, the Arab community of seventh-century Arabia that received the revelation did, as far as the Qur'an was concerned, represent the rest of humankind; in addressing them, God addressed all humankind. Fifth, humankind is now in need of, and ripe for, the early message of the Qur'an, which represents the only path through which men can solve their problems and realize their salvation.

The theory of a second message and the claim that abrogation can be reversed in favor of the earlier revelations raises the crucial questions of agency and authority: if there is a second message, and as a message requires a messenger (*rasul*), who then is its messenger? If parts of the Qur'an are to be abrogated and their rulings superseded, who then has the authority to perform such a task?

In tackling the first question, Taha's answer is inconsistent. Initially, he affirms that Muhammad is the messenger of both the first and second messages. Although the Prophet elaborated on the first message, he left the sec-

ond on a generalized level, and all that is required now is a fresh understanding of the Qur'an that uncovers the specifics of the second message
(RT 17, DH 34). Yet Taha also expressed the more radical view that the messenger of the second message is "a man to whom God has imparted an understanding of the Qur'an and has granted the authority to divulge [this
understanding]" (RT 11). To substantiate this claim he argues that the crucial verse, 33:40, which declares the end of "prophecy" *(nubuwwa)*, does not
likewise bring "messengerhood" *(risala)* to an end (RT 10). The ending of
prophecy has an objective reason and a subjective one. Objectively,
prophecy had to be concluded once the entirety of the Qur'an was revealed
to Muhammad—the "Qur'an" being a continuing revelation that started
with Adam and culminated with Muhammad, and encompassing all that
God wished to communicate to humankind. Subjectively, the ending of
prophecy meant that each human being has become the subject of divine
address—prophetic agency and election are replaced by a diffusion and
"democratization" of divine communion. The implication of this is that
prophecy is dispensable and bound to come to an end when humankind
reaches a certain point of maturity, but "messengerhood" is indispensable
and continuous. In accounting for Taha's initial circumspect stance and his
subsequent, more contentious position, it is possible that the secular, anti-
clerical shift of the early 1970s in the Sudan and the relative freedom and
expansion that his ideas and the Jumhuri movement enjoyed during that
period encouraged him to advance a more radical position. His aggressive
campaigns against the *'ulama'* and his constant disparagement of what he
described as the regressive and obscurantist nature of their ideas was an indirect way of asserting his own authority. But as far as he was concerned
(and for that matter as far as his followers were concerned), the ultimate
source of his authority was his claim and belief that through his mystical
experience he could engage in his *mi'raj* (ascent), meet God, and realize his
authenticity. It was by virtue of realizing this spiritual station *(maqam)* that
he was granted the *idhn* (permission, authority) to suspend the first message and call for the immediate implementation of the second message.
Taha's sense of his own special status and authority was extended to his followers, whom he perceived as the *ghuraba'* (the unfamiliar, the outsiders)
indicated by the prophetic tradition (DI 51).

A key theme in Taha's work is what he describes as the renewal of *tawhid*, or, as he puts it metaphorically, "the raising of the mast of *tawhid* to a new height" (RU 8). He uses the term *tawhid* in its ordinary sense of "unity" and "oneness" but also as shorthand for the doctrine of the Unity of Being. The notion of oneness is expressed in Islam through the formulaic expression of *La Ilaha ila 'l-Llah* (There is no god but God), which, according to Taha, is the center around which the whole of the Qur'an (and for that matter every religion) revolves (LL 11). The expression, in turn, has a center, namely, the word "God," but "God" is an abstraction that can only be grasped through the mediation of the formulaic expression. Taha holds that the very structure of the expression, involving negation and affirmation, underlines the nature of the dialectical movement that must be followed in order to reach God because Truth is neither in the act of negation nor in the act of affirmation (QF 37).

The new level of *tawhid* to which Taha refers is a reformulation of the doctrine of the Unity of Being in terms of an emphasis of a "unity of agency" *(wahdat 'l-fa'il)*, the central notion in Taha's thought. Yet, this notion remains a mere abstraction that has no bearing on Taha's radical program of economic, political, and social transformation rooted in a deep belief in and a conscious mobilization of a free human agency that reshapes history and directs it.

Socialism

The society of the second message is the society of Islam and Muslims in the ultimate sense of these words. This is a society whose hallmarks are the constitutional nature of its legal system and its three equalities, that is to say, the prevalence of economic, political, and social equalities. As a "good society" *(mujtama' salih)*, it represents one of two vital elements through which man can realize the unity of his divided self—the other being an "educational, knowledge-based approach through which the individual strives to liberate his natural potential from (the grip of) deep-rooted fear" (RT 143). Besides being law based, this society is also characterized by the liberal nature of its public opinion that celebrates individual and social diversity.

Taha stresses that the struggle between the "haves" and the "have-nots" will never cease until complete equality is achieved, and he further stresses that economic equality or socialism is the foundation on which other equalities rest. He defines socialism in its most basic sense as "the communal sharing of the wealth of the earth," and, like other Islamist thinkers who tried to situate socialism in an Islamic framework, he quotes in this respect a tradition according to which the Prophet said, "People share three in common: water, pasture, and fire." Although the tradition lays the foundation of Islam's socialist perspective, it expresses what Taha describes as a form of "primitive socialism" (DI 22). In identifying the socialism he advocates, he notably does not use the expression "Islamic socialism,"[60] but rather, à la Marx, "scientific socialism."[61] He is, however, quick to distance himself from Marx, whose atheism, in Taha's view, deals his entire system a fatal blow and renders his socialism "unscientific." Whereas in Marxism any socialism that grounds itself in religion is "idealistic" and hence "unscientific," Taha contends that Islam is a unique case among religions owing to its scientific nature: Islam provides a scientific method—that is, prayer and worship—by means of which one can realize one's liberation, and the second message is a scientific level of Islam that goes beyond mere belief to a higher, "scientific" *iqan* (certainty)-based realization.

Although Taha acknowledges the role of class struggle in history and the class basis of socialism, he does not seem to base his socialism on the interests of a particular class or a particular class alliance. He seems to think of socialism as a universal program that commands universal consensus, offering a dream that exercises equal pull on everyone. Although he acknowledges that legislation and planning are vital instruments in the building of socialism, he places a special emphasis on the moral element or the power of *damir* (conscience). When he deals with legislation, he exhibits an unmistakably condescending attitude: legislation is but a lower phase of regulation and education designed to help individuals evolve toward a higher phase where their actions are governed by morality (DI 31–32). On the basis of a simplistic assumption that fails to recognize morality outside religion, Taha asserts that the vital role played by moral sensibility is conclusive proof of the superiority of the socialism of the second message over Marxist socialism because men ultimately need a moral rather than a material incentive to produce surplus under a socialist economy.

Taha asserts that socialism is based on increased productivity on the one hand and equitable distribution of wealth on the other. There should be a minimum income that all citizens, including children, enjoy, and a maximum income not so high as to lead to the creation of an upper class.[62] Private ownership of the sources of production and its means should not be allowed. Private property is limited to "one's house and its surrounding garden, one's furniture, a car, and so on. There will be no exploitative use of another citizen's toil to increase one's income" (RT 147). Ownership is predicated on "use value," and the ultimate ownership of objects is vested in God and the community.

The increase of productivity in a socialist society leads to an increase in minimum and maximum incomes, but this should be managed in a manner of positive discrimination designed to bridge the income gap between those at the bottom and those at the top. Through this gradual process, income and class distinctions will ultimately be abolished and "full equality" be achieved. This full equality is the higher stage of communism (RT 147).

Taha claims that Muhammad lived in fact on a "communistic" level that made him stand apart from the members of his community. Whereas these members were required to spend a small percentage of what they owned (i.e., the *zakat* tax that Taha describes as "lesser *zakat*"), the Prophet lived on the level of what Taha describes as "greater *zakat*" (i.e., giving all that exceeded his immediate needs). The members of the formative community lived (and Muslims have since been living) in accordance with verse 9:103, which enjoins, "Of their wealth take alms [*sadaqa*], that so thou mightest purify and sanctify them." By contrast, the Prophet lived in accordance with verse 2:219, which says, "They will question thee concerning what they should expend. Say: 'The abundance [*al-'afw*].' " It is this verse and more specifically the word *'afw* that constitutes the Qur'anic basis of Taha's claim that Islam is socialistic and ultimately communistic.

The term *'afw* plays a central role in Taha's social thought. Classical exegetes disagreed on what the term meant. Al-Tabari provides us with several views that fall into a general category and a specific one. In the first category the following propositions are suggested for *'afw*: (1) giving what remains as surplus (*fadl*) after one's need is satisfied; (2) spending a small amount of what one possesses; (3) spending a small or substantial amount of what one possesses; and (4) spending moderately. In the second category the meaning of *'afw* assumes a narrower sense: one view identifies it with the specified *zakat* tax while another view shifts the focus to the quality of what is given, suggesting that *'afw* is about giving the best of what one possesses.[63] Among modern exegetes, Muhammad 'Abduh understands the term essentially in terms of "spending from one's surplus." He is not against a loose identification of the term with *zakat* (because *zakat* comes out of one's surplus), but he views it chiefly as an extra-*zakat* public tax or voluntary spending.[64] Another modern exegete, al-Tabataba'i, asserts that the term indicates "moderation in spending."[65]

Taha adopts the view that *'afw* is about giving the "surplus" *(fadl)*—that is, one's wealth or income beyond the minimum needed for subsistence. He strongly opposes saving such a surplus, basing this position on his claim that when prayer reaches its spiritual peak it then, in itself, becomes the means of one's *rizq,* or sustenance (see chapter 2). He frequently stresses that the question of *rizq* is at the very root of shirk (associationism), or as he puts it, "It has been said that man escapes his [*ajal*] (appointed time of death) and runs after his *rizq*. In reality, both *ajal* and *rizq* continually pursue man. Man cannot escape his *ajal,* nor can he escape his *rizq*. When man's certainty [*yaqin*] in God is complete, he knows that he will receive what was predestined for him to receive, even if he escapes from it" (RS 72). Muhammad, for whom *rizq* was no source of worry, was the paragon of this *yaqin*-infused consciousness. When the Prophet's companions wanted to perform voluntary fasting as much as he did, he forbade them and told them, "I am not like you, for God provides me with food and drink." Taha comments on this saying, "Of course he was not given [familiar food or drink]. He received the lights of certainty. It is by virtue of these lights that the difficulties of this life became insignificant in his eyes and it was easy for him to give all that was in excess of his immediate need without caring about what the future held, placing his complete trust in God" (QF 57). Taha argues that what the Prophet really wanted was a society where the poor had a right to economic equality rather than the humiliating pittance of *zakat* (RU 22–23). He highlights Muhammad's reportedly scornful attitude toward the *zakat*, which he described as "the filth of others."[66] It should be noted that Taha's image of a "communistic" and propertyless

Muhammad flies in the face of the historical Muhammad of the *sira* and the hadith material.[67]

In chapter 4 we have already seen Taha's use of verse 39:74 in connection with the notion of a "heavenly earth" or an "earthly paradise" that he identifies with the advent of Islamic communism. He asserts that the communism Marx foresaw and dreamed of could only be realized through the second message of Islam. The earthly paradise Taha foresees and dreams of is, according to him, captured by verses 15:45–48, which say, "But the god-fearing shall be amidst gardens and fountains: 'Enter you them, in peace and security!' We shall strip away all rancour that is in their breasts; as brothers they shall be upon couches set face to face; no fatigue there shall smite them, neither shall they ever be driven forth from there."

Yet these eschatological verses on which Taha forces an earthly context do not, after all, serve as an accurate reflection of what will ultimately befall men on earth. Here, Taha has to adjust his vision to the conventional Islamic portrayal of what will happen before the end of time. Men will end up being "driven forth from" their "earthly paradise," as "there will come a time in the future when humankind, having reached the peak of its achievement, starts to decline and [the verses of the first message] will be revived. . . . The human condition will inexorably degenerate until the hour comes and ruin prevails" (AJi 49). Taha's vision, however, does not lose its optimism, because this apocalyptic catastrophe is nothing but the birth of a new phase in man's journey to meet God.

Democracy

The provenance of Taha's concept of democracy is Western liberalism. However, ideologically, he owes more to a tradition that he never acknowledges, that is, the tradition of social democracy. Social democracy grew out of a revisionist rethinking of Marxism, rejecting violence and revolution as instruments of social change and advocating an evolutionary transition from capitalism to socialism through peaceful, democratic means.[68]

Taha points out that democracy, like socialism, is about the struggle between the "haves" and the "have-nots," but in the political rather than the economic domain. Stressing the *ought* aspect of the second message he insists that democracy and socialism are inseparable; they are "the two wings" without which society cannot fly. He defines democracy in terms of the following set of principles:

1. There is equality among all citizens;
2. Individuals are valued above the state;
3. The government acts in the service of the people;
4. Rule of law prevails;
5. The government relies on reason and accumulated experience;
6. While the majority rules, the rights of the minority are respected; and
7. Democratic procedures and means are employed to realize ends. (RT 151–52)

Yet, in the final analysis, democratic institutions and procedures are not an end in themselves but a means to realize the "dignity of man." This means that it is the second principle that constitutes the heart of democracy, for it is the individual who is the ultimate end. Both macrodemocracy and microdemocracy should complement each other: democracy should operate not only on the level of government but should also extend to become no less than a comprehensive way of life, permeating individual and family life and all the formations of civil society.

The greatest virtue of democracy is that its style of government allows individuals to learn and develop. Taha places a very high value on this characteristic owing to his belief that learning from one's mistakes is the best educational method. He contends that because under dictatorship citizens cannot act freely or take initiative, their intellectual, emotional, and moral development is stymied. Democracy, by contrast, is the only system that allows for a full development of one's potential because, in essence, it is "the right to err." Taha contends that the democratic ideal finds its highest expression in the prophetic tradition according to which, should humans fail to make errors and ask God for His forgiveness, God will put them away and bring a new creation of people who commit errors, ask for His forgiveness, and be forgiven. Although evidently the tradition is God centered in that its ultimate emphasis is on divine forgiveness, Taha shifts the tradition's center and emphasis to man and his erroneousness. This of course does not mean that one is supposed to commit errors for the sake of it. What Taha says in this respect intermeshes with the centrality of freedom and the necessity of carrying the existential burden of freedom seriously, or as he puts it, "Freedom implies choice between several paths of action. One cannot really act democratically unless one learns how to choose well and to correct the errors of choice one makes every now and then" (RT 152–53).

In considering the early period of Islam, Taha stresses the failure of the community of the *mu'minun* to be responsive to the democratic ideal. He contends that the ideal of free action and choice was encapsulated in verses 88:21–22, which say (addressing Muhammad), "Then remind them! Thou art only a reminder; thou art not charged to oversee them." The ideal was, however, withdrawn in favor of a guardianship instituted by verse 3:159, which says (again addressing Muhammad), "So pardon them, and pray forgiveness for them, and take counsel with them in the affair [*wa shawirhum fi 'l-amri*]; and when thou art resolved, put thy trust in God." The *shura* (consultation) process mentioned in this verse and verse 42:38 was identified by some modern Muslim thinkers with democracy, a view that Taha dismisses.

Taha views *shura* as a descent *(tanazzul)* from democracy and as such it operates on the subsidiary level of the earlier community. The *shura* to which the Qur'an referred and which the Prophet practiced did not bring into being a democratic system where the view of the majority was binding; rather, the *shura* was a consultative, optional act on the Prophet's part. The level of that community made it imperative that the Prophet exercise over them what Taha describes as the "rule of the rightly guided individual" and, as such, *shura* was "the rule of the mature [*rashid*] over the immature or the legally minor [*qasir*]" (DJ 26). Through the exercise of *shura*, the community was destined, in Taha's view, to reach eventually the mature level of democracy.[69]

Although Taha can see that there is an intrinsic incompatibility between the notions of individual freedom and guardianship, he is willing to make an exception in the case of Muhammad. In justifying this, he gives subjective criteria based on Muhammad's "higher moral rank" and "personal perfection," which provide the necessary safeguards against abuse of power. This raises on the theoretical level the following question: if Muhammad's guardianship is justifiable on account of his unique status, then what should happen, Islamically, after his demise? The clear and logical implication of Taha's theory is that no one else should have been entrusted with a guardianship over the community—not even Abu Bakr "who was at the forefront of the *mu'minun* community, yet the gulf between him and the Prophet was so vast" (RT 138).

Taha, however, does not apply his theory consistently. In assessing the caliphate after the Prophet's death, he applies a traditional perspective based on a simplistic distinction between *din* (religious, otherworldly commitment) and *dunya* (materialist, this-worldly commitment). Accordingly, the caliphates of Abu Bakr, 'Umar, and the early period of 'Uthman were committed to *din*, 'Ali's attempt to restore the regime of *din* failed, and with the triumph of Mu'awiya the regime of *dunya* gained mastery and the caliphate assumed the nature of "ravenous domination" *(mulk 'adud)*, as a prophetic tradition had purportedly predicted (TM 30). What Taha says in this respect shows a clear approval of the earlier period of the rightly guided caliphs despite the fact that his theory does not allow for their guardianship. Indeed, what his theory implies leads to a more extreme position than that of the Shi'ites, for as they would recognize the contested caliphate of 'Ali as the only legitimate caliphate, Taha's position would imply that the entire history of the caliphate was based on illegitimate guardianship.

When Taha speaks about "the rule of law" under democracy, he usually stresses the constitutional aspect. He defines constitutional law in terms of reconciling the seemingly incompatible claims of the individual and his society. For him the individual sees his primary interest in terms of stressing the value of freedom, whereas society perceives this interest in terms of giving priority to the value of justice; it is only constitutional law that can resolve this conflict. Constitutional law performs the dual function of reconciling these two values on the one hand and curbing abusive individuals on the other. Taha's constitutionalism is informed by a social democratic ideal that insists on the fusion of the individual and the social, the political, and the economic, democracy and socialism. It is on the basis of this ideal that he attacks both bourgeois "capitalistic democracy" and "communist democracy," for under the former, genuine democratic rights are open to the abuse and manipulation of the power of capital, and under the latter the rights and freedoms of individuals are trampled upon.

Despite what Taha says about democracy in earlier Qur'anic revelations, his ultimate ideal is the direct democracy of Greece. This is a "people's democracy" *(dimuqratiyya sha'biyya)* that embodies Abraham Lincoln's definition of democracy as "the rule of the people, by the people, for the people." Representative democracy falls short of the ideal because a majority bloc in a representative assembly could be voted in by nonmajority votes and because bills could be passed by the simple majority of those who attend sessions. Despite these drawbacks, Taha argues that representative democracy is a necessary stage paving the way for direct democracy (UD 18–19).

Taha's dream of a "federal, democratic, socialist" republic in the Sudan, outlined in a draft constitution he wrote in 1955 on the eve of independence, did not materialize. It is clear that the historical moment of independence charged him with a sense of great exhilaration and optimism. He views his document as a "Qur'an-based constitution" that the Sudanese could offer as a "global ideal" for the government of the rule of law. But what about the argument that democracy requires a high degree of literacy and political maturity and hence the Sudanese were still "not ready" for enjoying democratic rights and shouldering the responsibilities of a democratic polity? In responding to this, Taha offered his most convincing defense of democracy. He acknowledged that the Sudanese were "backward," particularly in rural areas, and that they were therefore in need of education, but he pointed out that this education cannot be entrusted to an absolutist regime because the educational policies of such a regime cannot teach people to value freedom. He asserts that the surest way to educate a nation is to "make it confront its problems and provide it with the chance to learn through trial and error" (UD 23).

Taha's own stance after independence was not consistent with his earlier, preindependence, unconditional commitment to democracy. His antagonism to the sectarian politics of the Ansar and the Khatmiyya was so intense that he was willing to contemplate the suspension of democracy by a secular military regime for the sake of undermining these forces. His reaction to the deficiencies and failures of Sudanese democracy turned into a harsh judgment, holding that the Sudanese needed a further period of reeducation to free them of sectarianism before they were ready for democracy. This effectively meant falling back on the notion of *wisaya* (guardianship) despite his assertion that it should no longer be operative.

Social Equality

Economic and political equalities lead to social equality, which Taha views as "the most difficult of equalities" and the crowning achievement of the civilizing process (RT 155). The basis of social equality is the total elimination of distinctions on account of birth, race, color, religion, or gender. Taha places social equality firmly at the heart of man's moral evolution from a lower, coercion-oriented moral sense and conduct to a higher, justice-oriented moral sense and conduct. Elaborating on this, he says, "The absence of discrimination against the vulnerable and the elimination of the distinctions between individuals and classes that arose out of the law of the jungle is the main task of the civilizing process *(tamadyun)*. A civilized society is a society where the rights of the vulnerable are safeguarded and respected, where women are free, protected, and honored, and where children are accorded rights, provided with care, and loved" (RT 157).

In demonstrating the Qur'anic basis of social equality, Taha cites verse 49:13, which declares, "O mankind, We have created you male and female, and appointed you races and tribes, that you may know one another. Surely the noblest among you [*akramakum*] in the sight of God is the most god-fearing of you [*atqakum*]." In reading the verse, he stresses that *karama* (nobility in the sight of God) hinges on knowledge *('ilm)* and moral character *(khulq)* because *taqwa* (piety, the state of godfearingness) is, after all, "[right] knowledge and [right] action informed by this knowledge" (RT 156). A problem that can evidently be raised in connection with the verse is that of the locus of human dignity: is man's worth and dignity rooted in his mere humanity, or in the quality of *taqwa*, that is, his relationship to God? Taha seems to say both. On the one hand, he emphasizes the values of *taqwa*, right knowledge, and right action. But on the other, he celebrates "the individual human being . . . even if he were mentally retarded" as the ultimate end (RT 156).

Taha elaborates on the role played by knowledge through his discussion of the respective roles of education *(ta'lim)* and cultural cultivation *(tar-*

biyya). Education aims at providing the individual with the knowledge, training, and skills that are required to achieve a specialization through which he or she contributes to the community. Distinctions of specialization, however, should not induce social distinctions. An element to which Taha attaches special importance in the schooling of every individual is the development of a manual skill. In his view, working with one's hands is important not only "as a means of earning a livelihood but, more notably, [as a means through which one brings] the brain, the eye, and the hand [into unity and harmony]. This will lead to the integration of those human forces through the unity of which life realizes its perfection, that is, the mind, the heart, and the body" (TK 8).

This unificatory function and objective of manual activity on the level of acquiring an educational skill overlaps with the broad objective of cultivating individuals. Whereas education is essentially about specialization and hence involves fragmentation, cultivation is about restoring one's wholeness. Cultivatory activity seeks to "liberate one's natural talents, namely the mind and the heart, from the bondage of deception and fallacies. When the heart is free of fear and when the mind is free of deception, then thought and feeling come to full life" (RT 159). This "fullness of life" is the ultimate objective of cultivation. On a more immediate and practical level, however, cultivation is about "civility" or socially responsible, proper, sensitive, and refined conduct.

Islam is presented by Taha through a dual perspective. On one level, it is ahistorical; it is the primordial and natural religion of humans from the moment of creation, so much so that all religious expressions are perceived as "degrees" of Islam. This ahistorical character is projected onto the future, and hence man ultimately meets God through Islam. What he describes as "the peak of the pyramid of Islam" will always be an unattainable and unrealizable spiritual state—beyond man in the realm of eternity and posteternity (RT 161). On another level, though, Islam is historical, and by virtue of this historicity it assumes a changeable and mutable nature that allows it not only to respond to the needs of past societies but also to the more complex needs of present-day global societies. As a first message, Islam operated on the level of the "subsidiary": it denied the polytheists their religious freedom and instituted jihad, it accepted a measure of discrimination against women, and it tolerated slavery and class distinctions. As a second message, Islam operates on the level of the "essential," embracing economic, political, and social equality. This is the original message that Muhammad envisaged from the start but history militated against it.

Taha's second message of Islam is in effect a paradigmatic shift. The traditional Islamic paradigm that privileges the prophetic moment that is seen as the culmination of human salvation history is rejected in favor of a paradigm that privileges a future moment. The golden age does not lie in the past but rather the future, when the second message is fully realized and when "the earth will be filled with equity and justice as it has been filled with inequity and injustice, and peace will prevail among all creatures" (AJii 64).

6 ✍

Evolution, Shari'a, and Art

THIS CHAPTER FOCUSES on three seemingly disparate though interconnected themes that are accorded varying degrees of importance in Taha's work. Taha's thought was greatly influenced by the notion of evolution; both his theory of prayer and his theory of a second message of Islam rest on an evolutionary assumption and scheme. In the case of prayer, the evolutionary process takes the form of an upward movement from collective spirituality to individual spirituality, from imitation to authenticity, from fragmentation to unity, from mediated communion to direct communion. Likewise, evolutionary logic is central in the formulation of the second message theory that conceives human history in terms of a progressive, spiral, upward movement from simplicity to complexity, from "lower" civilizational rungs to "higher" ones, from social conflict to social harmony, from the society of "believers" to the society of "Muslims." This evolutionary perspective provided Taha with the necessary foundation to reform some aspects of shari'a.

Although Taha did not deal with aesthetic subjects systematically, his mystical grounding made him open to the problem of conceptualizing and experiencing beauty. In September 1968 he gave a public talk to the staff and students of the College of Fine and Applied Art in Khartoum that was transcribed and later published. In the course of this talk he made his most serious effort to articulate an aesthetic theory and reconcile fine and other arts with shari'a. Owing to the increasing importance of the arts in modern Muslim societies and the special problems they pose for shari'a, a separate section in this chapter is devoted to the question of arts.

179

Modern Muslims and the Theory of Evolution

Regarding Charles Darwin's theory of evolution, modern Muslim thinkers fall into two camps: a majority camp that rejects evolution totally and denounces it and a minority camp that accepts it.[1] Taha belongs to the latter group.

One of the earliest opponents of evolutionary theory was Jamal al-Din al-Afghani (d. 1897). In 1879 he produced a book in Persian that came to be better known by its Arabic title, *al-Radd 'ala 'l-dahriyyin* ("The Refutation of the Materialists"), in which he devotes a section to an attack on Darwinism. Al-Afghani did not read Darwin, and his knowledge of Darwin's theory was based on secondary sources. In a short paragraph, he gives an outline of Darwinism as a theory stating that humans descend from apes and that successive centuries of evolution made them reach the stage of the higher ape orangutan from which humankind eventually sprang. Scoffing at Darwin, he says that "according to [his] view it would be possible that after the passage of centuries a mosquito could change into an elephant and an elephant, gradually, could change into a mosquito."[2] He did not accept factors such as the environment, or heredity, or geological timescales as plausible conditions for evolution. Above all and more importantly from his religious standpoint, the failure of Darwinism to see design and final purpose in nature instead of "blind necessity" was sufficient to demonstrate its falsity.[3]

Al-Afghani attacked Darwin in the context of a ferocious onslaught on materialists, past and present, particularly the ideas of his Indian contemporary Sayyid Ahmad Khan (d. 1898).[4] Sayyid Ahmad Khan was a modernist thinker who pursued a wide range of intellectual activities and was highly receptive to the ideas of modern science, which he eagerly wanted to reconcile to Islam. He was a man of remarkable intellectual independence and boldness. By virtue of his independence he refused to be shackled by the authority of Qur'anic literalism, hadith, or *fiqh*, and by virtue of his boldness he "was able to subject these to rational criticism, [rejecting] from them all that was in conflict with logic and nature."[5]

In reading the Qur'an, Sayyid Ahmad Khan adopted a metaphorical approach, strictly subjecting the scripture to the rationally proven truths of science and not allowing for any contradiction between the two. It was in the light of this approach that he read the biblico-Qur'anic stories of the Creation or the Flood or the miracles of Jesus as folkloric narratives that the scriptures had to resort to in order to "address the people among whom [they were] revealed . . . within [a] framework comprehensible to them."[6] Consequently, he argued that the Adam and Eve story is not meant to be taken literally; rather, the Fall is a metaphor about attaining moral maturity by virtue of being able to distinguish between good and evil. Adam and Eve are, hence, not real individuals but symbolic entities that stand for humankind. On the basis of such an understanding, a believing Muslim should have no quarrel with Darwin's theory of evolution.

Although Muhammad 'Abduh translated al-Afghani's *Refutation of Materialists* into Arabic in 1885, he himself expressed a more accommodating position on evolution than his master. In commenting on verse 4:1, which affirms the creation of humans from a "single soul" and "its mate," he dismisses the traditional interpretation that the references here are to Adam and Eve. In undermining this reading he deploys the claims of modern scholars and a particular traditional Islamic claim:

> There are people who do not know Adam and Eve and have never heard of them. . . . It was the Hebrews who claimed a continuous history uniting mankind with Adam and assigning for this history a recent time frame. . . . [Modern] knowledge and research dispute the Hebrew historical perspective. We Muslims are not obligated to believe in this history even if attributed to Moses because we do not trust that it is part of the Torah and has remained unaltered since the time of Moses.[7]

In the light of verse 2:251, which declares (after a description of the encounter between David and Goliath), "Had God not driven back the people, some by the means of others, the earth had surely corrupted," 'Abduh is willing to accept key evolutionary notions such as struggle for survival, survival of the fittest, and natural selection.

An early strong advocate of evolution was the Egyptian Isma'il Mazhar (d. 1962), who produced the first Arabic translation of Darwin's *The Origin of Species*. Mazhar was introduced to Darwinism by Shibli al-Shumayyil (d. 1917), a Lebanese of Christian background whose writings were controversial on account of his vigorous promotion of an evolutionary materialism.[8]

Mazhar did not embrace al-Shumayyil's materialism and was in fact at pains to show that the theory of evolution does not undermine faith. He stressed that the theory does not deal with the origins of life or make claims about its generation as being spontaneous or that its ultimate nature is materialistic. Adopting a teleological position and maintaining that the materialist standpoint is intrinsically incapable of explaining the essence of life, he aligns himself with the vitalistic views of Alfred R. Wallace, the codiscoverer of natural selection.[9]

This insistence that the theory of evolution is compatible with religious faith is also expressed by the Egyptian Muhammad Farid Wajdi (d. 1954), whose writings manifested a consistent preoccupation with the relationship between religion and science. His approach, however, is more akin to that of 'Abduh as he rereads certain Qur'anic verses in the light of evolutionary notions such as natural selection and survival of the fittest.[10] A similarly accommodating position was expressed by two Shi'ite scholars, namely, the Lebanese Husain al-Jisr (d. 1909) and the Iraqi Muhammad Rida al-Isfahani (d. 1943).[11]

This accommodative spirit was in stark contrast with a creationist position inspired by al-Afghani's earlier vehement attack on Darwinism. At the forefront was the prestigious and conservative al-Azhar University, which usually expresses the majority views of Sunnite orthodoxy. In one of his fatwas, the influential Mahmud Shaltut, the rector of al-Azhar from 1958 until his death in 1963 and noted for his liberal views on many issues, said the following about the theory of evolution:

> The theory of evolution . . . is not spurned by [Muslim] clerics out of prejudice or bigotry. Rather, they refute it on the basis of what is clearly affirmed by the scripture and on the basis of the religious principle to reject what has not been substantiated by proof or verified by experiment. What the Qur'an says about the creation of humans is clearly stated as it spoke about the creation of the first human, of the substance from which he was created, of the creation of his offspring, and of what substance they were and how they were. . . . This is what God veraciously states and it has been supported by miracles. God tells us that humans were created as an independent species that did not evolve out of another animal species. . . . If

humans were created through evolution out of another species, then it follows that what the Qurʾan says about human creation does not conform to the truth and is incompatible with reality.[12]

The thinkers of the popularly based and politically influential al-Ikhwan 'l-Muslimun (the Muslim Brothers) movement threw their weight behind the anti-Darwinist position. In his vitriolic denunciation of some Western thinkers, the contemporary Egyptian Muhammad Qutb saves his bitterest attack for Darwin, who is projected as the head of a philosophical trinity of evil whose other persons are Marx and Freud. Qutb argues that Darwin is the root of evil in modern Western civilization because his theory degrades humans by reducing them to animals.[13] Both Marx and Freud built on this Darwinian "animalization"—with Marx's historical materialism reducing human beings to "economic animals" motivated by the quest to satisfy their material wants and Freud's psychoanalysis reducing them to "sexual animals" driven by libidinal forces. Hence, for Qutb, the rejection of Darwinism is synonymous with the rejection of materialism and the affirmation of the humanity and uniqueness of humans as, essentially, spiritual and moral beings.[14]

The contemporary Iranian scholar Seyyed Hossein Nasr holds the same intense hostility toward Darwin, Marx, and Freud, although he shows a far greater degree of academic sophistication in dealing with their ideas. He attacks evolution as having "erased the final vestiges of Divine Wisdom from the face of nature and removed whatever ultimate significance natural forms might have by denying all ultimateness and finality and reducing all forms simply to a cross section of the stream of time and flow and process of matter."[15] Although he views evolution as "no more than a scientific hypothesis that has been parading itself for the past century as a scientific fact"[16] and as "metaphysically impossible and logically absurd,"[17] he nevertheless recognizes the great challenge it poses and wants to see a "serious and widely known Islamic response of a metaphysical and intellectual nature to the hypothesis of evolution."[18] This Islamic response involves the establishment of what Nasr describes as an "Islamic science." But what is this Islamic science and what characterizes it? Nasr characterizes it vaguely as a science that does not derive from human reason but rather from "the intellect, which is Divine" because, ultimately, the "seat of intellect is the heart rather than the head."[19]

The Evolutionism of Taha

While accepting the theory of evolution, Taha resituates it within a creationist framework, as his starting point is the Qur'anic creation story. His parting of ways with Muslim thinkers who reject evolution is his understanding of the nature of the Fall.

Despite his adoption on one level of Ibn 'Arabi's notion of the Unity of Being in the sense of conceiving all that exists *(wujud)* as a manifestation of God, Taha is willing, on another level, to anthropomorphize the unity of being and conceive all that exists as a manifestation of the human. Accordingly, he perceives humankind and the nature of all that exists in the following terms: "The human is an animal who has attained a special status of worthiness by virtue of reason [*'aql*]. Humankind is still evolving, and there will be no end of its evolution as it moves up the scale of perfection eternally. Animals also move up this scale, but the utmost they can realize is to reach the lowest degree of humanity. As such, the difference between the human and the animal is not of kind but rather of degree. . . . There is nothing in created existence but the human. All that we see and do not see in this existence is the human in different and successive [evolutionary] stages" (RS 10).

Taha perceives human evolution as falling into four broad stages: the first is purely organic, the second is marked by the emergence of living organisms, and the third is characterized by the appearance of humans on the scene of life. He holds that humankind is currently in the last phase of this third evolutionary stage. The fourth stage, which he describes as "the stage of perfection" *(marhalat 'l-kamal),* will come into existence with the rise of the sixth and seventh senses.

The first stage is indicated in the verse 21:30, which describes cosmic beginnings in terms of acts of *ratq* (contracting) and *fatq* (spreading out) involving the heavens and the earth. The contracted stuff of this verse is further indicated by verse 41:11, which describes God lifting himself to heaven "when it was smoke *(dukhan).*" Commenting on this, Taha says,

"Smoke here means water in a vaporized state as the heavens and the earth were a contracted gaseous cloud that was then spread out" (RS 11). The seed of humankind is to be found in the atoms of this gas.

Hence, the second stage—out of inorganic, inanimate material came organic matter and life as we know it: organisms that grow, move, metabolize, reproduce, feed, respire, and excrete. At the very bottom of this stage are the unicellular organisms and with their emergence "a new, extraordinary era was launched: the era of life and death" (RS 11). At the top of the evolutionary scale of the second stage stand the mammals. But can Taha cite any Qur'anic support for what he borrows from evolutionary theory? In this respect he cites three verses. The first is verse 15:26, which tells us about the stuff from which the human was created, "Surely We created man of a clay of mud moulded." In reading this verse, Taha blends human and cosmic beginnings: the primordial mud was exposed to the heat of the sun and thus hardened and turned into clay and that is "because the earth was part of the sun and on separating from it started to cool, solidify, and develop the conditions that sustain life" (RS 11). It was when this earthly stage was set that "life out of water and mud" emerged. This, in his view, is intimated by verses 76:1–2, which read, "Has there come on man a while of time when he was a thing unremembered? We created man of a sperm-drop, mingling, trying him; and we made him hearing, seeing." In reading the first verse he affirms that its mood is in fact declarative and not interrogative—the verse indicates the enormous temporal length of human evolution during the second stage. For the purpose of his reading, he bestows the term "sperm-drop" *(nutfa)* with a different denotation, that is, "clear water," and reads into the "mingling" act a connotative allusion to "mud." It is through these forced readings of these verses that Taha constructs a Qur'anic basis for the history of the evolution of life since its very beginnings till the moment when it was poised to give birth to humankind.

Taha's portrayal of the third stage involves two temporal perspectives. The first is a creationist perspective that firmly places the beginning of humankind in the divine act of creating Adam in paradise; the second is an evolutionary perspective that traces the beginning of Adam or humankind to the life processes of the second stage. The Adam to whom the Qur'anic story refers is Adam the vicegerent *(khalifa)*. Taha refers to this Adam as the

Perfect Adam *(Adam 'l-kamil)*, yet he is ambivalent about this perfection as he also refers to him as the Adam "who was created in the nearest form to perfection" (RS 12). This uncertainty on Taha's part is understandable as he has to account for Adam's capability of disobedience, a capability that detracts from his perfection as understood in religious terms. As the Qur'anic (and for that matter biblical) story tells us, this Adam was expelled from paradise and his fall is summed up in the Qur'an in verses 95:4–5 (also discussed in chapter 5 in connection with the loss of subjectivity): "We indeed created man in the fairest stature then We restored him the lowest of the low." What concerns us here is another sense that Taha bestows on the phrase "lowest of the low" *(asfala safilin)* and that he utilizes as the basis of his reconciliation of the Qur'anic creation story and the theory of evolution. He contends that this phrase indicates that the Fall was an act of "evolutionary regression": God punished Adam and Eve by sending them down the evolutionary scale to "the lowest of the low," that is, the simplest form of life, as a hydrogen atom (TK 25). This is the point where Taha weaves his temporal perspective into that of Darwinian evolution.

The Qur'an provides several descriptions of the primordial stuff from which the human was created: verse 21:30 declares, "and of water [We] fashioned every living thing," while verse 18:37 refers to human creation "of dust," and verse 15:26 asserts that the human was created "of a clay of mud moulded." Taha sees all these verses as variations that imply the unity of all creation because the ingredients mentioned in these verses can all be reduced to a hydrogen atom (QF 115). However, he moves on another level beyond the Qur'anic description of the primordial stuff in material terms to propose a spiritual stuff. Comparing the beginnings of angels and humans, he says, "[Angels] are created from the light of intellect [*nur 'l-'aql*], whereas humans are created from the light of heart [*nur 'l-qalb*], from the soul [*nafs*]" (LL 43). Taha argues for the moral excellence of humans over angels on account of their freedom to err. This claim is reinforced here by a further claim of an excellence of origin.

What verse 95:5 says about reducing the human to the "lowest of the low" is not affirmed as a universal statement—its subsequent verse makes a significant exclusion, "save those who believe, and do righteous things; they shall have a wage unfailing." Classical exegetes understood the passage comprised of verses 95:4–6 in terms of one of two "degradations": degradation through old age and senility or degradation through unbelief. For those who upheld the first interpretation, the exclusion of "those who believe and do righteous things" is of a retrospective nature: their former deeds during the time of their physical and mental strength would be the basis of their final reward. The proponents of the second interpretation offer the straightforward view that the exclusion is an affirmation that those who believe and do good acts will reap their reward.[20]

So, how does Taha account for this exclusion despite the universal implication of his interpretation? He refers to a particular post-Fall event underlined by the Qur'an, that is, that Adam and Eve showed their contrition and asked God for His forgiveness. This was in clear contrast to Satan, who only wanted to be "[respited] till the day [humans] shall be raised" (verse 7:14). Hence, contends Taha, "when they were all sent down to [the rank of] the lowest of the low, Satan was left there and God saved Adam and his wife and guided them, thanks to their belief, on the way of return" (RS 12). This contention leaves us with two further problems. Although the Qur'anic passage is specifically about humans, Taha extends its denotation to include Satan, and, on the basis of his understanding of what "the lowest of the low" means, then Satan has to be reconceptualized as a mere hydrogen atom. Such a reconceptualization is evidently in direct contradiction with the Islamic concept of Satan as a conscious and active agency of evil with selfhood. Taha does in fact accept this traditional concept because he maintains that Satan will be the last being to leave hell before its destruction (QF 137–38).

Taha attaches a special significance to the stage when homo sapiens became homo religiosus; this coincided with the "achievement of prophethood [*nubuwwa*] on earth" and becoming religiously responsible (*mukallaf*) and was hence humankind's first step to regain the vicegerency lost through disobedience. It was by virtue of this step that humans were no longer a "thing unremembered" (verse 76:1) but rather a "thing remembered in the spiritual world [*malakut*]" (DT 43). This religiously responsible "Adam," was, however, preceded by many other "failed" Adams. It was these repeated past failures that prompted the angels to protest when God told them that He was creating a vicegerent on earth. "What, wilt Thou set therein one who will do corruption there, and shed blood" (verse 2:30). God responds to the angels' opposition by declaring, "Assuredly I know that you know not."[21] This soon becomes clear when He teaches Adam "the names, all of them." When the angels fail to tell Him the names, He says, "Did I not tell you I know the unseen things of the heavens and earth?" (verses 2:31–32). It was at that point that the angels bowed themselves to Adam, for God had demonstrated to them "the perfection of human nature, which has the capability to evolve and constantly advance from ignorance to knowledge" (RS 12).

What Taha proposes can be summed up in the following two points: (1) the fall of Adam and Eve involved their reduction to a hydrogen atom, and it was from that basic form that humankind started its evolutionary journey back to God; and (2) the angels' objection to the creation of humans was based on their knowledge of a human history before the emergence of a successful Adam. The temporal perspective of what the angels refer to when they speak about "doing corruption" and "shedding blood" and the source of their knowledge about what humans would do were important problems that exercised the exegetes' minds. Some of them pushed their temporal perspective into yet an even further past preceding the creation of humans and constructed a history according to which "the first who inhabited earth were the jinn. They committed iniquities, shed blood, and killed each other."[22] Others adopted a humanized temporal perspective revolving around the moment of human creation and contended that God told the angels in advance about humans and how they will "do corruption" and "shed blood."[23]

By contrast, what Taha does with his temporal perspective is different. His reading assumes that the angels' objection is based on knowledge of a human post-Fall history they had actually witnessed. But would not such a reading be absurd because the angels express their objection before the Fall and hence before that crucial moment when Taha's evolutionary temporal perspective starts with the emergence of the hydrogen atom? It was possibly the awareness of such an absurdity that prompted the classical exegetes to suggest the extra-Qur'anic proposition that what the angels express has in fact been taught by God. So, how does Taha overcome this problem? Like his classical counterparts, he resorts to the suggestion of an extra-Qur'anic proposition: Adam was created three times, twice in the spiritual realm of intelligibles *('alam 'l-malakut)* and once in the material realm *('alam 'l-mulk)* (RS 13–14). As such, Adam was distanced twice from God: the first distancing *(iqsa')* was when he was sent down to the "lowest of the low" rank from which he evolved till he realized the rank of vicegerency *(khilafa)*. This is the point when Adam becomes the subject of the dialogue between God and the angels. This, as the Qur'anic story tells us, was followed by the Fall—an act of distancing that Taha describes as being less drastic than the earlier one. His proposition, however, raises a question that he never addresses: what happened in the first instance that made God decide to send humankind to the "lowest of the low"? It is of course possible for Taha to read the part of the creation story about paradise, the disobedience, and the expulsion as an earlier episode (verses 2:35–36), thus giving a Qur'anic basis for the sending of humankind to the "lowest of the low." Yet this is still unsatisfactory as it simply shifts the question to the second fall.

The third stage of evolution—the stage marking the rise of humankind—is accorded paramount importance owing to the emergence of a very special faculty—human intelligence or the intellect *('aql)*. In the light of verse 15:29, Taha defines the human intellect as "the divine breath that God blew into the human" (RS 26), a process that he regards as "ceaseless."[24] This breathing image serves to express the creation of Adam in God's image and of the world in Adam's image as God breathed His spirit in Adam and Adam's spirit in the world. His breathing in Adam was at the highest level and His breathing in the world at the lowest level. This divine breathing is described in terms of ascending, spiral, seven-level cycles that draw, on the upward way to God, ever closer to their axis. "When the breathing cycle comes to an end at the seventh level, it starts anew. The last level becomes a first in a new cycle, and so on to infinity" (RS 27). Taha's assignment of the number seven to the levels of the perfective spiral cycles he suggests is inspired by a reading of verses 23:12–13 and verse 7:54 according to which the divine breathing into the human and the world is of a septenary nature. The first passage describes the seven phases of fetal development in the womb, and the second is about the creation of the heavens and the earth.[25]

Taha's fourth evolutionary stage is one of "perfection," a stupendous mutational event that takes human life to an unfamiliar and unprecedented level. Whereas the first and second stages are characterized by their material nature and corporeality, the third is marked by the conflict between body and mind. The fourth stage will bring total harmony between body and mind. Evolution has so far been purely organic or organo-mental, and the fourth stage will launch a new type of purely mental evolution. But what happens at this stage? The human sensory perception will be expanded: the familiar five senses will be supplemented by a sixth and a seventh sense. The sixth sense is the "brain" *(dimagh),* which will unite all the other senses and equip the human sensory perception with a sharp, comprehensive sensibility—one would "sense, hear, see, taste, and smell things at the same time" (RS 18). The seventh sense is the "heart" whose function is "life" *(hayat).* This is the "original sense" in the service of which all the other senses are employed. In explaining the role and the emergence of the seventh sense, Taha says,

> Had it not been for fear, life would not have come into existence in the first place and would not have evolved in the second place. Yet, if life does not ultimately overcome fear it would not realize its perfection. This will happen when the sixth sense becomes mature enough to realize the truth [of things] and at that point it will become clear that fear is part of the ignorance and deficiency of the early beginnings of humans. When the sixth sense reaches this level, the seventh sense, the heart, will expand and relax. Being free of the inhibition generated by fear, the heart will vigorously pump the blood of life to all the body's cells—cells that were petrified by fear and turned into a shield to protect primitive life. The whole body becomes all sensible, all alive, all spiritualized, and all and most beautiful. That is the "earth" of the body the Qur'an describes when it says, "And thou beholdest the earth barren and lifeless, then, when We send down water upon it, it quivers, and swells, and puts forth every kind of radiant bloom [22:5]." (RS 18–19)

The seventh sense is inextricably bound up with the sixth sense: the purer the mind and sharper the thought, the sounder the heart and the more expansive and perfect is life (RS 19). The function of the seventh sense is the realization of the perfect life. Taha does not envisage this as a fixed objective but rather as an ever-advancing and expanding horizon whose final end is God. He refines his notion of the constant divine breathing into the human by contending that the locus of this breathing is neither the body nor the mind but rather the heart. Rejecting what modern physiology tells us about the heart as being a mere blood pump, he defends the traditional Muslim notion that the heart is in fact a seat of perception.[26] He divides the heart into an outer heart and an inner one *(fu'ad)*. Furthermore, he employs the terminology of psychoanalysis and calls the heart "the unconscious" *(al-'aql 'l-batin)*. He evidently uses the term in its conceptually descriptive rather than its ascriptive psychoanalytical sense: the heart is a mind *('aql)* by virtue of its cognitive faculty, yet the special knowledge it inheres or through which we can experience is "concealed" *(batin)*. Whereas the mind operates on the level of dual cognition *(idrak shaf'i)*, the heart operates on the level of unitary cognition *(idrak witri)*. When the latter cognition is realized, "the perceiver, the act of perception, and the perceived all become one" (RS 38).

To sum up, although Taha accepts the theory of evolution, he nonetheless Islamizes it by injecting it with a creationist dimension and by placing the human-God relationship at the heart of the story of life. Consequently, he depicts the future of life exclusively in terms of this relationship.

Taha's position on the theory of evolution is consistent with what appears to be the overall positive attitude he takes toward modern science. He often affirms that modern science and modern technology represent the appealing face of modern Western civilization and asserts that Muslim societies cannot advance without embracing them. But the modern science that Taha is willing to invite into Muslim societies has to undergo a radical change before it gains admissibility—it has to forego the notion of causality *(sababiyya)*. In rejecting causality, Taha shows the great influence that the Ash'arites and al-Ghazali exercised on him.[27]

Al-Ghazali viewed causality with suspicion because he believed that it undermined the notions of divine omnipotence and divine will. He had, hence, argued, "The conjunction between what is assumed to be cause and what is presumed as effect is not necessary. . . . This conjunction . . . is owing to what God had decreed through [a] succession *(tasawuq)* [of cause and effect] rather than necessitation."[28] Although our experience demonstrates that when cotton is exposed to fire it burns, al-Ghazali insists that this is not a matter of necessary causation. In his view it is perfectly possible for this not to take place under the exposure condition and it is perfectly possible for cotton to burn without being touched by fire.[29] In opting for this particular example, al-Ghazali lays the foundation for the possibility and validity of miracles—the example serves as a verification of the Qur'anic story about the throwing of Abraham into fire and the failure of the fire to burn him thanks to divine intervention (see verses 21:68–69).

In Taha's view, causality is a function of a superficial, exoteric mode of perception (what corresponds to the level of "shari'a consciousness"). When one moves beyond this perception to a deeper, esoteric level (what corresponds to the level of *haqiqa* consciousness), one would then realize that causality is an illusion. It is at this point that one would discover that "causes and effects are sequences of receptivity *(istiqbal)* from God on the part of a locus *(mahall)*" (AJi 39). Like al-Ghazali, Taha uses the Abraham story to underline the nonexistence of causality and demonstrates this by applying his logic of receptivity and locality: the expected receptivity (the act of burning) of fire (as a locus) was suspended, as God did not give it the permission *(idhn)* to act. As such, all causes lead to God as the ultimate cause and are dependent on his will.

Taha's anticausal logic can sometimes lead him to an absurd reading of seemingly historical events. According to the hadith material, the Prophet advised one year against pollinating palm trees, and when this led to crop failure, he reportedly said, "You have better knowledge of your worldly matters."[30] In another version of the tradition, his statement was more pointedly reported as "The matters of your world are for you [to decide] and the matters of your religion are for me [to stipulate]."[31] Although the Prophet acknowledged that his advice was a mistake and he decided not to extend his authority to the sphere of worldly or technical matters, Taha reads the tradition as expressing the failure and limitation of those who received the prophetic advice. In his view, the question here is one of operating either on a causality level or a transcausality level: when the Prophet counseled against the pollination of the palm trees, his advice was on the higher level of divine unity that saw the hand of God as the real cause behind things (AJi 41). The Prophet's companions, however, operated on the lower level of apparent causality; their failure to see the ubiquitous hand of God led to the failure of their crop. What Taha says in this respect presents us with an example of sophistry at its worst. Besides flouting the explicit and unambiguous meaning of the prophetic statement, Taha's logic leads to the projection of an inconsistent image of Muhammad. As Taha is aware that the companions operated on a lower level of unitary consciousness, it cannot be claimed that the Prophet was unaware of this when he gave his advice. This leads to the conclusion that the Prophet gave a piece of advice that violated the fundamental prophetic rule of addressing people "in accordance with their level of understanding"—a tradition that Taha often quotes elsewhere to demonstrate prophetic wisdom. Although Taha is at pains to stress that Islam and modern science are fully compatible, he fails to show the basis of this compatibility. His rejection of causality raises real problems, as it is not clear how in the absence of the notions of cause and effect it would be possible to develop a scientific method or a scientific theory that explains scientific data. Furthermore, his subscription on the one hand to a Platonic epistemological theory stressing recollection as the foundation of knowledge and his mystical elevation of worship as a means of attaining knowledge on the other militate against any real and meaningful acceptance of the method of science and the knowledge it provides.

Shari'a Between Permanence and Change

Shari'a is so central in Islam that the religion, as an envisaged comprehensive system expressing the will of God and requiring humans to conduct their lives according to what it dictates, may be characterized as nomocentric. The Qur'anic worldview does not allow for a "legal vacuum"—humankind has always been in possession of divine law from its very Adamic, social beginning. However, what should be noted about this worldview is that its frame of reference is regional as its notion of divine law is essentially limited to Judaism and Christianity—the universally shared Adamic beginning does not qualify all laws to be conceived as divine. Not only that, but the Qur'anic worldview went through a transition from a phase of relative legal inclusivism where the laws of the Torah and the New Testament were recognized alongside the Qur'an to an exclusivist phase where only Islamic shari'a was recognized.[32]

Origins of Law

Taha deals with law on the one hand as an abstract conceptual construct rooted in the notion of "natural law" *(al-qanun 'l-tabi'i)* and on the other as a concrete social construct arising in response to the specific needs of a specific society. Taha's exposition of the second aspect revolves around two issues: the origin of law and the nature of its development. According to him, the origin of law lies in the need of men to protect their property and their women, who were perceived and treated as property. Although Taha does not refer to Marxism in this respect, what he says about the origin of law suggests the influence of Engels's *The Origin of the Family, Private Property and the State* (1884). However, Taha does not share Engels's speculation that in the era of "primitive communism" the communal ownership of the forces of production meant that the family as such did not exist and men and women lived promiscuously. In his view, human society could not have been possible without the regulation of sex and private property (IS 21). He locates the power and authority of the laws governing the family and private property in a construction that could provide the ultimate sanction, namely, religion. These early beginnings are described by Taha in the following terms:

> Out of [the] fear and anticipation [of early humans] emerged intelligence *(dhaka')*, a faculty that made it possible to distinguish between what was appropriate and what was inappropriate. Then emerged the will, through whose power it was possible to restrain one's passions and perform one's duties and responsibilities. This entailed foregoing one's immediate pleasures, in preference for anticipated pleasures provided by the gods in this life or in an afterlife or the pleasure of gratifying the community and enjoying its appreciation and praise (RS 41).

Taha thus delineates a scheme where the interplay of the principles of the lawful *(halal)*, the unlawful *(haram)*, reward *(thawab)*, and punishment *('iqab)* leads to the rise of society as a fully functional system. What he says in this respect is closely associated with his distinction between the will to life and the will to freedom: following one's instinctual drives is a function of the will to life whereas curbing these drives for the sake of a higher pleasure is a function of the will to freedom.

When it comes to the issue of the nature of the development of law, Taha adopts an evolutionary perspective according to which law evolved from relatively lower levels of harshness, cruelty, and oppressiveness to relatively higher levels of leniency and humaneness. It is in this light that he reads the Qur'anic account in verses 37:101–8 of the commandment to Abraham to sacrifice his son and the subsequent ransoming of the son by an animal sacrifice. "This rule [of sacrificing individuals to appease the gods] was religiously and rationally acceptable [in early societies]. Abraham himself was commanded to sacrifice his son Ishmael[33]. . . . God, however, decreed the abrogation of this rule and, hence, humankind was ransomed with a lower animal. This was a [clear] proclamation that humankind had at last been elevated above its animality" (RT 30). This transition from what is relatively harsh to relatively lenient is the governing principle of legal evolution, and its spirit is encapsulated in verse 4:147, which affirms interrogatively, "What would God do with [punishing] you if you are thankful, and believe?" It is the application of this evolutionary principle to shari'a that sets Taha apart from his conservative opponents. He points out that he and his opponents agree that shari'a is "perfect" *(kamila)*, although they differ about what this perfection entails. Whereas his traditionalist opponents (the Salafiyyun)[34] insist that this means the system's immutability, he holds the opposite view, that perfection means change and coping with change to meet "the ever-changing needs of human society" (AJi 54–55).

Taha identifies natural law with the divine will that governs all existents. Using terms that carry Neoplatonic resonances, he defines natural law as the "imprint of the eternal mind from which the particular minds of humans derive [their laws]" (UD 36). He contends that natural law is best articulated by the Qur'an, which plays the unique role of providing human intelligence with access to divine intelligence.[35] The Qur'an can do so because the law it offers is the best approximation of the perfection and coherence of the natural law, which can liberate humans internally by uniting their conscious and unconscious minds and externally by bringing them to peace with their environment.

Shari'a and Haqiqa

The relationship Taha establishes between Qur'anic law and natural law reflects two other key relationships in his thought, that is, those of shari'a and *haqiqa* on the one hand and of individual and society on the other. Although he affirms the importance of shari'a and upholds it as the basis of social legal conduct, he places his ultimate emphasis on *haqiqa* as a higher basis for individual conduct. Whereas shari'a is an imperative in the realm of imitation, *haqiqa* requires authenticity because *haqiqa* is the shari'a of the individual who has met God. This individual shari'a constitutes the primary source *(asl)* from which all other laws flow and is hence above communal laws.

But can any conflict arise between the personal shari'a of what Taha describes as the "gnostic individual" *('arif)* and the communal shari'a of society? This should not arise in the shari'a sphere of *mu'amalat*, or what is due to other members of society, as here the conduct of all individuals (including the gnostic) is governed by the universal rule of desisting from harming others (QF 145). What Taha says in this respect is not particularly original or helpful. However, beyond this commonplace qualification, Taha's gnostic fully enjoys the fruits of his personal law *(shari'a fardiyya)*, that is, his freedom not to follow shari'a in the sphere of *'ibadat* or ritual acts directed toward God on account of his attainment to his personal religion.

An issue that Taha addresses through the perspective of his shari'a-*haqiqa* opposition is that of dietary prohibitions. On the basis of a comparison between the scale of these prohibitions in Judaism and Islam (but not, strikingly enough, between Islam and Christianity), he concludes that the divine message evolved toward a clear narrowing down of their scope. This is underlined by verse 2:173, whose theme is dietary prohibitions. Commenting on the verse, Taha stresses, "Prohibitions were all reduced to four [carrion, blood, the flesh of swine, and what has been hallowed to other than God] and even these were exempted and made permissible in case of dire necessity" (QF 141).

What this demonstrates, Taha points out, is that when the notion of unlawfulness is applied to things, it is in fact a conventional, shari'a-given construction and does not indicate a judgmental reprobation of the thing in itself. The Qur'anic ascription of "corrupt" *(khabith)* (as opposed to "good," *tayyib)* that is attached to certain forbidden things applies only in a relative sense as a function of ignorance and the restrictiveness that is associated with this state of ignorance. Once this ignorance is overcome through gnostic maturity, then all things attain their original goodness *(tiba)* and revert back to an original state of permissibility *(hill)* as indicated by verse 5:93, which declares, "There is no fault in those who believe and do deeds of righteousness what they may eat" (QF 140–41). In Taha's view, the goal of the prohibition of things is meant to serve as a means to the prohibition of wrong action *('uyub 'l-suluk,* lit. "defects of conduct"). Wrong action originates in desire or craving *(hawa 'l-nafs),* and it is through his "beneficial knowledge" *('ilm nafi')* that the gnostic can overcome craving and put an end to wrong action.

Taha is evidently impelled by a radical aspiration to elevate the Islamic prohibitory perspective and shift it from a narrow legalistic level to an essentially moral level. What he says about the conventional nature of the prohibition of certain things and about the eventual reversion of things to their original state of permissibility may raise a question in the minds of some about the things that are prohibited in verse 2:173 and whether they may end up being permissible. Although Taha does not directly address this issue and although the way he presents his case may give rise to such an implication, it would be absurd to suggest that his conception of the state of *haqiqa* allows for the eating of "carrion, blood, the flesh of swine, [and] what has been hallowed to other than God." In fact, Taha's conception of what one eats at a post-shari'a level is decidedly vegetarian. His interpretation of verse 49:12, which refers to the eating of "the flesh of [one's] dead brother," allows for the prohibition of eating animal flesh.

The Penal Code of Shari'a

The most crucial role that shari'a can play is the regulation of relations among the members of the Islamic community. This is the *mu'amalat* sphere of the legal system, covering family law, contracts, criminal law, procedural law, constitutional law, international law, commercial transaction, and laws concerning the public enforcement of shari'a precepts.

Taha maintains that his perception of shari'a as a living, evolving body that adapts to change applies only to the sphere of *mu'amalat* and does not touch on '*ibadat*. In saying this, he proposes a reform horizon similar to that of other modernist reformists. This, however, is not really the case when it comes to what he proposes, because his ultimate aim of realizing one's authenticity and following a personal shari'a renders the '*ibadat* temporary and surpassable. Furthermore, Taha maintains that although legislation in the sphere of *mu'amalat* is subject to change, this does not affect legislation for the offenses that fall under the categories of *hudud* and *qisas*. *Hudud* (lit. "limits, boundaries") refer to certain offenses that have been forbidden or sanctioned by punishments in the Qur'an. *Qisas* (retaliation) covers the offenses of killing and of nonfatal bodily harm. The category of *hudud* is perceived as being a right or claim of God *(haqq 'Llah)*, with the practical consequence that no pardon or settlement is acceptable once the case is brought to court. The pardon or settlement feature is what constitutes the crucial difference between *qisas* and *hudud*.

Jurists have disagreed on what constitutes the category of *hudud*. The followers of Abu Hanifa (d. 150/767) maintained that there were five *hudud* offenses, namely, theft *(sariqa)*, unlawful intercourse *(zina)*, drinking wine *(shurb)*, intoxication *(sukr)*, and false accusation of adultery *(qadhf)*.[36] Followers of other schools added other *hudud* offenses, such as highway robbery *(hiraba)*, insurrection *(baghy)*, apostasy *(ridda)*, and intentional murder that necessitates retribution *(qatl 'amd mujib li-l-qisas)*.[37] At the hands of jurists like the Malikite Ibn Juzayy, the category was extended to include acts like blasphemy against prophets and angels, failure to perform prayer and fasting, and witchcraft.

Taha tackles *hudud* and *qisas* and their attendant severe punishments within the general framework of what he perceives as the penal philosophy of shari'a. The operative notions here are freedom and reciprocity *(mu'awada)*: when an individual abuses his freedom, then that freedom has to be curbed. Such abuse can involve transgression against others or against oneself. If one transgresses against others, then one's freedom is to be curbed according to shari'a's law of reciprocity, summed up in verse 5:45: "And therein We prescribed for them: 'A life for a life, an eye for an eye, a nose for a nose, an ear for an ear, a tooth for a tooth, and for the wounds retaliation'; but whosoever forgoes it as a freewill offering, that shall be for him an expiation." If, on the other hand, the individual commits a transgression against his own self, then his freedom would be curbed in accordance with the law of reciprocity on the level of *haqiqa*, indicated in verses 99:7–8: "and whoso has done an atom's weight of good shall see it, and whoso has done an atom's weight of evil shall see it."

According to Taha, law on the level of *haqiqa* is "original" law that "covers every single minutia" and is characterized by its absolute preciseness (RT 82). Although law on the level of shari'a does not exhibit such characteristics, the closest it comes to the *haqiqa* level is in its *hudud* and *qisas* formulations. For Taha, the *hudud* category covers the five offenses of unlawful sexual intercourse, false accusation of adultery, theft, highway robbery, and intoxication. He places the first four offenses in a special subcategory as "they originate from the two principles of protecting one's family and protecting one's property, which were the first two laws that came into existence in primitive societies, making social life possible" (RT 83). What is notably absent from Taha's principles giving rise to the earliest laws in human communities is the basic principle of the protection of life (expressed in the "You shall not kill" commandment of the Mosaic Decalogue, coming before "You shall not commit adultery," "You shall not steal," and "You shall not bear false witness against your neighbor"). Such a failure on Taha's part is to be expected because in seeking to justify the special status of the *hudud* offenses he does not confine himself to what shari'a stipulates but goes on to appeal to an extra-shari'a anthropological speculation about the earliest two laws that arose in human society. The offense of intoxication, however, proves to be refractory as this speculative anthropology does not account for its inclusion in the *hudud* category.

The privileging of the *hudud* category as being "God's rights" correlates in the Islamic penal code with the exceptional extremity and harshness of the punishments meted out to transgressors. *Hudud* punishments include the death penalty either by stoning in the case of unlawful intercourse where the offender is a married person or by crucifixion or with the sword in the case of highway robbery with homicide; amputation of hand for theft and of hand and foot for highway robbery without homicide; and flogging in the cases of unlawful intercourse where the offender is unmarried, false accusation of adultery, and intoxication.

The notion of *qisas* in the general sense of retributive justice constitutes the basis of Taha's defense of the retention of *hudud* and their respective punishments. In reading verse 2:179, "In retaliation *(qisas)* there is life *(hayat-un)* for you, men possessed of minds; haply you will be godfearing," he maintains that "life" here means "growth of knowledge or realization" (RT 48). Defending the principle of *lex talionis* in shari'a he says,

> That the implementation of *qisas* results in a growth of realization is self-evident. An individual who infringes on the freedoms of others in the course of exercising his freedom does so only because of ignorance, stupidity, and lack of imagination. When such an individual pulls out another person's eye in a fit of anger, he does not commit such an act while fully aware of the enormous pain and damage he inflicts upon his victim. When he is punished by being put in the victim's place and his eye is pulled out in retaliation for his offense, then two objectives have been simultaneously achieved. First, the community's interests are protected as the offender has been deterred and made an example for others; second, the individual's imagination undergoes an expansion as he is provided with an opportunity to relive the harrowing experience he has inflicted upon another person. (RT 49)

Taha is so enthusiastic about this type of retributive justice that he is willing to project it as a solid foundation for the rebirth of a new, reformed individual who is more humanized owing to his expanded, postpunishment imagination and who not only desists from harming others but may even turn into a pious, righteous person who eagerly serves others. This logic of punishment-induced imaginational expansion reaches its crudest in Taha's defense of the amputation of hands for theft. In his view, stealing without being destitute or sick is a function of ignorance that requires a corrective measure operating on the level of the wrongdoer's consciousness. Hence, and owing to the intimate connection between the hand and the mind, the wisdom of God decreed that the offender's hand be cut off in order to activate the mind (RS 57–58).

Despite his subscription to an evolutionary perspective, Taha is rigidly dogmatic when it comes to the special status of the *hudud* offenses and the punishments they and *qisas* carry. Dealing with the history of the punishment of theft, he maintains that in early societies thieves were executed, but when these societies achieved a greater degree of development and "individuals reached a degree of maturity and intelligence that made it possible to deter them with less violence," this extreme measure was mitigated and replaced with amputation (RT 29). However, as far as Taha is concerned, juristic evolution should have been arrested at this amputation stage. The fact that amputation is not acceptable as a penal measure in the vast majority of Muslim countries and may be perceived by the rest of the world community as cruel is dismissed by Taha. When the Egyptian writer Mustafa Mahmud tried to infuse a greater degree of flexibility and sensitivity to public opinion into the debate about shari'a implementation by suggesting that repentance and expression of remorse could act as mitigating factors to exempt an offender from amputation, Taha sternly declared that this was a major mistake and reiterated the conventional position that "once the offense of theft reaches court and its elements are established, it is not possible to exercise pardon and the offender cannot be exempted from amputation. No one, even the noble Prophet himself, can suspend the amputation of a convicted thief" (QF 205).

Taha's endorsement of the conventional juristic position as regards theft does, however, undermine the justificatory foundation of his theory. An important element that the jurists, and Taha along with them, stipulate to convict a person of theft is *nisab*, a minimum quantity or value of what is stolen below which no amputation is allowed. This, and other preconditions, was the juristic way of circumventing the drastic results of a literal reading of verse 5:38 that could lead to amputation for the mere act of theft. Such a literal reading would not allow, for instance, for *nisab*. Nor should Taha's theory about the underlying wisdom of amputation allow for *nisab*. When he accuses a person who has stolen of suffering from a lack of imagination and a deficiency of intelligence that requires the exceptionally harsh and irreversible measure of cutting his hand off in order to stimulate his imagination and awaken his intelligence, he cannot justify the *nisab* stipulation, as such a quantitative element does not affect the intrinsic nature of the act of stealing. This is an inconsistency from which the traditional juristic position, which does not posit a theory of imagination to justify amputation, does not suffer. Furthermore, Taha's defense of hand amputation as the appropriate and "natural" punishment for theft because of the special connection between the hand and the mind does not account for the punishment the shari'a prescribes for another type of theft, namely, highway robbery where the offender would lose not only his right hand but also his left foot.

When it comes to unlawful intercourse or *zina,* Taha applies the same logic in justifying the exceptionally severe punishment of stoning. He establishes a close connection between the paramount importance of sex as "the greatest manifestation through which life preserves itself" and the utmost necessity to protect it. In his view, this special significance made sexual activity the subject of the first legislation that human society laid down and the subject of the first repression *(kabt)* that was forced on the unconscious. As in the case of theft, he employs a mechanical logic to justify stoning. He argues that because sexual impulses and wishes are forced back into the inner recesses of the conscious mind, the stipulation of lapidation that involves "pelting the brain with stones" is an appropriate punishment (TS 61).[38]

Again, Taha's logic runs into an inconsistency when we consider what shari'a actually stipulates. The fact that the punishment in the case of *zina* is determined by the offender's marital status suggests that what takes precedence here is the protection of the marriage institution rather than the control of the sexual drive. When Taha says that *zina* is a function of psychological repression acting on the level of the unconscious, he is evidently speaking about a psychological mechanism according to which an offender's marital status should have no relevance. By shifting the emphasis to the psychological aspect in order to justify stoning, Taha lays shari'a open to the charge of punishing the same offense with drastically different penalties.

Another argument Taha presents to justify stoning and flogging for *zina* is based on the notion of reciprocity: as the person who commits *zina* has sought pleasure at the expense of law, he has to be subjected to pain that acts as a corrective measure through which he can restore what is perceived as a lost balance. Using images drawn from verse 8:42, he says, "In the valley of the soul, pain is situated on the farther bank whereas pleasure is on the nearer bank. A soul that runs after its hedonistic lusts should be pulled back to pain—this will act as a counterpoise to achieve the soul's equilibrium and keep it away from thoughtless and impulsive acts" (RT 49–50). This may evidently be argued in the case of flogging, but how about stoning? To address this, Taha changes his strategy, abandoning his psychological logic in favor of a purely religious logic that invokes the Islamic belief in a hereafter. As such, the pain of stoning that the offender undergoes assumes a penitential nature that will help relieve his suffering in the afterlife (AJii 9).

In dealing with the offense of false accusation, Taha stresses that the gravity of the offense of *zina* necessitates a severe punishment against those who make false accusations concerning it. Quoting verse 24:4, which lays down the punishment of *qadhf* as a flogging of eighty stripes, he comments that "the most specific and scrupulous of the *hudud* offenses are those of *zina* and *qadhf*" (TS 61). The shari'a system is undoubtedly particularly severe in dealing with the offense of *qadhf*, so much so that its punishment is only twenty stripes less than that of the more serious offense of fornication.[39] It may be argued that the inclusion of *qadhf* in the *hudud* category and the relative severity of its punishment were owing to what is known in the *sira* history as "the affair of the lie" *(hadith 'l-ifk)*, a slanderous allegation against 'A'isha's chastity that was refuted by the Qur'an.[40] The limited scope of the Qur'anic notion of *qadhf* was, however, broadened by the jurists to cover a wider range of slanderous acts.[41]

Taha writes about *qadhf* in a traditional manner that underlines the Qur'an's dire warnings to slanderers, such as verse 24:24, which threatens them with a "mighty chastisement on the day when their tongues, their hands and their feet shall testify against them." The austere sensibility that Taha expresses in this respect is in relative contrast to a more lenient sensibility that characterized the stance of Shafi'ite and Hanbalite jurists who maintained that the offense of *qadhf* is a right of humans *(haqq adami)*, with the direct consequence that a plaintiff may pardon a defendant even after a case has been brought to court.[42] Taha's austere sensibility is further demonstrated by the view he holds as regards the Qur'anic injunction concerning the "casting down of one's eyes" *(ghadd 'l-basar)*, which is considered as a necessary measure to counter *zina*.[43] In a response to Mustafa Mahmud's suggestion that a literalist and stern understanding of the Qur'anic injunction should be abandoned in favor of a more flexible understanding that stresses "evil thoughts," Taha sticks to the traditionalist juristic position that "the first glance is yours (i.e., forgiven), but the second is held against you" (QF 144). What is notable in his treatment of *qadhf* is the absence of any attempt to rationalize the offense's specific punishment as he does in the cases of theft and *zina*.

Taha contends that the pain inflicted by shari'a's punishments is designed to restore a lost equilibrium, and he uses the same logic in justifying flogging in the case of the offense of intoxication. "When a person who drinks alcohol tries to blot out his consciousness, he is trying to escape his [bitter] reality to live in a world created by his illusions and sick fantasies. Hence, the purpose of the pain of flogging is to force him back to face his bitter reality and focus his consciousness on changing it" (RT 50). The image that Taha offers of the drinking of alcoholic beverages is highly stereotypical, and it is unlikely that moderate or social drinkers would recognize themselves in what he portrays. Furthermore, when it comes to the extreme category of alcoholics for whom drinking is a means of escape, Taha's assumption that the pain induced by their flogging would provide them with instant liberation and free them of their alcoholism is a grossly simplistic answer to a complex problem.

Constitutionalism and Shari'a Reform

Taha does not accept all aspects of shari'a, particularly as regards some laws that regulate the family. Consequently, he replaces shari'a as the ultimate source of the basic principles and laws with the modern notion of the constitution *(dustur)*. The constitution as the "legal formulation of a nation's ultimate ideal" strives, in his view, to reconcile the individual need for absolute freedom and the social need for total justice (UD 11). As such the constitution is the vehicle through which economic, political, and social equalities are realized.

In identifying the ultimate source of the constitution, Taha constructs a composite perspective that draws on humanism, Neoplatonism, and the Qur'an. So, on one level, he emphasizes that human nature *(al-tabi'a 'l-bashariyya)* inheres laws that correspond to the laws of nature and as such it is the ultimate source that determines constitutionalism (RM 34). These intrinsic laws are subsumed into the notion of natural law. On another level, the ultimate source is an eternal intelligence *('aql azali)*. This eternal intelligence is contrasted by a created intelligence *('aql muhdath)*; the former intelligence generates an eternal law to which all worlds are subject, and the latter intelligence produces its own law that aspires to identify itself with the eternal law. Furthermore, the Qur'an is conceived as the ultimate source of any constitution and as such it is the only constitution that is capable of reconciling absolute individual freedom and total social justice (UD 12).

When Taha speaks about the Qur'an as a constitution, he is careful to distinguish it from shari'a, which is not consistent with constitutionalism. He points out that the seed out of which constitutionalism grows is a principle not recognized by shari'a, namely, the right to freedom of thought *(hurriyyat 'l-ra'y)* (ZJ 13). However, it should be noted that when Taha speaks about the Qur'an as a constitution, he is using the term loosely as his theory of a second message presupposes that there is a constitutional, abrogated level in the Qur'an and another abrogating level that curbed freedoms in the past and has to be rendered null and void under an Islamic constitution. This Islamic constitution will mark the beginning of a new era because humankind, Taha tells us with all the confidence of an Islamocentric zeal, "has not yet attained to constitutional legislation" (TS 11).

Taha's call for the reform of shari'a should be placed within the broader project of modern Islamic reformism. Although he hardly recognizes the influence of other modernists on him, he is considerably indebted to those who espoused the cause of reform before him, particularly Muhammad 'Abduh.[44] 'Abduh was instrumental in reviving certain principles from the jurisprudence of the Hanbalite Najm al-Din al-Tufi (d. 716/1316) and the Malikite Ibrahim b. Musa al-Shatibi (d. 790/1388) that provided the cause of reform with a solid foundation. In his *usul 'l-fiqh* (principles of jurisprudence), al-Tufi stresses the principle of *maslaha* (public interest, utility) to the point of contending that if a conflict arises between *maslaha* on the one hand and the text of the law *(nass)* and consensus *(ijma')* on the other, then *maslaha* should take precedence.[45] Likewise, al-Shatibi lays great emphasis on *al-maslaha*, whose realization and advancement he views as a primary aim *(maqsad,* pl. *maqasid)* of shari'a. *Maslaha* is intimately linked to custom *('adat)* and hence al-Shatibi further insists that the law should adapt itself to the consideration of custom.[46] It was this juristic flexibility that provided the modernist project with its impetus and, hence, we find in 'Abduh for example an emphasis of the notion of *'urf* (custom) and an elevation of its legal force to a level comparable to that of the text of the law. Besides, 'Abduh recognizes that shari'a has to change in order to reflect changes of circumstances and that need *(haja)* carries a legal force equivalent to that of necessity *(darura).*[47]

Like 'Abduh, Taha attaches a great deal of significance to the notion of *'urf.* As already seen, he interprets the term *"ma'ruf,"* in verse 2:228, as a customary act that reflects a changing circumstance. Change in Taha's metaphysical perspective is synonymous with an upward, progressive movement. Accordingly, when shari'a recognizes and assimilates *ma'ruf,* it engages in an evolutionary process that Taha calls *tatwir* (reform, modernization). Yet, despite his recognition of the role of the external factor of change in this process of constant adaptation on the part of shari'a, Taha expresses on another level a shari'a-centric view according to which the adaptation of shari'a is no more than a transition within its system from one subsidiary text of the law to another, fundamental text. What Taha says in this respect may correspond to the assertion other reformists make when they insist that their reform proposals are in complete harmony with the higher objectives *(maqasid)* of shari'a or the higher interests *(masalih)* that shari'a is intended to protect.[48] It may further be argued that what Taha and the other reformists assert is intended to appease orthodox opinion.

The provenance of Taha's constitutionalism is Western. His most spirited defense of constitutionalism was prompted by the pamphlet that Hasan al-Turabi wrote to justify the dissolution of the Communist Party by the Constituent Assembly in November 1965. What is significant about Taha's line of argumentation is his appeal to the values of what he describes as "true" Western culture in expounding the meaning of constitutionalism and championing it. He accuses al-Turabi of a superficial understanding of

Western legal culture (despite his formal legal training in the West) and hence of a failure to grasp and appreciate the essence of constitutionalism. Taha quotes at length from Pericles's funeral oration about Athenian democracy following the war against Sparta in 430 B.C.E., cites Aristotle on natural law, and refers to the American Declaration of Independence (ZJ 10–12, 20, and 13 respectively).

When it comes to constitutionalism Taha's idealism goes beyond the boundaries of his own country, envisaging the establishment of an international government based on an international constitution (RMi 30–34). He expressed this internationalist commitment as early as the early 1950s, at a time when he was actively engaged in the struggle for independence and the attainment of national sovereignty. This idealism got the better of him, as he was willing to surrender national sovereignty (or at least part of it) to a United Nations government for the sake of world peace, justice, and the unity of humankind.

Arts Between Prohibition and Conditional Permission

One important area of Muslim life that the intervention of shari'a has historically devitalized is that of art, particularly the representational arts of painting and sculpture. Although Islamic civilization can boast highly sophisticated achievements in the fields of architecture and calligraphy and other fields such as ceramics, mosaic, carpets, textiles, and metalwork, intense religious hostility to *taswir* (representational art) continued unabated in premodern times, creating a charged and adverse climate that crippled representational creativity. It has rightly been suggested that "of the three great missionary religions of the world—Buddhism, Christianity, and Islam—each striving for the mastery of the world and endeavouring to win the allegiance of all men by various devices of propaganda, Islam alone has refused to call in the aid of pictorial art as a handmaid to religion."[49]

The roots of this antipathy go back to Muhammad's rejection of Arab idolatry *(wathaniyya)*. According to exegetical material, the debate between Meccans and Muhammad was echoed by verse 39:3 in which they justified their idolatry by saying, "We only serve them [i.e., the idols] that they may bring us nigh in nearness to God." This makes it clear that they shared Muhammad's belief in an ultimate reality but also believed that their idols had the special power of acting as mediators between them and that remote ultimate reality. The implication of what the verse attributes to the Meccans is that they did not identify their idols with God—they were far too sophisticated to hold such a simple belief. Rather, their idols were identifiable with the Judeo-Islamic mediatory institution of prophecy.

Yet the Qur'an also identifies the religion of the Meccans with *shirk*, that is, associationism or "partner-ism" in the sense of perceiving of the idols as partners *(shuraka')* of God or protectors *(awliya')*. The Qur'anic argument against associationism rests on the notion of creation: God creates whereas the polytheists' idols (or the powers they symbolize) are not capable of creation (see, for instance, verse 13:16). Hence, whereas the logic of verse 39:3 implies a competition between the intercessory role of idolatry and the mediatory role of prophecy, the logic of associationism implies a competition with divinity itself.

It is this rivalry with divinity that is invoked in the hadith material to condemn representational art. In his section on representational art, al-Bukhari provides the basic prophetic pronouncements that conditioned Muslim attitudes toward painting and sculpture. The harshest expression of prophetic condemnation is a hadith according to which the severest punishment on doomsday would be meted out to those who engage in representational art *(musawwirun)*.[50] Another hadith highlights the notion of rivalry: the makers of images will be asked in the process of their punishment to breathe life into the creatures they had depicted.[51] The consumption of the community of believers of what representational artists produced was actively discouraged in a hadith declaring that angels would not enter a house containing images.[52]

It has been suggested that these traditions reflected later attitudes and that "primitive Muslim society . . . does not appear to have been so iconoclastic as later generations became, when the condemnation of pictorial and plastic arts based on the Traditions ascribed to the Prophet had won general approval in Muslim society."[53] This is unlikely to be the case as the early period of fierce and bitter confrontation between Muhammad and his Meccan opponents provides more of a plausible context for the rise and hardening of Islamic iconoclasm than later periods when Islam was triumphant and secure.

This rigid, orthodox insistence on the interdiction of figurative art was ignored in practice by many later caliphs, princes, and authors, who adorned their palaces, houses, and books with paintings. The official patronage of figurative art reached a high point under the Timurid princes, the Mughal emperors, and the Ottoman sultans. In modern times and specifically since 1839, Muslim opinion was divided over the new challenge of photography. Rashid Rida issued a fatwa in 1908 prohibiting painting and photography, and this was echoed in a similar statement by Shaikh 'l-Islam in Istanbul in 1920, an attitude that was soon to change with the sanction of fatwas coming from al-Azhar.[54]

Another area of controversy and dispute was that of singing, music, and dancing, or what came to be known as *sama'* (listening). Here, jurists and mystics expressed competing and contradictory views. Lenient jurists who were inclined to accept *sama'* as religiously acceptable found themselves pitted against orthodox jurists who judged it as impermissible or at best reprehensible. Among those who fiercely defended the orthodox position was Ahmad b. Taimiyya (d. 728/1328) who insisted that "the lawful *sama'* that God prescribed concerned listening to His revelation."[55] Listening to the Qur'an can be the *sama'* experience par excellence as it can stimulate such overwhelming emotional and physical reactions as to cause exhilaration, ecstatic outbursts, loss of consciousness, and even death.[56] Attacking Sufi *dhikr* (recollection) in which the human voice was often accompanied by musical instruments, he asserts that when such an action is intended as a form of worship, it amounts to misguidance *(dalal)*. Relying on the authority of the hadith and the four founding fathers of the juristic schools of Sunnism, he declares that playing of all musical instruments is unlawful when the intention is pleasurable entertainment *(tamattu')* and amusement *(tala"ub)*.[57] Likewise, dancing is unlawful, and Ibn Taimiyya views it as a violation of a norm set by verse 25:63, which says, "The servants of the All-merciful are those who walk in the earth modestly."

Sufis expressed a different attitude. In his chapter on *sama'*, al-Qushairi invokes the authority of traditional *fiqh* to support the activity. Pointing out that the Prophet had listened to poetry being recited in his presence, he argues that it is possible to conclude accordingly that the admissibility of *sama'* in this case cannot be invalidated just because the recitation of poetry is accompanied by musical tunes. Deploying a host of Sufi traditions, al-Qushairi underscores the importance of *sama'* in Sufi experience and social life. According to one tradition, Abu 'l-Qasim al-Junaid was asked why a person becomes excited and ecstatic in a *sama'* session, and he said, "When God made His primordial covenant with men saying, 'Am I not your Lord?' and they responded saying, 'Yea! We do testify!' [verse 7:172], the sweetness of hearing the divine speech consumed their souls. In a *sama'* session, men are moved by this memory." [58] When it came to ecstatic outbursts in *sama'* sessions, the Sufis developed different attitudes. There were sober masters like al-Junaid who would not allow such outbursts and others who tolerated them. [59] Al-Daqqaq expressed a view of *sama'* through which he tried to reconcile the orthodox prohibitive position and Sufi permissiveness: "*Sama'* is prohibited to common people *('awam)* because of the lowliness of their souls, permissible to ascetics *(zuhhad)* because of their constant striving, and recommended to Sufis because their hearts are alive." [60] It was this attitude of what may be described as "spiritual elitism" that came to inform Taha's position on art.

In dealing with the shari'a-based prohibitions of sculpture, painting, photography, music, and singing, Taha deploys his familiar apologetic logic. He maintains that "the prohibition [of all these arts] was provisional. The reason [for imposing prohibition] was that people were close to the times of idolatry and *jahiliyya* and it was likely that they might [relapse] if statues were made. People were also close to the times of their lascivious entertainment *(lahw)* in the brothels of *jahiliyya* and to their dancing" (IF 37–38). Hence, during its formative period, Islam had to be strict because a "yearning to pagan symbols" could have easily been aroused. Taha points out that it would be absurd to suggest that if present-day Muslims legitimize sculpture on the basis of shari'a, this would entail a risk of reviving idolatry. [61] Despite this awareness of the difference between the society of early Islam and modern Muslim societies, however, Taha still maintains that shari'a prohibitions on certain arts are operative on a certain level and their lifting is subject to the fulfilment of certain conditions.

In Taha's view art is "the means by which the human expressive faculty [*malakat 'l-ta'bir*] realizes itself" (IF 2). This "expressive faculty" is no less than the totality of human life itself: movement, feeding, reproduction, poetry, prose, singing, dancing, sculpting, drawing, painting, acting, playing music, etc. Although Taha is inclined to consider any life activity an art, he perceives that this would lead to an imprecise and unhelpful generalization. He hence draws a distinction between art and life energy by valorizing the former: art is an activity that inheres a value *(qima)*. Accordingly, he contends that art is "the expression of the energy of life of itself through intelligences characterized by their systematicity, chastity, and power of perception. Art is an expression of the life of reflection and the life of emotion at the same time." As such, art is an expression of a "chastened desire" that is under the firm control of intelligence and "the proper rules of morality" (IF 3). What Taha says in this respect underlines a key feature of his position on art, that is, that the beautiful and the moral are intimately linked.

However, Taha is careful to distance himself from the position of those who still prohibit the production or enjoyment of certain arts. Yet, his willingness to embrace art is qualified. He advises his Sufi seeker to be wary of the harm that can be caused by art when he is still at the beginning of his spiritual journey. In his early stages, the seeker is subject to severe restrictions; he is required to focus all energies on his worship activity with the view of realizing the unity of his self. It is when the seeker has attained spiritual maturity that all restrictions are lifted and he may freely enjoy art. Taha avoids discussing what should happen on the level of Muslim public space, that is, whether painting, sculpture, music, dancing, and so on are allowed to be an integral part of the cultural staple diet of all modern Muslim societies or whether the familiar shari'a restrictions on these arts should be retained because they can also be distractive on the broader social level.

Taha's emphasis on the notion of peace on the one hand and the central role that the Qur'an plays in the act of worship on the other lays the foundation for his aesthetic. In defining beauty he says, "If one says that beauty is order and symmetry *(tanasuq)*, one is right but only partly. Initially, I would like to suggest that beauty is human justice. However, one should then go further to human love, to living with others in peace. In my view, beauty is undoubtedly peace. We cannot be at peace with others unless we are at peace with ourselves. This inner peace means putting an end to the disharmony within the human self" (IF 31). In realizing itself, the human expressive faculty responds to a natural drive to create and diffuse harmony *(tanghim)*.

Not surprisingly, in providing an underpinning for his aesthetic perspective, Taha turns to the Qur'an, which is endowed with the unique characteristic of "containing all the eternal and created worlds" and of being "the sublime and superior tune [*lahn*] that sets forth to map out man's path, starting from his source of origin, through his return journey, and back to his point of return, which is the divine essence" (IF 11). The Qur'an is "music" played on a string drawn tight between the departure point (or "human reality," *al-haqiqa 'l-'abdiyya*) and the return point (or "divine reality," *al-haqiqa 'l-ilahiyya*). Taha captures all this through his descent and ascent imagery while firmly placing it within his theory of prayer. As one speaks in music about a heptatonic scale, one can say that the descent of the divine essence from the level of the Truth *(al-haqq)* to that of Reality *(al-haqiqa)* down to the level of "the lowest of the low" *(asfala safilin)* assumes the character of a "heptatonic scale": God descends through the seven attributes of life, knowledge, will, power, hearing, sight, and speech and man ascends through the same seven attributes but in reverse order. This process is recreated through prayer, which was prescribed above seven heavens and in which the worshipper is required to perform in each prayer unit *(rak'a)* seven movements and prostrate himself on seven bones of his body.[62]

Taha claims that one can realize through prayer an inner peace through the ending of the fluctuating movement of thought. He recognizes that the moments of artistic creativity or appreciation can be similar to the moment of prayer in that the fluctuating movement of thought can stop and one can experience the present moment more fully. Comparing religion, science, and art, he maintains that while science is about external knowledge (the "horizon signs" of verse 41:53) and religion is about internal knowledge (the "soul signs" of the same verse), art provides us with knowledge that is both of the external and the internal, though more of the former. Unlike religion, art does not possess the required methodology to delve into the realm of internal knowledge in a systematic, sustained, and profound manner. This is why Taha asserts that prayer remains far superior in liberating and enriching thought. However, once prayer has yielded its fruits and the seeker has attained spiritual maturity, then art becomes one of his means in journeying to God. This is the case because, ultimately, God has no enemy and all that exists, even Satan, calls for Him (IF 38–39).

Taha's emphasis on the Qurʾan leads him to an ultimate emphasis on music as opposed to language or poetry. In his view, one starts with the word, the immediately accessible, the visible, the concrete, and advances to music, the unfathomable, the invisible, the abstract. Speaking about perception, music, and language, he says, "When your perception is open to the totality of existence, then music can be far more profound than words because it can express all that words have failed to communicate. Nevertheless, in the early stages of the path music can be confusing, and language gives definite meanings. This is why the Qurʾan initially fashions its music from language and then proceeds to the sublime music of the totality of existence" (IF 38).

In privileging music over language, Taha not only underlines the inherent expressive inadequacy of language but also its capability to create deception and illusion. It is in this connection that he discusses poetry and the relationship between the Qurʾan and poetry. The Qurʾan clearly draws a line between poetry and itself in verse 36:69, which reads, "We have not taught him poetry; it is not seemly for him. It is only a Remembrance and a Clear Qurʾan." Taha had initially upheld the traditional position that not only stresses the differentiation of the Qurʾan from poetry but also expresses an antipoetry sentiment resting on the identification of poetry with untruth. He modified his position, however, in favor of a more open perspective that perceives the Qurʾan as a special kind of poetry combining music and truth (IF 40).

The ideal for Taha is to bring religion and art together in a harmonious relationship that enriches life intellectually and emotionally. He recognizes the power of art and wants to channel it in the service of religion. In his view, the artist and the artist's audience suffer from an inner fragmentation (*inqisam*) that can only be addressed through the means of religion, particularly prayer. In the absence of resolving this fragmentation through internal unity, art not only fails to realize its purpose of enriching the lives of human beings but can also become an impediment in their spiritual path.

What Taha says about art undoubtedly expresses a more understanding and receptive position than that championed by the traditional defenders of orthodoxy. However, although he is willing to effect an immediate break with shari'a in certain other areas, he adopts a less radical position when it comes to art. The underlying reason for such a position can be understood in the light of his recognition that "art is without question the best of secular knowledge that can achieve most by way of a greater sense of morality, a level of inner harmony, and a measure of good relationship with life (or a measure of expansiveness [*si'a*])" (IF 39). It is this perceived competition between art and religion that prompts Taha to insist that art should always be subordinated to shari'a. Art, hence, cannot achieve its full aesthetic potential or transformative impact unless it recognizes its function as the handmaiden of religion.

Conclusion

ALTHOUGH TAHA BELONGS to the modern revivalist tradition of Islam, he did not succeed in building a movement as did, for instance, Hasan al-Banna, the founder of the Muslim Brothers' movement. He is more like Muhammad 'Abduh, who founded a school of thought and left an intellectual legacy aimed at revitalizing Islam to overcome its crisis in the modern age.

Similarly to other Muslim modernists, Taha does not accept that Islam itself is in a state of crisis; rather, the crisis lies in Muslims' understanding of their religion. This emphasis on understanding is in fact an emphasis on the key role that consciousness plays in constructing the world and bringing about change. Taha would agree with Marx that there is an intimate connection between consciousness and the material reality of human existence, but he does not accept the Marxist position that consciousness is ultimately determined by material reality. This emphasis on consciousness leads him to assert another view that is at variance with orthodox Marxism, namely, that the "individual is the end" and hence the individual should be given primacy over society. The individual is the locus of consciousness, freedom, and action, and it is, hence, individual understanding and action that transform the human condition.

Yet despite his assertions to the contrary, it is clear that Taha's reform project is a response to the crisis of Islam that resulted from its encounter with Western modernity and colonial hegemony. By virtue of his education, Taha belonged to an elite that was molded by European education and influenced by the values of Western liberalism. Although this led, in the case of the majority of this educated elite, to an acceptance of secular values and institutions, Taha was among those who believed that Islam had the essential resources to offer solutions not only to Muslim societies but also to the global community. In this respect Taha was not different from another Sudanese, Muhammad Ahmad al-Mahdi, who believed that the program of his Mahdism was of a global nature. Yet for Taha, Mahdism was a limited and dated concept that had to be replaced by a modernist messianism. It is this messianic element that makes the notion of "promise" central in his thought: God, as the Qur'an asserts, had sent Muhammad with the "true religion" *(din 'l-haqq)* in order "to make it triumph over every religion" (9:33, 48:28, 61:9). Taha's lifelong effort was to expound the precise nature of this "true religion." Unlike Mirza Ghulam Ahmad (d. 1908), the founder of the Ahmadiyya, he did not claim to be a Mahdi or a messiah. Nevertheless, he made another special claim that vested him, as far as he and his followers were concerned, with a special authority.

With his claim of being "authentic," Taha's authority assumed the nature of what may be described as "primary authority." Whereas other modernists such as Sayyid Ahmad Khan, Sayyid Amir 'Ali (d. 1928), and 'Abduh assumed a "secondary authority" that derived its legitimacy from the Prophet's primary authority and the pressing demands of modernity, Taha's claim of being authentic, of expounding a message that originated in a moment of direct communion with God, made him the possessor of a primary authority that not only made clear what the "true religion" was but could, procedurally, abrogate what the Prophet left in place. This does not mean that other modernists did not in effect abrogate what the Prophet left in place. What marks Taha, however, is his assertion that the Prophet is in fact a "veil" between the servant and God that should be removed—that imitating the Prophet, despite its necessity, is a function of spiritual immaturity and it is only when one has transcended this state of imitation that one can make the claim of having attained spiritual maturity. The implications of this are evidently sweeping and far reaching: a parallel authority to that of the Prophet could be established and a progressive process of going beyond the prophetic horizon could become established as a key mechanism in reconstructing Islam. This is a process that may be called "prophetic marginalization."

Prophetic marginalization is a logical and plausible consequence of the Sufi experience, which, by its nature, stresses the element of a personal communion with God. This is a characteristic that is pronounced in the Sufism of al-Bistami or al-Hallaj or Ibn 'Arabi, for example. It may, however, be argued that it is in Taha's theory of prayer that we find the culmination and most mature expression of prophetic marginalization. When he characterizes ordinary Muslim prayer as a prayer of "imitation" or "gestures" or "ascension," he in fact views it primarily in terms of a worshipper-Muhammad relationship. The worshipper who performs his prayer in accordance with Taha's theory is infused from the start with a sense of ritual-spiritual hierarchy: his ordinary prayer belongs to a lower plane beyond which there is the promise of a higher, "authentic" plane of a worshipper-God relationship. This means that the worshipper's relationship with Muhammad is in essence of a transitional nature. In underlining this, Taha, in conformity with a well-established Sufi tradition, employs the *mi'raj*-journey metaphor; the Lote-Tree assumes a central significance as a boundary experienced not just by the Prophet but also by every worshipper at the moment that marks his break with Muhammadan imitation.

Naturally enough, this prophetic marginalization led Taha to a distinctive approach to the Qur'an. He accepts the orthodox dogma that the Qur'an is God's word, although he sets out to subject the doctrine to a radical Sufi reconstruction. This he does by following two strategies. On the one hand he bestows upon the Qur'anic text what may be described as a translinguistic nature by contending that the text's language only reveals a surface, a partial meaning beyond which lies a realm of infinite meanings. In this connection, he identifies divine speech with divine essence; engaging the Qur'an and unfolding its endless semantic layers becomes in effect an esoteric "journey in God." On the other hand, Taha recasts the notion of divine speech to invest it with a transtextual sense: God's speech is the totality of the phenomenal world. So here, likewise, one's discovery of the world and understanding of it is in effect an exoteric journey in God.

What Taha says about divine speech is inextricably bound up with his notion of authenticity, which results in a state of direct reception from God (*al-talaqqi kifahan*). This means that inasmuch as the one who has realized authenticity has his own individual testimony, prayer, *zakat*, fasting, and pilgrimage, he also has his own *qur'an*. What Taha says in this respect "democratizes," as it were, the Islamic notion of direct reception from God, which tends to be identified with, and confined to, the institution of prophecy. Whereas prophecy is about election and an exclusive voice through which God declares His will and purpose, what Taha describes and promises is inclusion in the divine presence that gives every authentic worshipper a divine voice, a "personal *qur'an*," by virtue of "hearing" from God and being in direct receipt from Him. It should, however, be noted that Taha neither uses the term "personal qur'an" nor refers to a *qur'an* that could replace the Qur'an that was revealed to Muhammad. Rather, the notion of a personal *qur'an* is implicit in what he writes and can be deduced from his theory of authenticity, which entails a personal law or a personal religion.

When it comes to the Qur'anic text, Taha reads it in terms of a basic opposition of "essential" and "subsidiary" passages. This opposition is indebted to the orthodox doctrine of abrogation and its opposition of "abrogating" and "abrogated." Although Taha does not go into the specific details of abrogation as some modern Muslim scholars have done, he calls into question the general assumption that abrogation is a unidirectional process. Consequently, he overturns the historical consensus that the Qur'anic passages that were later revealed in Medina abrogated and superseded the earlier, pre-*hijra* Meccan passages once and for all. He asserts the possibility, indeed the absolute necessity, of a counterabrogation that repeals the prevailing rulings of Medinan revelations and revives the rulings of earlier, Meccan revelations. This he bases on the bold assumption that what was essential was revealed in the earlier rather than the latter phase of the Prophet's career. According to Taha, then, the historical perception that Muhammad succeeded in spreading the "message of Islam" is mistaken or, at best, inaccurate: what triumphed under Muhammad and his successors was not the real message of Islam but rather a watered down, accommodationist version of what God had originally intended for humankind. Hence, the promise of a Second Message of Islam that can, for the first time in the history of humankind, combine the ideals of democracy and socialism in one politico-social system and realize a complete social equality.

In arguing his case for a second message, Taha simultaneously seeks to historicize and dehistoricize the Qur'an: whereas the Medinan passages are historical in that they reflected and responded to the historical reality of the time of Muhammad's mission, the Meccan passages originated in a different plane and reflected a different, future reality. At the heart of the Qur'an is thus a spatio-temporal rupture: Medinan and Meccan revelations on the one hand, and present-oriented (or past-oriented from our vantage point) and future-oriented revelations on the other. This rupture had to take place because of the nature of the Prophet's age, which was characterized by its *ghilza* (lit. "thickness, coarseness"; Taha's term for extending a degree of the state of *jahiliyya* into the Islamic era), a state that came to influence the divine revelation and diminish its horizon. Taha holds this depreciative view of post-*hijra* Islam in the face of the orthodox consensus that Islam (without a differentiation between Meccan and Medinan messages) brought about a radical spiritual and social change, liberating its adherents from their depraved state of *jahiliyya*. Of course, Taha does not deny that Islam brought about significant change, but he does not accept the orthodox belief that the Prophet's time (and the time of his caliph successors in Medina) was the golden age of Islam and the highest point in human history.

In insisting that the Medina state represented a fall from the Qur'anic ideal and that a utopian golden age of Islam is still ahead, Taha adopts an evolutionary, progressivistic perspective that is evidently inspired by Marxism. An important issue that arises in this connection is the clear conflict between the evolutionary anthropology he espouses (which allows for the recognition of elementary forms of religious life as early, legitimate, and necessary steps toward monotheism) and the nonevolutionary Qur'anic perspective that assumes a primal Adamic monotheism constantly revived by a continuous chain of prophets culminating in, and ending with, Muhammad. Taha tries to resolve the conflict through a contrived reconstruction of the Qur'anic creation story according to which there was a long and turbulent human history of "failed Adams" that preceded the emergence of Adam the vicegerent to whom the Qur'an specifically refers. Yet, Taha's problem remains, as he fails to show how the evolutionary anthropology he adopts can be reconciled to Qur'anic anthropology that conceives human history in the light of a basic salvific scheme of continuous struggle between belief *(iman)* and unbelief *(kufr)*.

A key esoteric function with which Taha invests the Qur'an is that it is an expression of the descent of the divine essence from its absolute realm to the realm of the created world. On this level the Qur'an is atemporal and ahistorical. The general framework of this expression is the theory of the Unity of Being that Taha borrows from Ibn 'Arabi. The Unity of Being doctrine views every moment in creation as a moment of complete perfection because it represents the totality of the divine. Furthermore, Taha adopts an extreme position of what may be called an "ontological simultaneity," or the view that all things, whether in the past, present, or future, *are*. He neither elaborates on this nor does he show how it operates on the level of reading actual human history.

Taha's call for a counterabrogation that revives Meccan revelations provides what he deems as the Qur'anic foundation for his notion of a Second Message of Islam. Like some other modernists, he claims a Qur'anic foundation for concepts such as democracy, socialism, and gender and social equality, but unlike these modernists he views the specific Qur'anic passages dealing with these issues as suspended and inoperative, and it is only through the radical measure of abrogating the rulings of Medinan revelations and declaring them null and void that Islam can fully realize its liberative potential. Relying on the Qur'anic text (or for that matter the hadith material), Taha cannot present us with fully fledged formulations of democracy, socialism, or gender and social equality but only the most general of statements that are subjected to an eclectic interpretive reading. It should, however, be noted that for Taha's purpose, and for that matter for the purposes of other like-minded modernists, what really matters is what they perceive as Qur'anic sanction of these notions. Such sanction is sufficient for Taha to advance particular claims the details of which are derived from other sources.

When it comes to Taha's epistemology and position on science, it is important to note that despite his acceptance of modern science and his assertion that its findings do not undermine Islam, he is committed to a religious epistemology that privileges revelation and does not recognize causality. The term "revelation" should be understood here in the general sense of knowledge that is rooted in a human-divine encounter—an encounter not confined only to prophets but inclusive of all worshippers. When it comes to knowledge that is not claimed to have been revealed, Taha displays a marked ambiguity. On the one hand and in accordance with a notion of unity that predicates everything on divine will, all knowledge is perceived as of divine origin. On the other hand there is something such as false or untrue knowledge that he rejects and combats. A case in point is what Taha says about Marxist atheism, which he treats in one instance as God-willed (as no phenomenon could come into existence if not willed by God) yet contests throughout his work as "false knowledge."

A major tension in Taha's thought arises over the problem of freedom. Philosophically he defends the notion of absolute individual freedom. Yet on the theological level he is committed to a strong determinist position that insists on attributing all actions to God. These conflicting claims cannot be reconciled with another aspect of his thought—that is, his staunch defense of shari'a (albeit a reformed shari'a in some areas). Shari'a assumes moral and legal responsibility, and Taha's strong determinism effectively takes away that responsibility. He tries to overcome this by resorting to far-fetched and contrived argument based on an opposition of divine and human knowledge: since it is only God who knows future human actions, it follows that all that humans can do is to follow His law as laid down in shari'a. In arguing this, Taha does not take the implications of his determinism seriously, as the key question is not one of foreknowledge but concerns the mere power to perform an action. What should be stressed, however, is that when it comes to practice rather than theory, Taha deals with human actions and history from a perspective that presupposes human freedom and autonomy of will.

The active interplay between history and the word of God or history and religion is a major theme in Taha's thought, revealing both its creativity and limitations. On the mystical level his focus is on the word of God, which he identifies with the created world. As such, the word of God can also be identified with the totality of history. In contrast, religion is a concretized, historicized, and institutionalized expression of the word of God. The distinction between the word of God and religion is underlined by Taha in terms of his key distinction between belief ('aqida) and knowledge as a gnostic realization ('ilm): whereas 'aqida is particular, 'ilm is universal; whereas 'aqida conditions the mind in a manner that breeds bias and fragmentation, 'ilm liberates and unites the mind. As such, one can conceive of a universal religion that transcends the specificity of historical religions and offers a more liberating and comprehensive spiritual horizon. This is the level where for Taha Islam assumes a generic nature—it becomes *islam* in the basic sense of submission to God, total harmony with the divine scheme of things, a loss of one's human subjectivity in the all-encompassing divine subjectivity, a release and return from the exile of humanity to the origin and home of the spark of divinity inside every human.

This highly creative and essentially subversive religious imagination is, however, restrained by its framework. Taha insists on a gradualist and evolutionary approach that gives *'aqida* its due as an essential starting point: a universal religion has to be a culmination of a particular, institutionalized religion; a conscious servitude and bondage is an essential prerequisite for freedom. It is this position that lays the foundation for what has been described as Taha's Islamocentricism. Embracing the orthodox position, he insists that an unquestioning acceptance of the claims of Islam is the only path that leads to salvation and universal religion. This sums up his life-long dilemma, which may be that of many religious modernists whether Muslim or non-Muslim: while he seeks to expand the horizon of his religious tradition and make it coincide with a more expansive and inclusive horizon produced by modernity, he calls at the same time for an impregnation of this modernity with the values of his specific religious tradition, without which, he claims, it will lose its spirit and be condemned to alienation.

Throughout his life Taha was a controversial thinker who constantly challenged Muslims to reconsider their understanding of Islam on the level of individual spirituality. In addition, he offered on the social level a reformulation of a new message of Islam that he profoundly believed could meet the needs and challenges facing modern Muslim communities. His mystical vision and his reform project remain among the boldest and most original responses to the crisis of Islam in the modern world.

Notes

Bibliography

Index

 Notes

Background

1. On the background to this development, see Yusuf Fadl Hasan, *The Arabs and the Sudan from the Seventh to the Early Sixteenth Century* (Edinburgh: Edinburgh Univ. Press, 1967), 90–132.

2. On Funj origins, see O. G. S. Crawford, *The Fung Kingdom of Sennar* (Gloucester: John Bellows, 1951), 143–55; P. M. Holt, "Funj Origins: A Critique and New Evidence," *Journal of African History* 4, no. 1 (1963): 39–56; and Yusuf Fadl Hasan, *Muqaddima fi tarikh 'l-mamalik 'l-Islamiyya fi 'l-Sudan 'l-sharqi, 1450–1821* (Khartoum: Matba'at Jami'at 'l-Khurtum, 1989), 39–59.

3. James Bruce, *Travels to Discover the Source of the Nile* (Edinburgh: A. Constable and Co., 1813), 6:388.

4. On Islam as an important component of state ideology in the Funj Kingdom and as the ideological basis of the kingdom's corporate identity within the world of nations, see Jay Spaulding, *The Heroic Age in Sinnar* (East Lansing: African Studies Center of Michigan State University, 1985), 122–25.

5. On an analysis that stresses the role of the Funj Kingdom as an agent of Arabization, see 'Abd al-'Aziz Husain al-Sawi and Muhammad 'Ali Jadain, *Al-Thawra 'l-mahdiyya fi 'l-Sudan: Mashru' ru'ya jadida* (N.p.: Sharikat 'l-Farabi, 1990), 28–30.

6. Underlining a *shaikh*-community interdependence, Hofheinz says, "I would describe a *tariqa* as a social complex centering around a *shaykh* who transmits religious valuables—ritual guidance, knowledge, 'blessing'/Divine power *(baraka)*, etc.—to the community and its members and mediates between them and higher powers. While in the narrower sense it certainly is an association or even an organization which individuals join by taking the covenant of allegiance, it is important to realise that the practical implications of this oath usually remain latent. Only a few people usually practice the office assigned to them by the *shaykh;* to most, association with a brotherhood means only that they know to whom to turn for support in case of need." Albrecht Hofheinz, "Internalising Islam: Shaykh Muhammad Majdhub, Scriptural Islam, and Local Context in the Early Nineteenth-Century Sudan" (Ph.D. diss., University of Bergen, 1996), 18.

7. On the establishment of these orders in Sudan, see J. Spencer Trimingham, *Islam in the Sudan* (Oxford: Oxford Univ. Press, 1949), 217–24; and Ali Salih Karrar, *The Sufi Brotherhoods in the Sudan* (Evanston: Northwestern Univ. Press, 1992), 20–41.

8. Muhammad al-Nur Ibn Daif Allah, *Kitab 'l-tabaqat fi khusus 'l-awliya' wa 'l-salihin wa 'l-'ulama' wa 'l-shu'ara' fi 'l-Sudan*, ed. Yusuf Fadl Hasan (Khartoum: Matba'at Jami'at 'l-Khurtum, 1985), 212.

9. Ibid., 212.

10. Ibid., 71.

11. On the prevalent Islamic sciences and their sources during this period, see Yusuf Fadl Hasan, introduction to *Kitab 'l-tabaqat fi khusus 'l-awliya' wa 'l-salihin wa 'l-'ulama' wa 'l-shu'ara' fi 'l-Sudan*, by Muhammad al-Nur Ibn Daif Allah (Khartoum: Matba'at Jami'at 'l-Khurtum, 1985), 4–6. On the *khalwa* as an institution and on the methods and stages of learning, see 'Abd al-Majid 'Abdin, *Tarikh 'l-thaqafa 'l-'Arabiyya fi 'l-Sudan mundhu nash'atiha ila 'l-'asr 'l-hadith* (Beirut: Dar 'l-Thaqafa, 1967), 86–97. See also Bushra G. Hamad, "The Education System of the Funj Kingdom," *Sudan Notes and Records* 3 (1999): 25–44.

12. Ibn Daif Allah, *Kitab 'l-tabaqat*, 57.

13. On the political role of the *shaikh*s, see 'Abd al-Salam Sidahmad, *Al-Fuqaha' wa 'l-saltana fi Sinnar* (Prague: Babylon, 1991) particularly 85–114.

14. For a list of al-Bashir's works, see Hasan Muhammad al-Fatih Qarib Allah, *Al-Tasawwuf fi 'l-Sudan ila nihayat 'asr 'l-Funj* (Khartoum: The Graduate College at the University of Khartoum, 1987), 155–59.

15. On the sources of al-Bashir's thought, see 'Abd al-Qadir Mahmud, *Al-fikr 'l-sufi fi 'l-Sudan* (Cairo: Dar 'l-Fikr 'l-'Arabi, 1968), 72–89.

16. On al-Bashir's career, see Neil McHugh, *Holymen of the Blue Nile: The Making of an Arab-Islamic Community in the Nilotic Sudan, 1500–1850* (Evanston: Northwestern Univ. Press, 1994), 136–41.

17. P. M. Holt and M. W. Daly, *The History of the Sudan: From the Coming of Islam to the Present Day* (London: Wieden and Nicolson, 1979), 48.

18. Na"um Shuqair, *Tarikh 'l-Sudan 'l-qadim wa 'l-hadith wa jughrafiyatuhu* (Cairo: Matba'at 'l-Ma'arif, 1903), 3:4.

19. On the life and reform ideas of Ahmad b. Idris, see R. S. O'Fahey, *Enigmatic Saint: Ahmad Ibn Idris and the Idrisi Tradition* (London: Hirst and Company, 1990).

20. On the foundation of the Khatmiyya and its eventual Sudanization, see John O. Voll, "A History of the Khatmiyyah Tariqah in the Sudan" (Ph.D. diss., Harvard Univ., 1969), chapters 2 and 3.

21. On the arguments that the *'ulama'* raised against the Mahdism of Muhammad Ahmad, see 'Abd Allah 'Ali Ibrahim, *Al-Sira' baina 'l-Mahdi wa 'l-'ulama'* (Cairo: Markaz 'l-Dirasat 'l-Sudaniyya, 1994), 33–42; and Muhammad Ibrahim Abu Salim, *Al-Haraka 'l-fikriyya fi 'l-Mahdiyya* (Khartoum: Matba'at Jami'at 'l-Khurtum, 1989), 50–77.

22. Sulaiman b. al-Ash'ath Abu Da'ud, *Sunan Abi Da'ud,* ed. Muhammad 'Abd al-'Aziz al-Khalidi (Beirut: Dar 'l-Kutub 'l-'Ilmiyya, 1996), 3:110.

23. On the Mahdi's "lifting" *(raf')* of *madhhab*s and *tariqa*s, see Abu Salim, *Al-Haraka 'l-fikriyya,* 86–90.

24. This policy was inspired by Lord Cromer's religious policy in Egypt. See Gabriel Warburg, *Islam, Sectarianism and Politics in Sudan Since the Mahdiyya* (London: Hurst and Company, 2003), 57–58.

25. Holt and Daly, *History of the Sudan,* 124.

26. Peter Woodward, *Condominium and Sudanese Nationalism* (London: Rex Collings, 1979), 4.

27. On the rise of the Ansar during this period, see Gabriel Warburg, "British Policy To-wards the Ansar in Sudan: A Note on an Historical Controversy," *Middle Eastern Studies* 33, no. 4 (1997): 675–92; and Hassan Ahmed Ibrahim, "The Neo-Mahdists and the British, 1944–47: From Tactical Co-operation to Short-lived Confrontation." *Middle Eastern Studies* 38, no. 3 (July 2002): 47–72.

28. Ahmad Khair, *Kifah Jil: Tarikh harakat 'l-khirrijin wa tatawwuruha fi 'l-Sudan* (Khartoum: Al-Dar 'l-Sudaniyya, 1970), 18–19.

29. On Muhammad 'Abduh and his ideas, see Malcolm H. Kerr, *Islamic Reform: The Political and Legal Theories of Muhammad 'Abduh and Rashid Rida* (Berkeley, Ca.: Univ. of California Press, 1966), chaps. 1–4; and Hourani, Albert, *Arabic Thought in the Liberal Age, 1798–1939* (Cambridge: Cambridge Univ. Press, 1995), 130–60.

30. Khair, *Kifah Jil,* 21.

31. Muhammad Ahmad Mahjub, *Nahw 'l-ghad* (Khartoum: Matba'at Jami'at 'l-Khurtum, 1970), 134.

32. Nationalist consciousness often fuses the notions of "otherness" and "foreignness." An example of this from the Sudanese nationalist lore is about an encounter between a *kujur* (spiritual leader), who led a revolt in southern Sudan, and a colonial officer. When the officer asked him why he revolted, the *kujur* took a handful of dust, brought it close to the officer's nose, and asked, "Do you smell your father in this dust?" Khair, *Kifah Jil,* 91.

33. British colonial policy encouraged tribal identification, a matter that was opposed by the nationalists. A revealing incident concerns a group of nationalists who were involved in a prison revolt in 1924. In their interrogations they were asked about their *jins* (origin, nationality), and they all responded by saying they were "Sudanese." Their British interrogator subjected them to severe beatings until they relented and identified themselves "tribally." See Yoshiko Kurita, *'Ali 'Abd al-Latif wa Thawrat 1924: Bahth fi Masadir 'l-Thawra 'l-Sudaniyya,* trans. Majdi al-Na'im (Cairo: Markaz 'l-Dirasat 'l-Sudaniyya, 1997), 34–35.

34. On the events of 1924, see Hasan 'Abdin, *Early Sudanese Nationalism, 1919–1925* (Khartoum: Institute of African and Asian Studies, 1985); and Kurita, *'Ali 'Abd al-Latif.* For shorter treatments, see Muddathir 'Abd al-Rahim, *Imperialism and Nationalism in the Sudan: A Study in Constitutional and Political Development, 1899–1956* (Oxford: Oxford

Univ. Press, 1969), 102–8; and Tim Niblock, *Class and Power in Sudan: The Dynamics of Sudanese Politics, 1898–1985* (Albany: State Univ. of New York Press, 1987), 90–132.

35. Mahjub, *Nahw 'l-ghad,* 176.

36. On the founding of the Graduates' Congress and its activities, see Mohamed Omer Beshir, *Revolution and Nationalism in the Sudan* (London: Rex Collings, 1974), 153–65; and Bashir Muhammad Sa'id, *Al-Za'im al-Azhari wa 'asruhu* (Cairo: Al-Qahira 'l-Haditha li-'l-Tiba'a, 1990), 45–68.

37. The hostility against *ta'ifiyya* was particularly pronounced among those intellectuals who formed what came to be known as the Abu Rawf group (Abu Rawf being a quarter of Omdurman). In a sweeping attack on *ta'ifiyya,* a member of the group, Khidir Hamad, described it as the "prop that supports colonialism and acts as its agent in several areas." Quoted in Muhammad Sa'id al-Qaddal, *Tarikh 'l-Sudan 'l-hadith* (Cairo: Al-Amal li-'l-Tiba'a wa 'l-Nashr, 1993), 346.

1. The Context, the Man, and the Movement

1. On the Rikabiyyun, see H. A. MacMichael, *A History of the Arabs in the Sudan* (Cambridge: Cambridge Univ. Press, 1922), 1:333–34.

2. Ibn Daif Allah, *Kitab 'l-tabaqat,* 316–17.

3. The Qadiriyya was introduced into the Funj Kingdom by a certain Taj al-Din al-Bahari, who visited the country in 985/1577. According to legend, he told those who wanted to be initiated that they had to be slaughtered. Those who were willing to take up this ultimate sacrifice were taken aside, while hidden rams were slaughtered and their blood let out. One of these initiates was Muhammad al-Hamim. See Ibn Daif Allah, *Kitab 'l-tabaqat,* 108–9.

4. Ibid., 317. The Night of Power is the theme of chapter 97 in the Qur'an. It is traditionally believed to be a night in the month of Ramadan during which the entirety of the Qur'an was revealed to Muhammad. In popular Islam, this night is connected with a special and mysterious blessing that makes the realization of wishes possible. Being open to this blessing is expressed in terms of "seeing" the Night of Power.

5. Ibn Daif Allah, *Kitab 'l-tabaqat,* 301–2.

6. Ibid., 70–71.

7. Ibid., 71–72. This was such a radical step that even a modern scholar and Sufi *shaikh* finds it difficult to accept. Hasan al-Fatih Qarib Allah comments, "In our view, Abu Dulaiq was as illiterate as al-Hamim and had no inkling of who was fit to be *shaikh.* He did not think of the consequences of his act and what impact it would have on his disciples and followers. . . . Moreover, he did not at all take into account the rivalry between his own branch and other [Qadiriyya] branches and whether a member of another branch would bring an end to [al-Hamim's] branch by marrying the [female] *shaikh.*. . . . 'A'isha was not strong enough to defeat rivals and not bold enough to respond to points raised by debaters in public forums. Moreover, she was a single woman and as such needed assistance and sincere company. The branch met with ill fortune when 'A'isha was married by Shaikh Badawi Abu Dulaiq, an am-

bitious man who liked to be a leader. After her marriage, 'A'isha had to choose between looking after her family or assuming the responsibilities of the brotherhood. She chose the former. . . . As such she was the last *shaikh* of al-Hamim's branch." Qarib Allah, *Al-Tasawwuf fi 'l-Sudan*, 76–77.

8. Besides his family support, Taha was fortunate that he grew up in Rufaʿa. Rufaʿa is in a region that received modern education at an early stage during the condominium period. In 1907, elementary teacher training courses were started in Rufaʿa and Sawakin. The town was among the first five centers in which elementary schools for girls were established. See Mohamed Omer Beshir, *Educational Development in the Sudan, 1898–1956* (Oxford: The Clarendon Press, 1969), 45–46.

9. Taha did not write an autobiography. The basic biographical information in this chapter is based on Abdullahi Ahmed an-Naʿim's introduction to *The Second Message of Islam*, by Mahmud Muhammad Taha, trans. an-Naʿim (Syracuse, N.Y.:Syracuse University Press, 1987), 1–30. Taha's best biography to date is Edward Thomas's "Mahmud Muhammad Taha: His Life in Sudan" (Ph.D. diss., The Univ. of Edinburgh, 1999).

10. W. Stephen Howard, "Mahmoud Mohammed Taha: A Remarkable Teacher in Sudan." *Northeast African Studies* 10, no. 1 (1988): 85.

11. On the debate concerning tradition and modernity in Muslim societies, see Dale F. Eickelman and James Piscatori, *Muslim Politics* (Princeton, N.J.: Princeton Univ. Press, 1996), 22–45.

12. This notion of a triple heritage was expressed in 1941 by Muhammad Ahmad Mahjub in connection with the future of the intellectual movement in the country. See Mahjub, *Nahw 'l-ghad*, 209–34. On Arabism and Sudanese identity, see Heather Sharkey, "Colonialism and the Culture of Nationalism in the Northern Sudan, 1898–1956" (Ph.D. diss., Princeton Univ., 1998), 278–84.

13. Al-Ikhwan 'l-Jumhuriyyun, *Maʿalim ʿala tariq tatwwur 'l-fikra 'l-Jumhuriyya* (Omdurman: Republican Movement Publication, 1976), 35. Highlighting Taha's refusal to cooperate and the consequences of his imprisonment, the British intelligence report of May-June 1946 said the following: "On being convicted, [Taha] was invited to enter into a bond to keep the peace and to provide a couple of sureties. This he refused to do and was accordingly committed to prison, until he signed the bond. Every effort was made, unsuccessfully, to explain to him and to his friends that he was not being required to denounce his republican principles but merely to undertake to propagate them by legitimate means. He preferred the role of 'political martyr' and has been hailed as such by the Congress and local vernacular press. As a result of this advertisement, the Republican Party's shares have boomed and its membership risen to nearly 100." Sudan Political Intelligence Summary (SPIS), no. 57, par. 478, Public Records Office (PRO)/Foreign Office (FO) 371/53328.

14. The assembly's resolution was passed by eighteen votes to nine. Despite the perceived general resistance to the legislation among the population, the vote reflected the im-

mense success of the anticircumcision campaign in winning over the majority of legislative opinion. For the history of this campaign and an excellent account of the circumcision debate in the Sudan, see Lillian P. Sanderson, *Against the Mutilation of Women: The Struggle to End Unnecessary Suffering* (London: Ithaca Press, 1981), 70–111. Being fully cognizant of the delicate sensitivity of the issue and the likely resistance the legislation might spark, the Sudan government could not have embarked on this step without the backing of the influential political and religious forces. As early as 1940, the social program of the Graduates' Congress sought to combat "prostitution, public consumption of alcohol, and pharaonic circumcision." Beshir, *Revolution and Nationalism,* 157. In 1943, the mufti of the Sudan, Shaikh Ahmad al-Tahir, made a statement condemning the practice as un-Islamic. Likewise, 'Ali al-Mirghani and 'Abd al-Rahman al-Mahdi made statements calling on their supporters to end the practice.

15. In pharaonic circumcision the clitoris, labia minora, and labia majora are excised, whereas in the sunna type only the clitoris is excised. On the types of circumcision, see Asma el-Dareer, *Woman, Why Do You Weep? Circumcision and Its Consequences* (London: Zed Press, 1981), 1–8.

16. On a criticism of Taha's position, see Mohamed Mahmoud, "Mahmud Muhammad Taha and the Rise and Demise of the Jumhuri Movement," *New Political Science* 23, no. 1(2001): 72–74.

17. The dire seriousness of the situation was reflected by the decision of the authorities to send "a company of Sudan Defence Force troops . . . to Rufaa, where they stood by outside the town while Mohamed Mahmoud [*sic*] Taha and other ringleaders were arrested and taken to Hassaheissa." SPIS, no. 59, Aug.-Sept., 1946, par. 532, PRO/FO 371/53328.

18. Some of Taha's supporters either misunderstood his spiritual exercise or decided to exploit it politically. According to the intelligence report of November 1946, "Muhammad Mahmud [*sic*] Taha, the Republican leader, has been indulging in a religious fast in Madani gaol, eating only by night. His supporters have sent telegrams alleging him to be at death's door but public interest has subsided and he is regarded as having got his deserts. His health is quite satisfactory." SPIS, no. 61, par. 579, PRO/FO 371/53328.

19. In writing about the movement and its ideas, Paul J. Magnarella reflects this brief experimental phase and refers to it simultaneously as the "Republican Brothers" and the "New Islamic Mission." See his "The Republican Brothers: A Reformist Movement in the Sudan," *The Muslim World* 72, no. 1(1982): 14–24.

20. The description *Islamic fundamentalism* has generally been applied to traditional expressions of Islamism. Discussing the relevance of applying such a description to the Republicans, an-Na'im argues, "The term 'Muslim Fundamentalist' is currently popularly used to refer to those who demand the immediate implementation of historical Islamic shari'a law. Otherwise, the Republicans would claim to be fundamentalist in the sense of advocating a return to the fundamental sources of Islam to develop a modern version of Islamic law."

An-Na'im, in Taha, SMn 11. The Republicans' claim is evidently motivated by their wish to stress the credentials of their case. As what really matters here is the way the "fundamental sources" are read, and because the Republicans' goal is to develop a modern version of Islamic law, in sharp opposition to the readings of other Islamist movements, a distinction between the Republicans and these movements is in order. It is in the light of this distinction that the term *fundamentalist* is more accurately and appropriately applicable to the more orthodox and traditional movements that resist the development of modern versions of Islamic law. Taha's deep clash with fundamentalism led to his apostasy trials and was a crucial factor in his execution. Paradoxically, the distinction stressed here is also upheld by an-Na'im, who describes in another place the Islamists' approach as "fundamentalist and traditionalist" and Taha's approach as "modernist." See Abdullahi An-Na'im, "The Elusive Islamic Constitution: The Sudanese Experience," *Orient* 26, no. 3 (1985): 332.

21. This was clearly spelled out in a memorandum that the Federal Bloc, a southern party, submitted to the Sudan government in May 1955. See Mansour Khalid, *The Government They Deserve: The Role of the Elite in Sudan's Political Evolution* (London: Kegan Paul, 1990), 134.

22. On this mutiny, see Oliver Albino, *The Sudan: A Southern Viewpoint* (London: Oxford Univ. Press, 1970), 36–39.

23. Khalid, *The Government They Deserve*, 167.

24. See Haydar Badawi Sadig, "The Republican Brothers: A Religio-Political Movement in the Sudan" (M.A. diss., Univ. of Khartoum, 1988), 61–64; and Annette Oevermann, *Die "Republikanischen Brüder" im Sudan: Eine islamische Reformbewegung im Zwanzigsten Jahrhundert* (Frankfurt am Main: Peter Lang, 1993), 55–57.

25. On the role of the Communist Party during the 'Abbud period leading to the October uprising, see Gabriel Warburg, *Islam, Nationalism and Communism in a Traditional Society: The Case of Sudan* (London: Frank Cass, 1978a), 106–16; and Muhammad Sa'id al-Qaddal, *Ma'alim fi tarikh 'l-hizb 'l-Shuyu'i 'l-Sudani* (Beirut: Dar 'l-Farabi, 1999), 105–26.

26. On the incident that sparked the Muslim Brothers' campaign, see Hasan Makki, *Harakat 'l-Ikhwan 'l-Muslimin fi 'l-Sudan, 1944–1969* (Khartoum: Ma'had 'l-Dirasat 'l-Ifriqiyya wa 'l-Asyawiyya, 1982), 82–83; and al-Qaddal, *Ma'alim*, 152–53.

27. The government's loss of the legal battle and the resistance of leftist and liberal forces may have earned the Communists a legitimacy that the Right did not challenge again. During the democratic period of 1985–89, the Communist Party was a legitimate force whose full and active participation in the country's political life was not contested by the Islamists or any other force. Even under the current military Islamist regime (1989 to present), the Communists have not been singled out by a special set of laws on account of subscribing to an atheistic ideology. Although the 1991 penal code contains an article pertaining to apostasy *(ridda)*, this has not so far been invoked against the Communists.

28. Taha's anti-Communism informed many of his positions. For instance, he was vehe-

mently opposed to Nasser's nationalization of the Suez Canal, which he saw as a shortsighted measure that would thrust Egypt into the thick of the cold war and create a favorable climate for the Soviet Union to establish a firm foothold in the Middle East (MS 27–30).

29. *Hisba* is a concept and practice developed by jurists in connection with the Qur'anic injunction to "promote good and combat evil." Accordingly, it was argued that it is incumbent upon Muslims to do this through legal intervention (even in the absence of personal interest) or other means of intervention. Islamists have often invoked *hisba* against their opponents. For a succinct treatment of the concept's development, see the *Encyclopaedia of Islam* New Edition (hereafter *EI²*), (Leiden: Brill, 1960–2003), s.v. "*hisba*" 3:485–93.

30. Louis Massignon's three-volume work on al-Hallaj, *The Passion of al-Hallaj: Mystic and Martyr of Islam*, trans. Herbert Mason (Princeton: Princeton Univ. Press, 1982), remains the definitive work on him; for information on his life and times, see the first volume. See also Herbert W. Mason, *Al-Hallaj* (Richmond, Surrey: Curzon Press, 1995), 1–34; and 'Abd al-Salam Nur al-Din, *Al-Haqiqa wa 'l-shari'a fi 'l-fikr 'l-Sufi* (Nicosia: Dar Sawmar, 1992), 32–48. On the historical conflict between Sufism and orthodoxy, see Gerhard Böwering, "Early Sufism between Persecution and Heresy," in *Islamic Mysticism Contested: Thirteen Centuries of Controversies and Polemics*, ed. Frederick de Jong and Bernd Radtke (Leiden: Brill, 1999), 54–65. On the conflict between the Jumhuris and other Sufis, see Ibrahim M. Zein, "Religion, Legality, and the State: 1983 Penal Code" (Ph.D. diss., Temple Univ., 1989), 291–92; and Mansour Khalid, *Al-Fajr 'l-kadhib: Nimairi wa tahrif 'l-shari'a* (Cairo: Dar 'l-Hilal, 1986), 91. The legal attack on Taha went in tandem with a ferocious campaign that demonized him as an agent of imperialism and Zionism. On this campaign, see Jürgen Rogalski, "Mahmud Muhammad Taha—Zur Erinnerung an das Schicksal eines Mystikers und Intellektuellen im Sudan," *Asien Afrika Lateinamerika* 24 (1996): 49–50.

31. Eltayeb suggests that the Republican Party's campaign against the Muslim Brothers, the Umma Party, and the Nationalist Unionist Party (NUP) and their proposed Islamic constitution was a direct cause for this trial. Eltayeb H. M. Eltayeb, "The Second Message of Islam: A Critical Study of the Islamic Reformist Thinking of Mahmud Muhammad Taha (1909–85)" (Ph.D. diss., Univ. of Manchester, 1995), 75. This is inaccurate as there was no evidence that either the Umma Party or the NUP wanted to dissolve the Republican Party.

32. On the attitudes of Egyptian Islamists to the defeat of 1967, see Emmanuel Sivan, *Radical Islam: Medieval Theology and Modern Politics* (New Haven: Yale Univ. Press, 1990), 16–18. On the crisis of Arab nationalism and the rise of Islamist discourse after the defeat, see Gilles Kepel, *Jihad: The Trial of Political Islam*, trans. Anthony E. Roberts (London: I. B. Tauris, 2002), 62–63.

33. Khalid, *The Government They Deserve*, 242.

34. According to an-Na'im the active membership of the Republicans did not exceed one thousand. Abdullahi An-Na'im, "Sudan Republican Brothers: An Alternative Islamic Ideology," *Middle East Report* 17, no. 147 (1987): 41. Evidently, the hardcore Republicans were surrounded by many sympathizers. Rogalski estimates this circle of supporters and

sympathizers to be between five and ten thousand. Jürgen Rogalski, "Die 'Republikanischen Brüder' im Sudan: Ein Beitrag zur Ideolgiegeschichte des Islam in der Gegenwart" (M.A. diss., Free Univ. of Berlin, 1990), 53. On the other hand, Duran maintains that "the core activists rarely numbered more than 800, but sympathizers were counted in tens of thousands." Khalid Duran, "The Reform Theology of Mahmud M. Taha," *TransState Islam* 1, no. 3 (1995), 10. Whereas the numbers of core members can be ascertained with reasonable accuracy, it is clear that estimates of sympathizers tend to be highly speculative, although what Rogalski suggests sounds more reasonable than Duran's suggestion.

35. Although the social origin of the overwhelming majority of the Republicans placed them above the line of poverty, their socialist ideology made them identify with the poor, as Duran rightly observed. Khalid Duran, "Die 'Republikanischen Brüder' im Sudan—eine islamische Reformbewegung der Gegenwart." *SOWI* 10, no. 2 (1981), 69. In this respect, the Republicans stood in marked contrast to the Sudanese Muslim Brothers whose ideology has tended to defend capitalism and whose ethos has tended to celebrate making money.

36. Sadig points out that among the Republicans "there were practically no illiterates except among workers and other petty traders who constitute a small percentage [of the movement]." Sadig, "Republican Brothers," 18.

37. In Sadiq's sample 85 percent were between fifteen and forty years old. See his "Republican Brothers," 19.

38. In their *Sisters under the Sun,* Hall and Ismail speak about the astonishing "sight of young women modestly dressed in white robes walking in pairs along the main thoroughfares of the capital handing out leaflets and canvassing on behalf of the Republican Movement. Engaging passers-by in discussion about the aims of their movement, they persuasively seek to win converts to their cause." Marjorie Hall and Bakhita Amin Ismail, *Sisters Under the Sun: The Story of Sudanese Women* (London: Longman, 1981), 24. Hale points out, "When I first became aware of the Republicans in the 1970s, I was surprised at the extent to which women participated in the movement." Sondra Hale, *Gender Politics in Sudan: Islamism, Socialism, and the State* (Boulder: Westview Press, 1997), 86. See also Khalid Duran, "The Centrifugal Forces of Religion in Sudanese Politics," *Orient* 26, no. 4 (1985), 598.

39. On the events leading to the Aba attack, see Mansour Khalid, *Nimeiri and the Revolution of Dis-May* (London: Kegan Paul, 1985), 18–21.

40. On this coup, see Fu'ad Matar, *Al-Hizb 'l-shuyu'i 'l-sudani: Naharuhu am 'ntahar?* (Beirut: Dar 'l-Nahar, 1971), 32–71. See also 'Abd al-Salam Sidahmad, *Politics and Islam in Contemporary Sudan* (Richmond, Surrey: Curzon, 1997), 117–18.

41. Francis Deng, *War of Visions: Conflict of Identities in the Sudan* (Washington, D.C.: The Brookings Institution, 1995), 362.

42. On Islamic banking and the social context of its rise, see Nazih Ayubi, *Political Islam: Religion and Politics in the Arab World* (London: Routledge, 1991), 178–200. On Islamic banking in the Sudan, see Elfatih Shaaeldin and Richard Brown, "Towards an Understanding of Islamic Banking in Sudan," in *Sudan: State, Capital, and Transformation,* ed. Tony Barnett

and Abbas Abdelkarim (London: Croom Helm, 1988), 121–40; and Badreddin el-Beiti, "Participatory Islamic Finance and Entrepreneurship: A Theoretical Examination," *Sudan Notes and Records* 2 (1998): 175–86. See also Mansour Khalid, *Al-Nukhba 'l-Sudaniyya wa idman 'l-fashal* (Cairo: Sijil 'l-'Arab, 1993), 1:652–57.

43. Republican criticisms centered on economic mismanagement and the regime's "integration charter" with Egypt. For an exposition and defense of the Republican position, see Eltayeb, "Second Message," 79–81.

44. 'Abd Allah Jallab, "Mahmud Muhammad Taha yaqul," *al-Sahafa,* Dec. 11, 1972, www.alfikra.org. Warburg maintains that "the alliance between Numayri and Taha came to an end in 1977 as a result of Numayri's Islamic policy and his reconciliation with the Muslim Brothers and the Ansar, both of whom regarded Taha's views as heresy." Warburg, *Islam, Sectarianism and Politics,* 162. A reading of the memorandum, the national charter submitted by the Jumhuris, and their widely distributed booklet *al-Sulh khair* (Reconciliation Is Best) shows that this was not the case; see al-Ikhwan 'l-Jumhuriyyun, *Al-Sulh khair* (Omdurman: Republican Movement Publication, 1977). In 1977, Taha still believed in the regime and its anti-*ta'ifiyya* credentials and remained fully supportive of the regime despite the peace it made with his archenemies.

45. For the memorandum's full text, see al-Amin Da'ud, *Dajjal 'l-Sudan.* N. p.: n. p., 1978, 13–18.

46. On the *hudud* punishments, see chapter 6. On the regime's religious policies that laid the foundation for the imposition of shari'a, see Idris Salim el-Hassan, *Religion in Society: Nemeiri and the Turuq, 1972–1980* (Khartoum: Khartoum Univ. Press, 1993), 84–86.

47. Justifying the role the Muslim Brothers played in the imposition of shari'a, al-Turabi said, "Fellow Islamists outside the Sudan were puzzled and misjudged our position, asking whether it was justified for an Islamic movement to be reconciled with a military regime. They lacked the strategic outlook and ignored many other considerations which to us had important bearing on the regime. We were taken by surprise by Nimeiri's decision [to implement shari'a], although once it was made public we were not fooled by it, and we again tried to use it to our strategy's advantage. We mobilized the streets to project a more comprehensive understanding of Islamic society and turned the shari'ah from a political platform to a means for directing the popular trends more into line with our overall strategy." Al-Turabi, quoted in *The Making of an Islamic Political Leader: Conversations with Hasan al-Turabi,* by Mohamed Elhachmi Hamdi (Boulder: Westview Press, 1998), 25. On Islamization following Nimairi's reconciliation with the Muslim Brothers and the Umma Party, see Alexander S. Cudsi, "Islam and Politics in the Sudan," in *Islam in the Political Process,* ed. James Piscatori (Cambridge: Cambridge Univ. Press, 1983), 36–55. On a treatment covering Nimairi's Islamization until the regime's overthrow, see Carolyn Fluehr-Lobban, "Islamization in Sudan: A Critical Assessment," in *Sudan: State and Society in Crisis,* ed. John Voll (Bloomington: Indiana Univ. Press, 1991), 71–89. On a treatment with more focus on the

1983 penal code and a closer examination of specific cases, see Zein, "Religion, Legality, and the State."

48. An-Naʿim in Taha, SM 9.

49. An-Naʿim points out that the release of the Republicans could possibly have been a response to "mounting international pressure protesting the detention of the group" or "a deliberate trap to involve the Republicans in overt acts rendering them liable to prosecution under the new laws." An-Naʿim in Taha, SM 9–10. The assumption concerning the regime's sensitivity to international opinion and pressure in this case is implausible. In Taha's case Nimairi and his allies were apparently determined to carry out their plan and were completely impervious to international opinion. The second assumption is, hence, more likely.

50. Al-Ikhwan ʾl-Jumhuriyyun, *Al-Kaid ʾl-siyasi wa ʾl-mahkama ʾl-mahzala* (Omdurman: Republican Movement Publication, 1985), 11.

51. Abd ʿAllah Jallab, "Mahmud Muhammad Taha yaqul," *al-Sahafa,* Dec. 11, 1972, www.alfikra.org.

52. For the leaflet's text, see Rifʿat Sayyid Ahmad, *Limadha aʿdamani Nimairi?: Qiraʾa fi awraq ʾl-shaikh Mahmud Taha* (Cairo: Dar Alif, 1985), 107–9. For a translation of the text, see an-Naʿim in Taha, SM 10–12.

53. Ibid., 12.

54. Ibid., 12–13.

55. The four who were arrested with Taha were ʿAbd al-Latif ʿUmar Hasab Allah, Muhammad Salim Baʿshar, Khalid Babikir Hamza, and Taj al-Din ʿAbd al-Raziq Husain.

56. The explicit presidential sanction came as a belated remedial measure because the September 1983 laws did not provide for apostasy. Later, the Muslim Brothers were careful to address this omission, and al-Turabi included an apostasy provision in his draft penal code of 1988, which he submitted in his capacity as attorney general. This draft code later became the basis of the current 1991 Criminal Act. Article 126 of this act provides that apostasy is a capital offense. For an English translation of the act, see "Sudan's Criminal Act of 1991," *Arab Law Quarterly,* 9, no. 1 (1994): 32–80.

57. An-Naʿim in Taha, SM 14.

58. Judith Miller, *God Has Ninety Nine Names: Reporting From a Militant Middle East* (New York: Simon and Schuster, 1996), 12.

59. Ibid.

60. Burying victims in undisclosed graves is part of the culture of the Sudanese military. Prisoners of war in the south have reportedly been systematically killed and buried in undisclosed individual or mass graves. Human rights reports often mention the government's refusal to allow the International Committee of the Red Cross access to prisoners of war. This has led Human Rights Watch to conclude in its country report in 2000 that "failure to acknowledge holding rebel soldiers prisoner pointed to a continuing government policy of secret summary executions." In the wake of the collapse of the 1971 coup d'état against

Nimairi, officers and civilians who were executed were buried in undisclosed graves. Under the current regime of General 'Umar al-Bashir, a group of officers who attempted a coup in April 1990 were summarily executed and buried in undisclosed graves. It should, however, be noted that in Taha's case there was no demand by his family or his followers to disclose his grave and reclaim his body. According to an-Na'im, Taha "had left written instructions, during his self-imposed religious seclusion of 1948–51, that if he should die, he should be buried with the clothes he was wearing, without the usual rites of burial, and in an unmarked grave." An-Na'im in Taha, SM 17n 24.

61. Shortly after Taha's execution and in honor of his memory, the Arab Human Rights Organization declared January 18 as the Arab Human Rights Day.

62. For a text of the statement and a transcript of the session and the following court session, see al-Makashfi Taha al-Kabbashi, *Al-Ridda wa muhakamat Mahmud Muhammad Taha fi 'l-Sudan* (Khartoum: Dar 'l-Fikr, 1987), 206–41. The author was one of the leading judges in the implementation of *hudud* and in Taha's apostasy trial.

63. An-Na'im in Taha, SM 17. For an excellent treatment of the legal aspects of the trial, see Abdullahi An-Na'im, "The Islamic Law of Apostasy and Its Modern Applicability," *Religion* 16 (1986): 329–40.

64. The expectation rife within the Jumhuri community of a second coming of Christ was given a public articulation in 1980 when the Jumhuriyyun produced a pamphlet, *'Awdat 'l-Masih* (The Return of Christ)," depicting a very Jumhuri Christ who is committed to the unity of religion and Taha's program of reform. Al-Ikhwan 'l-Jumhuriyyun, *'Awdat 'l-Masih* (Omdurman: Republican Movement Publication, 1980).

65. Lichtenthäler points out that "Republicans would not be led by a non-Republican in prayer, neither would they pray in mosques." Gerhard Lichtenthäler, "Muslih, Mystic and Martyr, The Vision of Mahmud Muhammad Taha and the Republican Bothers in the Sudan: Towards an Islamic Reformation?" *Islam société au sud du Sahara*, 9 (1995): 66.

66. Taha's authority was summed up in his title, *al-ustadh* (the master, the teacher). He was the only person within the movement who was referred to by this title. The Republicans rarely used his name, as they would usually refer to him by his title, which was not merely honorific but in fact reflected his supreme spiritual rank.

67. These observations are based on the author's personal acquaintance with Taha in 1972–73. In meat-eating Sudan, vegetarianism is viewed as an eccentricity. Taha's vegetarianism had its roots in Sufi spirituality. Influenced by his example, many Republicans gave up eating meat. This aversion to meat and the country's mounting economic hardships led the Republicans in the early 1980s to call for the ending of the mass slaughter of sheep during the Festival of Sacrifice *('id 'l-adha)*.

68. In addition to the four Republicans arrested alongside Taha, about four hundred were later arrested throughout the country. Following Taha's execution, they signed pledges to desist from carrying out any political activity or propagating Taha's ideas. See el-Tayeb, "Second Message," 87.

69. Commenting on the killing of Che Guevara in 1967, Taha expressed a clearly negative view of martyrdom when he said, "Guevara was a genuine revolutionary who was faithful to his conception of socialism, as his revolutionary fervor went beyond the conventional boundaries of national states. The youth are fascinated by him. I do not believe he is the right model for the revolutionary youth in the future as revolutionary commitment should lead one to live for mankind rather than die for it." Taha, quoted in Mahjub Muhammad Sharif, "al-Wajh 'l-akhar li-Mahmud Muhammad Taha," *al-Hayat*, www.alfikra.org.

70. Writing about the movement's inaction even after the restoration of democracy in April 1985, an-Na'im remarks, "It remains to be seen whether this is due to the initial shock and the magnitude of the loss of the founder and leader of the movement or a permanent phenomenon." He then adds, "In rational and material terms, however, it would seem to be imperative that someone must continue to propagate the theory if it is to reach and be accepted by the masses of Muslims who can bring about its eventual practical implementation." However, an-Na'im does not seem to link the impact of Taha's thought to the revival of his movement. Rather, he shifts the emphasis to the likely impact of Taha's writings when "they are discussed, at the scholarly level, by students of Islam throughout the world." Abdullahi An-Na'im, "Mahmud Muhammad Taha and the Crisis in Islamic Law Reform: Implications for Interreligious Relations," *Journal of Ecumenical Studies* 25, no. 1 (1988): 19–20. This sentiment is shared by Mustapha Khayati, who says, "La pensée réformatrice de M. Taha, qui est presque totalement inconnue dans le monde arabe et musulman, dépasse largement le cadre du Soudan, et mérite d'être plus amplement connue." Mustapha Khayati, "Introduction à la pensée de Mahmud Muhammad Taha, réformiste et martyr ['Les Frères Républicains' au Soudan]," in *Sudan: History, Identity, Ideology*, ed. Hérve Bleuchot, Christian Delmet, and Derek Hopwood (Reading: Ithaca, 1991), 297.

71. See Muhammad b. 'Abd al-Jabbar al-Niffari, *Kitab 'l-mawaqif wa 'l-mukhatabat*, ed. A. J. Arberry (Cambridge: Cambridge Univ. Press, 1935); and Paul Nwyia, "Nusus ghair manshura li-'l-Niffari," in *Nusus sufiyya ghair manshura*, ed. Paul Nwyia (Beirut: Dar 'l-Mashriq, 1973), 193–324. Commenting on al-Niffari's work, Nwyia says, "L'oeuvre de Niffari a ceci de remarquable que la conscience soufie y passe du discours sur soi à un dialogue avec Dieu. En elle, ce n'est plus le mystique qui parle de sa proper expérience, mais Dieu qui l'interpelle constamment au sein de cette expérience et qui se manifeste à travers cetter interpellation." Paul Nwyia, ed., *Exégèse coranique et langue mystique* (Beirut: Dar 'l-Mashriq, 1986), 357. On al-Niffari as a "drunken" Sufi, see Serafim Sepälä, *In Speechless Ecstasy: Expression and Interpretation of Mystical Experience in Classical Syriac and Sufi Literature* (Helsinki: Finnish Oriental Society, 2003), 32–33.

72. 'Abd al-Rahman Badawi, *Shahidat 'l-'ishq 'l-ilahi Rabi'a al-'Adawiyya* (Kuwait: Wakalat 'l-Matbu'at, 1978), 92.

73. Ibid., 124.

74. It has been suggested that this was owing to a Hindu influence to which he was exposed through his Indian teacher Abu 'Ali al-Sindi. On the possible Hindu influence on

al-Bistami and an examination of his theopathic statements in the light of Hindu sources, see R. C. Zaehner, *Hindu and Muslim Mysticism* (London: Univ. of London, Athlone Press, 1960), 93–109.

75. 'Abd al-Rahman Badawi, *Shatahat 'l-sufiyya: Abu Yazid 'l-Bistami* (Cairo: Maktabat 'l-Nahda 'l-Misriyya, 1949), 1:68.

76. Ibid., 1:113.

77. Ibid., 1:115. Commenting on al-Bistami's theopathic statements, Fakhry wrote, "How a Muslim could make such extravagant claims . . . and yet go unscathed in the ninth century is truly surprising. However, a note made by later authors gives us the clue to this problem. When al-Bastami was accused of laxity in the performance of his ritual duties, we are told, he resorted to the expedient which other Sufis also employed: affected madness. This device apparently saved his life as well as the life of numerous fellow Sufis." Majid Fakhry, *A History of Islamic Philosophy* (New York: Columbia Univ. Press, 1970), 273.

78. Louis Massignon and Paul Kraus, eds., *Akhbar 'l-Hallaj* (Paris: Au Calame, 1936), 108.

79. Ibid., 21.

80. Massignon, *Passion of al-Hallaj*, 3:223.

81. On al-Suhrawardi's spiritual geography, see Seyyed Hossein Nasr, *Three Muslim Sages* (Delmar, New York: Caravan Books, 1976), 64–66.

82. See, for instance, A. E. Affifi, *The Mystical Philosophy of Muhyid Din-Ibnul 'Arabi* (Cambridge: Cambridge Univ. Press, 1939), 54–62.

83. In quoting this tradition, Ibn 'Arabi dismissed the consensus of orthodox traditionists who affirmed that it was a forgery. He insisted that although it was not verifiable through the traditional methods of hadith transmission, it was sound *(sahih)* on the basis of what he described as "prophetic unveiling" *(kashf)*. Muhyi al-Din Ibn 'Arabi, *Al-Futuhat 'l-Makiyya* (Beirut: Dar Sadir, n.d.), 2:399.

84. Muhyi al-Din Ibn 'Arabi, *Fusus 'l-hikam*, ed. Abu al-'Ila 'Afifi (Beirut: Dar al-Kitab 'l-'Arabi, n.d.), 48.

85. Ibid., 55.

86. According to Ibn 'Arabi's epistemology, there are three types of knowledge: speculative or rational knowledge *('ilm 'l-'aql)*; empirical or experiential knowledge *('ilm 'l-ahwal)*; and esoteric knowledge *('ilm 'l-asrar*, lit., "knowledge of mysteries"). Ibn 'Arabi, *Al-Futuhat*, 1:31.

87. On the reception of Ibn 'Arabi and the controversies raised by his work during medieval times, see Alexander D. Knysh, *Ibn 'Arabi in the Later Islamic Tradition: The Making of a Polemical Image in Medieval Islam* (Albany: State Univ. of New York Press, 1999).

88. Mahjub Karrar, "Mahmud Muhammad Taha fi hiwar Sufi ma'a Hodgkins," *al-Sahafa*, Dec. 16, 1972, www.alfikra.org.

89. See *al-Sahafa*, Dec. 16, 1972.

90. Ibid. In contrast to Taha's modest claims, Bashari writes the following, "He was an

avid reader in Arabic and English. He studied philosophical schools and all types of logic. . . . He has studies on the school of dialecticians from the German philosopher Hegel till Marx and the later writings of Marxist theoreticians. He has studies on mathematical logic and refutations of Whitehead and Russell. He also has refutations of Hegel." Mahjub 'Umar Bashari, *Ruwwad 'l-fikr 'l-Sudani* (Khartoum: Dar 'l-Fikr, 1981), 369. The source of Bashari's detailed information about Taha's early readings and purported studies is not clear. He may have been prompted by his immense regard and esteem for Taha and his own admiration for Western thought to project Taha as a widely and systematically read intellectual on the cutting edge of modern thought.

91. Assessing 'Abduh, Taha maintained that his reform left its impact on his generation and the following generations but fell "lamentably short of the requirements of our present day" (AJii 76). He never elaborated on what he meant by this. One of his disciples, however, produced a book in which he dealt with 'Abduh's views on women. While praising 'Abduh's overall progressive stance on women and particularly his opposition to polygyny, he criticizes his defense of the principle of male guardianship. See 'Umar al-Qarra'y, *Al-Fikr 'l-Islami wa qadiyyat 'l-mar'a* (Ft. Worth, Texas: Lonestar, n.d.), 93–95.

92. H. A. R. Gibb, *Modern Trends in Islam* (Beirut: Librairie du Liban, 1975), 33.

93. The ideological disagreements between Taha's understanding of Islam and that of the school of the Muslim Brothers were apparent from an early stage. In its early phase of development, the Sudanese Muslim Brothers' movement was faction ridden, and in a bid to resolve its crisis, Muhammad Yusif, a student leader of the group, traveled in 1951 to Rufa'a to meet Taha by way of exploring whether Taha could lead their movement. However, "after a lengthy discussion [Yusif] decided that Taha's views were too unorthodox for him to lead the movement." Abdelwahab el-Affendi, *Turabi's Revolution* (London: Grey Seal, 1991), 65.

94. Sayyid Qutb, *Ma'alim fi 'l-tariq* (Beirut: The Holy Koran Publishing House, 1978), 46–54.

2. Theory of Prayer: Worship, Individualism, and Authenticity

1. The English word *prayer* has a wider denotation than the Arabic word *salat*. Whereas the English word is used to denote prayer both in the narrow sense of a ritual act and the broad sense of invoking God in word or thought for help or support, Arabic reserves the word *salat* for the ritual sense and uses the word *du'a* (supplication) for the broad, open, invocatory sense.

2. Islam incorporated the pre-Islamic belief in a class of spirits called the *jinn* into its belief system. It is interesting to note that this verse does not mention the angels, the third category of rational beings that worship God. On *jinn* according to Muslim conception and popular belief, see *EI²*, s.v. *"djinn"* 2:546–50.

3. Muhammad b. Jarir al-Tabari, *Tafsir 'l-Tabari* or *Jami' 'l-bayan fi ta'wil 'l-Qur'an* (Beirut: Dar 'l-Kutub 'l-'Ilmiyya, 1992), 11:476.

4. Ibid. The same statement by Ibn 'Abbas is quoted by al-Qurtubi, but the word *'ibada* is

used instead. Muhammad b. Ahmad al-Ansari al-Qurtubi, *Al-Jami' li-Ahkam 'l-Qur'an,* ed. Ahmad 'Abd al-'Alim al-Barduni (Cairo: Dar 'l-Kitab 'l-'Arabi, 1952), 17:55. The terms were evidently treated as synonyms. In *Lisan 'l-'Arab* Ibn Manzur refers to *'ubuda, 'ubudiyya,* and *'abdiyya* as all holding the same meaning of "submission" *(khudu')* and "self-abasement" *(tadhallul).* To these, al-Firuzabadi added *'ibada* in his *al-Qamus 'l-muhit* and gave their meaning as "obedience" *(ta'a).*

5. Al-Qurtubi, *Al-Jami',* 17:55.

6. Al-Tabari, *Tafsir,* 11:27.

7. Al-Qurtubi, *Al-Jami',* 17:55.

8. Mahmud b. 'Umar al-Zamakhshari, *Al-Kashshaf* (Riyad: Maktabat al-'Ubaikan, 1998), 4:396.

9. 'Abd 'l-Karim al-Qushairi, *Al-Risala 'l-Qushairiyya,* ed. 'Abd al-Halim Mahmud and Mahmud Ibn al-Sharif (Cairo: Dar 'l-Kutub al-Haditha, 1972), 2:428.

10. Al-Qashani keeps al-Daqqaq's tripartite scheme but reformulates it in terms of *'ibada* and two levels of *'ubudiyya,* a lower one for the elect and a higher one for the super-elect. 'Abd al-Razzaq al-Qashani, *'Istilahat 'l-Sufiyya,* ed. Muhammad Kamal Ibrahim Ja'far (Cairo: al-Hai'a 'l-Misriyya al-'Amma li-'l-Kitab, 1981), 107.

11. Ibn 'Arabi, *Al-Futuhat,* 2:214.

12. Ibid., 3:40.

13. Annemarie Schimmel, *Mystical Dimensions of Islam* (Chapel Hill: Univ. of North Carolina Press, 1975), 24.

14. *Tawhid* is the science of divine unity. On a modern exposition of this science, its themes and arguments, see Muhammad 'Abduh, *Risalat 'l-tawhid,* in *Al-A'mal 'l-kamila li-'l-imam Muhammad 'Abduh,* ed. Muhammad 'Amara (Beirut: Al-Mu'assasa 'l-'Arabiyya li-'l-Dirasat wa 'l-Nashr, 1972), 3:353–476.

15. The revelation of the Qur'an was believed to have continued throughout Muhammad's prophetic career as he was believed to have had regular revelatory and nonrevelatory encounters with Gabriel. It was, however, his initial encounter with the archangel, during which he reportedly received the first verses of chapter 96, that came to occupy a central and unique position in Muslim imagination. For an account of this encounter, see 'Abd al-Malik Ibn Hisham, *Al-Sira 'l-nabawiyya* (Beirut: Dar 'l-Kutub 'l-'Ilmiyya, 2000), 1:169–70.

16. Ibid., 1:297.

17. Zamzam is a sacred well in Mecca.

18. Another hadith gives more details about the prophets Muhammad meets in his ascent through the seven heavens. Muhammad b. Isma'il al-Bukhari, *Sahih,* ed. Qasim al-Shamma'i al-Rifa'i (Beirut: Dar 'l-Qalam, 1987), 5:143–47.

19. Ibid., 4:353–56.

20. Ibid., 4:296.

21. Ibid., 1:278.

22. Al-Tabari, *Tafsir* 8:16.

23. Ibid., 11:512–14.

24. Ibid., 11:510–11.

25. The source of this image is apparently verse 55:76, which describes those in paradise as "reclining on green cushions [*rafraf akhdar*] and rich carpets of beauty."

26. Muslim sources say that whenever Gabriel saw Muhammad he took a human form. On the ascension, however, Muhammad saw Gabriel in his real awesome form and majesty, according to three prophetic traditions referring to verses 53:9, 53:11, and 53:18. According to one tradition, Muhammad saw Gabriel with six hundred wings. Abu al-Husain Muslim b. al-Hajjaj Muslim, *Sahih Muslim bi-Sharh al-Nawawi*, ed. Khalil Ma'mun Shiha (Cairo: al-Matba'a 'l-Misriyya, 1930), 3:3.

27. Al-Tabari, *Tafsir*, 11:514–15.

28. For a brief treatment of Sufi appropriation of the term *mi'raj*, see Su'ad al-Hakim, introduction to *Al-Isra ila 'l-maqam 'l-asra*, by Muhyi al-Din Ibn 'Arabi, 28–33 (Beirut: Dandara li-'l-Tiba'a wa 'l-Nashr, 1988). On viewing the notion of ascension in the wider context of Near Eastern mythology and religion, see Qassim al-Samarrai, *The Theme of Ascension in Mystical Writings: A Study of the Theme in Islamic and Non-Islamic Writings* (Baghdad: National Printing and Publishing Co., 1968), 65–90.

29. 'Ali b. 'Uthman al-Hujwiri, *The Kashf al-mahjub*, trans. Reynold A. Nicholson (New Delhi: Taj Company, 1982), 238.

30. Abu Nasr 'Abd Allah b. 'Ali al-Sarraj, *Al-Luma' fi 'l-tasawwuf* (Beirut: Dar al-Kutub 'l-'Ilmiyya, 2001), 375.

31. Ibid., 376.

32. Following al-Hallaj's execution, his close friend Abu Bakr al-Shibli (d. 334/946) saw the risk involved in provoking orthodox opinion and warned Sufis against making ecstatic utterances in public. Contrasting his own position with that of al-Hallaj, he said, "I and al-Husain b. Mansur were in the same state, but he revealed and I concealed." Louis Massignon, *Recueil de textes inédits concernant l'histoire de la mystique en pays d'Islam* (Paris: Librairie Orientaliste Paul Geuthner, 1929), 79.

33. 'Ali b. Muhammad al-Jurjani, *Kitab 'l-ta'rifat*, ed. Muhammad 'Abd al-Rahman al-Mar'ashli (Beirut: Dar 'l-Nafa'is, 2003), 132. For a brief treatment on the nature of *shath*, see Louis Massignon, *Essai sur les origines du lexique technique de la mystique musulmane* (Paris: Librairie orientaliste, 1922), 99–100. For an overview of *shath* in Sufi literature from its classical period until the eighteenth century, see Carl W. Ernst, *Words of Ecstasy in Sufism* (Albany: State Univ. of New York Press, 1985), 9–24.

34. Al-Hujwiri, *Kashf,* 238.

35. The use of the word *rufi'tu* is reminiscent of verse 4:158, which, in the context of affirming that Jesus was neither killed nor crucified, says, "God raised him up [*rafa'ahu*] to Him."

36. Badawi, *Shatahat,* 116.

37. Ibid., 128.

38. Ibn 'Arabi, *Al-Futuhat* 3:342.

39. Ibid., 3:343–44.

40. Ibid.

41. It may be argued in the light of this subjective element that the command to al-Bistami to "smear [his] eyes with the dust of [Muhammad's] feet and follow him continually" is incompatible with the tenor of his experience and is probably an interpolation inserted to temper a perceived extremism in his account.

42. Ibn 'Arabi, *Al-Futuhat* 3:346–50. For a partial English translation, see James W. Morris, "Ibn 'Arabi's Spiritual Ascension," in *Les Illuminations de La Mecque,* ed. Michel Chodkiewicz, 366–81 (Paris: Sindbad, 1988).

43. Ibn 'Arabi borrows his expression from verse 52:4, which is generally interpreted as referring to the Ka'ba.

44. Ibn 'Arabi, *Al-Futuhat,* 3:350.

45. Describing the Lote-Tree, Muhammad said, "Then I was made to ascend to *sidrat 'l-muntaha.* . . . Behold, its fruits were like the jars of Hajr [a place near Medina] and its leaves were as big as the ears of elephants." Al-Bukhari, *Sahih,* 4:550.

46. Verse 3:84 reads, "Say: 'We believe in God, and that which has been sent down on us, and sent down on Abraham and Ishmael, Isaac and Jacob, and the Tribes, and in that which was given to Moses and Jesus, and the Prophets, of their Lord; we make no division between any of them, and to Him we surrender.' " The same verse appears with minor variations as verse 2:136. Both verses open with the same command of "Say" but with a variation in the imperative verb: the verb in verse 3:84 is singular, second-person masculine *(qul),* while in verse 2:136 it is plural, second-person masculine *(qulu).* Although it is clear that the imperative verbs here are interchangeable, it may be argued that Ibn 'Arabi's choice of verse 3:84 was deliberate. The singular, personal address of this verse may have served his purpose better because he relates to it as a fresh revelation to him. He is in a state of direct communion with God and that, for all intents and purposes, excludes Muhammad's mediation.

47. Ibn 'Arabi, *Al-Futuhat* 3:350.

48. Ibid. 3:350.

49. Ibid. 3:350.

50. Ibid. 3:40. Ibn Qadib al-Ban (d. 1040/1630) was a later mystic who was influenced by Ibn 'Arabi. He claimed a spiritual ascension in the description of which he closely followed the traditional account of the prophetic ascension. For his account, see 'Abd al-Rahman Badawi, *Al-Insan 'l-kamil fi 'l-Islam* (Kuwait: Wakalat 'l-Matbu'at, 1976), 164–72.

51. The oral tradition of the Republican community, however, provides us with an ascension account, albeit limited by Taha's own standards. According to 'Ali Lutfi, Taha's brother-in-law, the latter told him that "he was in a lift, taken up very high, up to the clouds,

and he found huge fields and a man there—Muhammad. He said, 'Praise God, you have come to your farm, take your farm.' [Taha] accepted the farm." Quoted in Thomas, "Mahmud Muhammad Taha," 97.

52. Republican Brothers, Information Bureau, internal bulletin, May 21, 1982, 2.

53. Arberry renders verse 55:29 as "Every day He is upon some labour." Mindful of Taha's interpretation of the verse, an-Na'im renders it as "Every day He [reveals Himself] in a fresh state." An-Na'im in Taha, SM 39.

54. A *hadith qudsi* or *ilahi* or *rabbani* is a tradition whose content is attributed to God while its formulation is attributed to Muhammad. By contrast, a *hadith nabawi* (prophetic tradition) is a statement by Muhammad. The Qur'an, on the other hand, stands in a distinct category because both its content and form are believed to be of divine authorship. On *hadith qudsi*, see William Graham, *Divine Word and Prophetic Word in Early Islam: A Reconsideration of the Sources, with Special Reference to the Divine Saying or Hadith Qudsi* (The Hague: Mouton, 1977).

55. Al-Bukhari, *Sahih* 8:483.

56. Ibid. 9:834.

57. In another place, Taha quotes a tradition in which Muhammad reportedly said, "On the night of my ascension, my sight and insight were fused together and hence I saw God." See TK 31.

58. When Gabriel reached the Lote-Tree and was on the point of leaving Muhammad to meet God, the Prophet said, "Is this a place where one leaves one's friend?" Gabriel responded, "This is my station and if I proceed one more step I will burn." Quoted in TM 19.

59. Here Taha adds, "He came to them from the twentieth century." In identifying the future with the "twentieth century," the statement now sounds dated. Yet, what remains important is his general meaning rather than specific statement.

60. In referring to the worshipper, Taha generally uses the general Islamic term *'abd* (servant) and the Sufi term *salik* (wayfarer, seeker). Because he often refers to the human spiritual quest in terms of a "journey" metaphor, the use of the term *seeker* is undoubtedly more appropriate than *servant*.

61. The word *gharib* that the tradition uses can also be rendered "strange," "alien," "unusual," or "atypical." Those who make the revival of the "unfamiliar" possible are described by the tradition as *ghuraba'* (strangers, outsiders). In characterizing the "unfamiliar" aspect of what these future "brothers" do, Taha chooses a tradition variant that focuses on the revival of the sunna. There are other variants as well: a "silent" variant that does not specify what the *ghuraba'* will do (see, for instance, Muslim, *Sahih*, 2:176); a variant that refers to what they will do as "putting right when others do evil" (see Ahmad Ibn Hanbal, *Al-Musnad* [Beirut: Dar 'l-Kutub 'l-'Ilmiyya, 1993], 4:92); and another variant that characterizes them as people who leave their kith and kin, evidently for the sake of a higher cause, although the

nature of this cause is not specified (see, for example, Muhammad b. Yazid Ibn Maja, *Sunan*, ed. Muhammad Fu'ad 'Abd al-Baqi [Beirut: Dar 'l-Kutub 'l-'Ilmiyya, 1995], 2:1320).

62. See, for instance, Muhyi al-Din Ibn 'Arabi, *Al-Tanazzulat 'l-musaliyya fi asrar 'l-taharat wa 'l-salat wa 'l-ayam 'l-asliyya* (Cairo: Maktabat 'Alam 'l-Fikr, 1986), 169–93.

63. In the context of dealing with Ibn 'Arabi's cosmology, Chittick translates the final phrase of verse 41:53 as "till it is clear to them that it/He is the Real." In contrast, an-Na'im renders it in his translation of RT as "until it becomes manifest to them that He is the Truth" (SM 87). This is the case because, as Chittick points out, the antecedent of the pronoun *hu* (He or it) in *annahu 'l-haqq* is ambiguous. William C. Chittick, *The Self-Disclosure of God: Principles of Ibn al-'Arabi Cosmology* (Albany: State Univ. of New York Press, 1998), 6.

64. Although the Qur'an mentions in several verses that God created the heavens and the earth in six days, Taha imposes a seventh day of creation by counting the reference to God's sitting on the throne, a Qur'anic equivalent of the biblical seventh day when God rested "from all the work that he had done in creation" (Gen. 2:3).

65. See for instances verses 2:43, 9:72, 19:55, 31:4, 58:13, and 73:20.

66. See al-Tabari, *Tafsir*, 1:298.

67. The tradition reportedly says, *"inna 'l-shaitan yajri min ahadikum majra 'l-damm,"* which translates literally as "Satan flows inside each one of you like the flowing of blood." Although the statement can be read metaphorically, Taha is attracted by an essentially literalist reading because he wants to establish a "scientific" basis for fasting. Justifying fasting on medical grounds is a popular theme among modern Muslims. Muhammad Rashid Rida and Muhammad 'Abduh, for example, claim that "some Western medical authorities said that the fasting of one month detoxifies the body for a whole year." Rida, *Tafsir 'l-manar* (Beirut: Dar 'l-Ma'rifa, 1993), 2:148. See also 'Abd al-Razzaq Nawfal, *Al-Islam wa 'l-'ilm 'l-Hadith* (Cairo: Dar 'l-Ma'arif, 1958), 176–81.

68. Once he has pronounced "God is great" (the act of *takbir)* at the start of his prayer, the worshipper enters the state of *ihram* (prohibition), which means that he is prohibited from saying or doing anything that does not belong to prayer. Hence, with this formal utterance, he enters into a "presence of prohibition."

69. This is mentioned in verse 2:238. Most exegetes agreed that by "middle prayer," the verse refers to the *'asr* (late afternoon) prayer. Although Taha accepts this interpretation on one level, he extends the verse's connotation to cover the specific meaning advanced here.

70. This "presence" takes its name from the last words the worshipper utters when he concludes his prayer session, that is, *"al-salamu 'alaikum"* (Peace be upon you).

71. The word *din* also has the general meaning of "(good) character," "probity," and "righteousness."

72. This doctrine is expressed by a tradition according to which the Prophet said, "No one is saved through his [good] actions." When asked, "Not even you?" he responded, "Not even I, unless God encompasses me with [His] mercy." See, for instance, al-Bukhari, *Sahih* 8:469.

73. The Prophet reportedly stepped into the mosque with his right foot and out of it with his left foot. However, he reportedly reversed this order when he went to the toilet. He also reportedly lay on his right side and faced the direction of the Ka'ba when he went to sleep.

74. Taha reads the verses that stress following the Prophet, such as 3:31 and 59:7, as indicating imitation, whereas he reads verse 33:21 ("You have had a good example [*uswa*] in God's Messenger") as underlining the stage of emulation that for him is a postimitation stage.

75. In his *Kitab 'l-ri'aya*, al-Muhasibi deals with this subject under the theme of *riya'* (duplicity, deceitfulness). For al-Muhasibi, constant watchfulness against this state of duplicity, on even the subtlest levels, is the Sufi's main task, without which his spiritual life will always be deficient. Al-Harith b. Asad al-Muhasibi, *Kitab 'l-ri'aya li-huquqi 'Llah,* ed. Margaret Smith (London: Luzac, 1940), 84–139. Al-Kalabadhi characterizes Sufis as a "people of light" *(ta'ifa nuriyya)* by virtue of their purification of their outward being of *anjas* (defilements) and their inward being of *ahjas* ([impure] thoughts). Muhammad b. Ishaq al-Kalabadhi, *Al-Ta'arruf li-madhhab ahl 'l-tasawwuf,* ed. A. J. Arberry (Cairo: Matba'at 'l-Sa'ada, 1933), 7–8. In his *Al-Risala,* al-Qushairi often touches on this theme. In a chapter on *taqwa* (piety), he quotes a statement by Dhu al-Nun al-Misri in which he defines *taqwa* in terms of a complete identity of the outer self and the inner self. Al-Qushairi, *Al-Risala,* 1:308. Al-Ghazali devotes a great deal of space in his *Ihya'* to the theme of *riyadat 'l-nafs* (the spiritual training of the mind) and gives a detailed account of what the Sufi seeker should do to address the "maladies of the heart" *(amrad 'l-qalb).* Abu Hamid al-Ghazali, *Ihya' 'ulum 'l-din* (Beirut: Dar al-Ma'rifa, n.d), 3:48–414. His ideal is one of complete identity between the seeker's external conduct and the attitude of his mind. In his comprehensive mystical manual *'Awarif 'l-ma'arif,* 'Umar al-Suhrawardi characterizes the Sufi as someone who has realized this identity through the purification of the heart. 'Umar b. Muhammad al-Suhrawardi, *'Awarif 'l-ma'arif* (Beirut: Dar 'l-Kutub 'l-'Ilmiyya, 1999), 59.

76. Quoted in Massignon, *Passion of al-Hallaj* 3:42.

77. On the role of the *shaikh,* see Schimmel, *Mystical Dimensions,* 98–186.

78. On the Uwaisiyya as a Sufi expression, see A. S. Husaini, "Uways al-Qarani and the Uwaysi Sufis," *Muslim World* 57, no. 2 (1967): 103–13. On an imagined history of an Uwaisi mystical brotherhood, see Julian Baldwick, *Imaginary Muslims: The Uwaysi Sufis of Central Asia* (London: I. B. Tauris, 1993).

79. Republican Brothers, Internal Bulletin, May 21, 1982, 4.

80. Ibid., 7.

81. On the miracles associated with the Prophet's birth, see Ibn Hisham, *Al-Sira* 1:116–17. On a modern, uncritical, miracle-oriented portrayal of the event, see Muhammad Abu Zahra, *Khatam 'l-nabiyyin* (Beirut: al-Maktaba 'l-'Asriyya, 1979), 1:128–47.

82. On the implications of the failure to use Arabic in prayer and the hierarchical scheme of languages adopted by medieval Muslim scholars, see Muhyi al-Din b. Sharaf al-Nawawi,

Al-Majmu': Sharh 'l-Muhadhdhab, ed. Mahmud Matraji (Beirut: Dar 'l-Fikr, 2000), 3:244–45.

83. There was only one other claim of authenticity in the history of the Jumhuri movement, namely, that of Muhammad Khair Mihaisi. Mihaisi was a dedicated disciple who was dismissed from the Religious Institute of Omdurman (later Omdurman Islamic University) on account of his Republican commitment. His spiritual experience convinced him that he had attained his authenticity, a claim that was not recognized by Taha. He left the Republican movement and had no success in founding his own movement.

84. Regarding this, Taha uses the hadith about the *ghuraba'* (strangers, outsiders) who revive the sunna. See note 61 for this chapter.

3. The Qur'an and the Hermeneutics of Semantic Fluidity

1. Al-Darami, *Sunan* 2:435; quoted in RT 4.

2. Ibn 'Arabi, *Al-Futuhat* 2:107.

3. Some early authorities argued on the basis of verse 26:193—"Truly it is the revelation of the Lord of all Being, brought down by the Faithful Spirit ['l-ruh-u 'l-amin-u]"—that the meanings *(ma'ani)* of the Qur'an were communicated to Muhammad by the archangel Gabriel (the verse's "Faithful Spirit") and that the Prophet expressed these meanings in human language. This, however, was a minority view that was soon overwhelmed by the orthodox position, which insisted that both the verbal expression *(lafz)* and the meaning *(ma'na)* of the Qur'an were revealed. For early debates, see al-Suyuti, *Al-Itqan* 1:96–98; and for a modern treatment of the notion of revelation, see Nasr Hamid Abu Zaid, *Mafhum 'l-nass: Dirasa fi 'ulum 'l-Qur'an* (Beirut: al-Markaz 'l-Thaqafi 'l-'Arabi, 1998), 31–52.

4. Comparing the Qur'an with the Hebrew Bible or the Old and New Testaments, Taha says that the last two are similar to Muhammad's oral traditions, where the meanings were revealed by God but the language was expressed by humans. When it comes to the Qur'an, he rearticulates the traditional view that, in its case, both meaning and language were revealed by God, and Muhammad's role was confined only to the transmission *(tabligh)* of the divine message (QT 133).

5. On Ibn 'Arabi's defense of the soundness of this tradition, see p. 238, n. 83, above.

6. Ignaz Goldziher, *Die Richtungen der Islamischen Koranauslegung* (Leiden: E. J. Brill, 1920), 183–84.

7. Abu Hamid al-Ghazali, *Mishkat 'l-anwar wa misfat 'l-asrar,* ed. 'Abd al-'Aziz Izz al-Din al-Sairawan (Beirut: 'Alam 'l-Kutub, 1986), 165–71.

8. To these seven attributes of essence (or essential attributes) some authorities added other active attributes. See 'Abd al-Qahir al-Baghdadi, *Kitab usul 'l-din* (Istanbul: Matba'at 'l-Dawla, 1928), 90; and Muhammad b. al-Tayyib al-Baqillani, *Kitab 'l-tamhid,* ed. Richard J. McCarthy (Beirut: al-Maktaba 'l-Sharqiyya, 1957), 272. In distinguishing between essential and active attributes, theologians argued that the former belong to a set of attributes the opposites of which cannot be asserted in connection with God. So, when one says that God is

living one is also implicitly affirming that it would not be possible to apply the opposite attribute of "nonliving" when speaking about God. By contrast, active attributes belong to a set that can be either applicable or not applicable to God. In effect, active attributes are not fundamental in our conceptualization of God. See 'Ali b. Isma'il al-Ash'ari, *Maqalat 'l-Islamiyyin wa 'khtilaf 'l-musallin*, ed. H. Ritter (Wiesbaden: Franz Steiner Verlag, 1980), 508.

9. On the collection of the Qur'an, see Subhi al-Salih, *Mabahith fi 'ulum 'l-Qur'an* (Beirut: Dar 'l-'Ilm li-'l-Malayin, 1972), 117–224.

10. See Ibn 'Arabi, *Al-Futuhat* 3:160.

11. The term *furqan* occurs in seven places in the Qur'an. Verses 8:29 and 8:41 use it in a general sense. The first verse addresses the believers and announces that if they fear God He will grant them a *"furqan."* This, as al-Tabari tells us, was interpreted as granting them either a way out, a deliverance, or a criterion to help them distinguish between right and wrong. Al-Tabari, *Tafsir,* 6:223. The second verse mentions the "day of *furqan*," which is further characterized as "the day the two hosts encountered," a reference generally interpreted as an allusion to the Battle of Badr that took place in 2/624. See al-Tabari, *Tafsir* 6:254–55. In two verses, the term is used in connection with the Mosaic event in the Qur'an. Verse 2:53 points out that God gave Moses "the Book [*al-kitab*] and the *furqan*," and verse 21:48 states that God granted Moses and Aaron "the *furqan*." The word has commonly been interpreted in both verses as the "criterion on the basis of which one judges right from wrong." See al-Tabari, *Tafsir,* 1:323–24 and 9:34 respectively. In two of the other three verses there is a clear relationship between the word and what was revealed to Muhammad. Verse 25:1 says, "Blessed be He who has sent down the *furqan* upon His servant, that he may be a warner to all beings." In verse 2:185, the *furqan* is an aspect of what the all-comprehensive Qur'an offers, "the month of Ramadan, wherein the Koran was sent down to be a guidance to the people, and as clear signs of the Guidance and the *furqan*." In 3:3–4 we read, "He has sent down upon thee the Book with the truth, confirming what was before it, and He sent down the Torah and the Gospel aforetime, as guidance to the people, and He sent down the *furqan*." The word *furqan* here indicates an independent entity or revelation that corresponds to the Book (the Qur'an), the Torah, and the Gospel. Here, its use is similar to that in a prophetic tradition according to which Muhammad said in praise of the opening chapter of the Qur'an that "nothing comparable to it was revealed in the Torah or the Gospel or the Psalms or the *furqan*." Muhammad b. 'Isa al-Tirmidhi, *Sunan*, ed. Mahmud Nassar (Beirut: Dar 'l-Kutub al-'Ilmiyya, 2000), 4:3. After reviewing the views held by some Western scholars on the origin and meaning of the term, Jeffery expresses the highly speculative view that "it seems clear that *furqan* is a word that Muhammad himself borrowed to use as a technical term, and to whose meaning he gave his own interpretation. The source of the borrowing was doubtless the vocabulary of the Aramaic-speaking Christians, whether or not the word was also influenced by Judaism." Arthur Jeffery, *The Foreign Vocabulary of the Quran* (Lahore: al-Biruni, 1938), 229.

12. Verse 7:180 refers to God's "Names Most Beautiful" *(al-asma' 'l-husna).* On the basis

of a prophetic tradition, these names were designated as being ninety-nine in number, and as a result a list of divine names was compiled. On the meanings and classification of the Beautiful Names, see Abu Hamid al-Ghazali, *Al-Maqsad 'l-asna fi sharh ma'ani asma' 'Llah 'l-husna*, ed. Fadlou A. Shehadi (Beirut: Dar 'l-Mashriq, 1971), 63–162. On a treatment of these names in English, see M. I. Siddiqi, *Ninety Nine Names of Allah* (Delhi: Adam Publishers and Distributors, 1988). The Sufi notion of the Perfect Human as a bearer of divine attributes contrasts with the belief of the Mu'tazilites Ahmad b. Khabit (d. 232/846) and al-Fadl al-Hadathi (d. 257/870) that Jesus is the bearer of divine attributes or the incarnation of God. In their view verse 2:210, which poses the question, "What do they look for, but that God shall come to them in the cloud-shadows," refers in fact to Jesus. See Muhammad b. 'Abd al-Karim al-Shahrastani, *Al-Milal wa 'l-nihal*, ed. Muhammad Sayyid Kilani (Beirut: Dar Sa'b, 1986), 1:60. Taha reads the reference in the verse to God as a reference to the Perfect Human, and the implied notion of incarnation as a reference to the Second Coming (QF 45).

13. For a treatment of this doctrine in the context of the Mu'tazilite and Ash'arite debate, see W. Montgomery Watt, *Early Islam: Collected Articles* (Edinburgh: Edinburgh Univ. Press, 1990), 86–93.

14. Quoted in RT 56. For the full version of the tradition, see, for instance, al-Bukhari, *Sahih*, 8:391; and Ibn Hanbal, *Al-Musnad*, 2:421. There was considerable disagreement about the referent of the pronominal suffix of *"suratihi."* In one hadith in Muslim's *Sahih*, the statement is placed within the context of prophetic advice that should a Muslim be engaged in a violent fight he ought to avoid striking the face for "God had created Adam in its image." Muslim, *Sahih* 16:165–66. Another point of view maintained that the reference was to Adam himself. It was perhaps this ambiguity that led to the rise of another version of the tradition that said, "God created Adam in the image of the Merciful [*al-rahman*]." This version was rejected by the traditionists. Ibn 'Arabi, deploying his device of "prophetic unveiling," insisted that the tradition was sound. See Ibn 'Arabi, *Al-Futuhat* 1:106. For him this image consisted of a manifestational aspect *(sura zahira)* involving the phenomenal world and its realities and an immanental aspect *(sura batina)*, which is in the divine image. The divine tradition holds that God privileges the servant who engages in supererogatory works by becoming the "hearing by which he hears" and "the sight by which he sees." This tradition is used by Ibn 'Arabi to demonstrate the distinction between these two aspects as God uses the terms *hearing* and *sight* rather than *ear* and *eye*. See Ibn 'Arabi, *Fusus*, 55. As a fuller version of the hadith refers to God being the servant's "hand" and "leg" (see al-Bukhari, *Sahih* 8:483), Ibn 'Arabi's logic works only partially. In another place, he uses the fuller version in the context of discussing Sufi experiential knowledge that, despite being attained through different faculties, stems in reality from one source. Hence, according to him, what God asserts in the hadith is that His "identity *(huwiyya)* is the same as that of the limbs that constitute the very identity of the servant." Ibn 'Arabi, *Fusus*, 107.

15. On the orthodox interpretations of *umm 'l-kitab*, see al-Tabari, *Tafsir*, 11:165–66.

16. Ibn 'Arabi, *Al-Futuhat*, 2:67. On the parallelism that Ibn 'Arabi establishes between the world and man on the one hand and man and God on the other, see Nasr Hamid Abu Zaid, *Falsafat 'l-ta'wil: Dirasa fi ta'wil 'l-Qur'an 'inda Muhyi al-Din Ibn 'Arabi* (Beirut: Dar 'l-Tanwir, 1993), 157–62.

17. The Jahmites were the followers of Jahm b. Safwan (d. 128/746). On the Jahmites' agreement with the Mu'tazilites as regards the createdness of the Qur'an, see Abd al-Rahim b. Muhammad b. 'Uthman al-Khayyat, *Kitab 'l-intisar wa al-radd 'ala Ibn al-Rawandi 'l-mulhid*, ed. H. S. Nyberg (Cairo: Dar 'l-Kutub 'l-Misriyya, 1925), 188.

18. Fakhry, *History*, 73.

19. According to al-Ash'ari the Mu'tazilites divided into six factions as to whether God's speech was substance or not. One faction maintained that God's speech is nothing but created substance. Another faction contrasted human speech with divine speech: while the former is accidental by virtue of entailing movement, the latter is a substance consisting of an "articulated, arranged, and audible voice" *(sawt muqatta' mu'allaf masmu')* that is none other than God's action and creation. A third faction argued that God's speech is not substance but a created accident that could exist in several places at the same time through its recitation and writing. By contrast, a fourth faction, while agreeing with the third faction that God's speech is a created accident, held that it could not exist in two places at the same time. A fifth faction argued that the Qur'an is an accident. They further maintained that accidents are generated by either living beings or dead beings. As in their view it is impossible for God to generate accidents, then the Qur'an could not have been generated by Him. As such the Qur'an is the action *(fi'l)* of the place, which serves as its locus: if it is heard from a tree, then it is the action of that tree. A sixth faction held that God's speech is a created accident that exists in several places at the same time. See al-Ash'ari, *Maqalat*, 192–93.

20. Verses 85:21–22 read, "Nay, but it is a glorious Koran, in a guarded tablet." Some exegetes identified this "guarded tablet" with the inscrutable Qur'anic notion of *umm 'l-kitab*. The imagination of 'Abd Allah b. 'Abbas (d. 68/687) was credited with the following tradition: "The guarded tablet is made out of a red ruby the upper part of which is attached to the throne and the bottom of which is in the lap of an angel called Matriyun. . . . God looks into it every day three hundred and sixty times. Each time He does what he wishes: He elevates a lowly person or lowers a person of lofty stature; He enriches a poor person or impoverishes a rich one; He gives life or death." To Anas b. Malik (d. between 91/709 and 93–711) and Mujahid (d. between 100/718 and 104/722) is attributed a tradition that throws its weight behind another archangel, namely, Israfil, on whose forehead stands the guarded tablet. See al-Qurtubi, *Al-Jami'*, 19:296.

21. The Mu'tazilite-leaning caliph al-Ma'mun (d. 218/833) decided to impose belief in the createdness of the Qur'an as an official dogma to be adopted by all state officials. The same policy was zealously followed by his successors, al-Mu'tasim (d. 227/842) and al-Wathiq (d. 232/847). The harshness of this policy and the inquisitorial manner with which it was imposed earned it the name of *mihna* (trial) in Islamic history. It was under

al-Mutawakkil (d. 247/861) that this policy was eventually reversed, and since then the Mu'tazilite view has been anathematized, and the position championed by Ahmad b. Hanbal came to express the majority orthodox view. On the doctrinal basis of 'l-Ma'mun's policy, see some of his letters in Muhammad b. Jarir al-Tabari, *Tarikh 'l-umam wa 'l-muluk* (Beirut: Dar 'l-Kutub 'l-'Ilmiyya, 2001), 5:186–89. On general surveys of Ibn Hanbal's plight, see 'Abd al-Halim al-Jindi, *Ahmad b. Hanbal: Imam ahl 'l-sunna* (Cairo: Dar 'l-Ma'arif, 1977), 379–414; and Walter M. Patton, *Ahmed Ibn Hanbal and the Mihna* (Leiden: E. J. Brill, 1897), 124–30.

22. On the one hand, the fierce opposition of Ibn Hanbal and other orthodox scholars to allegorization was intimately bound up with their affirmation of de-anthropomorphism *(tanzih)*. Their insistence on the latter aspect led them to rule that if a person moves his hand when reading "that I created with My own hands" (verse 38:75) or points with his fingers when quoting the prophetic tradition "The heart of the believer is between two of God's fingers" (see, for instance, Ibn Maja, *Sunan*, 2:1260), the person's hand or fingers should be cut off. See al-Shahrastani, *Al-Milal*, 1:104. (This apparently was an extreme pietistic reaction against a gesticulatory practice by some as attested by the example of al-A'mash, one of the transmitters of the tradition in Ibn Maja's *Sunan*, who, on conveying the tradition, made a sign with his fingers.) But on the other hand, Ibn Hanbal had a clearly anthropomorphic side and was willing to defend the notion of a god who has a face, eyes, and hands, sits on a throne, and descends at times to the lower heavens. See Ahmad Ibn Hanbal, *Al-Radd 'ala 'l-Jahmiyya wa 'l-Zanadiqa*, ed. 'Abd al-Rahman 'Umaira (Riyad: Dar 'l-Liwa', 1977). It is, however, important to distinguish between Ibn Hanbal's Sunnite literalism and anthropomorphism and other more extreme expressions of the same tendency. Some anthropomorphists constructed an image of a God whom one can touch, shake hands with, see in this world, and pay a visit to. To Da'wud al-Jawaribi was attributed the statement, "Spare me from talking about the genitals [*farj*] and the beard and ask me about anything else." According to him, God has body, flesh, and blood; He has organs such as hands, legs, a head, a tongue, eyes, and ears. But, still, He did not resemble any of His creatures, and none of His creatures was like Him. To al-Jawaribi was also attributed the belief that God is hollow from His upper part to His chest and solid in the rest of His body and that He has short black curly hair collected together upon the head. See al-Shahrastani, *Al-Milal* 1:105. In formulating their views, these anthropomorphists drew on the Qur'an, the hadith material, and other sources. It is noteworthy that some Muslim anthropomorphists also exhibited an anthropopathic tendency and made statements such as that God cried after Noah's flood till His eyes were inflamed. In this respect, al-Shahrastani accused them of having drawn on Jewish sources. Al-Shahrastani, *Al-Milal,* 1:106.

23. On the orthodox position on this point, see al-Shahrastani, *Al-Milal,* 1:92.

24. Ibn Hanbal did not hesitate to assume an extreme judgmental role when it came to this issue, as the following passage against the Jahmites demonstrates, "The Qur'an is God's uncreated speech. He who claims that it is created is an unbelieving [*kafir*] Jahmite. And he

who says that the Qur'an is God's speech without completing his statement and affirming whether it is created or uncreated is even worse than the first type. He who claims that our articulation and recitation of the Qur'an is created while the Qur'an is God's speech is a Jahmite. And he who does not judge all these people as unbelievers is himself an unbeliever." Ibn Hanbal, quoted in Ahmad b. 'Abd al-Halim Ibn Taimiyya, *Dar' ta'arud 'l-'aql wa 'l-naql,* ed. Muhammad Rashad Salim (Cairo: Maktabat Ibn Taimiya, n.d), 1:260 n1. On Ibn Hanbal's rebuttal of Jahmite views, see his *Al-Radd 'ala 'l-Jahmiyya,* particularly 114–26 regarding the createdness of the Qur'an.

25. Quoting, for instance, verse 16:40, which declares, "The only words We say to a thing, when We desire it, is that We say to it 'Be,' and it is," al-Ash'ari argues, "If the Qur'an were created then it should have been addressed by 'Be' and then it is. If God were to utter the speech item [*qawl*] 'Be,' then [the Qur'an which is] speech would be addressed through speech. This implies one of two things: either that God's speech is uncreated or that each speech is created by another speech ad infinitum, which is absurd." 'Ali b. Isma'il al-Ash'ari, *Al-Ibana 'an usul 'l-diyana,* ed. Fawqiyya Husain Mahmud (Cairo: Dar 'l-Ansar, 1977), 65.

26. The notion of "mental speech" is expressed by al-Baqillani as "a sense that exists in the mind" *(ma'na qa'im bi-'l-nafs).* See al-Baqillani, *Al-Tamhid,* 251. 'Abd al-Rahman Badawi comments that this "mental speech" is in fact the Greek logos in its essential sense of thought and mind. See 'Abd al-Rahman Badawi, *Madhahib 'l-islamiyyin: Al-Mu'tazila wa 'l-Asha'ira* (Beirut: Dar 'l-'Ilm li-'l-Malayin, 1971), 1:733.

27. 'Abd al-Malik b. 'Abd Allah b. Yusuf al-Juwaini, *Kitab 'l-irshad ila qawati' 'l-adilla fi usul 'l-i'tiqad,* ed. Muhammad Yusuf Musa and 'Ali 'Abd al-Mun'im 'Abd al-Hamid (Cairo: Maktabat 'l-Khanji, 1950), 132.

28. Ibid., 135.

29. The word *ummi* and its plural *ummiyyun* occur in several places in the Qur'an. Referring to the Jews, verse 2:78 states, "And some there are of them that are *ummiyyun* not knowing the Book, but only fancies and mere conjectures." Verse 3:75 attributes to the Jews the statement "There is no way over us as to the *ummiyyun.*" Here, the term is applied by the Jews to non-Jews. By contrast, in verse 62:2 the term is appropriated by the Qur'an to describe the Prophet's community. In dealing with the meaning of the word *ummi,* al-Tabari adduces several authoritative statements concurring that the word means "unlettered," "illiterate." To this effect he cites a tradition according to which the Prophet said, "We are a community of *ummiyyun* who neither write nor compute." Al-Tabari maintains that the word is derived from *umm* (mother) because literacy was a male preoccupation and hence illiteracy may be connected with the mother rather than the father. Al-Tabari, *Tafsir* 1:417. Although al-Shahrastani agrees that the word means "illiterate," he invests it with a religious significance to signify ancient Arabian faith. He says that whereas the religion of the People of the Book was "Israelite" in nature, the religion of the Arab *ummiyyun* was "Ishmaelite" in nature. See al-Shahrastani, *Al-Milal,* 1:208–9. The implication of what al-Shahrastani says is echoed by Wensinck, who argues that "when Muhammad called himself *ummi,* he meant . . . that he

was the Arabian Prophet of the gentiles, speaking to the gentiles to whom no Apostle had ever been sent before." A. J. Wensinck, *The Muslim Creed: Its Genesis and Historical Development* (London: Frank Cass & Co., 1965), 6. Taha not only sticks to the traditional understanding of the word as "unlettered" but, not unlike some modern Muslim thinkers, romanticizes this state of unletteredness, describing it in the following celebratory terms: "Islam is the religion of the unlettered; its Prophet was unlettered and so was its community *(umma)*. . . . Unletterdness indicates the innocence of one's natural state *[fitra]* from distractive study, confused sophistry, and presumptuousness that usually go hand in hand with education" (AJi 34–35).

30. See, for instance, verses 51:20–21.

31. On Plato's theory of learning as recollection, see his *Protagoras and Meno,* trans. W. K. C. Guthrie. (Harmondsworh, Middlesex: Penguin Books, 1980), 128–30.

32. Responding to Taha's views, the Sudanese poet and educator Muhammad Muhammad 'Ali (d. 1970) put to him the question, "If your fanciful description applies to the Qur'an, would it not be equally applicable to all sacred books, arts, and mythology?" Taha replied by saying, "All sacred books, arts, and mythology are ascending ladders toward the Truth *[al-haqq]* (God), though they vary in nearness and distance from [that Truth]. The only thing is that the Qur'an is superior to all of them as it brings together all the truths that are scattered in them" (RMii 8).

33. Muhammad Muhammad 'Ali might have been the first to point out the Platonic provenance of what Taha argued about knowledge as recollection. Taha dismissed what 'Ali suggested and insisted that the source of his view was Qur'anic (see RMii 7–8). This claim is characteristic of his attitude throughout his work as he always insists on a Qur'anic basis for all his views.

34. According to Taha's religious imagination, Qur'anic music has permeated the physical world from its very beginning and has played a decisive role in prodding human evolution. "The music of the Qur'an has accompanied thought since the [primordial] moment when human beings were still in . . . an inorganic state. This continued until inorganic matter became organic, evolving into a unicellular organism. It continued attending thought, taking care of it, and churning it, as one would churn butter out of milk, until it produced present-day mankind. It will continue going along with it, tending to it, cultivating it, and promoting it till it reaches the level of the Perfect Human" (IF 17). In accounting for the origin of this Qur'anic music, Taha offers metaphysical categories: "The music of the Qur'an is played on a string taut between two ends with a point moving along. These two points are untruth *[batil]* and the Truth *[haqiqa]* . . . and the moving point is truth *[haqq]* in its quest and upward movement toward the Truth" (IF 18).

35. The term *mathani* occurs twice in the Qur'an. The other place is verse 15:87, "And We have bestowed upon thee the seven *mathani* and the mighty Koran." The term has puzzled exegetes. Al-Tabari gives a good account of the different points of view. Some exegetes maintained that the "seven *mathani*" of verse 15:87 refers to the first seven chapters of the

Qur'an, which also happen to be the longest. According to these exegetes the word *mathani* pertains to a "doubling" or "repetition" feature in the Qur'an because Qur'anic parables *(amthal),* stories *(akhbar),* and moral lessons *('ibar)* are repeated in these chapters. This view was rejected by other exegetes, who argued that this could not be the case because the verse was revealed before the revelation of the seven long chapters in question. Another exegetical point of view holds that "seven *mathani*" refers to the meanings of the Qur'an. Other exegetes argued that the phrase refers to the opening chapter of the Qur'an. As this chapter contains in fact six verses, the exponents of this view had to resort to the exceptional measure of counting the *basmala* formula at the chapter's head as a verse. According to them the "seven" verses of this chapter are *"mathani"* because they are oft-repeated in prayer. Al-Tabari favors this position and argues that it is amply supported by the Prophet's traditions in one of which he declares that this chapter is "the mother of the Book, the mother of the Qur'an, and the seven *mathani.*" Al-Tabari, *Tafsir,* 7:533–41. Although Taha maintains that the entire Qur'an exhibits a *mathani* quality in that it has different semantic levels, he concurs with the orthodox position that the "seven *mathani*" phrase refers specifically to the opening chapter of the Qur'an (see QF 52). On the views of some Western scholars regarding an assumed foreign origin of *mathani,* see Jeffery, *Foreign Vocabulary,* 257–58.

36. There are several verses in the Qur'an that suggest that the earth's shape is flat. For example, verse 13:3 confirms that "it is He who stretched out the earth" *(madda 'l-arda).* Some modern Muslim apologists who claim that the Qur'an is fully consistent with scientific knowledge insist that it does in fact confirm that the earth is spherical. The employment of verse 79:30 has been particularly popular in defending this claim. See, for instance, 'Abd al-Razzaq Nawfal, *Baina 'l-din wa 'l-'ilm* (Cairo: Maktabat Wahba, n.d.), 167.

37. The concept of the earth as round was introduced into Muslim geographical thought during the third-fifth/ninth-eleventh centuries with the exposure of geographers to Indian, Iranian, and Greek geographical sciences. The question of the shape of the earth was raised by Greeks interested in general geography (as opposed to regional geography). The spherical shape of the earth was accepted by philosophers, and by Aristotle's time (d. ca. 230 B.C.E.), the proofs put forward are similar to those we find in modern textbooks. In connection with the earth's shape, al-Idrisi (ca. 560/1165) writes, "What has come [to us] from the statements of philosophers, the majority of the learned, and those who study geography is that the earth is as round as a ball and that water clings to it, being attached to it in a natural way." Muhammad b. Muhammad b. 'Abd Allah al-Idrisi, *Kitab nuzhat 'l-mushtaq fi 'khtiraq 'l-afaq* (Leiden: E. J. Brill, 1970), 7. On the history of Muslim geography, see J. H. Kramer, "Geography and Commerce," in *The Legacy of Islam,* ed. Thomas Arnold and Alfred Guillaume (Oxford: Clarendon Press, 1931), 79–107; and Nafis Ahmad, *Muslim Contribution to Geography* (New Delhi: Adam Publishers and Distributors, 1945), particularly 16–44.

38. Like the Greeks, the Arabs assigned numerical values to the letters of the alphabet, according to their position. The twenty-eight letters were divided into three sets of nine each: units (from 1 to 9), tens (from 10 to 90), hundreds (from 100 to 900), and one thou-

sand. On the numerical value of the letters, see *EI²*, s.v. "abdjad." On the specific numerical values of the respective letters, see W. Wright, *A Grammar of the Arabic Language*, 3rd ed. (Cambridge: Cambridge Univ. Press, 1988), 1–2.

39. For example, verse 22:47 affirms, "and surely a day with thy Lord is as a thousand years of your counting." Another verse Taha quotes in this respect is verse 70:4, which states, "To Him the angels and the Spirit mount up in a day whereof the measure is fifty thousand years." Taha does not allow the latter value to affect his logic, insisting on one thousand as his basic unit.

40. Among the most accomplished classical expositions of the theory of *i'jaz* were the works of al-Baqillani and 'Abd al-Qahir al-Jurjani (d. 471/1078). On what al-Baqillani considers the most salient aspects of Qur'anic *i'jaz*, see Muhammad b. al-Tayyib al-Baqillani, *I'jaz 'l-Qur'an*, ed. 'Imad al-Din Ahmad Haidar (Beirut: Mu'assasat 'l-Kutub 'l-Thaqafiyya, 1986), 57–72. Al-Jurjani's treatment of the subject in his *Kitab dala'il 'l-i'jaz fi 'ilm 'l-ma'ani*, ed. Muhammad 'Abdu, Muhammad Mahmud al-Shinqiti, and Rashid Rida (Cairo: Dar 'l-Manar, 1946) is characterized by its sophistication and subtlety. On a modern exposition of al-Jurjani's views on the *i'jaz* of the Qur'an, see Navid Kermani, *Gott is schön: Das ästhetische Erleben des Koran* (Munich: Verlag C. H. Beck, 1999), 253–89; and for a general exposition of his theory of construction *(nazm)*, see Kamal Abu Deeb, *Al-Jurjani's Theory of Poetic Imagery* (Warminster, Wilts.: Aris and Phillips, 1979), 24–64. On a modern treatment of *i'jaz* that applies the notion to the Prophet's use of language, see Mustafa Sadiq al-Rafi'i, *I'jaz 'l-Qur'an* (Cairo: al-Maktaba 'l-Tijariyya 'l-Kubra, 1965).

41. Al-Bukhari, *Sahih*, 8:369.

42. Ibid., 8:366.

43. See, for instance, al-Qurtubi, *Al-Jami'* 13:145–50. On a rhetorician's spirited rebuttal of the antipoetry position, see al-Jurjani, *Dala'il 'l-i'jaz*, 9–22. On the views of Sufis concerning *sama'* or the combination of poetry recitations with singing and the playing of music, see al-Qushairi, *Al-Risala*, 2:637–59.

44. For a review of classical exegetical views on these letters, see al-Tabari, *Tafsir*, 1:118–28; and Fakhr al-Din al-Razi, *Al-Tafsir 'l-kabir* (Cairo: al-Matba'a al-Bahiyya al-Misriyya, n.d.), 2:2–12. For a succinct account of the meanings suggested for them, see Muhammad b. Abd Allah al-Zarkashi, *Al-Burhan fi 'Ulum 'l-Qur'an* (Beirut: Dar 'l-Ma'rifa, 1994), 1:262–67. Although modern exegetes may favor a particular interpretation, they tend to avoid the abstruse discussions associated with these letters. Muhammad 'Abduh throws his weight behind the view that the letters are in fact the titles of their respective chapters. Muhammad Rashid Rida (d. 1935), 'Abduh's disciple and companion, supplemented this by trying to establish forced connections between the disjoined letters and the dominant themes of the chapters they preface. See Rida, *Tafsir 'l-manar*, 8:296–99. Although al-Tabataba'i is of the same view in that he also sees a connection between these letters and the contents of their chapters, he avoids offering any specific suggestions of what these connections might be. After reviewing the exegetical views about the letters and expressing his

dissatisfaction with them, he concludes by saying that these letters are "signs [*rumuz*] between God and His prophet [with meanings] that are not revealed to us. Our modest powers of comprehension have no access to their meanings except insofar as we sense some special connection between them and the contents of the chapters to which they belong." Muhammad Husain al-Tabataba'i, *Al-Mizan fi tafsir 'l-Qur'an* (Beirut: Mu'assasat 'l-A'lami li-'l-Matbu'at, 1970), 18:7–9. His final verdict is thus not dissimilar to that attributed to al-Sha'bi (d. between 103/721 and 110/728) when he advised an inquirer not to waste his time trying to understand what these letters meant. See Jalal al-Din 'Abd al-Rahman al-Suyuti, *Al-Durr 'l-manthur fi 'l-tafsir bi-'l-ma'thur* (Beirut: Dar al-Kutub 'l-'Ilmiyya, 2000), 1:56.

45. Al-Razi cites a few traditions to this effect. To Abu Bakr, for instance, is attributed a tradition according to which he said, "In each Book, God has a mystery and His mystery in the Qur'an is the [lettered] beginnings of the chapters." Similar statements are attributed to 'Ali, Ibn 'Abbas, and al-Sha'bi. Al-Razi also gives an account of a theory of knowledge transmission expounded by some exegetes. Commenting on a part of verse 13:17 that reads, "He sends down out of heaven water, and the wadis flow each in its measure," these exegetes maintained that "God, with whom reside seas of knowledge, gives [His] prophets wadis full of knowledge. From their wadis, the prophets give learned people ['*ulama'*] rivers of knowledge. These learned people then give common people [*al-'amma*] streams of knowledge according to their capacity. The common people, in their turn, give brooks of knowledge to their own folks." Al-Razi, *Tafsir*, 2:3.

46. As a linguistic expression defining God's concreteness, the word *Allah* describes God's unicity (*ahadiyya*), but the same word, when applied to the Absolute, turns into a sign indicating God's ineffability (QF 47).

47. The terms *external speech* and *inner speech* are borrowed from the Russian psychologist Levi Semenovich Vygotsky. On his treatment of these notions, see his *Thought and Language*, ed. and trans. Eugenia Hanfmann and Gertrude Vakar (Cambridge, Mass.: The Massachusetts Institute of Technology Press, 1977), 44–51, 130–53.

48. When Taha speaks about alphabetical letters, he is, like his Sufi predecessors who dealt with the subject of letters, Arabic-centric in that he invariably refers to the twenty-eight letters of the Arabic alphabet. Furthermore, he is Qur'an-centric in that he privileges the fourteen letters that comprise the disjoined letters. These letters are described as "light letters" (*huruf nuraniyya*). By contrast, the rest of the alphabet comprises what is described as "dark letters" (*huruf zulmaniyya*) (QF 48). The special distinction given to the disjoined letters is a theme found in the works of many Sufis, notably those of Ibn 'Arabi's. Ibn 'Arabi invests letters with ontological properties. He claims that, like humans, letters are "communities" (*umam*) that are addressed by God (*mukhatab-un*) and charged with obligations (*mukallaf-un*). For Ibn 'Arabi they inhabit a universe similar to the universe of Sufi imagination, with its hierarchical descent from the world of '*azama* (majesty) to the uppermost (*a'la*) world to the world of sovereignty (*malakut*) to the world of power (*jabarut*) and then the lower world of manifestation (*shahada*). Moreover, he subjects letters to the tradi-

tional spiritual Sufi hierarchy that distinguishes between the commonalty *('amma)*, the elect *(khassa)*, and the elect of the elect *(khassat 'l-khassa)*. He places the disjoined letters at the rank of election. See Ibn 'Arabi, *Al-Futuhat*, 1:58. On Ibn 'Arabi's theory of letters and its significance in his thought, see Abu Zaid, *Falsafat 'l-ta'wil*, 297–331. On the science of letters and its use in magic and Sufism, see 'Abd al-Rahman Ibn Khaldun, *Tarikh Ibn Khaldun* (Beirut: Dar 'l-Kutub 'l-'Ilmiyya, 1992), 1:558–68. For an English translation, see Ibn Khaldun, *The Muqaddimah: An Introduction to History*, trans. Franz Rosenthal (London: Routledge and Kegan Paul, 1958), 3:171–82.

49. Taha uses the words *tafsir* and *ta'wil* in a Sufi technical sense. The term *tafsir* occurs once in the Qur'an in verse 25:33, addressing Muhammad: "They bring not to thee any similitude but that we bring thee the truth, and better in exposition [*ahsan-a tafsir-an*]." On the other hand, the term *ta'wil* occurs seventeen times in the Qur'an. In all these instances, with the exception of two places where it is used idiomatically, the word means "interpretation" or "explanation." Classical scholars used *tafsir* and *ta'wil* interchangeably, and al-Tabari called his Qur'anic commentary a *ta'wil*. It was the Sufis who felt the need to distinguish between the two terms, and so *tafsir* came to designate in their terminology orthodox, exoteric interpretation, whereas *ta'wil* was reserved for their own esoteric hermeneutic approach. On early debates on whether *ta'wil* is a divine province or open to humans, see Nasr Hamid Abu Zaid, *Al-Ittijah 'l-'aqli fi 'l-tafsir: Dirasa fi qadiyyat 'l-majaz fi 'l-Qur'an 'inda 'l-Mu'tazila* (Beirut: Dar 'l-Tanwir, 1983), 141–63.

50. Taha is echoing here the already familiar divine tradition in which the divine voice declares, "I was a hidden treasure." See page 36 above.

51. See, for instance, al-Tabari, *Tafsir*, 7:589.

52. Verse 7:204 urges of believers that when the Qur'an is recited they should lend their ears to it *(fa-'stami'u lahu)* and listen *(wa ansitu)*. In interpreting this verse, al-Tabari reads the phrase *"fa-'stami'u lahu"* to mean "hearken to it so that you understand its verses and take warning from its exhortations." He reads the phrase *"wa ansitu"* to mean "so that you may comprehend. You should not speak [during its recitation] lest you fail to comprehend it." It is possible to detect in what he says a distinction between *'istima'* as primarily an auditory experience and *insat* as a reflective experience. His understanding of the phrase *"wa ansitu"* is based on the material concerning the verse's occasion of revelation; apparently early Muslims used to speak during the performance of their prayers, and this verse was revealed to put an end to this practice. See al-Tabari, *Tafsir*, 6:161–65.

53. Mustafa Mahmud, *Al-Qur'an: Muhawala li-fahm 'asri li-'l-Qur'an* (Beirut: Dar 'l-Shuruq, 1970), 85.

54. The very concrete images of paradise in the Qur'an and the hadith material are sometimes counterbalanced by a tendency to push the notion of paradise into the realm of the indescribable. Hence, in commenting on verse 32:17, which affirms, "No soul knows what comfort is laid up for them secretly, as a recompense for that they were doing," the hadith material furnishes a tradition in which Muhammad reports that God said that He had

prepared for the righteous "what no eye had ever seen, no ear had ever heard of, and no heart had ever envisioned." Al-Bukhari, *Sahih,* 6:481.

55. On this type of literalism, see note 22 to chapter 3, above.

56. See al-Qushairi, *Tafsir,* 2:255. Ibn 'Arabi discusses the symbolism of the putting off of the shoes in the context of discussing the meaning of the disjoined letters *alif-lam-mim* with which chapter 2 opens. See Ibn 'Arabi, *Al-Futuhat,* 1:63.

57. In Islamic sources, the Second Coming involves the return of Jesus as Muhammad's successor and his presiding over a time of destruction to be followed by a time of construction. See Ahmad b. Muhammad al-Tha'labi, *Qisas 'l-anbiya'* (Beirut: al-Maktaba 'l-Thaqafiyya, n.d.), 363.

4. Determinism, Free Will, and Divine Punishment

1. The exegetes were naturally concerned to explain the manner of divine intervention in connection with the declaration of verse 8:17. Those who maintained that the Battle of Badr was the verse's occasion of revelation explained the slaying in view of, for example, what verse 8:9 mentions about the participation of the angels in fighting. See al-Tabari, *Tafsir,* 6:188–91. They explained the reference to throwing by producing accounts replete with miracles. According to one account, the Prophet threw three stones at the Meccans, who were completely routed at the throwing of the last one. Another account involves Gabriel, who appeared to Muhammad and ordered him to take a fistful of sand and throw it at the Meccans' faces. See al-Tabari, *Tafsir,* 6:203–4. Those who argued that the context of the verse's occasion of revelation was the Battle of Uhud in 3/625 highlighted a particular incident, that is, the attempt of Ubayy b. Khalaf to kill Muhammad, and his death after being injured by a spear that the Prophet threw at him. On the incident and its setting, see Muhammad b. 'Umar al-Waqidi, *Kitab 'l-maghazi,* ed. Marsden Jones (London: Oxford Univ. Press, 1966), 1:250–52. It may be argued that when verse 8:17 is read within the larger context of the passage made up by verses 8:15–19, the second proposition seems to be more likely as an occasion of revelation. Verses 8:15–16 could be read as a commentary on the Muslims' setback at Uhud, and a plausible link can be established between the specific reference to the act of throwing in verse 8:17 and the Ubayy b. Khalaf incident.

2. Al-Tirmidhi, *Sunan,* 3:390.

3. Al-Bukhari, *Sahih,* 4:551–52.

4. Al-Shahrastani, *Al-Milal,* 1:85.

5. For a brief and stimulating account of Jahmite theology, see W. Montgomery Watt, "Early Discussions about the Qur'an," *The Muslim World* 40, no. 1 (1950): 27–40, 28–33.

6. Al-Ash'ari, *Maqalat,* 279.

7. 'Abd al-Halim Mahmud, *Al-Tafkir 'l-falsafi fi'l-Islam* (Cairo: Dar 'l-Ma'arif, 1984), 145.

8. Ibn al-Murtada includes al-Basri in the third class of the Mu'tazilites. In a letter he sent to the caliph 'Abd al-Malik (r. 65–86/685–705), al-Basri expressed a clearly Qadarite po-

sition. He argued that one cannot attribute to God what He has forbidden, such as unthankfulness *(kufr)*. See Ahmad b. Yahya Ibn al-Murtada, *Kitab Tabaqat 'l-Mu'tazila,* ed. Susanna Diwald-Wilzer (Beirut: Dar Maktabat 'l-Hayat, n.d.), 19–20. Al-Basri's view is summed up in an anecdote. Passing by a crucified thief, al-Basri asked him why he stole, and when the thief said it was God's decree, he retorted, "Liar! Would God decree that you steal and then decree that you get crucified!" Ibid., 21. There were, however, counter accounts that emphasized al-Basri's refusal to express an explicit opinion on the question of *qadar.* Ibn al-Murtada dismisses these accounts and maintains that al-Basri had to be wary and circumspect on account of the oppressiveness of the Umayyad regime. Ibid., 24.

9. Al-Shahrastani, *Al-Milal,* 1:47.

10. Ibid., 1:51.

11. See ibid., 1:54; and al-Ash'ari, *Maqalat,* 555.

12. Al-Shahrastani, *Al-Milal,* 1:65; al-Ash'ari, *Maqalat,* 574.

13. Al-Ash'ari, *Maqalat,* 549–50.

14. Ibid., 539.

15. W. Montgomery Watt, *Free Will and Predestination in Early Islam* (London: Luzac and Company, 1948), 83.

16. Al-Ash'ari's newfound distrust of total reliance on reason in understanding God's ways was articulated through a hypothetical situation he posed to his teacher. He proposed three brothers: a believing righteous one, an unbelieving sinful one, and a child. Then he asked al-Jubba'i, "What would God's decree be in their case when they have died?" The master answered that the righteous would go to heaven, the unbelieving to hell, and the child would be sent to a safe place. Al-Ash'ari then asked, "Would the child be allowed if he wanted to join the righteous brother in heaven?" Al-Jubba'i said, "No! He would be told that his brother earned his place on account of his good works and that he did not perform such works." Al-Ash'ari asked, "What if the child said, 'That is not my fault. You did not grant me a longer life and hence allow me to obey you.'" The master answered, "God would say, 'I knew that had you lived you would have disobeyed and would have deserved a grievous punishment and hence I took care of you.'" Al-Ash'ari then asked, "And if the unbelieving brother said, 'O God! You also knew that I would disobey. Why did You take care of him but not of me?'" We are told that al-Jubba'i was dumbfounded and could not come up with an answer. See Shams al-Din Ahmad Ibn Khallikan, *Wafayat 'l-a'yan wa anba' 'l-zaman,* ed. Ihsan 'Abbas (Beirut: Dar Sadir, 1977), 4:267–68. On disputing the authenticity of this debate, see W. Montgomery Watt, *The Formative Period of Islamic Thought* (Edinburgh: Edinburgh Univ. Press, 1973), 305.

17. Some orthodox authorities tended to ground al-Ash'ari's defection from the cause of Mu'tazilism in a miraculous event, and we are hence told about a dream (or dreams) in which he met the Prophet, who firmly enjoined him to "champion the schools [*madhahib*]" that were based on his authority. See 'Ali b. al-Hasan Ibn 'Asakir, *Tabyin kadhib 'l-muftari fi-ma nusiba ila 'l-imam Abi al-Hasan al-Ash'ari* (Damascus: Matba'at 'l-Tawfiq, 1928),

39–43. This is further enforced by an independent account of a man who saw the Prophet in a dream. When he asked the Prophet about the createdness of the Qur'an, the Prophet endorsed the Ash'arite view. Ibn 'Asakir, *Tabyin,* 166. Commenting on al-Ash'ari's dream stories, Watt says, "These stories would seem to be symbolically true, and may even have an element of factual truth." Watt, *Formative Period,* 305. Leaving what he describes as "symbolic truth" aside, there is no substantial basis for assuming that there is "factual truth" in what is attributed to al-Ash'ari. It is more likely that the dream stories were invented to enhance al-Ash'ari's position on the one hand and to vilify the Mu'tazila on the other. If we take into account that al-Ash'ari's father was a traditionist and that he himself remained a follower of Shafi'ism as a religious rite (despite al-Shafi'i's hostility to *kalam*), it is reasonable to assume that he was torn in his intellectual loyalties and that his final break with Mu'tazilism was in fact a resolution of this inner conflict in favor of his orthodox convictions.

18. Al-Ash'ari, *Al-Ibana,* 44.

19. 'Ali b. Isma'il al-Ash'ari, *Kitab 'l-luma' fi 'l-radd 'ala ahl 'l-zaigh wa 'l-bida',* ed. Richard J. McCarthy (Beirut: Imprimerie Catholique, 1953), 38–39.

20. Ibid., 98.

21. Ibid., 71.

22. Al-Ghazali, *Ihya',* 1:110–11.

23. Commenting on Ibn 'Arabi's determinism, 'Afifi maintains that it is not "a mechanical or materialist determinism derived from inanimate nature. Rather, it is similar to the notion of 'pre-established harmony' in Leibniz." Ibn 'Arabi, *Fusus,* 2:22.

24. Ibid., 1:106.

25. Ibid., 1:108. On a critical treatment of Ibn 'Arabi's views on determinism and free will, see Affifi, *Mystical Philosophy,* 153–56.

26. Ibn 'Arabi, *Al-Futuhat,* 1:162–63.

27. 'Abd al-Karim b. Ibrahim al-Jili, *Al-Insan 'l-kamil fi ma'rifat 'l-awakhir wa 'l-awa'il* (Cairo: Mustafa al-Babi al-Halabi, 1956), 81.

28. Ibid., 56.

29. Ibid., 57.

30. For Muhammad 'Abduh's treatment of the issue of free will and determinism, see his *Risalat 'l-tawhid,* 3:386–99. See also Kerr, *Islamic Reform,* 110–16.

31. Quoted in Taha, RMi 49–50.

32. For a brief critical comment on Freud's views by 'Abbas Mahmud al-'Aqqad, see his *Allah: Kitab fi nash'at 'l-'aqida 'l-ilahiyya* (Cairo: Dar 'l-Ma'arif, 1966), 20–21.

33. Taha's emphasis is usually on the human need for God. Ibn 'Arabi, by contrast, also underlines the need of God for humans and the world. God created the world in order to see Himself as "the seeing of a thing of itself by itself is not like the seeing of itself in something else that acts as a mirror. . . . God had brought out the entire world as a form with no spirit, and it was hence like an unpolished mirror. . . . It was consequently necessary to polish the world's mirror, and Adam was the very polished mirror and the spirit of the [world's] form.

The angels were part of this world form described by the Sufis as the 'great human' [*al-insan 'l-kabir*]." Ibn 'Arabi, *Fusus*, 1:48–49.

34. This is a formula that Muslims may pronounce when disaster strikes or when faced with a situation they cannot control.

35. Verse 33:72 reads, "We offered the trust to the heavens and the earth and the mountains, but they refused to carry it and were afraid of it; and man carried it. Surely he is *zalum-an*, very *jahul-an*." Arberry renders *zalum* as "sinful" and *jahul* as "foolish." An-Na'im, mindful of Taha's interpretation of the terms, renders *zalum* as "unfair" and *jahul* as "ignorant" (SM 80). Classical exegetes offered several meanings for the ambiguous word *amana* (trust, responsibility, wardship). See al-Tabari, *Tafsir*, 10:339–42. Taha's contention that what God offered to the world and to humankind was "will" contradicts the verse's internal logic as the divine offer here presupposes the presence of will in the world and humankind who could choose either to accept carrying the *amana* or not. When it comes to the negative epithets *zalum* and *jahul*, it is not clear whether they are a judgment on humankind's decision to carry the *amana*, or a post-*amana* judgment concerning humankind's subsequent performance, or a general pronouncement about humankind's intrinsic nature. Taha reads the epithets as expressive of a negative judgment of humankind's post-*amana* performance: humankind is *zalum* by virtue of falsely claiming what does not belong to it and *jahul* on account of believing that humans have a will (RT 57). In another place, he maintains that the epithets are "praise masked in admonitory language" (RT 96), a positive judgment that is not altogether consistent with his earlier reading of the terms' connotations.

36. On Sigmund Freud's notions of ego and id and the relationship between them, see his *Two Short Accounts of Psycho-Analysis,* trans. James Strachey (Harmondsworth, Middlesex: Penguin Books, 1972), 104–8 and 113–16.

37. The notion is based on verse 36:82, which affirms, "His command, when He desires a thing, is to say to it, 'Be,' and it is."

38. The word *tashri'i* comes from shari'a and broadly covers several types of command: positive ("thou shalt") commands, negative ("thou shalt not") commands, and ethical (ought) commands. The term "*ought*-command" is used to cover all types of shari'a commands.

39. This view about Satan's disobedience was also expressed by former Sufis, notably al-Hallaj. In reconstructing Satan's disobedience and his arguments, al-Hallaj's tone betrays an unmistakable admiration of him as a true and uncompromising monotheist who would bow only to God. Hence, he recounts, "Moses met Satan on Mt. Sinai and said to him: 'O Satan! What keeps you from bowing down?'—'What keeps me from doing it is my preaching of a Single Adored One; if I had bowed down, I would have become like you. For you were summoned only once, "Look toward the mountain!" and you looked; while I was called a thousand times, "Bow down!" and I did not bow down, because my declaration had to uphold the intention which had uttered it to me.' " Massignon, *Passion of al-Hallaj*, 3:311; for the Arabic original, see al-Husain b. Mansur al-Hallaj, *Kitab 'l-tawasin* (Paris: Librairie Paul

Geuthner, 1913), 45–46. On a treatment of this imagined encounter in Sufi literature, see Peter J. Awn, *Satan's Tragedy and Redemption: Iblis in Sufi Psychology* (Leiden: E. J. Brill, 1983), 129–34. In this regard Taha is closer to the letter and spirit of the Qur'an in expressing a sterner judgment on Satan. See, for instance, RT 76–77. For a modern, highly sympathetic and nuanced depiction of Satan, see Sadiq Jalal al-'Azm, *Naqd 'l-fikr 'l-dini* (Beirut: Dar 'l-Tali'a, 1997), 55–87.

40. This is in marked contrast to the Qur'anic attitude, which is negative about what Adam did (as verse 20:115 demonstrates) without being negative about the pre-Fall state in the garden, the return to which is what constitutes the Qur'anic notion of salvation.

41. Ibn Hanbal gives a fuller version of this tradition in the first part of which the Prophet says, "If you had erred (or committed sins) till your sins filled the space between heaven and earth and then asked God for His forgiveness, He would forgive you." Ibn Hanbal, *Al-Musnad*, 3:291. On Taha's further use of this tradition as a basis for democracy in Islam, see p. 172.

42. On the disagreement between orthodox theologians on the one hand and Mu'tazilites and philosophers on the other about the relative excellence of humans and angels, see *EI²*, s.v. *"mala'ika"* 6:216–19.

43. Taha's use of the word *mystery* is retrospective in effect. He points out that the Sufis knew this mystery but were not allowed to divulge it as the time was not ripe. As he had decided that his own time was ready to receive what he disclosed, it was evidently no longer a mystery.

44. As a technical term the word *sabiqa* is derived from the tradition, quoted on page 106, in which the Prophet asserts foreordination by using the expression "and then his book takes precedence" *(fa-yasbiq-u 'alai-hi kitabu-hu)*.

45. This total identification with God, realizing a state of annihilation *(fana')*, whereby one loses the sense of a separate self, is one of the claims of radical Sufis. Al-Bistami gives one of the boldest and most striking accounts of such an identificatory mystical experience. He says, "I looked at my Lord with the eye of certainty [*'ain 'l-yaqin*] after He had taken my attention away from everything save Him and made me shine with His light. He showed me wonders of His mysteries. He showed me His He-ness [*huwiyyatahu*]. By His He-ness I looked at my I-ness [*ana'iyati*], which then vanished. My light was from His light, my glory was from His glory, and my power was from His power. I saw my I-ness by His He-ness, my majesty by His majesty, and my sublimity by His sublimity. Then I looked at Him with the eye of truth [*'ain 'l-haqq*] and said to Him, 'Who is this?' He said, 'This is I and no one but I. There is no god but I.' Then He transformed me from my I-ness to His He-ness. He obliterated my he-ness by His He-ness. He showed me His He-ness by His particularity and so I looked at Him by His He-ness. When I looked at the Truth *(al-Haqq)* by the Truth I saw the Truth by the Truth. I stayed in the Truth by the Truth for some time *(zaman-an)* without breath, or tongue, or ear, or knowledge. So God gave me knowledge out of His knowledge, a tongue out of His speech, sight out of His light. I looked at Him by His light, knew by His

knowledge, and talked to Him with the tongue of His grace." Badawi, *Shatahat,* 138. Comparing al-Bistami's passage with what Taha says, we note that while al-Bistami uses a theopathetic and highly personal language Taha employs an impersonal language. However, what Taha says in this passage is the closest he comes to the language of Sufi theopathetic utterances.

46. Al-Bukhari, *Sahih,* 8:511. Several versions of this tradition are given by al-Tabari in dealing with verses 92:5–10, which say, "And for him who gives and is godfearing and confirms the reward most fair, We shall surely ease him to the Easing. But as for him who is a miser, and self-sufficient, and cries lies to the reward most fair, We shall surely ease him to the Hardship." In one version the prophetic assertion of preordination was challenged by a Bedouin who responded by saying, "So why did I come traveling over all the way from such and such a valley?" This apparently placed the Prophet in a dilemma, as he started "scratching up the ground [with a stick] till people thought he wished he had not said what he had to say. Then he recited, "Each of you is eased for what he has been created." See al-Tabari, *Tafsir,* 12:615–17.

47. Taha expressed this view in connection with the French philosopher Roger Garaudy, who stated in the course of a talk in Cairo that he was an atheist. In responding to Garaudy's public declaration of his atheism, Taha declared that someone like Garaudy should not give public talks "on any level" because he had "a problem to whose solution he should attend before giving talks to others" (TM 9). Taha sometimes espoused an "intellectual paternalism" over "common Muslims" (*al-ʿamma*) who, in his view, should not be exposed to too much knowledge or to the views of atheists, which might confuse them (AJi 30). When we take the context of Garaudy's statement, it becomes evident that Taha's intellectual paternalism extended beyond the common, impressionable Muslims to include intellectuals. This, however, was a view that did not agree with Taha's liberalism and that he later changed. In an interview with *al-Wadi* magazine in March 1983, he said that people had the right to believe in any ideas (including atheism) and had the right to propagate their ideas democratically. See www.alfikra.org.

48. On the first characteristic, see verse 50:30, and on the second, see, for example, verse 2:25. For a modern systematic portrayal of Qur'anic eschatological scenes, see Sayyid Qutb, *Mashahid 'l-qiyama fi 'l-Qur'an* (Cairo: Dar 'l-Maʿarif, 1961).

49. Al-Shahrastani, *Al-Milal,* 1:87.

50. Al-Jahiz, quoted in Al-Shahrastani, *Al-Milal,* 1:75.

51. Farhad Daftary, *The Ismaʿilis: Their History and Doctrines* (Cambridge: Cambridge Univ. Press, 1990), 66–67.

52. Ibn ʿArabi, *Al-Futuhat,* 2:93.

53. Ibn ʿArabi, *Fusus,* 1:94.

54. Ibn ʿArabi, *Al-Futuhat,* 1:290. Ibn ʿArabi's use of the sleep image along with the enveloping presence of divine mercy brings to mind Psalm 139:8, which says, "if I make my bed in She'ol, behold, thou art there." For Ibn ʿArabi on the cooling of hellfire, see William C.

Chittick, *Imaginal Worlds: Ibn al-'Arabi and the Problem of Religious Diversity* (Albany: State Univ. of New York Press, 1994), 113–19.

55. In explaining the meaning of *al-Muntaqim* as a Beautiful Name of God, al-Ghazali says that it means "the one who breaks the back of the recalcitrant, punishes criminals, and intensifies the punishment of the oppressor—but only after excusing and warning them, and after giving them the opportunity and the time to change." As with many other divine names, he goes on to show the human being's share in this name and the name's mystical significance: "Human vengeance is praiseworthy if it takes vengeance on the enemies of God the most high, and the worst such enemy is one's own lower soul. So it behooves him to take vengeance on it inasmuch as it yields to disobedience or fails in its duty of worship. As it is reported regarding Abu Yazid . . . that he said: 'My soul was so lazy one night as to keep me from a litany, so I punished it by depriving it of water for a year.' In this way should one pursue the path of vengeance." Abu Hamid Al-Ghazali, *The Ninety Nine Beautiful Names of God,* trans. David B. Burrell and Nazih Daher (Cambridge: The Islamic Texts Society, 1992), 138.

56. Al-Tabari, *Tafsir,* 1:84–85.

57. Ibn 'Arabi, *Fusus,* 1:151.

58. Al-Zamakhshari, *Al-Kashshaf,* 1:108.

59. In this debate we can distinguish between a primary, hermeneutical issue and a secondary, exegetical one. The insistence of exegetical authorities in the past and the present to draw a clear distinction between the two words rests on the hermeneutic assumption that although the words derive from the same root they cannot be synonymous because this would entail superfluity, which is inadmissible in the Qur'an. Having established this, then the exegetical questions of the denotations of the respective terms were raised. The terms served as vehicles for preconceived ideas. The denotative reversal we have seen in Taha's case can also be seen in the case of another modernist. Muhammad 'Abduh, starting from a consideration of the adjectival forms of the two words, argues that al-Rahman is an accidental attribute signifying agency, whereas al-Rahim is an essential attribute pertaining to the source *(mansha')* of this agency. In arguing this, 'Abduh was following Ibn al-Qayyim (d. 751/1350) but with a reversal of what the terms denoted for the latter. See Rida, *Tafsir 'l-manar,* 1:47–48.

60. In doing this Taha takes the verse out of its textual context, which elaborates on what will happen on the Day of Judgment. He uses the same verse to advance the secular and entirely noneschatological notion of "Islamic communism" (see chapter 5).

61. The verse within which this phrase occurs, verse 21:104, reads, "On the day when We shall roll up heaven as a scroll is rolled for the writings; as We originated the first creation, so We shall bring it back again—a promise binding on Us; so We shall do." The verse and the larger passage within which it occurs are about eschatological scenes. For the eschatological details concerning this verse, see al-Tabari, *Tafsir,* 9:94–97.

62. Verse 19:71 gave rise not only to exegetical disagreements but also apparently to states of persistent somberness and downheartedness among some early Muslims. The latter point is most poignantly illustrated by a story cited by al-Tabari. A man asked his colleague,

"Have you not already been told that you shall go down to hell?" When the colleague answered in the affirmative, the man asked, "Have you been told that you shall be delivered from it?" The colleague answered in the negative, and the man then wondered, "Then how can one ever laugh?" We are told that the colleague was "never seen laughing till the day he met his Maker." Al-Tabari, *Tafsir,* 8:367. Exegetically the verse was read either in isolation or in conjunction with the following verse, which reads, "Then we shall deliver those that were godfearing; and the evildoers We shall leave there, hobbling on their knees." The story of the despondent man (and other similar traditions) indicates that the deliverance verse was a later addition to the Qur'anic material. Yet, even when the verse was taken on its own, it did not distress all exegetes. The nonlaughing, hell-oriented, and pessimistic outlook of some commentators was opposed by another outlook that offered a confident, heaven-oriented, and optimistic reading of the verse. Some maintained that the verse could only have referred to the inevitable punishment of the unbelievers as no believer could conceivably go to hell. Others held that the verse was a universal proposition that referred to both unbelievers and believers but with the crucial difference that the believers would only pass through hellfire transiently. See al-Tabari, *Tafsir,* 8:364–69.

5. From the First to the Second Message of Islam

1. On the history of the Muslim Brothers in Sudan by movement members, see Hasan al-Turabi, *Al-Haraka 'l-islamiyya fi 'l-Sudan: al-Tatawwur wa 'l-kasb wa 'l-manhaj* (Cairo: al-Qari 'l-'Arabi, 1991); Makki, *Harakat 'l-Ikhwan 'l-Muslimin fi 'l-Sudan, 1944–1969*; Hasan Makki, *Al-Haraka 'l-Islamiyya fi 'l-Sudan, 1969–1985* (Khartoum: Ma'had 'l-Buhuth wa 'l-Dirast 'l-Ijtima'iyya and Bait 'l-Ma'rifa, 1990); and el-Affendi, *Turabi's Revolution.* On a critical examination of the movement, see al-Hajj Warraq Sidahmad, *Harakat 'l-Turabi* (Cairo: al-I'lamiyya li-'l-Nashr, 1997).

2. On these stories, see W. Montgomery Watt and Richard Bell, *Introduction to the Qur'an* (Edinburgh: Edinburgh University Press, 1970), 127–31.

3. On exegetical discussions of the phrase *khatam 'l-nabiyyin,* see al-Tabari, *Tafsir,* 10:305.

4. The Qur'an uses the terms *rasul* (messenger, apostle) and *nabi* (prophet, seer) in reference to prophets. Muslim authorities have made a technical distinction between the two terms: both the *rasul* and the *nabi* are in direct communion with God, but the former is charged with a mission *(risala)* to preach God's word publicly. As such, whereas every *rasul* is a *nabi,* not every *nabi* is a *rasul.* Muhammad is described by the Qur'an as both a *rasul* and a *nabi,* which might sound superfluous in light of the fact that prophethood is logically subsumed by messengerhood.

5. See Ibn 'Arabi, *Al-Futuhat,* 3:38–39.

6. Al-Bukhari, *Sahih,* 5:60–61.

7. On the Second Coming, see, for instance, al-Bukhari, *Sahih,* 4:633; Muslim, *Sahih,* 2:189–90; and Abu Da'ud, *Sunan,* 3:121–22.

8. See, for instance, Abu Da'ud, *Sunan*, 3:110; and Ibn Hanbal, *Al-Musnad*, 3:46.

9. On verse 21:104, see note 61 on page 263, above.

10. On social Darwinism's impact on the thought of some reformists, such as 'Abduh, see 'Aziz Azmeh (al-'Azma), *Al-'Almaniyya min manzur mukhtalif* (Beirut: Markaz Dirasat 'l-Wahda 'l-'Arabiyya, 1992), 148–49; or his *Islams and Modernities* (London: Verso, 1996), 105. On social Darwinism in general, see Peter Dickens, *Social Darwinism: Linking Evolutionary Thought to Social Theory* (Buckingham: Open Univ. Press, 2000).

11. Taha quoted Sartre's statement approvingly from an article by Kamal Shantair in *al-Ra'y al-'Am* newspaper on Mar. 9, 1961 (RMii 61). In his *Existentialism and Humanism*, Sartre argues, "If existence precedes essence, one will never be able to explain one's action by reference to a given and specific human nature; in other words, there is no determinism—man is free, man *is* freedom. Nor, on the other hand, if God does not exist, are we provided with any values and commands that could legitimise our behaviour. Thus we have neither behind us, nor before us in a luminous realm of values, any means of justification or excuse. We are left alone, without excuse. That is what I mean when I say that man is condemned to be free. Condemned, because he did not create himself, yet is nevertheless at liberty, and from the moment that he is thrown into this world he is responsible for everything he does." Sartre, *Existentialism and Humanism*, trans. Philip Mairet (London: Methuen, 1973), 34.

12. Taha's claim requires a recasting of the historical Muhammad into the Sufi ideal of someone whose external state *(zahir)* and internal state *(batin)* are in complete correspondence. To what extent can such a claim be "historical"? (And "historical" it should be, in the interest of Taha's theory, which projects the Prophet as an ultimate, universal prototype for humankind.) Such a claim about the Prophet should be critically examined, for instance in the light of verse 33:37: "When thou saidst to him whom God had blessed and thou hadst favoured, 'Keep thy wife to thyself, and fear God,' and thou wast concealing within thyself what God should reveal, fearing other men; and God has better right for thee to fear Him." This reproachful verse concerns Muhammad's falling in love with Zainab bint Jahsh, who was married to his adoptive son Zaid b. Haritha. Here we encounter a different portrayal of Muhammad from that given by Taha—one in which Muhammad's outward and inward states are different.

13. On the classical theories of abrogation and its modes, see chapters 2, 3, 4, 5, and 7 in John Burton, *The Sources of Islamic Law: Islamic Theories of Abrogation* (Edinburgh: Edinburgh Univ. Press, 1990).

14. In distinguishing between the Meccan and Medinan periods, Taha shows the probable influence of al-Shatibi (d. 790/1388). However, the two differ on two key points. In discussing the sources of the law, al-Shatibi argues that the shari'a is made up of universals *(kulliyat)* and particulars *(juz'iyyat)*. The universals were revealed in Mecca, while later Medinan revelations served as particulars that elaborated on these universals. These universals comprise five fundamentals *(usul,* sing. *asl)*, whose protection is the primary function of the law: religion *(din)*, life *(nafs)*, mind *('aql)*, progeny *(nasl)*, and property *(mal)*. Ibrahim

b. Musa al-Shatibi, *Al-Muwafaqat fi usul 'l-ahkam,* ed. Muhammad 'Abd al-Qadir al-Fadili (Beirut: al-Maktaba al-'Asriyya, 2000), 3:29. Al-Shatibi identifies these universals as absolute necessities *(daruriyyat)* that are recognized by the laws of all cultures. Besides these necessities, shari'a fosters other interests that al-Shatibi classifies into two levels: needs *(hajiyyat)* (those which contribute to the amelioration of hardship) and enhancements *(tahsinat)* (those which promote the betterment of life and its fulfillment). *Al-Muwafaqat,* 2:8–9. Although he recognizes abrogation, al-Shatibi is at pains to limit its application. One important point he makes is that "there was no abrogation as far as the universal principles of necessities, needs, and enhancements were concerned. Abrogation involved only particulars." *Al-Muwafaqat,* 3:77. The first key difference between al-Shatibi and Taha concerns their understanding of what constitutes the ultimate message of Islam. Al-Shatibi's understanding of universals is embedded in the juristic tradition of shari'a as developed up to his time. His is a late-fourteenth-century sensibility, whereas Taha's is a twentieth-century sensibility positing a radically different set of values within a radically different epistemological and ethical context. For Taha, the broader values of freedom, social justice, and social equality become the universals of Islam, outweighing al-Shatibi's traditional, narrower juristic concerns. The second key difference is predicated on the first. Taha can readily see that Islam is in the midst of a crisis, and in his bid to invest it with the values of his age he is willing to disconnect all post-Meccan revelations and history from the real message that Islam intended for humankind. To do this Taha had to accept a theory of abrogation that suspends the universals rather than the particulars—an assumption that al-Shatibi cannot entertain.

15. For a full version of the tradition, see, for instance, Muslim, *Sahih,* 1:156–60; and al-Tirmidhi, *Sunan,* 3:349–440.

16. The hadith material offers two versions of this tradition: a minimalist version in which the Prophet imposes only the condition of professing that "there is no god but God"—in short, a formal turning away from polytheism to monotheism (see, for instance, al-Bukhari, *Sahih,* 4:457–58); and a maximalist version that stipulates a formal acceptance of Islam and a full observance of its rituals and obligations (see, for instance, al-Bukhari, *Sahih,* 1:75). Taha usually quotes the maximalist version (see RT 109, 120; RU 27; TS 42).

17. In his public talks, Taha liked to explain these notions by using a demonstrative illustration. An urbanite tells a country person about bananas, which the latter has never seen. Because the country person trusts the urbanite, he accepts that there is an object such as bananas that exists. This corresponds to *'ilm 'l-yaqin.* On a visit to the urban center, the country man is shown bananas that he can see and touch. This is the stage of *'ain 'l-yaqin.* Then he eats a banana. This is the stage of the positive certainty of *haqq 'l-yaqin.* See DJ 22–23.

18. Taha's use of the adjectives *first* and *second* here is subject to his own convention. Although the Meccan message did historically precede the Medinan message, he designates it as the Second Message of Islam.

19. This same verse also occurs as verses 9:33 and 61:9 with a different closing phrase: "though the unbelievers be averse."

20. See, for instance, al-Bukhari, *Sahih*, 6:480.

21. On a modern exposition of this theme, see 'Abd al-'Aziz Jawish, *Al-Islam din 'l-fitra wa 'l-hurriyya* (Cairo: Dar 'l-Hilal, n.d.).

22. Verse 9:5 is commonly referred to as the "sword verse." Some authorities have, however, held that the sword verse is verse 9:36, which enjoins, "And fight the unbelievers totally even as they fight you totally." See Rida, *Tafsir 'l-manar*, 10:199.

23. Verses like 22:39, which proclaims, "Leave is given to those who fight because they were wronged," and 2:190, which exhorts, "And fight in the way of God with those who fight with you, but aggress not: God loves not the aggressors," were evidently no longer applicable after the revelation of verse 9:5.

24. The sword verse establishes what may be described as the Islamic theory of jihad in its starkest form: a polytheist is to be presented with the basic choice between the "word of God" and the "sword." Actual Islamic practice was different, however, and reflected the complexity of a human situation. As a statesman, Muhammad was willing to enter into negotiations with his polytheist adversaries and even make compromises. One notable example was the treaty of al-Hudaibiya in the year 6/628, which was initially opposed by 'Umar b. al-Khattab. On the events leading to the treaty and its details, see al-Waqidi, *Kitab 'l-maghazi*, 2:579–618; and Ibn Hisham, *Al-Sira*, 3:183. Verse 9:60 included among the beneficiaries of the alms tax a category described as "those whose hearts are brought together" *(wa 'l-mu'allafati qulubuhum)*. These were leading and influential polytheists who were paid to induce them to be favorably inclined to Islam. This practice apparently continued under Muhammad and was stopped either by Abu Bakr or, more probably, 'Umar b. al-Khattab. So, although some Qur'anic and hadith texts might project a stern and unaccommodating position, the actual prophetic and postprophetic dealings with polytheists were characterized by pragmatism.

25. For a recent treatment that views jihad in terms of a transition from a "mundane" war motivated by material gain to a "holy" war where religious or ideological commitment through identification with the newly forged *umma* takes precedence, see Reuven Firestone, *Jihad: The Origins of Holy War in Islam* (New York: Oxford Univ. Press, 1999). Firestone's transitional scheme is artificial. It is hard to separate the materialist from the religious as far as jihad wars were concerned, so much so that the otherworldly, religious reward for martyrdom—namely, paradise—is depicted in terms of materialist pleasures.

26. Abu Da'ud, *Sunan*, 2:221.

27. Al-Bukhari, *Sahih*, 4:410.

28. Ibid., 4:417.

29. This is what Ibn 'Arabi also calls "general struggle" *(jihad 'am)*, which covers any human act that involves effort. In the specific context of Islamic jihad and its conflicts, it can refer to those who engaged in jihad with the view of acquiring material gain, which was an important driving force for many Muslims.

30. In connection with this class, Ibn 'Arabi quotes verse 29:69, which says, "Those who

jahadu fina, surely We shall guide them in Our ways." The clause *"jahadu fina"* is rendered by Arberry as "struggle in Our cause" and by Abdullah Yusuf Ali as "strive in Our (Cause)." The fact that Ali brackets the word *cause* suggests that he might have initially felt inclined to render the phrase as "in Us" but decided against it. It is this "in Us" sense that Ibn 'Arabi stresses because God Himself can be a goal of jihad in the mystical sense of struggling to come ever close to Him.

31. Ibn 'Arabi, *Al-Futuhat,* 2:145. Ibn 'Arabi contrasts this command, which occurs in verse 22:78, with the command of verse 3:102, "O believers, fear God, as He should be feared [*haqqa tuqatihi*]." He maintains that the verses are interconnected and that the latter verse operates on the level of practical implementation *(taklif).*

32. Ibn 'Arabi, *Al-Futuhat,* 2:148.

33. The *sira* material furnishes us with a list of Muhammad's slaves (including two women concubines). See Ibn Sa'd, *Al-Tabaqat 'l-Kubra,* ed. Muhammad 'Abd al-Qadir 'Ata (Beirut: Dar 'l-Kutub 'l-'Ilmiyya, 1997), 1:385–87; and al-Tabari, *Tarikh,* 2:216–18.

34. According to one tradition, a Medinan man decided to manumit all six of his slaves on the event of his death. As these slaves comprised all the property that the man was to leave at his death, the Prophet interfered and revoked his decision, manumitting two slaves and allowing the others to be inherited by his heirs. See al-Tirmidhi, *Sunan,* 2:351–52.

35. Muslim, *Sahih,* 2:58.

36. For a defense of this position, see, for instance, Ameer Ali, *The Spirit of Islam* (London: Methuen, 1965), 262–67; and Muhammad Qutb, *Shubhat hawl 'l-Islam* (Cairo: Maktabat Wahba, 1964), 30–55.

37. Taha's use of the word *kuffar* (infidels) here is misleading. Although the word applied to all non-Muslims, the treatment of polytheists was different from that of scripturaries (Jews and Christians). What Taha describes above applies to the latter group but not to the polytheists, whose religious beliefs were never recognized by Islam. In his translation of RT, an-Na'im adds a footnote that makes this distinction clear (see SM 137).

38. Taha weaves into his text here verse 78:26, which is part of an eschatological passage describing the tortures of hell awaiting the infidels.

39. The speculative suggestion implied in Taha's argument—that the abolition of slavery would lead to economic disintegration and social chaos—is challenged by Bawla, who contends that there is no evidence that supports such an assumption. 'Abd Allah Bawla, ['Abd Allah Ahmad al-Bashir], "Muhawala li-'l-Ta'rif bi-musahamat 'l-ustadh Mahmud Muhammad Taha fi harakat 'l-tajdid fi 'l-fikr 'l-Islami 'l-mu'asir," *Riwaq 'Arabi,* no. 4 (October 1996): 42–43.

40. The same can be said about the position of an-Na'im, whose reform project is inspired by Taha. An-Na'im is too sceptical to adopt Taha's argument about slavery as a spiritualizing agent drawing its victim nearer to God, but, like other Muslim modernists, he takes it for granted that "given the entrenched position of slavery throughout the world at the time, Islam had no choice but to recognize the institution of slavery in that historical context

and do its best to improve the conditions under which slaves were to endure their unfortunate status." Abdullahi An-Na'im, *Toward an Islamic Reformation: Civil Liberties, Human Rights, and International Law* (Syracuse, N.Y.: Syracuse Univ. Press, 1990), 174. Like Taha, an-Na'im wants to see a radical Islamic reform according to which a modernized shari'a "prohibit[s] slavery forever." It is not clear how the inner resources of shari'a (or, for that matter, Islam, to adopt a Jumhuri distinction) can provide for such a leap, if the Qur'an, the sunna, the historical practice of the Prophet and his companions, and the juristic tradition have consistently sanctioned slavery. It may be argued that since modern Muslim societies have abolished slavery and delegitimized it despite shari'a, then the turning of shari'a against itself to outlaw what it has historically held to be lawful and to declare the abolition of what has already been abolished by secular laws is a belated, empty gesture. An-Na'im insists that this is essential to combat "negative social attitudes toward former slaves and segments of the population that used to be a source of slaves" and to stem "secret practices akin to slavery." An-Na'im, *Toward an Islamic Reformation*, 175. It is not clear, though, why shari'a, rather than secular values and laws, should be a source of such liberation and utility. Another scholar inspired by Taha is al-Baqir al-Afif Mukhtar, who expresses a position similar to that of an-Na'im. Al-Baqir al-Afif Mukhtar, "Human Rights and Islamic Law: The Development of the Rights of Slaves, Women and Aliens in Two Cultures" (Ph.D. diss., Univ. of Manchester, 1996), 347–51.

41. On the conflict between Abu Dharr al-Ghifari and those who "were niggardly towards God," see A. J. Cameron, *Abu Dharr al-Ghifari: An Examination of His Image in the Hagiography of Islam* (London: The Royal Asiatic Society, 1982), 62–119. On Abu Dharr as an early Socialist and a representative of the Left, see 'Abd al-Hamid Juda al-Sahhar, *Abu Dharr al-Ghifari 'l-Ishtraki 'l-zahid* (Cairo: Maktabat Misr, 1978); and Ahmad 'Abbas Salih, *Al-Yamin wa 'l-yasar fi 'l-Islam* (Beirut: al-Mu'assasa 'l-'Arabiyya li-'l-Dirasat wa 'l-Nashr, 1972).

42. Daftary, *The Isma'ilis*, 119.

43. Sufi sayings and narratives consistently denigrate materialism and praise the renunciation of property. Al-Ghazali gives a typology of poverty at the top of which he places *zuhd* (asceticism), which he defines as "a state where one loathes money, is offended by it, and escapes from it in horror and full cognizance of its evil." Al-Ghazali, *Ihya'*, 4:190. Sufi literature is replete with stories that demonstrate this renunciatory attitude. A classic example is the Buddha-like story of Ibrahim b. Adham (d. 161/777–78), who was the son of a "king of Khurasan" and who, on deciding to follow the Sufi path, exchanged his princely attire for a shepherd's coarse wool garment and went off to Mecca. See Muhammad b. Husain al-Sulami, *Kitab Tabaqat 'l-Sufiyya*, ed. Johannes Pedersen (Leiden: E. J. Brill, 1960), 37. The high esteem in which asceticism was held gave rise to a sense of spiritual competition among Sufis. An example demonstrating this is the following account. "Someone said: I saw a vision of Doomsday. An announcement came that Malik b. Dinar and Muhammad b. Wasi' [mystics of the second/eighth century] be allowed into paradise. I watched closely to see who

would enter first. Muhammd b. Wasiʻ preceded. I asked why, and I was told that he had only one garment, whereas Malik had two." Al-Qushairi, *Al-Risala*, 2:546.

44. On a treatment of what Islam prescribes as regards capitalism, see Maxime Rodinson, *Islam and Capitalism* (Harmondsworth, Middlesex: Penguin Books, 1977), 12–27. For a discussion of some Western works on the topic of Islam and capitalism, see Leonard Binder, *Islamic Liberalism: A Critique of Development Ideologies* (Chicago: The Univ. of Chicago Press, 1988), 206–42.

45. In arguing this, Taha is evidently informed by the modernist values of his own time. This same sensibility informs his assessment of the status of women in Arabia with the coming of Islam. Taha, along with other modernists, emphasizes a profound, universal transformation in their status. This widespread view is trenchantly criticized by Leila Ahmed, who contends, "The argument made by some Islamists . . . that Islam improved the position of women in all respects, seems both inaccurate and simplistic. In the first place, the situation of women appears to have varied among the different communities in Arabia. Moreover, although Jahilia marriage practices do not necessarily indicate the greater power of women or the absence of misogyny, they do correlate with women's enjoying greater sexual autonomy than they were allowed under Islam. They also correlate with women's being active participants, even leaders, in a wide range of community activities, including warfare and religion. Their autonomy and participation were curtailed with the establishment of Islam, its institutions of patrilineal, patriarchal marriage as solely legitimate, and the social transformation that ensued." Leila Ahmed, *Women and Gender in Islam* (New Haven: Yale Univ. Press, 1992), 42.

46. Rida, *Tafsir 'l-manar*, 4:349.

47. An aspect that Taha and modern reformers fail to mention in this respect is that the limiting of the number of wives to four only concerned "free" women. When it came to slave women, there was no limit to the number of women a man could possess and sexually exploit through the concubinage institution. See *EI²*, s.v. "*ʻabd*," 1:24–40.

48. Taha's position in this respect is similar to that of the Egyptian modernist Khalaf Allah, who argued that the practice may be necessary at times. Muhammad Ahmad Khalaf Allah, *Dirasat fi 'l-nuzum wa 'l-tashriʻat 'l-Islamiyya* (Cairo: Maktabat 'l-Anjlu 'l-Misriyya, 1977), 200–206. In adopting this position, Khalaf Allah was positioning himself in a middle ground between ʻAbduh, who wanted the practice to be banned, and Mahmud Shaltut, the modernist rector of al-Azhar University, who defended polygyny. Mahmud Shaltut, *Al-Islam ʻaqida wa shariʻa* (Cairo: Dar 'l-Shuruq, 1983), 223ff.

49. The phrase here is quoted from verse 9:32.

50. Ahmad b. ʻAli al-Razi al-Jassas, *Ahkam 'l-Qurʼan*, ed. ʻAbd al-Salam Muhammad ʻAli Shahin (Beirut: Dar 'l-Kutub 'l-ʻIlmiyya, 1994), 3:483. On a systematic treatment of the veiling verses in the Qurʼan in the context of a modernist refutation of the revival of the practice, see Husain Ahmad Amin, *Dalil 'l-Muslim 'l-hazin* (Cairo: Maktabat Madbuli, 1987), 242–50.

51. The expressions *public domain* and *public space* are used here to indicate different

spaces. *Public domain* is a social category; it is an empowering, active social space where a woman acts and interacts as an agent. By contrast, *public space* is a physico-spatial category, the spaces shared by everyone as opposed to private, domestic spaces.

52. Al-Tabari, *Tafsir,* 10:332.

53. Ibid., 10:331–32.

54. Al-Jassas, *Ahkam,* 3:486.

55. Al-Tabari, *Tafsir,* 9:310.

56. This was given legitimacy through an "election" doctrine expressed by some prophetic traditions. According to one such tradition, the Prophet said, "From the offspring of Ibrahim, God elected Isma'il; from the offspring of Isma'il, He elected Banu Kinana; from the offspring of Banu Kinana, He elected Quraish; from the offspring of Quraish, He elected Banu Hashim, and from Banu Hashim, He elected me." Al-Tirmidhi, *Sunan,* 4:420.

57. On juristic debates on equality in marriage, see Wahba al-Zuhaili, *Al-Fiqh 'l-Islami wa adilatuhu* (Damascus: Dar 'l-Fikr, 1989), 7:230–33.

58. On another level, this patriarchal bias has its impact on Taha's notion of citizenship. In the draft constitution he drew up in 1955, he defines a Sudanese citizen as "someone who is born to a Sudanese father" (see UD 24).

59. These words are part of verse 4:165 (see discussion in chapter 4). The statement occurs within a context justifying the sending of prophets. Taha takes this part of the verse out of its context and applies it specifically to the Meccan period.

60. One of the earliest expressions of an Islamist commitment to a radical change in the lot of peasants and workers was Sayyid Qutb's *Al-'Adala 'l-ijtima'iyya fi 'l-Islam* (Social Justice in Islam), which came out in 1949. During the 1960s, some Islamist activists and thinkers tried to combat Marxist socialism and Arab socialism by advocating an "Islamic socialism." In Sudan, Babikir Karrar founded the Islamic Socialist Party. In Syria, Mustafa al-Siba'i recast the ideology of the Muslim Brothers along Socialist lines, forming the Socialist Front and publishing in 1960 his major book *Ishtirakiyyat 'l-Islam* (The Socialism of Islam) (Damascus: Mu'asassat 'l-Matbu'at 'l-'Arabiyya, 1960), in which he argued that property should not be allowed to be a means of oppression and exploitation. The Egyptian Mahmud Shalabi sought to prove that socialism was an integral part of Islam from its very beginnings and so he produced *Ishtirakiyyat Muhammad* (The Socialism of Muhammad) (Cairo: Maktabat 'l-Qahira 'l-Haditha, 1962), *Ishtirakiyyat Abi Bakr* (The Socialism of Abu Bakr) (Cairo: Maktabat 'l-Qahira 'l-Haditha, 1963), and *Ishtirakiyyat 'Umar* (The Socialism of 'Umar) (Cairo: Maktabat 'l-Qahira 'l-Haditha, 1964). This trend, however, proved unpopular among the majority of Islamists, who clung to a position stressing the uniqueness of Islam in being a middle road between capitalism and socialism. One of the best formulations of this position is given by Muhammad Baqir al-Sadr, who claims that the economic theory and system of Islam are based on a principle of "dual property" (private and public), limited economic liberalism, and social justice. See Muhammad Baqir al-Sadr, *Iqtisaduna* (Beirut and Cairo: Dar 'l-Kitab 'l-Lubnani and Dar 'l-Kitab 'l-Misri, 1977), 257–68.

61. According to Frederick Engels, what justifies calling Marxist socialism "scientific" is Marx's discovery of "the materialistic conception of history and the revelation of the secret of capitalistic production through surplus value. . . . With these discoveries socialism became a science." Frederick Engels, *Socialism: Utopian and Scientific* (London: Lawrence and Wishart, 1973), 411.

62. In his *Al-Islam,* Taha maintains that the "difference between minimum income and maximum income should not exceed seven folds" (IS 36). Although he does not explain why "seven folds" in particular, it may be argued that his stipulation is governed by the perceived esoteric significance of the number seven, which figures in his own discussion of the seven stages of life or of Islam, for example. Writing thereafter in *Al-Risala 'l-thaniya* about the same theme of income differences, Taha does not mention this stipulation.

63. On the different exegetical views, see al-Tabari, *Tafsir,* 2:376–79.

64. Muhammad 'Abduh, quoted in Rida, *Tafsir 'l-manar,* 2:337.

65. Al-Tabataba'i, *Al-Mizan,* 2:196.

66. See, for instance, Muslim, *Sahih,* 7:179.

67. Muslim sources tend to place great emphasis on Muhammad's asceticism, usually in the context of underlining the fact that he acted as a prophet rather than as a man of temporal power. This, however, was not perceived as incompatible with the fact that he had property. Historically, Muhammad's property came to the attention of the Muslim community immediately after his death when a bitter dispute broke out between his daughter Fatima and the first caliph, Abu Bakr. The caliph refused to distribute Muhammad's estate, saying that the Prophet had stipulated his property be treated as alms *(sadaqa).* Ibn Kathir tells us that this property included "houses in which his wives lived, women slaves, men slaves, horses, camels, goats . . . [and] land taken from Banu al-Nadir, besides land taken in Khaibar and Fadak." Imad al-Din Isma'il Ibn Kathir, *Al-Sira 'l-nabawiyya,* ed. Mustafa 'Abd al-Wahid (Beirut: Dar 'l-Ma'rifa, 1976), 4:564–65.

68. Taha does not seem to be fully aware of Marx's and Engels's position on democracy. In *The Communist Manifesto* (1848), Marx stressed the opposition between "proletarian dictatorship" and "bourgeois dictatorship." However, "by the time of the First International (1864–76), he and Engels had modified their standpoint sufficiently to allow for the democratic conquest of power, and eventually this became the conventional outlook of Marxist Social Democracy." George Lichtheim, *A Short History of Socialism.* (London: Fontana, 1983), 94–95. On the revisionist debate and the arguments of social democracy, see Eduard Bernstein, *Evolutionary Socialism: A Criticism and Affirmation* (New York: Schocken Books, 1961), particularly 142–51, for his rejection of a revolutionary approach and espousal of a gradualist, democratic path. On an early theoretical expression of Bernstein's revisionism, see Peter Gay, *The Dilemma of Democratic Socialism: Eduard Bernstein's Challenge to Marx* (New York: Collier Books, 1962), 244–50. On an overview of the revisionist controversy, see David McLellan, *Marxism after Marx: An Introduction* (London: The Macmillan Press, 1980), 20–41. In assessing revisionist social democracy, Kolakowski maintains, "Thus was

created the ideological foundation of a new social democracy, the further development of which had very little to do with the history of Marxist doctrine. Although this form of socialism derives genetically from Marxism, in part at least, its origin soon became unimportant. The new doctrine was a compromise between liberalism and Marxian socialism, or a socialist variant of liberalism." Leszek Kolakowski, *Main Currents of Marxism* (Oxford: Oxford Univ. Press, 1978), 2:114.

69. The celebration of *shura* either as synonymous with democracy or at least as a democratic measure is widespread among modernist Muslim thinkers. The influential Muhammad 'Abduh effectively identifies it with democracy. Commending Western democracy and stressing its suitability as a model for Egypt, he fuses the notions of public opinion and *shura*, arguing that "the best and most desirable of laws are those that rest on the nation's public opinion, i.e., laws that are based on the principle of *shura*." Muhammad 'Abduh, *Al-A'mal 'l-kamila li-'l-imam Muhammad 'Abduh*, ed. Muhammad 'Amara (Beirut: Al-Mu'assasa 'l-'Arabiyya li-'l-Dirasat wa 'l-Nashr, 1972), 1:364–65. Muhammad Iqbal does not share 'Abduh's admiration for Western democracy, which he attacks as materialistic. Fazlur Rahman argues that Iqbal's criticism was not a rejection of the democratic ideal as such but only its Western manifestation and contends that *shura* could offer a democracy superior to that of the West because of the nature of the "global moral mission" with which it is charged. Fazlur Rahman, "The Principle of Shura and the Role of the Ummah in Islam," in *State Politics and Islam*, ed. Mumtaz Ahmed (Indianapolis, Ind.: American Trust Publications, 1986), 94–95. Hossein Modarressi draws a distinction between *shura* in its general sense, which is unbinding, and a binding "executive *shura*" that takes place within a legislative body of experts such as "lawyers, politicians, economists, and so on." Hossein Modarressi, "The Legal Basis for the Validity of the Majority Opinion in Islamic Legislation," in *Under Siege: Islam and Democracy*, edited by Richard C. Bulliet (New York: The Middle East Institute of Columbia Univ., 1994), 90–91. The Egyptian Islamist al-'Awwa accepts the substance of democracy but finds the word itself anathema. Muhammad Salim al-'Awwa, *Fi 'l-nizam 'l-siyasi li-'l-dawla 'l-Islamiyya* (Cairo: Dar 'l-Shuruq, 1989), 202. The Iranian reformist Soroush, on the other hand, embraces the term *democracy* and argues for what he describes as a "democratic religious government" that rests on a "convergence of reason [*'aql*] and revelation [*shar'*]." Abdolkarim Soroush, *Reason, Freedom, and Democracy in Islam* (Oxford: Oxford Univ. Press, 2000), 126. The view expressed by Taha, and other classical and modern thinkers, that *shura* is consultative in nature is rejected by the Egyptian Islamist Fathi Osman, who accuses them of having overlooked the spirit of the *shura* institution. Fathi Osman, "The Contract for the Appointment of the Head of an Islamic State: Bai'at al-Imam," in *State Politics and Islam*, ed. Mumtaz Ahmed (Indianapolis, Ind.: American Trust Publications, 1986), 77. For a critique of Taha's view along the same lines, see Bakri Muhammad Khalil, "Al-Fikr 'l-falsafi 'ind 'l-Jumhuriyyin fi 'l-Sudan" (M.A. diss., Univ. of Baghdad, 1996), 176–78. For the problematic of Islam and democracy, see Hamid Enayat, *Modern Islamic Political Thought: The Response of the Shi'i and Sunni Muslims to the Twenti-*

eth Century (London: Macmillan Press, 1982), 125–39; and for modern debates on *shura* and democracy in the Arab world, see Haidar Ibrahim 'Ali, *Al-Tayyarat 'l-Islamiyya wa qadiyyat 'l-dimuqratiyya* (Beirut: Markaz Dirasat 'l-Wahda 'l-'Arabiyya, 1996), 139–84.

6. Evolution, Shari'a, and Art

1. An argument the proevolution camp raises is that Darwinism is a modern, scientific expression of evolutionist tendencies that could be traced in the thought of medieval Muslim thinkers such as Miskawaih (d. 421/1030) and Ibn Khaldun (d. 808/1406). See Muhammad al-Talbi, *Ummat 'l-wasat: Al-Islam wa tahaddiyat 'l-'asr* (Tunis: Cérès li-'l-Nashr, 1996), 95–114.

2. Jamal al-Din al-Afghani, "The Refutation of the Materialists," trans. Nikki R. Keddie and Hamid Algar, in *An Islamic Response to Imperialism: Political and Religious Writings of Jamal Ad-Din "al-Afghani,"* ed. Nikki R. Keddie (Berkeley: California Univ. Press, 1968), 136.

3. Ibid., 136.

4. For a detailed treatment, see Abdullah Omar A. al-Omar, "The Reception of Darwinism in the Arab World" (Ph.D. diss., Harvard Univ., 1982), 104–48.

5. Wilfred Cantwell Smith, *Modern Islam in India: A Social Analysis* (Lahore: Minerva Book Shop, 1943), 14.

6. Aziz Ahmad, *Islamic Modernism in India and Pakistan* (London: Royal Institute of International Affairs and Oxford Univ. Press, 1967), 46.

7. Rida, *Tafsir 'l-manar,* 4:324. Although 'Abduh does not explicitly mention it, he is likely to be referring here to Archbishop Ussher's (d. 1664) claim that on the basis of his calculations from the Genesis story, he reckoned that creation had taken place in 4004 B.C. This was refined by John Lightfoot, vice-chancellor of the University of Cambridge, who claimed that the final act by which man was created took place at 9 A.M. on Sunday, October 23, 4004 B.C. Peter J. Bowler, *Evolution: The History of an Idea* (Berkeley, Ca.: Univ. of California Press, 1989), 4. By the eighteenth century, geologists and paleontologists had dismissed this calculation as they realized that the earth must be very old.

8. On al-Shumayyil, see Adel A. Ziadat, *Western Science in the Arab World: The Impact of Darwinism, 1860–1930* (London: Macmillan, 1986), 30–38.

9. Isma'il Mazhar, *Malqa 'l-sabil fi madhhab 'l-nushu' wa 'l-irtiqa'* (Cairo: al-Matba'a 'l-'Asriyya, 1926), 58.

10. See, for instance, Muhammad Farid Wajdi, *Al-Islam fi 'asr 'l-'ilm* (Cairo: al-Maktaba 'l-Tijariyya, 1932), 91–92.

11. On the responses of these scholars to the theory of evolution, see Ziadat, *Western Science,* 91–108.

12. Mahmud Shaltut, *Al-Fatawa* (Cairo: Dar 'l-Shuruq, 1991), 402–3.

13. Qutb's moral abhorrence is no different from that of many Victorians in England who "hated evolutionism because they saw it as being grossly immoral—something that

would undercut the social system and leave everything in a morass of animal bestiality." Michael Ruse, *Darwinism Defended: A Guide to the Evolution Controversies* (Reading, Mass.: Addison-Wesley Publishing Company, 1982), 265.

14. Muhammad Qutb, *Ma'rikat 'l-taqalid* (Cairo: Dar 'l-Shuruq, 1973, 53–74.

15. Seyyed Hossein Nasr, *Religion and the Order of Nature* (New York: Oxford Univ. Press, 1996), 145.

16. Seyyed Hossein Nasr, *Islam and the Plight of Modern Man* (London and New York: Longman, 1975), 8.

17. Ibid., 139.

18. Ibid., 140.

19. Seyyed Hossein Nasr, *Islam and Contemporary Society* (London: Longman Group, 1982), 179. Commenting critically on this, the Pakistani physicist Hoodbhoy says, "Any science which claims to derive 'from the intellect which is Divine and not human reason' is certainly excellent if practitioners of that science have direct access to the Divine intellect, but otherwise could be very contentious and problematic indeed. The success of Dr. Nasr's new 'Islamic' science is obviously contingent upon finding interpreters of the Divine intellect, who are presumably to be chosen from among the holy and the pious." Pervez Hoodbhoy, *Islam and Science: Religious Orthodoxy and the Battle for Rationality* (London: Zed Books, 1991), 73.

20. Al-Tabari, *Tafsir*, 12:637–42.

21. In the light of the story's dramatic logic, what the angels say can be read, on the one hand, as an expression of opposition and, on the other, as an expression of surprise, puzzlement, or bafflement. Taha reads this as an expression of opposition (RS 13). But does not such a reading detract from the Islamic image of angels as creatures whose obedience to God is absolute? See, for instance, verse 66:6. Some classical exegetes were aware of this problem and so Ibn Juraij (d. 150/767), for instance, says, "The angels spoke with what God had taught them about what humans would do. . . . The angels said, 'Wilt Thou set therein one who will do corruption there, and shed blood?' because God gave them permission to enquire about this. . . . The angels expressed their surprise [*ta'ajjub*] and asked Him, 'How, O Lord, do they disobey You while You are their Creator?' God answered by telling them, 'Assuredly I know that you know not.' " Other exegetes maintained that the angelic statement was by way of *istirshad* (seeking to know about a particular question). See al-Tabari, *Tafsir*, 1:245–46.

22. Al-Tabari, *Tafsir*, 1:239.

23. Ibid., 1:243.

24. See page 68 above.

25. In describing the manner of divine creation, the Qur'an adopts a gradualist, biblical notion on the one hand and a principle of instantaneous creation on the other. In this verse the Qur'an says that God created the heavens and the earth in six days and "then sat Himself

upon the Throne," echoing the biblical account of God creating the world and humankind in six days and resting on the seventh day. In contrast, verse 2:117 declares, "The Creator of the heavens and the earth; and when He decrees a thing, He but says to it 'Be,' and it is."

26. On the heart as a locus for knowledge in Ibn 'Arabi, for instance, see William C. Chittick, *The Sufi Path of Knowledge: Ibn al-'Arabi's Metaphysics of Imagination* (Albany: State Univ. of New York Press, 1989), 106–9.

27. On the Ash'arites and causality, see Ignaz Goldziher, *Introduction to Islamic Theology and Law,* trans. Andras Hamori and Ruth Hamori (Princeton: Princeton Univ. Press, 1981), 112–14.

28. Abu Hamid al-Ghazali, *Tahafut 'l-falasifa,* ed. Sulaiman Dunya (Cairo: Dar 'l-Ma'arif, 1987), 239.

29. Ibid., 239.

30. Muslim, *Sahih,* 15:116–18.

31. For instance, Ibn Maja, *Sunan,* 2:825.

32. An explicit expression of this is found in verse 5:48 in which it is declared, "To every one of you We have appointed a right way and an open road. If God had willed, He would have made you one nation; but that He may try you in what has come to you. So be you forward in good works; unto God shall you return, all together; and He will tell you of that whereon you were at variance."

33. The Qur'an is ambivalent about the identity of Abraham's son. The exegetes were divided on this, as some maintained it was Isaac and others held it was Ishmael. See al-Tabari, *Tafsir,* 10:510–14. Taha, without embroiling himself in the details of the argument, adopts the latter position.

34. In Egypt, Muhammad 'Abduh, who would agree with Taha's view of shari'a as an evolving, changing system, used the term *Salafiyyun* (the followers of *al-salaf 'l-salih,* the Righteous Forefathers) to describe his school. In Sudan, however, the term acquired a different denotation as it came to be applied to those who project shari'a as an unchanging, rigid system.

35. A similar view was expressed in Christianity by the Italian monk Gratian (d. before 1159), who equated the natural law with the law of the Old and the New Testaments, particularly the Christian version of the Golden Rule. See Charles E. Curran, "Absolute Norms in Moral Theology," in *Norm and Context in Christian Ethics,* ed. Gene H. Outka and Paul Ramsey (London: SCM Press, 1968), 143–44.

36. Al-Zuhaili, *Al-Fiqh 'l-Islami,* 6:13.

37. Ibid., 6:13.

38. What Taha says in this respect reflects the view of some who maintained that stoning involves forcing the convicted person into a hole and then pelting him or her with stones. This, however, was at variance with the majority opinion as far as men were concerned. According to this view, men are to be stoned while they are in a standing position. When it

comes to women, the Hanafites maintained that placing the convicted in a hole was a matter left to the discretion of the executive authority. The Shafi'ites favored holing, whereas the Malikites and Hanbalites rejected the procedure on account of lack of stipulation. See al-Zuhaili, *Al-Fiqh 'l-Islami*, 6:60–61.

39. Verse 24:2 stipulates, "The fornicatress and the fornicator—scourge each one of them a hundred stripes." Apparently there were debates among early Muslims about which sin was graver than the other, *zina* or *qadhf*, as indicated by a question put to Sa'id b. Jubair (d. 95/714). See al-Tabari, *Tafsir*, 9:265.

40. On this affair see Ibn Hisham, *Al-Sira*, 3:169–76.

41. For the range of slanderous offenses according to the jurists, see al-Zuhaili, *Al-Fiqh 'l-Islami*, 6:70–77.

42. Ibid., 6:81–82.

43. On the "casting down of one's eyes," see verses 24:30–31.

44. Assessing 'Abduh's legacy, Taha says, "Mohamed Abdu was a great man. He was a product of al-Azhar. . . . He had a Sufi turn of mind. He tried to bridge the gap between the traditional thinking of his Institute and life in his own day. He met with great opposition from his contemporary Azharites. Posthumously, he was recognized as a great Muslim thinker. His ideas at reform left their effect on his own day and in the days since, but they fall lamentably short of the requirements of our present day" (AJii 5, English Section).

45. See Najm al-Din al-Tufi, *Risala fi ri'ayat 'l-maslaha*, ed. Ahmad 'Abd al-Rahim al-Sayih (Cairo: al-Dar 'l-Misriyya l-Lubnaniyya, 1993).

46. Al-Shatibi, *Al-Muwafaqat*, 2:215.

47. Rida, *Tarikh 'l-Ustadh*, 1:614.

48. On the juristic employment of the notions of *maqasid* and *masalih* in modern Islamic jurisprudence, see Nur al-Din Buthuri, *Maqasid 'l-shari'a: Al-Tashri' 'l-Islami 'l-mu'asir baina tumuh 'l-mujtahid wa qusur 'l-ijtihad* (Beirut: Dar 'l-Tali'a, 2000).

49. Thomas Arnold, *Painting in Islam: A Study of the Place of Pictorial Art in Muslim Culture* (New York: Dover Publications, 1965), 4. On Islamic attitudes toward the arts, see Oleg Grabar, *The Formation of Islamic Art* (New Haven: Yale Univ. Press, 1987), 72–73. On a detailed discussion of Qur'anic verses in connection with the arts and crafts of the Prophet's time, see Ahmad Y. Ghabin, "The Qur'anic Verses as a Source of Legitimacy or Illegitimacy of the Arts in Islam," *Der Islam* 75, no. 2 (1998): 193–225.

50. Al-Bukhari, *Sahih*, 7:307.

51. Ibid.

52. Ibid.

53. Arnold, *Painting in Islam*, 8.

54. *EI²*, s.v. "*taswir*," 10:364a.

55. Ahmad b. 'Abd al-Halim Ibn Taimiyya, *Majmu' fatawa Ahmad b. Taimiyya*, ed. 'Abd al-Rahman b. Muhammad al-Qasimi (N.p.: n.p., n.d.), 11:557–58.

56. Ibid., 11:562. Ibn Taymiyya does not attribute such conduct to the Prophet's companions. Rather, it is the generation of those who followed the companions *(tabi'un)* who exhibited such conduct.

57. Ibn Taimiyya, *Fatawa*, 11:576.

58. Al-Qushairi, *Al-Risala*, 2:644.

59. Al-Qushairi cites the following incident. "There was a young man who was an associate of al-Junaid. Whenever this young man heard the *dhikr*, he used to scream in ecstasy. Al-Junaid said to him one day, 'If you do this again you can longer be with me!' The young man tried to control himself—an effort so stressful that he would sweat all over. One day he let out a scream and fell dead." Al-Qushairi, *Al-Risala*, 2:652. On the other hand, Khair al-Nassaj (d. 322/934), the teacher of al-Shibli, expresses a different attitude through the following tradition. "While Moses was once narrating a story to his people, one of the men let out an ecstatic scream. Moses scolded the man. God then said to Moses, 'O Moses, it is my fragrance that they diffuse, it is my love that they declare, it is my ardor that makes them scream—let them be!' " Ibid., 2:656.

60. Ibid., 2:644.

61. Modern exponents of orthodoxy reject this view and insist that even today the danger of reviving idolatry is present. The Egyptian Yusuf al-Qaradawi argues, "There are still those who worship cows and goats. . . . There are people in Europe who are no worse than pagans. . . . People still believe in superstitions. The mind has an intrinsic weakness and can accept unbelievable things. Even intellectuals can accept the most absurd falsities." Yusuf al-Qaradawi, *Min hadyi 'l-Islam: Fatawa mu'asira* (Beirut: al-Maktab 'l-Islami, 2000), 738.

62. When the worshipper prostrates himself in prayer, he does this on "seven bones": the forehead, the hands, the knees, and the toes (IF 18).

✍ Bibliography

'Abd al-Rahim, Muddathir. *Imperialism and Nationalism in the Sudan: A Study in Constitutional and Political Development 1899–1956*. Oxford: Oxford Univ. Press, 1969.

'Abdin, 'Abd al-Majid. *Tarikh 'l-thaqafa 'l-'Arabiyya fi 'l-Sudan mundhu nash'atiha ila 'l-'asr 'l-hadith*. Beirut: Dar 'l-Thaqafa, 1967.

'Abdin, Hasan. *Early Sudanese Nationalism, 1919–1925*. Khartoum: Institute of African and Asian Studies, 1985.

'Abduh, Muhammad. *Al-A'mal 'l-kamila li-'l-imam Muhammad 'Abduh*. Edited by Muhammad 'Amara. 4 vols. Beirut: al-Mu'assasa 'l-'Arabiyya li-'l-Dirasat wa 'l-Nashr, 1972.

Abu Da'ud, Sulaiman b. al-Ash'ath. *Sunan Abi Da'ud*. Edited by Muhammad 'Abd al-'Aziz al-Khalidi. 3 vols. Beirut: Dar 'l-Kutub 'l-'Ilmiyya, 1996.

Abu Deeb, Kamal. *Al-Jurjani's Theory of Poetic Imagery*. Warminster, Wilts.: Aris and Phillips, 1979.

Abu Salim, Muhammad Ibrahim. *Al-Haraka 'l-fikriyya fi 'l-Mahdiyya*. Khartoum: Matba'at Jami'at 'l-Khurtum, 1989.

Abu Zahra, Muhammad. *Khatam 'l-nabiyyin*. Beirut: al-Maktaba 'l-'Asriyya, 1979.

Abu Zaid, Nasr Hamid. *Falsafat 'l-ta'wil: Dirasa fi ta'wil 'l-Qur'an 'inda Muhyi al-Din Ibn 'Arabi*. Beirut: Dar 'l-Tanwir, 1993.

———. *Al-Ittijah 'l-'aqli fi 'l-tafsir: Dirasa fi qadiyyat 'l-majaz fi 'l-Qur'an 'inda 'l-Mu'tazila*. Beirut: Dar 'l-Tanwir, 1983.

———. *Mafhum 'l-nass: Dirasa fi 'ulum 'l-Qur'an*. Beirut: al-Markaz 'l-Thaqafi 'l-'Arabi, 1998.

el-Affendi, Abdelwahab. *Turabi's Revolution*. London: Grey Seal, 1991.

Affifi, A. E. *The Mystical Philosophy of Muhyid Din-Ibnul 'Arabi*. Cambridge: Cambridge Univ. Press, 1939.

al-Afghani, Jamal al-Din. "The Refutation of the Materialists." Translated by Nikki

R. Keddie and Hamid Algar. In *An Islamic Response to Imperialism: Political and Religious Writings of Jamal Ad-Din "al-Afghani,"* edited by Nikki R. Keddie, 101–87. Berkeley: California Univ. Press, 1968.

Ahmad, Aziz. *Islamic Modernism in India and Pakistan.* London: The Royal Institute of International Affairs and Oxford Univ. Press, 1967.

Ahmad, Nafis. *Muslim Contribution to Geography.* New Delhi: Adam Publishers and Distributors, 1945.

Ahmad, Rif'at Sayyid. *Limadha a'damani Nimairi?: Qira'a fi awraq 'l-shaikh Mahmud Taha.* Cairo: Dar Alif, 1985.

Ahmed, Leila. *Women and Gender in Islam.* New Haven: Yale Univ. Press, 1992.

Ajmal, Mohammad. "Sufi Science of the Soul." In *Islamic Spirituality,* edited by Seyyed Hossein Nasr, 294–307. London: Routledge and Kegan Paul, 1987.

Albino, Oliver. *The Sudan: A Southern Viewpoint.* London: Oxford Univ. Press, 1970.

Ali, Abdullah Yusuf, trans. *The Holy Qur'an: Text, Translation and Commentary.* Beirut: Dar 'l-'Arabiyya li-'l-Tiba'a wa 'l-Nashr wa 'l-Tawzi', 1968.

Ali, Ameer. *The Spirit of Islam.* London: Methuen, 1965. First published 1922.

'Ali, Haidar Ibrahim. *Al-Tayyarat 'l-islamiyya wa qadiyyat 'l-dimuqratiyya.* Beirut: Markaz Dirasat 'l-Wahda 'l-'Arabiyya, 1996.

———, ed. *Al-Ustadh Mahmud Muhammad Taha: Ra'id 'l-tajdid 'l-dini fi 'l-Sudan.* Casablanca: Markaz 'l-Dirasat 'l-Sudaniyya, 1992.

'Amara, Muhammad. *Al-Islam wa 'l-funun 'l-jamila.* Cairo: Dar 'l-Shuruq, 1991.

Amin, Husain Ahmad. *Dalil 'l-Muslim 'l-hazin.* Cairo: Maktabat Madbuli, 1987.

Anawati, Georges C., and Louis Gardet. *Mystique Musulmane: Aspects et tendances, expériences et techniques.* Paris: Librairie Philosophique J. Vrin, 1961.

al-'Aqqad, 'Abbas Mahmud. *Allah: Kitab fi nash'at 'l-'aqida 'l-ilahiyya.* Cairo: Dar 'l-Ma'arif, 1966.

Arberry, Arthur J., trans. *The Koran Interpreted.* London: Oxford Univ. Press, 1964.

Arnold, Thomas. *Painting in Islam: A Study of the Place of Pictorial Art in Muslim Culture.* New York: Dover Publications, 1965.

al-Ash'ari, 'Ali b. Isma'il. *Al-Ibana 'an usul 'l-diyana.* Edited by Fawqiyya Husain Mahmud. Cairo: Dar 'l-Ansar, 1977.

———. *Kitab 'l-luma' fi 'l-radd 'ala ahl 'l-zaigh wa 'l-bida'.* Edited by Richard J. McCarthy. Beirut: Imprimerie Catholique, 1953.

———. *Maqalat 'l-Islamiyyin wa 'khtilaf 'l-musallin.* Edited by H. Ritter. Wiesbaden: Franz Steiner Verlag, 1980.

Awn, Peter J. *Satan's Tragedy and Redemption: Iblis in Sufi Psychology.* Leiden: E. J. Brill, 1983.

al-ʿAwwa, Muhammad Salim. *Fi 'l-nizam 'l-siyasi li-'l-dawla 'l-Islamiyya.* Cairo: Dar 'l-Shuruq, 1989.

Ayubi, Nazih. *Political Islam: Religion and Politics in the Arab World.* London: Routledge, 1991.

al-ʿAzm, Sadiq Jalal. *Naqd 'l-fikr 'l-dini.* Beirut: Dar 'l-Taliʿa, 1997.

Azmeh (al-ʿAzma), ʿAziz. *Al-ʿAlmaniyya min manzur mukhtalif.* Beirut: Markaz Dirasat 'l-Wahda 'l-ʿArabiyya, 1992.

———. *Islams and Modernities.* London: Verso, 1996.

Badawi, ʿAbd al-Rahman. *Al-Insan 'l-kamil fi 'l-Islam.* Kuwait: Wakalat 'l-Matbuʿat, 1976.

———. *Madhahib 'l-Islamiyyin: Al-Muʿtazila wa 'l-Ashaʿira.* Beirut: Dar 'l-ʿIlm li-'l-Malayin, 1971.

———. *Shahidat 'l-ʿishq 'l-ilahi Rabiʿa al-ʿAdawiyya.* Kuwait: Wakalat 'l-Matbuʿat, 1978.

———. *Shatahat 'l-Sufiyya: Abu Yazid al-Bistami.* Cairo: Maktabat 'l-Nahda 'l-Misriyya, 1949.

al-Baghdadi, ʿAbd al-Qahir. *Kitab usul 'l-din.* Istanbul: Matbaʿat 'l-Dawla, 1928.

al-Baihaqi, Ahmad b. al-Husain. *Dala'il 'l-nubuwwa.* Edited by ʿAbd al-Rahman Muhammad ʿUthman. 2 vols. Damascus: Dar 'l-Fikr, 1983.

Baldwick, Julian. *Imaginary Muslims: The Uwaysi Sufis of Central Asia.* London: I. B. Tauris, 1993.

al-Baqillani, Muhammad b. al-Tayyib. *I'jaz 'l-Qur'an.* Edited by ʿImad al-Din Ahmad Haidar. Beirut: Mu'assasat 'l-Kutub 'l-Thaqafiyya, 1986.

———. *Kitab 'l-tamhid.* Edited by Richard J. McCarthy. Beirut: al-Maktaba 'l-Sharqiyya, 1957.

Bashari, Mahjub ʿUmar. *Ruwwad 'l-fikr 'l-Sudani.* Khartoum: Dar 'l-Fikr, 1981.

Bawla, ʿAbd Allah [ʿAbd Allah Ahmad al-Bashir]. "Muhawala li-'l-taʿrif bi-musahamat 'l-Ustadh Mahmud Muhammad Taha fi harakat 'l-tajdid fi 'l-fikr 'l-Islami 'l-muʿasir." *Riwaq ʿArabi*, no. 4 (October 1996): 29–47.

el-Beiti, Badreddin. "Participatory Islamic Finance and Entrepreneurship: A Theoretical Examination." *Sudan Notes and Records* 2 (1998): 175–86.

Bernstein, Eduard. *Evolutionary Socialism: A Criticism and Affirmation.* New York: Schocken Books, 1961.

Beshir, Mohamed Omer. *Educational Development in the Sudan, 1898–1956.* Oxford: The Clarendon Press, 1969.

————. *Revolution and Nationalism in the Sudan.* London: Rex Collings, 1974.

Binder, Leonard. *Islamic Liberalism: A Critique of Development Ideologies.* Chicago: The Univ. of Chicago Press, 1988.

Böwering, Gerhard. "Early Sufism between Persecution and Heresy." In *Islamic Mysticism Contested: Thirteen Centuries of Controversies and Polemics,* edited by Frederick de Jong and Bernd Radtke, 45–67. Leiden: Brill, 1999.

Bowler, Peter J. *Evolution: The History of an Idea.* Berkeley, Ca.: Univ. of California Press, 1989.

Brohi, Allahbakhsh K. "The Spiritual Dimension of Prayer." In *Islamic Spirituality,* edited by Seyyed Hossein Nasr, 131–43. London: Routledge and Kegan Paul, 1987.

Bruce, James. *Travels to Discover the Source of the Nile.* Edinburgh: A. Constable and Co., 1813.

al-Bukhari, Muhammad b. Isma'il. *Sahih.* Edited by Qasim al-Shamma'i al-Rifa'i. 9 vols. Beirut: Dar 'l-Qalam, 1987.

————. *Sahih.* Translated by Muhammad Muhsin Khan. 9 vols. New Delhi: Kitab Bhavan, 1987.

Burton, John. *The Collection of the Qur'an.* Cambridge: Cambridge Univ. Press, 1977.

————. *The Sources of Islamic Law: Islamic Theories of Abrogation.* Edinburgh: Edinburgh Univ. Press, 1990.

Buthuri, Nur al-Din. *Maqasid 'l-shari'a: Al-Tashri' 'l-Islami 'l-mu'asir baina tumuh 'l-mujtahid wa qusur 'l-ijtihad.* Beirut: Dar 'l-Tali'a, 2000.

Cameron, A. J. *Abu Dharr al-Ghifari: An Examination of His Image in the Hagiography of Islam.* London: The Royal Asiatic Society, 1982.

Chittick, William C. *Imaginal Worlds: Ibn al-'Arabi and the Problem of Religious Diversity.* Albany: State Univ. of New York Press, 1994.

————. *The Self-Disclosure of God: Principles of Ibn al-'Arabi Cosmology.* Albany: State Univ. of New York Press, 1998.

————. *The Sufi Path of Knowledge: Ibn al-'Arabi's Metaphysics of Imagination.* Albany: State Univ. of New York Press, 1989.

Chodkiewicz, Michel, ed. *Les illuminations de La Mecque.* Paris: Sindbad, 1988.

Crawford, O. G. S. *The Fung Kingdom of Sennar.* Gloucester: John Bellows, 1951.

Cudsi, Alexander S. "Islam and Politics in the Sudan." In *Islam in the Political Process,* edited by James Piscatori, 36–55. Cambridge: Cambridge Univ. Press, 1983.

Curran, Charles E. "Absolute Norms in Moral Theology." In *Norm and Context in Christian Ethics,* edited by Gene H. Outka and Paul Ramsey, 139–73. London: SCM Press, 1968.

Daftary, Farhad. *The Isma'ilis: Their History and Doctrines.* Cambridge: Cambridge Univ. Press, 1990.

Dali, Ahmed E. "A Step Towards Constructing a Foundation for a Philosophy of Education: A Sufi Perspective." Ph.D. diss., Ohio Univ., 1996.

el-Dareer, Asma. *Woman, Why Do You Weep? Circumcision and Its Consequences.* London: Zed Press, 1981.

al-Darimi, 'Abd Allah b. 'Abd al-Rahman. *Sunan 'l-Darimi.* 2 vols. Damascus: Matba'at 'l-I'tidal, 1930.

Da'ud, al-Amin. *Dajjal 'l-Sudan.* N. p.: n. p., 1978.

Deng, Francis. *War of Visions: Conflict of Identities in the Sudan.* Washington, D.C.: The Brookings Institution, 1995.

Dickens, Peter. *Social Darwinism: Linking Evolutionary Thought to Social Theory.* Buckingham: Open Univ. Press, 2000.

Duran, Khalid. "The Centrifugal Forces of Religion in Sudanese Politics." *Orient* 26, no. 4, 572–600 (1985).

————. "Die 'Republikanischen Brüder' im Sudan—eine islamische Reformbewegung der Gegenwart." *SOWI* 10, no. 2, 69–74 (1981).

————. "The Reform Theology of Mahmud M. Taha." *TransState Islam* 1, no. 3, 10–17 (1995).

Encyclopaedia of Islam (EI²). New Edition. Leiden: Brill, 1960–2003.

Eickelman, Dale F., and James Piscatori. *Muslim Politics.* Princeton, N.J.: Princeton Univ. Press, 1996.

Enayat, Hamid. *Modern Islamic Political Thought: The Response of the Shi'i and Sunni Muslims to the Twentieth Century.* London: The Macmillan Press Ltd, 1982.

Engels, Frederick. *Socialism: Utopian and Scientific.* London: Lawrence and Wishart, 1973.

Ernst, Carl W. *Words of Ecstasy in Sufism.* Albany: State Univ. of New York Press, 1985.

Fakhry, Majid. *A History of Islamic Philosophy.* New York and London: Columbia Univ. Press, 1970.

Firestone, Reuven. *Jihad: The Origins of Holy War in Islam.* New York: Oxford Univ. Press, 1999.

al-Firuzabadi, Majd al-Din Muhammad b. Ya'qub. *Al-Qamus 'l-muhit.* Edited by Muhammad 'Abd al-Rahman al-Mar'ashli. 2 vols. Beirut: Dar Ihya' 'l-Turath 'l-Arabi, 1999.

Fluehr-Lobban, Carolyn. "Islamization in Sudan: A Critical Assessment." In *Sudan: State and Society in Crisis,*, edited by John Voll, 71–89. Bloomington and Indianapolis: Indiana Univ. Press, 1991.

Freud, Sigmund. *Two Short Accounts of Psycho-Analysis.* Translated by James Strachey. Harmondsworth, Middlesex: Penguin Books, 1972.

Gay, Peter. *The Dilemma of Democratic Socialism: Eduard Bernstein's Challenge to Marx.* New York and London: Collier Books, 1962.

Ghabin, Ahmad Y. "The Qur'anic Verses as a Source of Legitimacy or Illegitimacy of the Arts in Islam." *Der Islam* 75, no. 2 (1998): 193–225.

al-Ghazali, Abu Hamid. *Ihya' 'ulum 'l-din.* Beirut: Dar al-Ma'rifa, n.d.

———. *Al-Maqsad 'l-asna fi sharh ma'ani asma' 'Llah 'l-husna.* Edited by Fadlou A. Shehadi. Beirut: Dar 'l-Mashriq, 1971.

———. *Mishkat 'l-anwar wa misfat 'l-asrar.* Edited by 'Abd al-'Aziz Izz al-Din al-Sairawan. Beirut: 'Alam 'l-Kutub, 1986.

———. *The Ninety Nine Beautiful Names of God.* Translated by David B. Burrell and Nazih Daher. Cambridge: The Islamic Texts Society, 1992.

———. *Tahafut 'l-falasifa.* Edited and introduced by Sulaiman Dunya. Cairo: Dar 'l-Ma'arif, 1987.

Gibb, H. A. R. *Modern Trends in Islam.* Beirut: Librairie du Liban, 1975.

Goldziher, Ignaz. *Die Richtungen der Islamischen Koranauslegung.* Leiden: E. J. Brill, 1920.

———. *Introduction to Islamic Theology and Law.* Translated by Andras Hamori and Ruth Hamori. Princeton: Princeton Univ. Press, 1981.

Grabar, Oleg. *The Formation of Islamic Art.* New Haven: Yale Univ. Press, 1987.

Graham, William. *Divine Word and Prophetic Word in Early Islam: A Reconsideration of the Sources, with Special Reference to the Divine Saying or Hadith Qudsi.* The Hague: Mouton, 1977.

Guillaume, A. *The Life of Muhammad: A Translation of Ishaq's Sirat Rasul Allah.* Karachi: Oxford Univ. Press, 1980.

Hale, Sondra. *Gender Politics in Sudan: Islamism, Socialism, and the State.* Boulder: Westview Press, 1997.

Hall, Marjorie, and Bakhita Amin Ismail. *Sisters Under the Sun: The Story of Sudanese Women.* London: Longman, 1981.

al-Hallaj, al-Husain b. Mansur. *Kitab 'l-tawasin*. Paris: Librairie Paul Geuthner, 1913.

Hamad, Bushra G. "The Education System of the Funj Kingdom." *Sudan Notes and Records* 3 (1999): 25–44.

Hamdi, Mohamed Elhachmi. *The Making of an Islamic Political Leader: Conversations with Hasan al-Turabi*. Boulder: Westview Press, 1998.

Hasan, Yusuf Fadl. *The Arabs and the Sudan from the Seventh to the Early Sixteenth Century*. Edinburgh: Edinburgh Univ. Press, 1967.

———. *Muqaddima fi tarikh 'l-mamalik 'l-Islamiyya fi 'l-Sudan 'l-sharqi, 1450–1821*. Khartoum: Matba'at Jami'at 'l-Khurtum, 1989.

El Hassan, Idris Salim. *Religion in Society: Nemeiri and the Turuq, 1972–1980*. Khartoum: Khartoum Univ. Press, 1993.

Hofheinz, Albrecht. "Internalising Islam: Shaykh Muhammad Majdhub, Scriptural Islam, and Local Context in the Early Nineteenth-Century Sudan." Ph.D. diss., Univ. of Bergen, 1996.

Holt, P. M. "Funj Origins: A Critique and New Evidence." *Journal of African History* 4, no. 1 (1963): 39–55.

Holt, P. M., and M. W. Daly. *The History of the Sudan: From the Coming of Islam to the Present Day*. London: Wieden and Nicolson, 1979.

Hoodbhoy, Pervez. *Islam and Science: Religious Orthodoxy and the Battle for Rationality*. London: Zed Books, 1991.

Hourani, Albert. *Arabic Thought in the Liberal Age 1798–1939*. Cambridge: Cambridge Univ. Press, 1995.

Howard, W. Stephen. "Mahmoud Mohammed Taha: A Remarkable Teacher in Sudan." *Northeast African Studies* 10, no. 1 (1988): 83–93.

al-Hujwiri, 'Ali b. 'Uthman. *The Kashf al-mahjub*. Translated by Reynold A. Nicholson. New Delhi: Taj Company, 1982.

Husaini, A. S. "Uways al-Qarani and the Uwaysi Sufis." *Muslim World* 57, no. 2 (1967): 103–13.

Ibn 'Abd al-Barr, Yusuf b. 'Abd Allah. *Al-Isti'ab fi ma'rifat 'l-ashab*. Edited by 'Ali Muhammad al-Bijawi. 4 vols. Beirut: Dar 'l-Jil, 1992.

Ibn 'Arabi, Muhyi al-Din. *Fusus 'l-hikam*. Edited by Abu al-'Ila 'Afifi. Beirut: Dar 'l-Kitab 'l-'Arabi, n.d.

———. *Al-Futuhat 'l-Makiyya*. 4 vols. Beirut: Dar Sadir, n.d.

———. *Al-Isra ila 'l-maqam 'l-asra*. Edited by Su'ad al-Hakim. Beirut: Dandara li-'l-Tiba'a wa 'l-Nashr, 1988.

———. *Al-Tanazzulat 'l-musaliyya fi asrar 'l-taharat wa 'l-salat wa 'l-ayam 'l-asliyya.* Cairo: Maktabat 'Alam 'l-Fikr, 1986.

Ibn 'Asakir, 'Ali b. al-Hasan. *Mukhtasar tarikh Dimashq.* 29 vols. Damascus: Dar 'l-Fikr, 1990.

———. *Tabyin kadhib 'l-muftari fi-ma nusiba ila 'l-imam Abi al-Hasan al-Ash'ari.* Damascus: Matba'at 'l-Tawfiq, 1928.

Ibn Daif Allah, Muhammad al-Nur. *Kitab 'l-tabaqat fi khusus 'l-awliya' wa 'l-salihin wa 'l-'ulama' wa 'l-shu'ara' fi 'l-Sudan.* Edited by Yusuf Fadl Hasan. Khartoum: Matba'at Jami'at 'l-Khurtum, 1985.

Ibn Hanbal, Ahmad. *Al-Musnad.* 6 vols. Traditions numbered by Muhammad 'Abd al-Salam 'Abd al-Shafi. Beirut: Dar 'l-Kutub 'l-'Ilmiyya, 1993.

———. *Al-Radd 'ala 'l-Jahmiyya wa 'l-Zanadiqa.* Edited by 'Abd al-Rahman 'Umaira. Riyad: Dar 'l-Liwa', 1977.

Ibn Hisham, 'Abd al-Malik. *Al-Sira 'l-nabawiyya.* 4 vols. Beirut: Dar 'l-Kutub 'l-'Ilmiyya, 2000.

Ibn Kathir, 'Imad al-Din Isma'il. *Al-Sira 'l-nabawiyya.* Edited by Mustafa 'Abd al-Wahid. 4 vols. Beirut: Dar 'l-Ma'rifa, 1976.

———. *Tafsir 'l-Qur'an 'l-'azim.* 7 vols. Beirut: Dar 'l-Andalus, 1996.

Ibn Khaldun, 'Abd al-Rahman. *The Muqaddimah: An Introduction to History.* Translated by Franz Rosenthal. 3 vols. London: Routledge and Kegan Paul, 1958.

———. *Tarikh Ibn Khaldun.* 7 vols. Beirut: Dar 'l-Kutub al-'Ilmiyya, 1992.

Ibn Khallikan, Shams al-Din Ahmad. *Wafayat 'l-a'yan wa anba' 'l-zaman.* Edited by Ihsan 'Abbas. Beirut: Dar Sadir, 1977.

Ibn Maja, Muhammad b. Yazid. *Sunan.* Edited by Muhammad Fu'ad 'Abd al-Baqi. 2 vols. Beirut: Dar 'l-Kutub 'l-'Ilmiyya, 1995.

Ibn Manzur, Muhammad b. Mukarram. *Lisan 'l-'Arab.* Edited by Amin Muhammad 'Abd al-Wahhab and Muhammad al-Sawi al-'Ubaidi. 18 vols. Beirut: Dar Ihya' 'l-Turath, 1999.

Ibn al-Murtada, Ahmad b. Yahya. *Kitab Tabaqat al-Mu'tazila.* Edited by Susanna Diwald-Wilzer. Beirut: Dar Maktabat 'l-Hayat, n.d.

Ibn Sa'd, Muhammad. *Al-Tabaqat 'l-Kubra.* Edited by Muhammad 'Abd al-Qadir 'Ata. 8 vols. Beirut: Dar 'l-Kutub 'l-'Ilmiyya, 1997.

Ibn Taimiya, Ahmad b. 'Abd al-Halim. *Dar' ta'arud 'l-'aql wa 'l-naql.* Edited by Muhammad Rashad Salim. 11 vols. Cairo: Maktabat Ibn Taimiya, n.d.

———. *Majmu' fatawa Ahmad b. Taimiyya.* Edited by 'Abd al-Rahman b. Muhammad al-Qasimi. 37 vols. N.p.: n.p. , n.d.

Ibrahim, 'Abd Allah 'Ali. *Al-Sira' baina 'l-Mahdi wa 'l-'Ulama'.* Cairo: Markaz 'l-Dirasat 'l-Sudaniyya, 1994.

Ibrahim, Hassan Ahmed. "The Neo-Mahdists and the British, 1944–47: From Tactical Co-operation to Short-lived Confrontation." *Middle Eastern Studies* 38, no. 3 (July 2002): 47–72.

al-Idrisi, Muhammad b. Muhammad b. 'Abd Allah. *Kitab nuzhat 'l-mushtaq fi 'khtiraq 'l-afaq.* Leiden: E. J. Brill, 1970.

Jallab, 'Abd Allah. "Mahmud Muhammad Taha yaqul." *Al-Sahafa,* Dec. 11, 1972. www.alfikra.org

al-Jassas, Ahmad b. 'Ali al-Razi. *Ahkam 'l-Qur'an.* Edited by 'Abd al-Salam Muhammad 'Ali Shahin. 3 vols. Beirut: Dar 'l-Kutub 'l-'Ilmiyya, 1994.

Jawish, 'Abd al-'Aziz. *Al-Islam din 'l-fitra wa 'l-hurriyya.* Cairo: Dar 'l-Hilal, n.d.

Jeffery, Arthur. *The Foreign Vocabulary of the Quran.* Lahore: al-Biruni, 1938.

al-Jili, 'Abd al-Karim b. Ibrahim. *Al-Insan 'l-kamil fi ma'rifat 'l-awakhir wa 'l-awa'il.* Cairo: Mustafa al-Babi al-Halabi, 1956.

al-Jindi, 'Abd al-Halim. *Ahmad b. Hanbal: Imam ahl 'l-sunna.* Cairo: Dar 'l-Ma'arif, 1977.

al-Jumhuriyyun, al-Ikhwan 'l-Jumhuriyyun. *'Awdat 'l-Masih.* Omdurman: Republican Movement Publication, 1980.

———. *Al-Kaid 'l-siyasi wa 'l-mahkama 'l-mahzala.* Omdurman: Republican Movement Publication, 1985.

———. *Ma'alim 'ala tariq tatwwur 'l-fikra 'l-Jumhuriyya.* Omdurman: Republican Movement Publication, 1976.

———. *Al-Sulh khair.* Omdurman: Republican Movement Publication, 1977.

al-Jurjani, 'Abd al-Qahir. *Kitab dala'il 'l-i'jaz fi 'ilm 'l-ma'ani.* Edited by Muhammad 'Abdu, Muhammad Mahmud al-Shinqiti, and Rashid Rida. Cairo: Dar 'l-Manar, 1946.

al-Jurjani, 'Ali b. Muhammad. *Kitab 'l-ta'rifat.* Edited by Muhammad 'Abd al-Rahman al-Mar'ashli. Beirut: Dar 'l-Nafa'is, 2003.

al-Juwaini, 'Abd al-Malik b. 'Abd Allah b. Yusuf. *Kitab 'l-irshad ila qawati' 'l-adilla fi usul 'l-i'tiqad.* Edited by Muhammad Yusuf Musa and 'Ali 'Abd al-Mun'im 'Abd al-Hamid. Cairo: Maktabat 'l-Khanji, 1950.

al-Kabbashi, al-Makashfi Taha. *Al-Ridda wa muhakamat Mahmud Muhammad Taha fi 'l-Sudan.* Khartoum: Dar 'l-Fikr, 1987.

al-Kalabadhi, Muhammad b. Ishaq. *Al-Ta'arruf li-madhhab ahl 'l-tasawwuf.* Edited by A. J. Arberry. Cairo: Matba'at 'l-Sa'ada, 1933.

Karrar, Ali Salih. *The Sufi Brotherhoods in the Sudan.* Evanston: Northwestern Univ. Press, 1992.

Karrar, Mahjub. "Mahmud Muhammad Taha fi hiwar Sufi ma'a Hodgkins." *Al-Sahafa,* Dec. 16, 1972. www.alfikra.org.

Kepel, Gilles. *Jihad: The Trial of Political Islam.* Translated by Anthony E. Roberts. London: I. B. Tauris, 2002.

Kermani, Navid. *Gott is schön: Das ästhetische Erleben des Koran.* Munich: Verlag C. H. Beck, 1999.

Kerr, Malcolm H. *Islamic Reform: The Political and Legal Theories of Muhammad 'Abduh and Rashid Rida.* Berkeley, Ca.: Univ. of California Press, 1966.

Khair, Ahmad. *Kifah Jil: Tarikh harakat 'l-khirrijin wa tatawwuruha fi 'l-Sudan.* Khartoum: al-Dar 'l-Sudaniyya, 1970.

Khalaf Allah, Muhammad Ahmad. *Dirasat fi 'l-nuzum wa 'l-tashri'at 'l-Islamiyya.* Cairo: Maktabat 'l-Anjlu 'l-Misriyya, 1977.

Khalid, Mansour (Mansur). *Al-Fajr 'l-kadhib: Nimairi wa tahrif 'l-shari'a.* Cairo: Dar 'l-Hilal, 1986.

———. *The Government They Deserve: The Role of the Elite in Sudan's Political Evolution.* London: Kegan Paul, 1990.

———. *Nimeiri and the Revolution of Dis-May.* London: Kegan Paul, 1985.

———. *Al-Nukhba 'l-Sudaniyya wa idman 'l-fashal.* 2 vols. Cairo: Sijil 'l-'Arab, 1993.

Khalil, Bakri Muhammad. "Al-Fikr 'l-falsafi 'ind 'l-Jumhuriyyin fi 'l-Sudan." M.A. diss., Univ. of Baghdad, 1996.

Khayati, Mustapha. "Introduction à la pensée de Mahmud Muhammad Taha, réformiste et martyr ['Les Frères Républicains' au Soudan]." In *Sudan: History, Identity, Ideology,* edited by Hérve Bleuchot, Christian Delmet, and Derek Hopwood, 287–98. Reading: Ithaca, 1991.

al-Khayyat, Abd al-Rahim b. Muhammad b. 'Uthman. *Kitab 'l-intisar wa al-radd 'ala Ibn 'l-Rawandi 'l-mulhid.* Edited by H. S. Nyberg. Cairo: Dar 'l-Kutub 'l-Misriyya, 1925.

Knysh, Alexander D. *Ibn 'Arabi in the Later Islamic Tradition: The Making of a Polemical Image in Medieval Islam.* Albany: State Univ. of New York Press, 1999.

Kolakowski, Leszek. *Main Currents of Marxism.* 3 vols. Oxford: Oxford Univ. Press, 1978.

Kramer, J. H. "Geography and Commerce." In *The Legacy of Islam,* edited by Thomas Arnold and Alfred Guillaume, 79–107. Oxford: Clarendon Press, 1931.

Kurita, Yoshiko. *'Ali 'Abd al-Latif wa thawrat 1924: Bahth fi masadir 'l-thawra 'l-*

Sudaniyya. Translated by Majdi al-Na'im. Cairo: Markaz 'l-Dirasat 'l-Sudaniyya, 1997.

Lichtenthäler, Gerhard. "Muslih, Mystic and Martyr, The Vision of Mahmud Muhammad Taha and the Republican Bothers in the Sudan: Towards an Islamic Reformation?" *Islam société au sud du Sahara,* 9 (1995): 57–81.

Lichtheim, George. *A Short History of Socialism.* London: Fontana, 1983.

MacMichael, H. A. *A History of the Arabs in the Sudan.* 2 vols. Cambridge: Cambridge Univ. Press, 1922.

Magnarella, Paul J. "The Republican Brothers: A Reformist Movement in the Sudan." *The Muslim World* 72, no. 1(1982): 14–24.

Mahjub, Muhammad Ahmad. *Nahw 'l-ghad.* Khartoum: Matba'at Jami'at 'l-Khurtum, 1970.

Mahmoud, Mohamed. "Knowledge, Authority, and the 'Second Message': Mahmud Muhammad Taha's Response to the Crisis of Modern Islam." *Annals of Japan Association for Middle East Studies* 21, no. 1 (2005): 75–94.

———. "Mahmud Muhammad Taha and the Rise and Demise of the Jumhuri Movement." *New Political Science* 23, no. 1(2001): 65–88.

———. "Mahmud Muhammad Taha's Second Message of Islam and His Modernist Project." In *Islam and Modernity: Muslim Intellectuals Respond,* edited by John Cooper, Ron Nettler, and Mohamed Mahmoud, 105–28. London: I. B. Tauris, 1998.

———. "Sufism and Islamism in the Sudan." In *African Islam and Islam in Africa: Encounters between Sufis and Islamists,* edited by David Westerlund and Eva Evers Rosander, 162–92. London: Hurst & Company, 1997.

Mahmud, 'Abd al-Halim. *Al-Tafkir 'l-falsafi fi'l-Islam.* Cairo: Dar 'l-Ma'arif, 1984.

Mahmud, 'Abd al-Qadir. *Al-fikr 'l-Sufi fi 'l-Sudan.* Cairo: Dar 'l-Fikr 'l-'Arabi, 1968.

Mahmud, Mustafa. *Al-Qur'an: Muhawala li-fahm 'asri li-'l-Qur'an.* Beirut: Dar 'l-Shuruq, 1970.

Makki, Hasan. *Al-Haraka 'l-Islamiyya fi 'l-Sudan, 1969–1985.* Khartoum: Ma'had 'l-Buhuth wa 'l-Dirast 'l-Ijtima'iyya and Bait 'l-Ma'rifa, 1990.

———. *Harakat 'l-Ikhwan 'l-Muslimin fi 'l-Sudan, 1944–1969.* Khartoum: Ma'had 'l-Dirasat 'l-Ifriqiyya wa 'l-Asyawiyya, 1982.

Mason, Herbert W. *Al-Hallaj.* Richmond, Surrey: Curzon Press, 1995.

Massignon, Louis. *Essai sur les origines du lexique technique de la mystique musulmane.* Paris: Librairie orientaliste, 1922.

———. *La passion d'al-Hosayn-Ibn-Mansour al-Hallaj martyr mystique de l'Islam.* 2 vols. Paris: Geuthner, 1922.

————. *The Passion of al-Hallaj: Mystic and Martyr of Islam.* Translated by Herbert Mason. 3 vols. Princeton: Princeton Univ. Press, 1982.

————. *Recueil de textes inédits concernant l'histoire de la mystique en pays d'Islam.* Paris: Librairie Orientaliste Paul Geuthner, 1929.

Massignon, Louis, and Paul Kraus, eds. *Akhbar 'l-Hallaj.* Paris: Au Calame, 1936.

Matar, Fu'ad. *Al-Hizb 'l-Shuyu'i 'l-Sudani: Naharuhu am 'ntahar?* Beirut: Dar 'l-Nahar, 1971.

Mazhar, Isma'il. *Malqa 'l-sabil fi madhhab 'l-nushu' wa 'l-'irtiqa'.* Cairo: al-Matba'a 'l-'Asriyya, 1926.

McHugh, Neil. *Holymen of the Blue Nile: The Making of an Arab-Islamic Community in the Nilotic Sudan, 1500–1850.* Evanston: Northwestern Univ. Press, 1994.

McLellan, David. *Marxism after Marx: An Introduction.* London: The Macmillan Press, 1980.

Miller, Judith. *God Has Ninety Nine Names: Reporting From a Militant Middle East.* New York: Simon and Schuster, 1996.

Mills, C. Wright. *The Marxists.* Harmondsworth, Middlesex: Penguin Books, 1973.

Modarressi, Hossein. "The Legal Basis for the Validity of the Majority Opinion in Islamic Legislation." In *Under Siege: Islam and Democracy,* edited by Richard C. Bulliet, 81–92. New York: The Middle East Institute of Columbia Univ., 1994.

Morris, James W. "Ibn 'Arabi's Spiritual Ascension." In *Les Illuminations de La Mecque,* edited by Michel Chodkiewicz, 366–81. Paris: Sindbad, 1988.

al-Muhasibi, al-Harith b. Asad. *Kitab 'l-ri'aya li-huquqi 'Llah.* Edited by Margaret Smith. London: Luzac, 1940.

Mukhtar, al-Baqir al-Afif. "Human Rights and Islamic Law: The Development of the Rights of Slaves, Women and Aliens in Two Cultures." Ph.D. diss., Univ. of Manchester, 1996.

Muslim, Abu al-Husain Muslim b. al-Hajjaj. *Sahih Muslim bi-Sharh al-Nawawi.* Edited by Khalil Ma'mun Shiha. 18 vols. Cairo: al-Matba'a 'l-Misriyya, 1930.

An-Na'im, Abdullahi. "The Elusive Islamic Constitution: The Sudanese Experience." *Orient* 26, no. 3 (1985): 329–40.

————. Introduction to *The Second Message of Islam,* by Mahmud Muhammad Taha, trans. an-Na'im, 1–30. Syracuse, N.Y.: Syracuse Univ. Press, 1987.

————. "The Islamic Law of Apostasy and Its Modern Applicability." *Religion* 16 (1986): 197–223.

————. "Mahmud Muhammad Taha and the Crisis in Islamic Law Reform: Implications for Interreligious Relations." *Journal of Ecumenical Studies* 25, no. 1 (1988): 1–21.

―――. "Sudan Republican Brothers: An Alternative Islamic Ideology." *Middle East Report* 17, no. 147 (1987): 40–42.

―――. *Toward an Islamic Reformation: Civil Liberties, Human Rights, and International Law.* Syracuse, N.Y.: Syracuse Univ. Press, 1990.

Nasr, Seyyed Hossein. *Islam and Contemporary Society.* London: Longman Group, 1982.

―――. *Islam and the Plight of Modern Man.* London and New York: Longman, 1975.

―――. *Religion and the Order of Nature.* New York: Oxford Univ. Press, 1996.

―――. *Three Muslim Sages.* Delmar, New York: Caravan Books, 1976.

al-Nawawi, Muhyi al-Din b. Sharaf. *Al-Majmu': Sharh 'l-Muhadhdhab.* Edited by Mahmud Matraji. 22 vols. Beirut: Dar 'l-Fikr, 2000.

Nawfal, 'Abd al-Razzaq. *Baina 'l-din wa 'l-'ilm.* Cairo: Maktabat Wahba, n.d.

―――. *Al-Islam wa 'l-'ilm 'l-Hadith.* Cairo: Dar 'l-Ma'arif, 1958.

Niblock, Tim. *Class and Power in Sudan: The Dynamics of Sudanese Politics, 1898–1985.* Albany: State Univ. of New York Press, 1987.

al-Niffari, Muhammad b. 'Abd al-Jabbar. *Kitab 'l-mawaqif wa 'l-mukhatabat.* Edited by A. J. Arberry. Cambridge: Cambridge Univ. Press, 1935.

Nur al-Din, 'Abd al-Salam. *Al-Haqiqa wa 'l-shari'a fi 'l-fikr 'l-Sufi.* Nicosia: Dar Sawmar, 1992.

Nwyia, Paul, ed. *Exégèse coranique et langue mystique.* Beirut: Dar 'l-Mashriq, 1986.

―――. *Nusus Sufiyya ghair manshura.* Beirut: Dar 'l-Mashriq, 1973.

Oevermann, Annette. *Die "Republikanischen Brüder" im Sudan: Eine islamische Reformbewegung im Zwanzigsten Jahrhundert.* Frankfurt am Main: Peter Lang, 1993.

O'Fahey, R. S. *Enigmatic Saint: Ahmad Ibn Idris and the Idrisi Tradition.* London: Hirst and Company, 1990.

al-Omar, Abdullah Omar A. "The Reception of Darwinism in the Arab World." Ph.D. diss., Harvard Univ., 1982.

Osman, Fathi. "The Contract for the Appointment of the Head of an Islamic State: Bai'at al-Imam." In *State Politics and Islam,* edited by Mumtaz Ahmed, 51–85. Indianapolis, Ind.: American Trust Publications, 1986.

Patton, Walter M. *Ahmed Ibn Hanbal and the Mihna.* Leiden: E. J. Brill, 1897.

Plato. *The Dialogues of Plato.* Translated by B. Jowett. 4 vols. Oxford: The Clarendon Press, 1953.

―――. *Protagoras and Meno.* Translated by W. K. C. Guthrie. Harmondsworh, Middlesex: Penguin Books, 1980.

al-Qaddal, Muhammad Saʿid. *Maʿalim fi tarikh ʾl-hizb ʾl-Shuyuʿi ʾl-Sudani.* Beirut: Dar ʾl-Farabi, 1999.

———. *Tarikh ʾl-Sudan ʾl-hadith.* Cairo: al-Amal li-ʾl-Tibaʿa wa ʾl-Nashr, 1993.

al-Qaradawi, Yusuf. *Min hadyi ʾl-Islam: Fatawa muʿasira.* Beirut: al-Maktab ʾl-Islami, 2000.

Qarib Allah, Hasan Muhammad al-Fatih. *Al-Tasawwuf fi ʾl-Sudan ila nihayat ʿasr ʾl-Funj.* Khartoum: The Graduate College at the Univ. of Khartoum, 1987.

al-Qarraʾy, ʿUmar. *Al-Fikr ʾl-Islami wa qadiyyat ʾl-marʾa.* Ft. Worth, Texas: Lonestar, n.d.

al-Qashani, ʿAbd al-Razzaq. *ʾIstilahat ʾl-Sufiyya.* Edited by Muhammad Kamal Ibrahim Jaʿfar. Cairo: al-Haiʾa ʾl-Misriyya al-ʿAmma li-ʾl-Kitab, 1981.

al-Qurtubi, Muhammad b. Ahmad al-Ansari. *Al-Jamiʿ li-Ahkam ʾl-Qurʾan.* Edited by Ahmad ʿAbd al-ʿAlim al-Barduni. 20 vols. Cairo: Dar ʾl-Kitab ʾl-ʿArabi, 1952.

al-Qushairi, ʿAbd ʾl-Karim. *Al-Risala ʾl-Qushairiyya.* Edited by ʿAbd al-Halim Mahmud and Mahmud Ibn al-Sharif. 2 vols. Cairo: Dar ʾl-Kutub ʾl-Haditha, 1972.

———. *Tafsir ʾl-Qushairi: Lataʾif ʾl-Isharat.* Edited by ʿAbd al-Latif Hasan ʿAbd al-Rahman. 3 vols. Beirut: Dar ʾl-Kutub al-ʿIlmiyya, 2000.

Qutb, Muhammad. *Maʿrikat ʾl-taqalid.* Cairo and Beirut: Dar ʾl-Shuruq, 1973.

———. *Shubhat hawl ʾl-Islam.* Cairo: Maktabat Wahba, 1964.

Qutb, Sayyid. *Al-ʿAdala ʾl-ijtimaʿiyya fi ʾl-Islam.* N.p., 1949.

———. *Maʿalim fi ʾl-tariq.* Beirut: The Holy Koran Publishing House, 1978.

———. *Mashahid ʾl-qiyama fi ʾl-Qurʾan.* Cairo: Dar ʾl-Maʿarif, 1961.

al-Rafiʿi, Mustafa Sadiq. *Iʿjaz ʾl-Qurʾan.* Cairo: al-Maktaba ʾl-Tijariyya ʾl-Kubra, 1965.

Rahman, Fazlur. "The Principle of Shura and the Role of the Ummah in Islam." In *State Politics and Islam,* edited by Mumtaz Ahmed, 87–96. Indianapolis, Ind.: American Trust Publications, 1986.

al-Razi, Fakhr al-Din. *Al-Tafsir ʾl-kabir.* 32 vols. Cairo: al-Matbaʿa ʾl-Bahiyya ʾl-Misriyya, n.d.

Rida, Muhammad Rashid. *Tafsir ʾl-manar.* 12 vols. Beirut: Dar ʾl-Maʿrifa, 1993. [Coauthor Muhammad ʿAbduh died before publication of this work.]

———. *Tarikh ʾl-ustadh ʾl-imam ʾl-shaikh Muhammad ʿAbduh.* 3 vols. Cairo: Matbaʿat ʾl-Manar, 1931.

Rodinson, Maxime. *Islam and Capitalism.* Harmondsworth, Middlesex: Penguin Books, 1977.

Rogalski, Jürgen. "Die ʿRepublikanischen Brüderʾ im Sudan: Ein Beitrag zur Ideolgiegeschichte des Islam in der Gegenwart." M.A. diss., Free Univ. of Berlin, 1990.

―――. "Mahmud Muhammad Taha—Zur Erinnerung an das Schicksal eines Mystikers und Intellektuellen im Sudan." *Asien Afrika Lateinamerika* 24 (1996): 47–61.

Ruse, Michael. *Darwinism Defended: A Guide to the Evolution Controversies.* Reading, Mass.: Addison-Wesley Publishing Company, 1982.

Sadig, Haydar Badawi. "The Republican Brothers: A Religio-Political Movement in the Sudan." M.A. diss., Univ. of Khartoum, 1988.

al-Sadr, Muhammad Baqir. *Iqtisaduna.* Beirut and Cairo: Dar 'l-Kitab 'l-Lubnani and Dar 'l-Kitab 'l-Misri, 1977.

al-Sahhar, 'Abd al-Hamid Juda. *Abu Dharr 'l-Ghifari 'l-Ishtraki 'l-zahid.* Cairo: Maktabat Misr, 1978.

Sa'id, Bashir Muhammad. *Al-Za'im al-Azhari wa 'asruhu.* Cairo: al-Qahira 'l-Haditha li-'l-Tiba'a, 1990.

al-Sakandari, Ibn 'Ata' Allah. *Al-Hikam 'l-'Ata'iyya.* Edited by Paul Nwyia. Beirut: Dar 'l-Mashriq, 1986.

Salih, Ahmad 'Abbas. *Al-Yamin wa 'l-yasar fi 'l-Islam.* Beirut: al-Mu'assasa 'l-'Arabiyya li-'l-Dirasat wa 'l-Nashr, 1972.

al-Salih, Subhi. *Mabahith fi 'ulum 'l-Qur'an.* Beirut: Dar al-'Ilm li-'l-Malayin, 1972.

al-Samarrai, Qassim. *The Theme of Ascension in Mystical Writings: A Study of the Theme in Islamic and Non-Islamic Writings.* Baghdad: National Printing and Publishing Co., 1968.

Sanderson, Lillian P. *Against the Mutilation of Women: The Struggle to End Unnecessary Suffering.* London: Ithaca Press, 1981.

al-Sarraj, Abu Nasr 'Abd Allah b. 'Ali. *Al-Luma' fi 'l-tasawwuf.* Beirut: Dar 'l-Kutub 'l-'Ilmiyya, 2001.

Sartre, Jean-Paul. *Existentialism and Humanism.* Translated and introduced by Philip Mairet. London: Methuen, 1973.

al-Sawi, 'Abd al-'Aziz Husain, and Muhammad 'Ali Jadain. *Al-Thawra 'l-Mahdiyya fi 'l-Sudan: Mashru' ru'ya jadida.* N.p.: Sharikat 'l-Farabi, 1990.

Schimmel, Annemarie. *Mystical Dimensions of Islam.* Chapel Hill: Univ. of North Carolina Press, 1975.

Sepälä, Serafim. *In Speechless Ecstasy: Expression and Interpretation of Mystical Experience in Classical Syriac and Sufi Literature.* Helsinki: Finnish Oriental Society, 2003.

Shaaeldin, Elfatih, and Richard Brown. "Towards an Understanding of Islamic Banking in Sudan." In *Sudan: State, Capital, and Transformation,* edited by Tony Barnett and Abbas Abdelkarim, 121–40. London: Croom Helm, 1988.

al-Shahrastani, Muhammad b. ʿAbd al-Karim. *Al-Milal wa ʾl-nihal.* Edited by Muhammad Sayyid Kilani. 2 vols. Beirut: Dar Saʿb, 1986.

Shalabi, Mahmud. *Ishtirakiyyat Abi Bakr.* Cairo: Maktabat ʾl-Qahira ʾl-Haditha, 1963.

———. *Ishtirakiyyat Muhammad.* Cairo: Maktabat ʾl-Qahira ʾl-Haditha, 1962.

———. *Ishtirakiyyat ʿUmar.* Cairo: Maktabat ʾl-Qahira ʾl-Haditha, 1964.

Shaltut, Mahmud. *Al-Fatawa.* Cairo: Dar ʾl-Shuruq, 1991.

———. *Al-Islam ʿaqida wa shariʿa.* Cairo: Dar ʾl-Shuruq, 1983.

Sharif, Mahjub Muhammad. "Al-wajh ʾl-akhar li-Mahmud Muhammad Taha." *Al-Hayat,* n.d. www.alfikra.org.

Sharkey, Heather. "Colonialism and the Culture of Nationalism in the Northern Sudan, 1898–1956." Ph.D. diss., Princeton Univ., 1998.

al-Shatibi, Ibrahim b. Musa. *Al-Muwafaqat fi usul ʾl-ahkam.* Muhammad ʿAbd al-Qadir al-Fadili. 4 vols. Beirut: al-Maktaba ʾl-ʿAsriyya, 2000.

Shuqair, Naʿʿum. *Tarikh ʾl-Sudan ʾl-qadim wa ʾl-hadith wa jughrafiyatuhu.* 3 vols. Cairo: Matbaʿat ʾl-Maʿarif, 1903.

al-Sibaʿi, Mustafa. *Ishtirakiyyat ʾl-Islam.* Damascus: Muʾasassat ʾl-Matbuʿat ʾl-ʿArabiyya, 1960.

Sidahmad, ʿAbd al-Salam (Sidahmed, Abdel Salam). *Al-Fuqahaʾ wa ʾl-saltana fi Sinnar.* Prague: Babylon, 1991.

———. *Politics and Islam in Contemporary Sudan.* Richmond, Surrey: Curzon, 1997.

Sidahmad, al-Hajj Warraq. *Harakat ʾl-Turabi.* Cairo: al-ʿIlmiyya li-ʾl-Nashr, 1997.

Siddiqi, M. I. *Ninety Nine Names of Allah.* Delhi: Adam Publishers and Distributors, 1988.

Sivan, Emmanuel. *Radical Islam: Medieval Theology and Modern Politics.* New Haven: Yale Univ. Press, 1990.

Smith, Margaret. *An Early Mystic of Baghdad: A Study of the Life and Teaching of Harith b. Asad al-Muhasibi A.D. 781–857.* London: Sheldon Press, 1977.

Smith, Wilfred Cantwell. *Modern Islam in India: A Social Analysis.* Lahore: Minerva Book Shop, 1943.

Soroush, Abdolkarim. *Reason, Freedom, and Democracy in Islam.* Oxford: Oxford Univ. Press, 2000.

Spaulding, Jay. *The Heroic Age in Sinnar.* East Lansing: African Studies Center of Michigan State Univ., 1985.

Sudan Political Intelligence Summary (SPIS), no. 57, par. 478, Public Records Office (PRO)/Foreign Office (FO) 371/53328.

"Sudan's Criminal Act of 1991." *Arab Law Quarterly,* 9, no. 1 (1994): 32–80.

al-Suhrawardi, 'Umar b. Muhammad. *'Awarif 'l-ma'arif.* Beirut: Dar 'l-Kutub 'l-'Ilmiyya, 1999.

al-Sulami, Muhammad b. Husain. *Kitab Tabaqat 'l-Sufiyya.* Edited by Johannes Pedersen. Leiden: E. J. Brill, 1960.

al-Suyuti, Jalal al-Din 'Abd al-Rahman. *Al-Durr 'l-manthur fi 'l-tafsir bi-'l-ma'thur.* 7 vols. Beirut: Dar 'l-Kutub 'l-'Ilmiyya, 2000.

———. *Al-itqan fi 'ulum 'l-Qur'an.* 2 vols. Beirut: Dar 'l-Kutub 'l-'Ilmiyya, n.d.

al-Tabari, Muhammad b. Jarir. *Tafsir 'l-Tabari* or *Jami' 'l-bayan fi ta'wil 'l-Qur'an.* 12 vols. Beirut: Dar 'l-Kutub 'l-'Ilmiyya, 1992.

———. *Tarikh 'l-umam wa 'l-muluk.* 6 vols. Beirut: Dar 'l-Kutub 'l-'Ilmiyya, 2001.

al-Tabataba'i, Muhammad Husain. *Al-Mizan fi tafsir 'l-Qur'an.* 20 vols. Beirut: Mu'assasat 'l-A'lami li-'l-Matbu'at, 1970.

Taha, Mahmud Muhammad. *As'ila wa ajwiba: al-Kitab 'l-awwal.* Omdurman: Jumhuri Publication, 1970.

———. *As'ila wa ajwiba: al-Kitab 'l-thani.* Omdurman: Jumhuri Publication, 1971.

———. *Bainana wa baina mahkamat 'l-ridda.* Omdurman: Jumhuri Publication, 1968.

———. *Al-Da'wa 'l-Islamiyya 'l-jadida.* Omdurman: Jumhuri Publication, 1974.

———. *Al-Din wa 'l-tanmiyya 'l-ijtima'iyya.* Omdurman: Jumhuri Publication, 1974.

———. *Al-Dustur 'l-Islami: Na'am wa la.* Omdurman: Jumhuri Publication, 1968.

———. *Al-Islam.* 2nd ed. Omdurman: Jumhuri Publication, 1968. First published 1960.

———. *Al-Islam bi-risalatihi 'l-ula la yasluh li-insaniyyat 'l-qarn 'l-'ishrin.* Omdurman: Jumhuri Publication, 1969.

———. *Al-Islam wa 'l-funun.* Omdurman: Jumhuri Publication, n.d.

———. *Al-Islam wa insaniyyat 'l-qarn 'l-'ishrin.* Omdurman: Jumhuri Publication, 1973.

———. *Khatwa nahw 'l-zawaj fi 'l-Islam.* Omdurman: Jumhuri Publication, n.d.

———. *La illaha illa 'Llah.* Omdurman: Jumhuri Publication, 1969.

———. *Al-Markisiyya fi 'l-mizan.* Omdurman: Jumhuri Publication, 1972.

———. "Min daqa'iq haqa'iq 'l-din." Omdurman: Jumhuri Publication, 1976.

———. *Mushkilat 'l-sharq 'l-awsat.* Omdurman: Jumhuri Publication, 1967.

———. *Qul hadhihi sabili.* 3rd ed. Omdurman: Jumhuri Publication, 1976. First published 1952.

———. *Al-Qur'an wa Mustafa Mahmud wa 'l-fahm 'l-'asri.* Omdurman: Jumhuri Publication, 1971.

———. *Rasa'il wa maqalat: al-Kitab 'l-awwal.* Omdurman: Jumhuri Publication, n.d.

———. *Rasa'il wa maqalat: al-Kitab 'l-thani.* Omdurman: Jumhuri Publication, 1973.

———. *Al-Risala 'l-thaniya min 'l-Islam.* 3rd ed. Omdurman: Jumhuri Publication, 1969. First published 1967.

———. *Risalat 'l-salat.* 7th ed. Omdurman: Jumhuri Publication, 1979. First published 1966.

———. *The Second Message of Islam.* Translated by Abdullahi an-Na'im. Syracuse, N.Y.: Syracuse Univ. Press, 1987.

———. *Al-Sifr 'l-awwal.* 3rd ed. Omdurman: Jumhuri Publication, 1976. First published 1945.

———. *Ta'allamu kaifa tusallun.* 2nd ed. Omdurman: Jumhuri Publication, 1973.

———. *Al-Tahaddi 'lladhi yuwajih 'l-'Arab.* Omdurman: Jumhuri Publication, 1967.

———. *Tariq Muhammad.* 8th ed. Omdurman: Jumhuri Publication, 1975. First published 1966.

———. *Tatwir shari'at 'l-ahwal 'l-shakhsiyya.* Omdurman: Jumhuri Publication, 1974.

———. *Al-Thawra 'l-thaqafiyya.* Omdurman: Jumhuri Publication, 1972.

———. *Usus dustur 'l-Sudan.* 2nd ed. Omdurman: Jumhuri Publication, 1968. First published 1955.

———. *Za'im Jabhat 'l-Mithaq 'l-Islami fi mizan (1) 'l-thaqafa 'l-gharbiyya, (2) al-Islam.* Omdurman: Jumhuri Publication, n.d.

al-Talbi, Muhammad. *Ummat 'l-wasat: Al-Islam wa tahaddiyat 'l-'asr.* Tunis: Cérès li-'l-Nashr, 1996.

el-Tayeb, Eltayeb H. M. "The Second Message of Islam: A Critical Study of the Islamic Reformist Thinking of Mahmud Muhammad Taha (1909–85)." Ph.D. diss., Univ. of Manchester, 1995.

al-Tha'labi, Ahmad b. Muhammad. *Qisas 'l-anbiya'*. Beirut: al-Maktaba 'l-Thaqafiyya, n.d.

Thomas, Edward. "Mahmud Muhammad Taha: His Life in Sudan." Ph.D. diss., The Univ. of Edinburgh, 1999.

al-Tirmidhi, Muhammad b. 'Isa. *Sunan*. Edited by Mahmud Nassar. 5 vols. Beirut: Dar 'l-Kutub al-'Ilmiyya, 2000.

Trimingham, J. Spencer. *Islam in the Sudan*. Oxford: Oxford Univ. Press, 1949.

al-Tufi, Najm al-Din. *Risala fi ri'ayat 'l-maslaha*. Edited by Ahmad 'Abd al-Rahim al-Sayih. Cairo: al-Dar 'l-Misriyya 'l-Lubnaniyya, 1993.

al-Turabi, Hasan. *Al-Haraka 'l-Islamiyya fi 'l-Sudan: al-Tatawwur wa 'l-kasb wa 'l-manhaj*. Cairo: al-Qari 'l-'Arabi, 1991.

Voll, John O. "A History of the Khatmiyyah Tariqah in the Sudan." Ph.D. diss., Harvard Univ., 1969.

Vygotsky, Levi Semenovich. *Thought and Language*. Edited and translated by Eugenia Hanfmann and Gertrude Vakar. Cambridge, MA: The Massachusetts Institute of Technology Press, 1977.

Wajdi, Muhammad Farid. *Al-Islam fi 'asr 'l-'ilm*. Cairo: al-Maktaba 'l-Tijariyya, 1932.

al-Waqidi, Muhammad b. 'Umar. *Kitab 'l-Maghazi*. Edited by Marsden Jones. 3 vols. London: Oxford Univ. Press, 1966.

Warburg, Gabriel. "British Policy Towards the Ansar in Sudan: A Note on an Historical Controversy." *Middle Eastern Studies* 33, no. 4 (1997): 675–92.

———. *Islam, Nationalism and Communism in a Traditional Society: The Case of Sudan*. London: Frank Cass, 1978.

———. *Islam, Sectarianism and Politics in Sudan Since the Mahdiyya*. London: Hurst and Company, 2003.

Watt, W. Montgomery. "Early Discussions about the Qur'an." *The Muslim World* 40, no. 1 (1950): 27–40.

———. "Early Discussions about the Qur'an." *The Muslim World* 40, no. 2 (1950): 96–105.

———. *Early Islam: Collected Articles*. Edinburgh: Edinburgh Univ. Press, 1990.

———. *The Formative Period of Islamic Thought*. Edinburgh: Edinburgh Univ. Press, 1973.

———. *Free Will and Predestination in Early Islam*. London: Luzac and Company, 1948.

Watt, W. Montgomery, and Richard Bell. *Introduction to the Qur'an*. Edinburgh: Edinburgh Univ. Press, 1970.

Wensinck, A. J. *The Muslim Creed: Its Genesis and Historical Development*. London: Frank Cass & Co., 1965.

Woodward, Peter. *Condominium and Sudanese Nationalism*. London: Rex Collings, 1979.

Wright, W. *A Grammar of the Arabic Language*. 3rd ed. Cambridge: Cambridge Univ. Press, 1988.

Zaehner, R. C. *Hindu and Muslim Mysticism*. London: Univ. of London, Athlone Press, 1960.

al-Zamakhshari, Mahmud b. 'Umar. *Al-Kashshaf*. 6 vols. Riyad: Maktabat al-'Ubaikan, 1998.

al-Zarkashi, Muhammad b. Abd Allah. *Al-Burhan fi 'Ulum 'l-Qur'an*. 4 vols. Beirut: Dar 'l-Ma'rifa, 1994.

Zein, Ibrahim M. "Religion, Legality, and the State: 1983 Penal Code." Ph.D. diss., Temple Univ., 1989.

Ziadat, Adel A. *Western Science in the Arab World: The Impact of Darwinism, 1860–1930*. London: Macmillan, 1986.

al-Zuhaili, Wahba. *Al-Fiqh 'l-Islami wa adilatuhu*. 8 vols. Damascus: Dar 'l-Fikr, 1989.

 Index